Arabic–Islamic Cities

Building and Planning Principles

This is a pioneering study of how traditional towns and cities were conceived, organized, and developed over long periods of time following simple rules that were based on religious and ethical values. Sources were used that date back to the fourteenth century and earlier. Although the study is embedded in the Arab-Islamic culture of North Africa and the Middle East, its implications are universal particularly in light of scientific discoveries of natural processes and the underlying principles of complexity theory and the processes that bring about emergence. Generative processes that shaped urban form are clearly demonstrated in the book. The study also sheds light on the implications of responsibility allocation to the various parties who are involved in the development process and the resulting patterns of decision-making that affect change and growth in the built environment. All of these issues are of significance when trying to understand the concepts that relate to various aspects of sustainability, the future potential of eco-cities, and the nature of policies and programs that are required for the immediate present and for the future. This work is a major contribution for enhancing the theories and practice of urban planning and design.

> *"This is a substantial, innovative work."*
> Journal of Architectural and Planning Research.

> *"This volume is an essential reference for all who are interested in the history and future of urban design."* Third World Planning Review.

> *"In general this study makes a significant contribution, of interest in itself but also important as a potential stimulus to similar studies of rule systems in other cultures."* Journal of Architectural Education.

Besim S. Hakim, architect and urban designer, has worked as professor/scholar and as a consultant/practitioner. He is Fellow of the American Institute of Certified Planners, and Member of the American Institute of Architects. His education in architecture was at Liverpool University, UK, and urban design at Harvard. He has researched and uncovered the underlying processes, rules, codes, and management systems of traditional towns since 1975. This book and subsequent other studies are a result of that work and have been, since its first publication in 1986, influential on numerous studies undertaken in academia and in professional practice.

Arabic–Islamic Cities

Building and Planning Principles

Besim Selim Hakim

To my parents and my children:

Omar, Lena, Sara, and Malak

First published in 1986 by Kegan Paul International Limited, London, England

Second edition 1988

This is the 2008 edition with a Postscript dated June 2008 and the addition of a 20-page article by the author published in 1994 that is highly relevant to the contents of the book.

ISBN: 0-9683-1842-8 (paperback), ISBN: 0-9683-1843-6 (hardback)
ISBN-13: 978-0968318423 (paperback), ISBN-13: 978-0968318430 (hardback)

Library of Congress Control Number: 82074252

Book cover design by Angie Underwood, www.bookcoverpro.com

To order additional copies visit www.booksurge.com, or www.amazon.com

Contents

List of illustrations

Figures in the text

All drawings, unless otherwise stated, were developed by the author.

Plates

All photographs, unless otherwise stated, were taken by the author. The Tunis photos were taken during 1974–77.

Acknowledgements

However resourceful and independent a researcher wants to be, it is nevertheless unavoidable and imperative that he seek assistance from various institutions and individuals. Primarily two types of assistance were essential to this work: facilitation and information. I would like to thank sources for both types.

At the top of the list is the Technical University of Nova Scotia (previously Nova Scotia Technical College), my employer from September 1967 to August 1980 and to whom I will always be indebted, as a facilitator for my research and consulting activities and hence professional development and maturity. I thank also the college's 'Studies Abroad' programme, which made it possible for me and ten of my students to spend the autumn term of 1975 in Tunisia undertaking a detailed study of the village of Sidi Bou Sa'id — the results of which were published as a monograph in 1978.

I owe thanks to al-Sharif Ibrahim, Abdullah Sulaiman Abu Saloom, and Abdulhamid al-Zantani for arranging a 1-week visit to the Arab Development Institute. To the Institute I am grateful for partially funding the expenses of my ambitious research project and for their total trust in my abilities and the objectives of the project as outlined in my initial research statement. Specifically I would like to thank Dr Sa'ad Ben-Hamid (the previous director general), Dr Ali Ben-Alashhar, Hadi Raghei, Hussein al-Muntasser and Abdulaziz Mursi.

In Tunisia, the site of Tunis Medina, the case study I used for developing the parameters of this research and for sharpening my findings, I am grateful to the friendliness and openness of the Tunisian people, and to many individuals in all walks of life. I would like specifically to extend my appreciation to the following individuals: Massimo Amodei, Jerome Woodford, Zoubeida Akkari, all of the District de Tunis and to Jamila Binous of the Association Sauvegarde de la Medina. I appreciate the insights and assistance of Slimane Mustafa Zbiss, Luigi Barocci, Abulkassim Karro, Wassim Ben Mahmoud, Moncef Bouhadra and Tahar Ben-Lagha. For the assistance and the information provided by the Office de la Topographie et de la Cartographie in Tunis and for the photographs of Abdelhamid Kahia.

The following libraries and individuals provided important assistance for which I am grateful: the Bibliothèque Nationale de Tunisie-to Salah Douar, Abdessalem Jomaa and Tahir Kobaisa; Nova Scotia Technical College library, M.R. Hussain, librarian, Mrs J.C. MacDonald, interlibrary loan officer, and Gwen Ling; Islamic Studies Library at McGill University, Montreal-Canada, the late Muzaffar Ali, librarian and Salwa Ferahian; and to the Widener Library, Harvard University, David H. Partington, head of the Middle Eastern Collection.

I am grateful to Professors Oleg Grabar, Wilhelm von Moltke and Wilfred C. Smith, all of Harvard University, for their interest in my work and their assistance in locating sources and introducing me to potential assistants. The following people have generously provided photographs, information, and general assistance: Selim Hakim, Wisam Hakim, Paul Vaughan, and Gamal Badawi. I must thank my assistants without whose help it would have been impossible to complete the work in the short span of three years: Paul C. Parshley, Maria Jones, Yee-on Tse and Homayoon Kassaian for assistance in research; Azim Nanji, Douglas I. Chard, Eva Huber and Judith Bode for translation work; for transliteration from the Maghribi to contemporary Arabic script; Lotfi Mohamed and Mohamed el-Maaroufi both from Morocco; for the skill and patience in typing the final manuscript, I am specially grateful to my former wife, Fatina S. Hijab. To her, and our three children, Omar, Lena and Sara, I will always be grateful for their patience and forebearance during almost four years while I undertook this work under the same roof.

Introduction

Since my final year as an architecture student in 1962 I have been interested in the factors that shaped 'vernacular' cities and villages. To pursue this interest effectively and fully utilize my background, sensitivities and skills, I decided to concentrate on the region of the Middle East and North Africa molded by the Arabic–Islamic civilization since the mid-seventh century.

Instigated by the accelerated building and construction activity in that region since 1973, I outlined, in August 1974, a research concept for which I began to seek support and which ultimately created this study. Implicit in undertaking this work was the conviction that building and urban development accomplished within the framework of Arabic-Islamic civilization achieved a high level of sophistication and merited thorough study and evaluation in terms of our current needs. The goal set out for the research was to provide the necessary information and techniques to help bridge the gap between current practice in the Arab and Islamic world (primarily imported from the West) and the traditional experience which developed continuously over a period of at least 1,000 years. Accordingly three specific objectives were set out to accomplish that goal:

1 To identify and record the building and planning principles which shaped the traditional Arabic–Islamic city.

2 To evaluate, recycle and test the traditional principles (or derivates) via a contemporary urban design project to determine their validity and usefulness today and for the foreseeable future.

3 To document the findings in a systematic and clear format so that others may benefit directly.

This book documents the results of implementing objectives 1 and 3. Objective 2 was partially undertaken by testing the organization/design system inherent in the traditional experience with the design of a prototype neighbourhood suitable for most arid conditions in the Middle East and North Africa. The project consists of 428 units and supporting community facilities on a typical, flat site of 17.67 hectares. For various reasons the decision was made not to include the test design in this publication, but I would like to mention that even though the test uses traditional physical features and is only part of the findings available to us, it nevertheless proves that with minor adaptations those features are suited to our contemporary needs and can create an attractive and viable alternative to present models.

Before indicating the approach followed in achieving objectives 1 and 3, it would be helpful to highlight a few of the historical facts that have affected the selection of the title for this book. During the years 1/622–133/750, (approximately by the end of the Umayyad dynasty) the geographic area extending from Spain to India embraced the religion of Islam, and constituted what is referred to today as the Muslim World. During the first three centuries of Islamic history (i.e., by the year 288/900), the foundations and principles of the social, economic, and legislative frameworks were accomplished. Building and urban activity occurred at a relatively accelerated pace during those years, and building activity — with its unavoidable problems — created the demand for guidelines and a legislative framework to regulate and adjudicate on those problems. In this way, a remarkable body of information was generated in various regions of the Islamic world, and this was actively exchanged by learned men on their travels, students seeking knowledge, and the acquisition of manuscripts.

The uniform legislative guidelines, and the almost identical socio-cultural framework created by Islam — in addition to the similarity of climatic conditions and construction techniques within most of the Islamic world — helped produce remarkable similarities in approach to the city-building process. This resulted in the frequent occurrence of the familiar beehive urban pattern throughout this vast geographic area. Deviations from this basically uniform urban pattern did occur owing to the modifying influences of micro-climates, economic conditions, available building materials and localized stylistic approaches and influences.

We find that this long tradition of building and urban development (which achieved its maturity by the year 288/900 and continued for the next ten centuries) came to a rather abrupt stop around the turn of this century, finally ending with the collapse of the Ottoman Empire in 1337/1918.

Why then is this book titled *Arabic–Islamic Cities* instead of just *Islamic Cities*? The primary reasons can be summarized thus:

1 Islam emerged from the heartland of Arabia, which had strong pre-Islamic Arab traditions in various spheres of life including building practice. Many of the traditions that were not compatible with Islamic values were prohibited but others, with modifications, became part of Islamic civilization. I believe that various aspects of pre-Islamic building practice were absorbed and modified and emerged with a distinct Islamic character. Some of those influences could be traced back to earlier Semitic and Arab civilizations particularly in the region of Mesopotamia.

2 The language of the Qur'an is Arabic, which became the most important language for communicating and generating knowledge within the Islamic world. Thus prime sources in various disciplines are in Arabic.

3 Of the predominant five schools of law in the Islamic world (four Sunni and one Shi'i), the Maliki School of Law, attributed to Imam Malik, is the one closest to the traditions and practices in Medina-Arabia, the Prophet's city. The foundations of those traditions were established during the decade before the Prophet's death in 11/632. Societal framework, attributes, and the experiences gained during that decade by the first Arab–Islamic community under the leadership and guidance of the Prophet were (and still are) considered by many the model to emulate.

4 Even though numerous Islamic cities were founded and built by Arab leaders in non-Arabic-speaking territories during the seventh and eighth centuries, there is no doubt that local building traditions and the nature of pre-Islamic cities must have had considerable influence, particularly in the eastern regions of the Islamic world. However, the region that exerted the least influence on emerging Islamic cities was in the Maghrib (the region extending from Libya to Spain). Thus cities founded by Arab-Islamic leaders in the western regions of the Islamic world were the 'purest' in terms of their general Islamic framework and their specific Arabic attributes. Although the lack of local influence was important in this regard, the teachings and outlook of the Maliki School were possibly more crucial.

Given the above reasons, it would have been feasible to entitle this book *Maghribi Islamic Cities* or *North African Cities* or even *Moorish Cities*; however, I believe the title *Arabic–Islamic Cities* is historically and culturally more accurate.

The approach I pursued in achieving the objectives mentioned earlier was directly influenced by the availability and type of information I could acquire. Even though I outlined an initial approach in my first research proposal, a clearer one soon emerged which partly confirmed my earlier intentions. The work had to be pursued within the following two areas:

1 The detailed study and analysis of an existing traditional Arabic–Islamic city which has undergone minor modification owing to recent technological influences. Within the Maghrib region the city of Tunis proved to be an excellent candidate.
2 Investigation of ancient Arabic manuscripts and historical records which would shed light on the city-building process. The area of Islamic law (Fiqh) proved the best source for that, as the problems arising from the city-building process were well recognized and addressed within the framework of Islamic values and ethics.

The vigour with which I pursued this work was also influenced by my conviction that the bulk of the values and experiences embodied in the theory and practice of modern architecture are rooted in a small segment of man's experience in building and urban development. This experience has been, to date, dependent solely on monumental buildings as works of art. The bulk of man's experience as builder of his habitat — popularly described by modern architects as 'architecture without architects' — has hardly influenced the shaping of values and theories of contemporary architecture. This historical fact has harmed the development of cities in Western countries as well as, more recently, those in other cultures. Luckily there are efforts in the West today to enlarge this narrow viewpoint, but it might take years before the damage caused by current practices can be fully recognized and rectified.

This study is therefore primarily addressed to architects, urban planners, city administrators and elected or appointed officials who have direct or indirect influence on urban development and government. It is also for those involved academically in the same areas. I hope the results of this work will also be of benefit to historians, archeologists, anthropologists and lawyers, on whose disciplines I drew a great deal in studying various aspects of the traditional city in the context of the Arabic–Islamic civilization.

This brings us to the problem of information, which was the most difficult task confronting me. I literally had to piece together sentences, paragraphs, portions of maps — in the form of a jigsaw puzzle — to reconstruct a clear picture of what happened. In doing so I utilized sources from four languages: Arabic, English, French and German.

I approached the research with an open mind and with no biases. I also assumed that the most remote and unexpected sources could provide a clue to the truth of what happened in history. This open-minded policy paid off handsomely as I found that valuable information existed in sources which, as an architect, I could not possibly have foreseen or imagined. One fact emerged: the type of sources we usually use in architecture and city planning for explaining historical phenomenon are relatively unhelpful in seeking reality.

Another useful strategy I pursued during the three years of research (1975–77) was constantly to seek out information as the work was progressing. This input allowed for continuous verification and/or modification of the findings. Accordingly I can say with full confidence that the results of this work represent the essential core of knowledge — within the limitations of one case study — of:

1 the principles and guidelines used during the building *process*, and
2 the organizational framework and associated techniques utilized in creating the urban form, or the built *product*.

Future research using other case studies will no doubt sharpen these findings and provide insight into similarities and subtle differences which existed from city to city and region to region, particularly as a result of the application of building principles and guidelines derived from Islamic values.

The work is grouped in four chapters, and four appendices. The first chapter details the first of two major areas of knowledge about the factors that shaped the Arabic-Islamic city — namely the neighbourhood building guidelines which were generated by Islamic jurists and administered/implemented by *Kadis* (judges) in cases of conflict. It is supplemented by Appendices 1, 2 and 3 which present integral components of the information.

Chapter 2 sets out the physical organizational system used in achieving the familiar beehive urban form. The components of the system are based on a hierarchy of identifiable urban and building scale elements which function together as a versatile design language. Chapters 1 and 2 therefore explain the essence of the 'why' and 'how' of the traditional Arabic–Islamic city as demonstrated by the case of Tunis.

Chapter 3 is interpretative and its purpose is to illuminate the interaction of the two fundamental mechanisms identified as building process and product (i.e., Chapters 1 and 2). Qualitative and quantitative elaboration and interpretation of the Medina of Tunis as a case study is undertaken, and examples are selected at both the city and neighbourhood scales. Appendix 4 points out some benefits which could be derived from the traditional experience for our contemporary use, in terms of the building process and the primary urban form components.

Chapter 4, the conclusion, summarizes the findings of the study and indicates areas for further related research to fill the gaps in the knowledge and experience of the past century that have occurred in the Arab and Islamic world, and no doubt in other cultures as well. This knowledge is crucial for a sucessful linkage between past, present, and future in the area of building and urban development.

Besim Hakim
7 Ramadan 1399/31 July 1979

Chapter 1

Islamic law and neighbourhood building guidelines

The basic principles and guidelines of the building process and its framework were derived from the essence and spirit of Islam. It can safely be asserted that the development of these basic principles and guidelines started in 1 AH or 622 AD (referred to as 1/622 in future) when the Prophet Mohammed settled in Medina.

The development of building and urban design principles centred primarily around housing and access. Their development paralleled that of Islamic law, and soon became semi-legislative in nature. Since building and the development of communities is a continuous process, related rules and guidelines were in demand constantly.

The multitude of cases due to conflicts between neighbours had to be resolved expeditiously and fairly. The resulting cases attracted the attention of interested judges, master masons and others, and were soon used as precedents. In this way, the development of Islamic law responded well in fulfilling the demand for building/urban design guidelines and a framework for adjudicating related conflicts. Research indicates that the development and maturity of these guidelines did, in fact, coincide with the development of Islamic law. The spread of Islam produced a great deal of intellectual activity and knowledge particularly related to the conduct of life as prescribed by religious principles and codes.

Many great scholars spent their lifetime studying, teaching and writing on the subject. Some of these scholars developed their work to such an extent that they soon formed schools of law (Madhhab) based on their teachings. Although numerous schools of law arose, only five have survived: the Hanafi, Maliki, Shafi'i, Hanbali and Jaffari. The first four are Sunni Schools and the fifth is Shi'i.

The lives of the schools' founders reflect the historical timeframe within which their work developed. Most of the development occurred within the first 200 years of Islam, and each school of law created its own geographic sphere of influence, though in some cases overlap did occur. However, it should be noted that these spheres of influence have not remained stationary during the past 1,300 years. For instance, the Maliki School spread from the Prophet's city 'Madina' in Arabia via Egypt to the Maghreb region and to Al-Andalus (Muslim Spain). To this day Morocco and Algeria subscribe only to the Maliki School. On the other hand, however, the Hanafi School was introduced to Tunisia and Libya in the mid-sixteenth century by the Ottoman Turks. Today most of the population in both countries are still Malikis, even though both Madhhabs have equal status.

Differences and similarities exist between the schools of law (although they will not be discussed here) but they were all influenced, and subsequently shaped by, the teachings of Muhammad Ibn-Idris al-Shafi'i who established the *Sunna* (practice of the Prophet Mohammad) as the second source of law after the *Qur'an*. A brief account of al-Shafi'i's legal theory is important as it will clarify subsequent material to be presented.

According to al-Shafi'i there are four major sources or roots (*usul*) of law:
the *Qur'an*, the *Sunna* (the divinely inspired behaviour of the Prophet Mohammad), the *Ijma'* (the consensus of the entire Muslim community), and *Qiyas* or *Ijtihad* (the use of human reason in the elaboration of law). Al-Shafi'i's legal theory is presented in his *Risala* which he wrote during the five years before his death in 204/819. It was drawn along simple, yet bold and uncompromising lines and was an innovation the value of which lay not in the introduction of any entirely original concepts but in giving existing ideas a novel connotation and emphasis and combining them within a systematic scheme.[1]

The Qur'an, apart from its substantive provisions, also indicated the means by which some of its material is to be interpreted and supplemented. In particular, the repeated command to 'obey God and his Prophet' established the precedents of Prophet Mohammad as a source of law second only to the word of God. The recognition of the Traditions (*Hadith*, precedents of the Prophet) as a source of the divine will complementary to the Qur'an is the supreme contribution of al-Shafi'i to Islamic jurisprudence. His arguments proved irrefutable, and once they were accepted, traditions could no longer be rejected by objective criticism of their content; their authority was binding unless the authenticity of the report itself could be denied.[2]

In Ijma, he takes up an existing notion and gives it a new connotation designed to achieve uniformity in the law. Denying that the agreement of the scholars of a particular locality had any authority, he argues that there could be only one valid consensus, that of the entire Muslim community, lawyers and lay members alike. Qiyas (or reasoning by analogy, in its widest sense) is the use of human reason in the elaboration of the law. It was also termed Ijtihad (effort or the exercise of one's own judgment) and covered a variety of mental processes, ranging from the interpretation of texts to the assessment of the authenticity of traditions. Qiyas or analogical reasoning, then, is a particular form of Ijtihad, the method by which the principles established by the Qur'an, Sunna and consensus are to be extended and applied to the solution of problems not expressly regulated therein. The role of juristic reasoning is thus completely subordinate to the dictates of divine revelation. Analogical deduction must have its starting point in a principle of the Qur'an, Sunna or consensus, and cannot be used to achieve a result that contradicts a rule established by any of these three primary sources.[3]

The following is a statement by al-Shafi'i which summarizes his legal theory:

> On points on which there exists an explicit decision of God or a Sunna of the Prophet or a consensus of the Muslims, no disagreement is allowed. On the other points scholars must exert their own judgment in search of an indication in one of these three sources; he who is qualified for this research is entitled to hold the opinion which he finds implied in the Qur'an, Sunna, or consensus; if a problem has two solutions, either opinion may be held as a result of systematic reasoning, but this occurs only rarely.[4]

Later jurisprudence modified al-Shafi'i's ideas of the relationship between the component parts of this theory, but his fundamental theory was never seriously challenged.

In the century that followed the death of al-Shafi'i in 204/819, the Sunna of the

Prophet became the focus of attention, and by the year 288/900 Muslim jurisprudence as a whole had succeeded in absorbing al-Shafi'i's teaching in a generally acceptable form.[5] The outstanding feature of this period is the growth of a separate science of traditions with a literature of its own. Specialist scholars devoted themselves to the process of collecting, documenting, and classifying traditions. Once the trustworthiness of their reporters was established, traditions were classified in varying grades of authority according to the strength of their *Isnads*. If the continuity of transmission was broken — for example, where two successive links in the chain of reports could not historically have been in contact with each other — this naturally detracted from, although it did not necessarily wholly destroy, the authority of the tradition. Apart from such considerations the criterion was the number of transmitters in each generation.

During the latter part of the third Islamic century (250–300/864–912) scholarship in this field claimed to have sifted the genuine from the false. Two such manuals in particular, those of al-Bukhari (died 257/870) and Muslim (died 262/875), have always enjoyed a high reputation in Islamic jurisprudence as authentic accounts of the practice of the Prophet.[6]

By the beginning of the fourth century of Islam (about 900 AD), the scholars of the surviving schools felt that all essential questions had been thoroughly discussed and finally settled, and a consensus gradually established itself that from that time onwards no one could be deemed to have the necessary qualifications for independent reasoning in law, and that all future activity would have to be confined to the explanation, application and, at the most, interpretation of the doctrine as it had been laid down once and for all. It followed that from then on every Muslim had to belong to one of the recognized schools. After this 'closing of the door of independent reasoning,' as it was called, the doctrine had to be derived not independently from the Qur'an, the Sunna, and the consensus, but from the authoritative handbooks of the several schools.[7] The activity of jurists was subsequently no less creative, within the limits set, than that of their predecessors. New sets of facts constantly arose in life, and they had to be mastered and moulded with the traditional tools provided by legal science. This activity was also carried out by the *muftis*.[8]

Tunis, the subject of the case study, reached development maturity during the period of the Hafsids (627/1229–982/1574). As mentioned before, the only school of law at that time which was followed in all the Maghreb region including Al-Andalus was the Maliki School. Although the Turks introduced the Hanafi School of Law in Tunis during their period of rule, its influence in matters relating to building law and guidelines was minimal. Concentrating on the study of the Maliki School would therefore be the most beneficial for understanding the underlying principles and practice related to building and urban design in Tunis.

The father of the Maliki School is Malik ben Anas Al-Asbahi who was born in Madina in 93/711, lived there most of his life, and died there in 179/795. His primary written contribution is the Muwatta which is a collection of Hadith and Fatawi (plural of Fatwa, in other words the opinions and cases of important contemporaries). Appendix 2 presents a chronological list of significant persons who spread the teaching of Malik and his school. They were identified as the basic sources used by Ibn al-Rami, who is the author of the fourteenth-century manuscript upon which the cases in this chapter are based. They represent the chain from Malik to Ibn al-Rami's period.[9]

Two factors need emphasis:

1 The first fourteen men after Malik lived during the first 260 years of Islam. Their work, therefore, was the basis and reference point for subsequent generations, as we shall see in our study of specific cases within the eighth century AH in Tunis (fourteenth century AD).
2 Al-Shafi'i's influence was widespread and well accepted by the year 288/900, so that the Sunna of the Prophet became the focal point of attention after his death in 204/819.

This chapter will continue in the following format: first I will present a selection of principles and behavioural guidelines which I have identified and specified by the interpretation of the material available from the eighth entury AH (fourteenth century AD) Tunis. They have never been presented in this format. They could be viewed as the general 'performance specifications' followed by the local Kadis and master masons in Tunis and elsewhere. All principles and guidelines are, whenever appropriate, identified with the Qur'anic verses and sayings of the Prophet from which they were derived or influenced. All appropriate verses and sayings are presented in Appendix 1.

The verses were selected because of their direct or indirect meaning, influence, and guidance to matters affecting urban living. The selection of sayings or Hadith have had direct influence on conduct and decision making within the urban milieu. Most were used by religious scholars and Kadis for setting principles and guidelines to be followed in the activity of urbanism.

Secondly, I will present a selection of cases and Fatawi (opinions by muftis) from the Hafsid period in Tunis, specifically from the late seventh and eighth centuries AH (late thirteenth and early fourteenth centuries AD). These are grouped and presented within a framework, devised for this purpose, of five categories of factors that shape urban form and tissue.

Referring to the chart in Figure 1, we note that the dynamic decision-making process operating in the city was primarily based on decisions by rulers and citizens. Rulers' decisions were macro in nature, creating in most cases a 'planned' effect on the urban fabric, or initiating the building of a Jami, a Madrassa, or extending a road, and so on. In other words these decisions had relatively obvious manifestations.

Citizens' decisions were of a micro nature, with less discernible effects than the decisions of rulers, but their aggregate

Figure 1 Conceptual model of selected factors that shaped the traditional Arabic–Islamic city

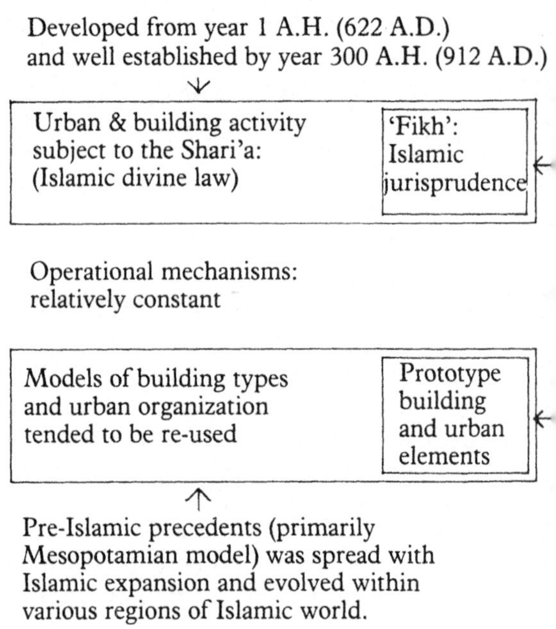
Developed from year 1 A.H. (622 A.D.)
and well established by year 300 A.H. (912 A.D.)
Urban & building activity
subject to the Shari'a:
(Islamic divine law)
'Fikh':
Islamic
jurisprudence
Operational mechanisms:
relatively constant
Models of building types
and urban organization
tended to be re-used
Prototype
building
and urban
elements
Pre-Islamic precedents (primarily
Mesopotamian model) was spread with
Islamic expansion and evolved within
various regions of Islamic world.

impact on the city was ultimately more significant, and affected the lives of most people directly. This aspect of the history of the city has been ignored by most contemporary urban historians, with a devastating effect on the theory and practice of the Modern Movement of Western architecture during this century. Since World War II this negative effect has spread to other cultures in the world, including the Arab and most Islamic countries.

Principles and behavioural guidelines

The following principles and guidelines common in Tunis during the eighth century AH (fourteenth century AD) were used by the local Kadis in resolving conflicts among neighbours and others. They would therefore represent the core of the building principles and guidelines of the Maliki School affecting the 'Micro urban decisions by citizens' (see Figure 1). These were also followed, where applicable, by rulers and others undertaking building activity (classified as 'Macro urban decisions by rulers' in the same chart).

Each principle/guideline is cross referenced with the relevant Qur'anic verse (V) and/or saying of the Prophet (S) in Appendix 1:

1 **Harm**. V: 6, 18, 19; S: 34, 35. The essence is that one should exercise one's full rights in what is rightfully his providing the decision/action will not generate harm to others. Likewise others should exercise their full rights in what is rightfully theirs providing their decision/action will not harm others.
2 **Interdependence**. V: 1, 2, 4, 5; S: 7, 8, 12, 13, 14, 15, 33, 39, 40, 42, 44, 45. This principle reinforces our contemporary

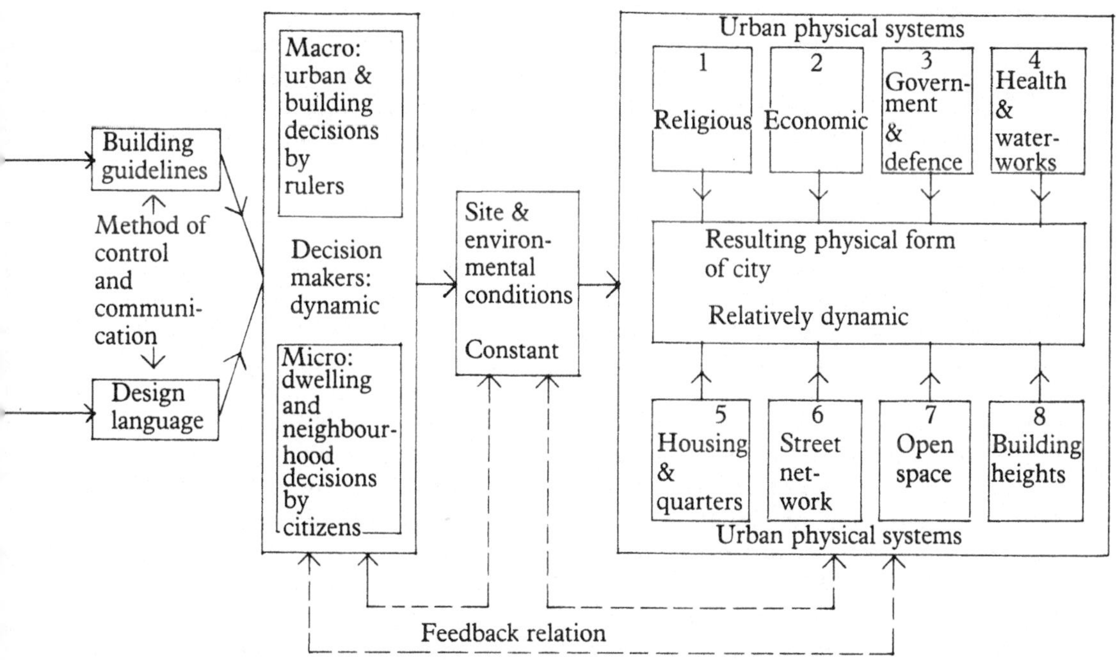

knowledge of the science of ecology and values emanating from it. A framework based on this principle is crucial for generating building 'solutions' to the special requirements of the built-form prevalent in Islamic cities. Note that Verse 5 prescribes the policing of this principle by encouraging self-regulatory behaviour. It is one of the pillars of the Islamic Hisba institution.

3 **Privacy**. V: 13, 14, 15, 16; S: 29, 30, 31, 32. In physical terms it refers to personal clothing and the private domain of the home. It also refers to the privacy of communication. The privacy of others must be respected and its invasion is prohibited, such as via direct visual corridors into the private domain of others. The Qur'an prescribes various behaviour patterns including those designed to respect the privacy of others, such as the manner of announcing one's presence to the occupants of a house, and others.

4 **Rights of original (or earlier) usage**. S: 17, 18, 19, 20. Ownership pattern across time creates rights of earlier ownership or usage, in effect granting certain rights to older and established facts. For example, this principle is used in resolving disputes related to the ownership and rights of party walls, the location of windows, etc.

5 **Rights of building higher within one's air space, even if it excludes air and sun from others**. V: 17; S: 26, 44. The Maliki School followed the prescription in Verse 17 and allowed the owner of a property or building to maximize its utilization for personal benefit by allowing, for example, the extension of the structure within the property's vertical air space. This is allowed even if the extension harms a neighbour by the exclusion of air and sun, and is the only exception to the principle of harm. However this allowance was waived when there was evidence that the intent to build higher was to harm a specific neighbour.

6 **Respect for the property of others**. V: 17; S: 10, 11, 16. The ownership and integrity of a property (land, building or any other item) must be respected and no action is allowed which will depress its value or usefulness or create nuisance to its owner.

7 **Pre-emption**. S: 46, 47, 48, 49, 50, 51. Pre-emption is the right of a neighbour or partner to purchase an adjacent property or structure when offered for sale by another neighbour or partner. The Prophet prescribed the application of pre-emption on primarily physically indivisible items. The intent is to protect the neighbour or partner from the potential harm or inconvenience of a stranger becoming a joint owner of an indivisible property, such as a party wall or garden.

8 **Seven cubits as the minimum width of public thoroughfares**. S: 4. The basis for this width is to allow two fully loaded camels to pass. The cubit ranges from 46 to 50 cm. The width, therefore, ranged from 3.23 to 3.50 m. From my research I found that the minimum vertical height of a public through street is also 7 cubits. This corresponds to the maximum vertical height of a camel with the highest load, see Figure 2(a). Therefore a through public street should have a minimum dimension of 3.23 to 3.50 m horizontally and vertically.

9 **Any public thoroughfare should not be obstructed (by temporary or permanent obstructions)**. S: 5, 6.

10 **Excess of water should not be barred from others**. S: 12, 13, 14, 15. The Prophet prescribed that people

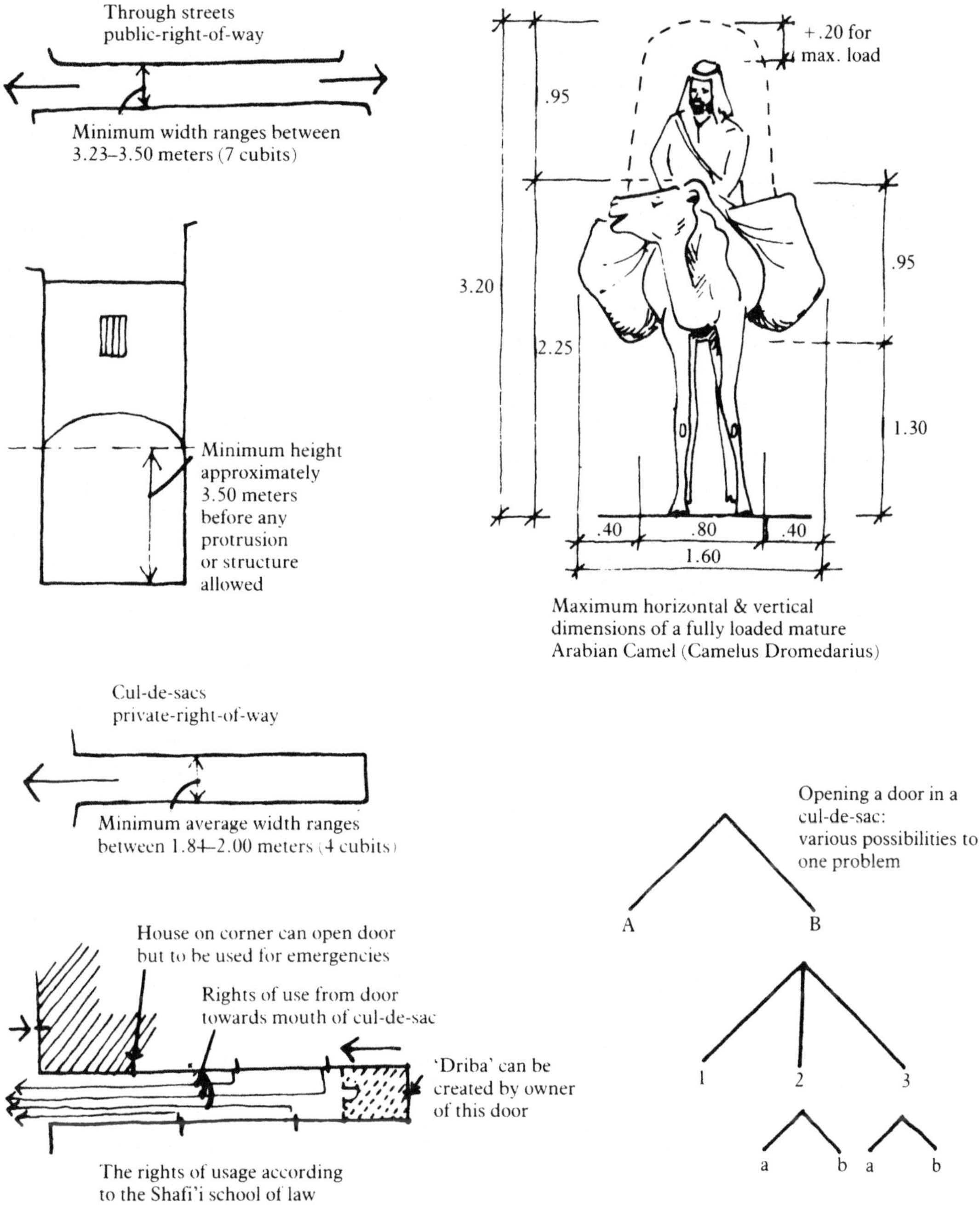

Through streets
public-right-of-way
Minimum width ranges between
3.23–3.50 meters (7 cubits)
Minimum height
approximately
3.50 meters
before any
protrusion
or structure
allowed
+ .20 for
max. load
.95
3.20
2.25
.95
1.30
.40
.80
.40
1.60
Maximum horizontal & vertical
dimensions of a fully loaded mature
Arabian Camel (Camelus Dromedarius)
Cul-de-sacs
private-right-of-way
Minimum average width ranges
between 1.84–2.00 meters (4 cubits)
Opening a door in a
cul-de-sac:
various possibilities to
one problem
A
B
1
2
3
a
b
a
b
House on corner can open door
but to be used for emergencies
Rights of use from door
towards mouth of cul-de-sac
'Driba' can be
created by owner
of this door
The rights of usage according
to the Shafi'i school of law

Figure 2(a) Streets: thoroughfares and cul-de-sacs

must share water, and that its owner should give to others any surplus he has for drinking or irrigation. This principle resulted in the familiar public water fountain in the streets of Islamic cities.

11 **The right for usage of the exterior Fina belongs to the owner of the house or building which abuts it.**[10] The Fina is defined and discussed in detail on pages 27–29.

12 **Sources of unpleasant smell, and uses that generate noise should not be located adjacent to or near mosques.** V: 10; S: 9. This principle influenced the layout and product distribution in the Suq or market which typically was built adjacent to or surrounding the major city mosque.

The following were values and societal guidelines of accepted behaviour that had a self-regulating effect on people:

1 **Encouragement to keep things clean, including the interior and exterior Fina.** (This principle was self-regulating by inspiring guilt and shame in the person who did not practice it, particularly with regards the exterior Fina). V: 5; S: 1, 2, 3.
2 **Encouragement to feel responsible and sense of public awareness** (such as removing obstacles in public right-of-ways). V: 5, 12; S: 5, 6, 7, 8.
3 **Beauty without arrogance.** V: 7, 10, 11, 13; S: 23, 24, 25, 26, 27.
4 **Trust, respect and peace amongst neighbours.** V: 7, 14, 15; S: 36, 37, 38, 39, 40, 41, 42, 43, 44, 45, 46, 47.
5 **Defects should be announced and not hidden when selling a property.** V: 6, 8; S: 52, 53, 54, 55.

It should be noted that the principle of harm was one of the most frequently quoted and used in building matters. Its roots are in the Prophet's saying number 34 (Appendix 1), which is interpreted in the Fiqh as 'No person or party to be harmed for another to benefit'.[11] Another interpretation of this saying is communicated by Isa ben Mousa ben al-Imam al-Tutaily (d. 386 AH/996 AD), who says that Mohammad ben Abd al-Selam al-Khocheni of Cordoba commented thus on the 'La dharar wa la dhirar': No infringement, whether profitable or not. The Dharar (ضرر) is the act of one who wrongs someone else with no profit to himself, and the Dhirar (ضرار) is the act of one who wrongs someone else for his own profit.[12]

According to the interpretation of Muhammad al-Tahir b. Ashour, harm can be classified in two general categories:

1 harm which should be avoided and/or prevented at all costs (he provides examples of six types); and
2 harm which is unavoidable and allowable.

The former hurts the party being harmed, whereas the latter prevents the occurrence of a potential benefit. An interesting example cited by Ashour of the first category is the necessary distinction that should be made between two identifiable harmful consequences originating from the same problem, and then categorizing them if possible into higher and lesser harms. The latter being the lesser of the two, is allowable if unavoidable.[13]

The cases presented in this chapter will refer to these principles and guidelines and should clarify further their intent and application.

Selected cases and Fatawi

Finding appropriate concrete cases and Fatawi (opinions by Muftis) to help us understand the processes of growth and change that shaped the traditional Arabic-Islamic city was no easy task. The macro urban decisions can be extracted by a careful analysis of historical facts with the necessary supporting maps. This would at best provide only a rough outline sketch of the structure of the city.

The bulk of the city comprising the housing, supporting neighbourhood facilities, and related access (streets and cul-de-sacs) needs to be understood, to appreciate the three-dimensional nature and quality of the Arabic-Islamic city. This quality is admired by most twentieth-century architects who have visited these cities or studied aerial photographs and other visual information about them. So far this admiration has only taken the form of visual essays under the general title of 'Architecture without Architects.'[14]

A key article written by the French Islamist, Robert Brunschvig, in 1945[15] opened the door for locating and studying two Arabic manuscripts on the subject of building 'solutions' (*Ahkam*) based on Islamic principles and guidelines, with special emphasis on the rights and obligations of adjacent neighbours. The first and earlier manuscript by the Andalusian Isa ben Mousa[16] (d. 386/996) is less comprehensive than the second and later manuscript by Ibn al-Rami.[17] However, both manuscripts illuminate three things: the remarkable similarity of 'solutions' 350 years apart, the dependency on similar earlier references within the Maliki School of Law, and the similarity of solutions across the vast geographic area of North Africa and Al-Andalus (Muslim Spain), resulting in a consistent urban design approach modified by variations in response to local siting, climate variation, and the availability of building materials.

I have also had the opportunity to study other Maghribi sources which confirmed the consistency and even the repetition of some of the cases or examples cited by Ibn al-Rami. An important earlier source is 'al-Mudawana al-Kubra' which is Sahnoun's version of Malik's teachings as interpreted by Ibn al-Qassim (d. 191/806). The former lived from 160/777 to 240/854.

Two other sources examined were by al-Burzuli, an eminent Maliki mufti of Tunis who was born seven years after Ibn al-Rami's death and lived 100 years (741/1340–844/1440), and al-Wansharisi, a Maliki Fekih born about 100 years after Ibn al-Rami's death and died in 914/1508. He spent the first forty years of his life in Tlemcen and the last forty in Fez. His work, including building solutions, was extremely influenced by al-Burzuli's writings on the subject. Both sources display the astonishing similarity of content with Ibn al-Rami's work.

The cases presented in this chapter are therefore primarily from Ibn al-Rami's manuscript. The author/compiler[18] was a literate and refined master mason from Tunis, who practised and died there in 734/1334. He was the student of Kadi abou Ishaq b. Abdul-Rafi[19] who died in 733/1332 in Tunis (the birth year of the famous historian Ibn Khaldoun). The advantages of Ibn al-Rami's manuscript include the following:

1 It is the work of a master mason providing insight to the approach and the priorities of particular cases from a master mason's point of view.

2 It clarified the interdependency that existed between the owner of a property (when protesting harm or when accused of doing harm), the judge (Kadi), and the master mason as an expert arbitrator when all three came together to address a problem requiring a 'solution'.

3 Ibn al-Rami lived in the first forty-four years of the 350 years of prosperous Hafsid rule in Ifriqiya. It is within the Hafsid period that the city of Tunis took

its final form, in terms of its overall framework and size, and more importantly the detailed tissue of the city. The structure and form of the city as we see it today has its foundations in that period.

4 In compiling his manuscript, Ibn al-Rami used extensive references to precedent and to previous cases either directly or indirectly in illuminating current cases in Tunis with which he had experience as an expert master mason. He also makes adequate reference to Kadi (judge) Abdul-Rafi's documents.[20]

The cases and 'solutions' presented in this chapter are grouped under the following framework which I devised for the purposes of clarity, and according to the priority and scale of factors that shape the bulk of the city tissue which I have referred to earlier:

1 Streets: thoroughfares (through streets), cul-de-sacs and related elements.
2 Locational restrictions of uses causing harm, for example due to smoke, offensive odour, and noise.
3 Overlooking: visual corridors generated by doors, windows, openings, and heights.
4 Walls between neighbours: rights of ownership and usage.
5 Drainage of rain and waste water.

Streets

(Relevant illustrations are Figures 2(a) and 2(b) and Plates 1 and 2.)
All the references consulted point out two classifications of streets:

1 *The street* (Shari) or thoroughfare i.e. through street (Tariq Nafidh) both are used for the same conceptual pattern — an open and continuous street. This type of street is the public right-of-way; it is open to everybody. It is referred to in ancient manuscripts as 'Tariq al-Muslimeen', but in fact it is open to all the population whether Muslim or not.
2 *The cul-de-sac* or 'the no-exit street' referred to as Derb Ghair Nafidh, Sikka Munsadat al-Asfal, Sikka Ghair Nafidha, Zuqaq, Zanqa. This type of access is not public and belongs in co-ownership to adjacent or bordering residents. There is no conflict regarding the above two classifications between the Maliki and, for instance, the Shafi'i schools.[21]

The following is an elaboration of each street classification (or type) with an exposition of 'solutions' (Ahkam), followed by discussing street-related concepts and elements.

The Street

Width

The minimum width of 7 cubits (minimum dimension of 3.23–3.50 m) was established by the Prophet (see Saying 4, Appendix 1). I have earlier indicated this condition as one of the important general principles which governed the three-dimensional quality of the Arabic–Islamic city.

Height

There was no specific saying of the Prophet that regulated this dimension, but the Fuqaha seem to agree that a person riding a camel should be able to pass through without obstruction. With reference to principle 8 (and its related note), the height of a fully loaded camel with a rider, or with a riding box for women corresponds to 7 cubits. This dimension was verified by studying various conditions from a number of Arab cities, particularly where there is a Sabat (air right structure) over a street (see Plate 1).

Plate 1 (*above left*) A thoroughfare showing a Sabat (room bridging street), a projecting portion of an upper room, and a prominent door. Note that the clearance height for the Sabat and the projection is similar, and the protrusion of the latter is within its Fina space. The Sabat is representative of a short type, in contrast to some which are very long. *Location*: Tunis; Rue du Tresor and on the right foreground Rue el-Khomsa.

Plate 2 (*above right*) A cul-de-sac showing buttressing arches, high windows, and a channel which is used for rainwater drainage. The sidewalk portions represent the width of the Fina for each side. *Location*: Rabat, Morocco. (Photo: Papini, M.H.A.T., Rabat)

Plate 3 (*right*) A tannery is usually located on the outskirts of a town. The photo shows a tannery just inside the Sur or city wall. Note the Burj or fortified towers along the ramparts. *Location*: Marrakech, Morocco. (Photo: Papini, M.H.A.T., Rabat)

Plate 4 (*left*) Windows are usually placed above eye level on the street side, usually the sill is approximately 1.75 m above street level. Note doors on either side of street are set back from each other. *Location*: Tunis; Rue el-Mufti.

Plate 5 (*below*) A window overlooking the private domain of a neighbour can be ordered to be built-up. This example indicates that the window was built-up to prevent overlooking, but a narrow strip was kept to allow light and possibly some ventilation. *Location*: Hotel Bou Faris, Sidi Bou Sa'id, Tunisia. (Photo: George Guimond, 1975)

Plate 6 (*left*) Roofs of houses that are actively used must be screened with parapets to prevent overlooking the private domain of neighbours. The photo shows clustered houses on the right with adequately screened roofs. On the left the roofs of a row of shops which will not be used and therefore do not require screening. *Location*: Fez, Morocco. (Photo: Papini, M.H.A.T., Rabat)

Plate 7 (*below*) The significance of ownership and usage rights of walls between neighbours is the outcome of the organizational nature of clustered courtyard housing. This factor is illuminated by studying typical aerial photos of traditional Arabic–Islamic cities. *Location*: A quarter in Marrakech, Morocco. (Photo: Papini, M.H.A.T., Rabat)

Plate 8 (*right*) Rainwater was allowed to be discharged on streets. One method was to collect the unused rainwater inside the house and channel it to the exterior by an opening under the main door. *Location*: Tunis; a door on the Rue des Tamis. Note the hole under the sill.

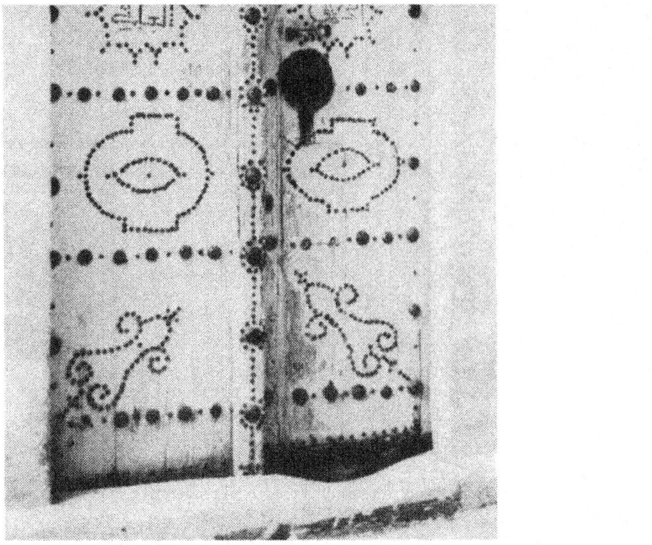

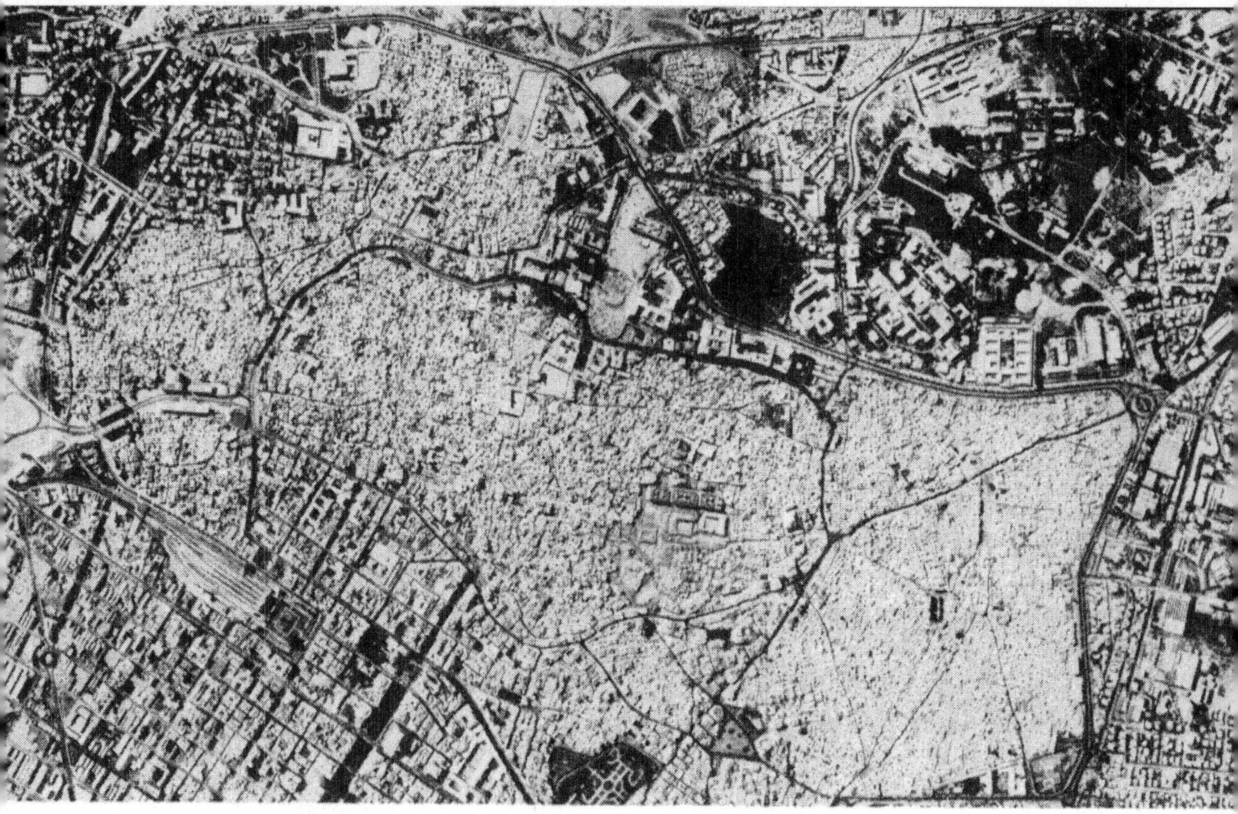

Plate 9 (*above*) The traditional city of Tunis is the primary case study used in this book. This aerial photo taken in 1975 shows the Medina Central flanked on the north (right) and south (left) by the Rabad or suburb, which were later additions in the historical growth of the city. Note that contemporary roads were built to follow the location of the ramparts, most of which were torn down. Also note that the pattern of the European city in the east (bottom) in contrast to the traditional pattern. It was built by the colonial French government during the first half of this century. (Photo: Office de la Topographie et de la Cartographie, Tunis)

Plate 10 (*below*) The Kasbah of Alhambra in Granada, Spain, as photographed by the author in 1963. The photo shows the predominant location relative to the Medina on the right.

The case of someone who protrudes or makes a protrusion into a street (Tariq al-Muslimeen).[22]

First possibility: If the protrusion harms people then it should be demolished, regardless of its size.

Second possibility: If no harm is done and the street is very wide, there are three solutions:

1 Demolish it.
2 Retain it.
3 If the street is less than 7 cubits, then the protrusion should be demolished. If the street is wider it can be retained.

Generally, solutions of this problem require demolition, and most of the cases substantiate that.

The following example was frequently referred to by those Kadis or Faqihs requiring demolition: Malik narrated a case involving Caliph Omar b. Al-Khattab:

> Omar passed by Abu Sufian while he was building his house in Madina, and he noticed that the foundation of the exterior wall protruded into the street. Omar said, 'Abu Sufian you have exceeded your rights and protruded into the rights of others, so remove your wall'; Abu Sufian obeyed Omar and began to remove the foundation stones until completed, then asked Caliph Omar where he wanted him to place the wall. Omar replied, 'I want what is right'.[23]

Unprotested infringement for a lengthy period of time

Among other Maliki jurists, Sahnoun condemned all infringement of a public right-of-way and ordered demolition except under the following conditions:[24] the protrusion in question was there for many years, such as 60 years, without anyone protesting, and the exact origin for the protrusion and occupation was unknown.

It should be noted that under these conditions, the intent is to protect the current occupant's rights, but not to sanction protrusion and occupations. This type of occupation of the public right-of-way usually tended to occur at times of weak public authority because of turmoil, political instability and war.

What is disallowed and allowed in streets[25]

Examples of disallowance in streets:

1 Planting of trees in a public right-of-way.
2 Building columns or pillars ('Stiwan, plural Asateen) in a public right-of-way.
3 The narrowing of a right-of-way for storage purposes by placing such items as wood, food and various loads. The exception is for unloading and service to houses when no harm is done.
4 Tying animals of burden on the street for a length of time and creating a nuisance to passers-by, particularly due to the excrement of 'parked' animals. Mounting and dismounting is exempted and allowed.
5 In the Suq (market) areas the following is disallowed: slaying an animal in front of a butcher's shop and polluting street with blood. Slaying should be done within the butcher's premises.
6 Disposing of items on the street, which might cause people to slip, such as garbage, watermelon skins, excessive spraying with water.
7 In narrow streets (presumably less than 7 cubits), not allowing downspouts and water outlets from walls to empty directly in streets, as they create splashing and cause harm to passers-by. This is allowed in wider streets (presumably over 7 cubits).
8 Melting snow should not be allowed to settle in streets without sweeping, and the sweeping is the responsibility of all

adjacent residents. When water accumulates in a street from a specific spout or rain pipe then it is the obligation of its owner to sweep the accumulated water as goodwill toward the public. However, he should not be ordered to do it, but only reminded politely.

The case of a mature tree which has extended into a public right-of-way[26]
If a tree does cause harm to passers-by within a public right-of-way, then those portions of the tree that cause harm should be trimmed or cut.

The cul-de-sac

Width and height
This is agreed to, depending on the nature and purpose of the cul-de-sac, by the first builders/residents. It is usually 4 cubits (1.84–2.00 m) but sometimes narrower, with the general principle that one fully loaded camel can enter.[27] The height usually follows the restrictions relating to Sabats and projections, see Plate 2. Since the cul-de-sac is owned jointly by all occupants who use it (i.e., common property — Mulk mushtarak, Shirka), agreement between all owners is essential in matters affecting the nature and usage of the cul-de-sac.

A general principle is observed in the usage of cul-de-sacs within the Shafi'i School:[28] every resident is entitled to use the cul-de-sac from its entrance (mouth) to his doorway, so that a person whose doorway is at the end can use all the cul-de-sac for access. In some cases the person who lived at the end of the cul-de-sac was allowed to move his door forward if it did not obstruct other doors, and, in effect, create a *Driba* to his house. The movement of doors was only possible in one direction, that is, from the end side toward the entrance (mouth) of the cul-de-sac. The houses at the mouth of the cul-de-sac whose main entrance is on the public street might be allowed to have a side door on the cul-de-sac if it is used for an occasional emergency only (see Figure 2a).

The following are general guidelines and related Maliki cases which were followed in most instances.

The case of the person who wants to open a door in a cul-de-sac and is prevented by his neighbour[29]
First possibility: if he will harm his neighbour, then he should be prevented and ordered to build up the door opening created.
Second possibility: when opening a door will create no harm to his neighbour, three situations should be observed:

1. If he secures the consent of all occupants on the cul-de-sac, then he can open the door, and they cannot rescind this agreement collectively or individually.
2. When some of the occupants living at the end of the cul-de-sac who always by-pass the door under question agree and others don't, there are two opinions: (a) All occupants have to agree to be able to open a door in a cul-de-sac. (b) If the occupants who agree live at the end of the cul-de-sac and always by-pass the proposed door, then it can be opened regardless of the others who refused.
3. If all occupants refuse the opening of a door, there are three opinions: (a) He can open a door if it is not located opposite a neighbour's door, or directly adjacent to a neighbour's door. (b) He cannot open a door which clearly creates harm to a neighbour by forcing that neighbour to relocate his door. This can be ascertained

by the available space adjacent to the neighbour's door which is used for loading and unloading animals of burden and for other such uses. (c) He can open a door if he uses it to replace the older one, providing no harm is done to the neighbour, such as creating a space for unloading which was not there before (see Figure 2a).

The case of the co-owners of a cul-de-sac who want to repair and maintain it, and other co-owners refuse[30]

It is the duty of all co-owners to share in fixing and maintaining their cul-de-sac, therefore those who refuse should be persuaded to agree. According to Kadi Abdul Rafi, no fixing or maintenance can proceed unless all co-owners' consensus is reached.[31] However, according to Maliki law a co-owner cannot be forced to follow other co-owners' wishes.

When consensus is reached, how will funding be allocated? [32]

Ibn al-Rami asked the Faqih Abou Abdallah b. al-Ghamaz and he answered:

> Usually it is only the richer owners who speak and demand the conversion of their cul-de-sac into a Driba for purposes of general protection and security from burglary, and the poor man is usually not afraid of burglars. Another factor is that fortification (i.e., the creation of a Driba) increases the value of the houses within the Driba. For the above reasons funding should be allocated on a proportional scale based on the richest to the poorest owner of each house.

The case of converting a cul-de-sac into a Driba by adding a door to the mouth of the cul-de-sac[33]

This can only be done with the agreement of all co-owners of the cul-de-sac. This rule was clearly illustrated by the following case in Tunis: A man who owned all the houses on a cul-de-sac except one, converted it to a Driba. The owner of the only other house protested to the Kadi. Master mason Ibn al-Rami was sent to remove the gate, and when he saw no one (i.e., the owner of the other houses made himself unavailable), he went ahead and hired a labourer, took down the gate, and paid the labourer with the money made from selling the remains. This procedure was carried out according to the Kadi's instructions.

Related street elements

1 *Al-Fina*

This term is used for the interior courtyard of a house and to the exterior space immediately adjacent to the exterior wall or walls of a house. The latter type is allocated for the daily temporary use of the inhabitant of the house to which it abuts, without allowing occupation of the space. Allowed uses are the loading and unloading of beasts of burden and the temporary parking of such animals (e.g., a camel, horse, or donkey). In this section the exterior Fina is discussed as it relates to streets and cul-de-sacs.

Caliph Omar b. al-Khattab ruled that the use of Finas belong to the owners (or users) of the houses to which they abut.[34] They can be used for sitting, parking of certain animals, and mobile vendors could also use them to sell their products. Finas should not be incorporated into its adjacent building or a wall built to surround them.

Criteria for recognizing the width of a Fina[35]

1 The contact of rainwater with the ground from gargoyles and spouts should occur within the Fina of the house from which the rainwater originates.
2 The protrusion or length of a gargoyle varies, but one opinion accepts that the

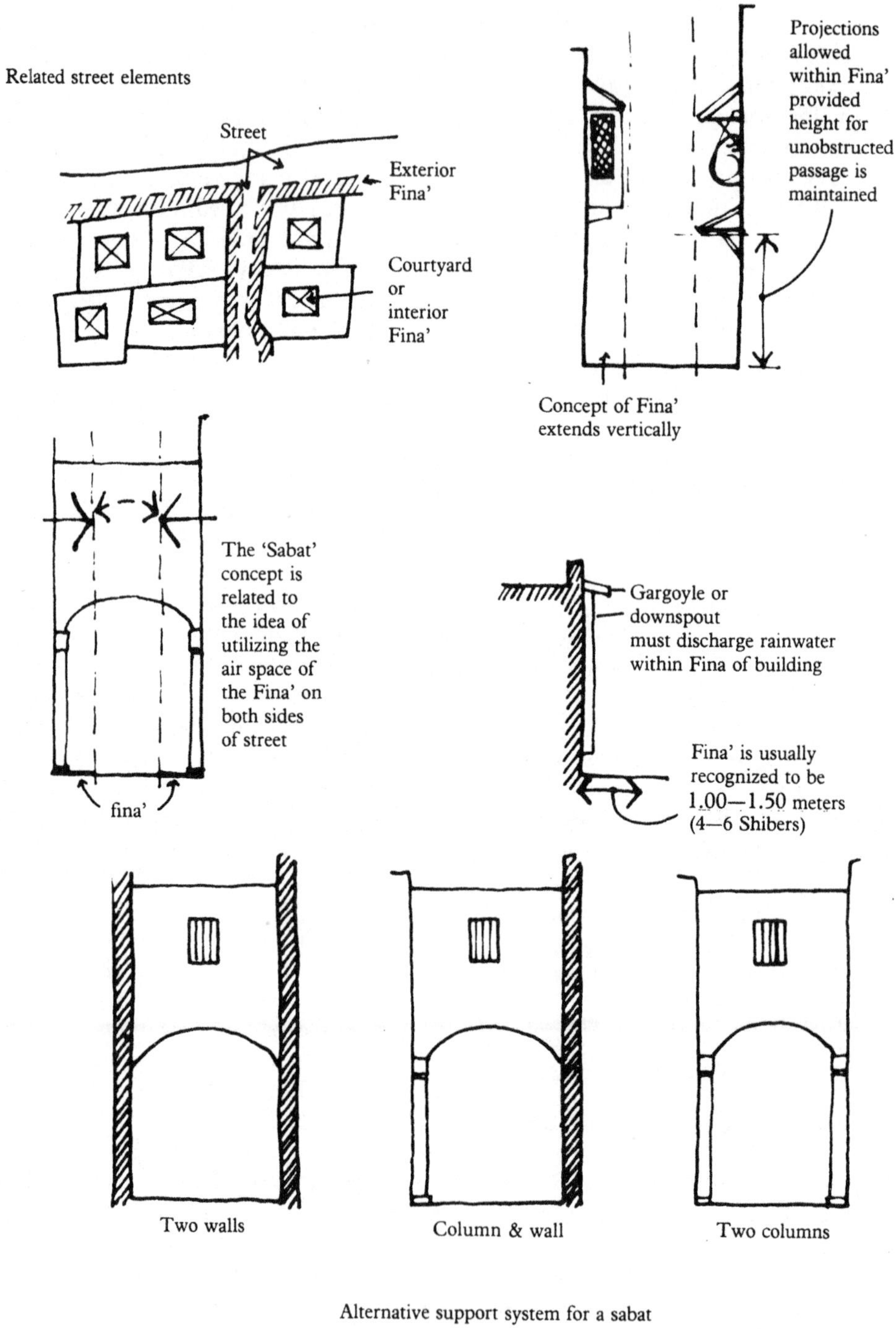
Related street elements
Street
Exterior Fina'
Courtyard or interior Fina'
Projections allowed within Fina' provided height for unobstructed passage is maintained
Concept of Fina' extends vertically
The 'Sabat' concept is related to the idea of utilizing the air space of the Fina' on both sides of street
fina'
Gargoyle or downspout must discharge rainwater within Fina of building
Fina' is usually recognized to be 1.00—1.50 meters (4—6 Shibers)
Two walls
Column & wall
Two columns
Alternative support system for a sabat

Figure 2(b) Streets: related elements

width of the Fina should be between 4 and 6 shibers (i.e., anywhere from 1.00 m to 1.50 m of the width of the street or cul-de-sac).

3 When there are closely adjacent properties such as in the case of cul-de-sacs and small squares, then Finas are jointly shared by respecting the principle that one man's usage should not cause harm to his neighbour.

Demarcation of Finas and renting their use[36]

This is not preferred by the Fuqaha and jurists, as it will decrease from their general effectiveness and will restrict riders of beasts of burden. However, recognition is given to the rightful owners of Finas to make decisions within their rights affecting the use of their Finas, particularly when consensus among neighbours is reached. Resulting common decisions are acceptable to jurists if they do not create harm to others.

Extension of a building into a street without causing harm to anybody[37]

Three approaches:

1 allowance (*Jawaz*);
2 dislike (*Karaha*); and
3 prohibition (*Tahrim*).

An example for allowance was a person who built a Mesjed within his house using his own funds and wanted to extend it partially into the street. Malik said that if the action would not create harm to the public right-of-way, then it could be allowed. Another similar case by a later Maliki jurist disallowed it, even when the Fina was wide.

An example for allowance and dislike: was a person who demolished parts of his house for purposes of rebuilding and incorporating parts of his wide Fina. If the Fina is wide and his action does not create harm to the street then he may be allowed, but Malik disliked it.

2 *High-level protrusions onto streets and air-right structures (Sabats) over streets:*

The concept of the Fina on the ground is also reflected in the air. Projections from houses towards the street are allowed provided they do not obstruct passage of maximum height.[38] Building a room over a street joining two structures owned by the same person is also allowed; these air-right structures are called *Sabat* (plural *Sawabeet* or *Sabatat*). Their height clearance over street level is also governed by the minimum dimension required applicable to projections. The Shafi'i and Maliki Schools allow projections and Sabats.[39]

Asbagh, Mutarrif and Ibn Majiun mention that:

> Such a usage had always existed, and one could not prevent anyone from doing it, provided that they [protrusions, overhangs and Sabats] are placed high enough not to hinder those passing underneath, riders, pedestrians, and those carrying burdens. If such a projection, overhang, or Sabat does not conform to this requirement, then it should be demolished.[40]

Sahnoun was asked about a man who owns two houses opposite each other across a street who wanted to join them with a room. He said that if he created no harm then he should be allowed, but if he created harm to the street, such as by narrowing it, then he should be prevented.[41] Ibn al-Rami reports that he asked the opinion of Shaikh Ibn al-Ghamaz about a protrusion which was too low and caused accidents because people's heads touched it:

> Could the situation be corrected by digging and ramping the street under so that enough clearance is created? The answer was no, it should be demolished and raised adequately to allow free passage of pedestrians and the highest mounted person.[42]

The case of two houses across a street owned by the same person who built a Sabat across the street

After his death the two houses were sold to separate buyers. The first bought one house without the Sabat. The second bought the house across the street with the Sabat. The wall which belongs to the house without the Sabat is the property of the owner of that house and is not a commonly owned wall. The owner of the house with the Sabat has only a neighbour's privilege of using that wall for support.[43]

Further examination of the Sabat in terms of streets (public right-of-ways) and cul-de-sacs (privately co-owned access) reveal the following:

1 When locating on streets, two possibilities occur: (a) one owner of the two sides of the street; or (b) two owners of the two sides of the street. In the first case the owner can construct the Sabat provided he does not cause harm to the street and does not hinder passers-by (as discussed previously). In the second case the owner of the house who wants to construct the Sabat and wants to use the exterior wall of the opposite house for support can do so only if he acquires authorization from the opposite owner. This authorization is considered a tolerance and can be revoked at any time by the owner of the wall who gives authorization. It can only constitute a right if it has been accorded a property title.

2 When locating on cul-de-sacs, the person who wants to build a Sabat must secure the permission and agreement of all co-owners of the cul-de-sac. This agreement is not essential when a person wants to build a Sabat as an extension to his house in the interest of the public good, such as a Kouttab, a children's school for the teaching of the Qur'an and religion.[44]

Some Sabats are built on columns on one or both sides of a street. This option is open when an opposite owner is not willing to allow his exterior wall to be used to support a Sabat. Owners of both sides of a street also use this technique assuming that their property might be divided in the future and the option will exist to sell one or both sides of the houses on the street without worrying about joint ownership of walls and related potential conflicts. The columns are usually built touching the exterior walls of the opposite houses to minimize protrusion and obstruction of the street.

Widths of other street types

For streets meant for public passage the width should be 7 cubits, and if it is not to be so used, then one should seek to leave the matter to the residents. For streets meant for cattle and sheep it should be 20 cubits, as the jurists have decided. The Prophet has said nothing on the subject. Footpaths where few people pass, and which are not classed as a public route, should be 4 cubits wide.[45]

Finally it should be noted that the Arabic–Islamic city was self-policing to a large extent, in terms of informing the authorities of any wrongdoing, such as the unlawful protrusions into streets and the misuse of the Fina. Any passer-by or neighbour who feels that harm has been done can inform the authorities. This self-regulating societal behaviour is sanctioned in the Qur'an.[46]

In Tunis during the early fourteenth cenury AD Kadi Abdul-Rafi used to send his master mason consultant Ibn al-Rami to walk through the city and report any unlawful protrusions or actions and also the condition of weak, dilapidated walls which might cause danger to pedestrians in case of sudden collapse. The Kadi would then order those unlawful protrusions and unsafe walls demolished.

Locational restrictions of uses causing harm

(Relevant illustrations are Figure 3 and Plate 3.)
In addition to an accepted tradition of land-use allocation on a macro scale, the Arabic–Islamic city followed principles affecting land or building use on a micro scale. The essential concept behind the principles followed is that of harm.

Within the framework of micro-locational restrictions, harm was viewed in two ways. It may have been existing or already established (referred to in Arabic as 'old' (*Qadim*), its impact felt due to an adjacent recent phenomenon. This category was usually not ordered to change. Or its uses might still have to have been established, adjacent to other uses which would have been creating nuisance and/or harm to those already established uses. Some were allowed, and others disallowed, according to the nature and duration of the harm to be caused.

Uses which create smoke

Smoke was viewed as emanating from two types of uses:

1 From buildings that are to be disallowed from locating adjacent to houses and other uses that might be harmfully affected by smoke, for example from public baths, bakeries, mills in Suqs or houses used to fry barley and other similar uses.
2 From activities which should not be disallowed due to their importance: for example, from within houses such as baking pits (*Tannur*), kitchens and other similar uses.

The following cases are for further clarification

If a person owns a plot of land adjacent to a house and wants to build on it a public bath or bakery, can the neighbour disallow it? [47]
Opinions differed when direct harm to the neighbour cannot be established. Those who said that it should be disallowed based their opinion on the grounds that the value of the house would depreciate, owing to the danger of fire from without, and the large number of people using the facility. Frequent reference is made to a verse in the Qur'an which specifically prohibits the injury or the diminishing of people's property.[48] Other opinions allow the location of such a facility when direct harm from smoking is not evident.

The case of the increase in the quantity of smoke[49]
A man had an oven with one source of fire and constructed another source of fire to increase the heating capacity of his oven and used the existing chimney to evacuate the smoke from both fires. The neighbours protested on the grounds that more smoke was being generated and therefore causing more harm. They complained to the Kadi who agreed with their complaint, and he ordered the man to remove his recently constructed additional source of fire.

When is a tenant responsible for a fire caused by a baking pit? [50]
If a tenant rents a house with a baking pit and is allowed to use it and a fire occurs which burns down the house and/or the neighbours' houses, he would not be responsible. However, if a tenant rents a house with the agreement that he should not

use the baking pit, then he would be held responsible for all damages in the event of a fire from that baking pit.

Uses that create offensive odour

Ibn al-Rami specifically mentions that the principle followed is to remove garbage, effluence, and sources of offensive smells (see Plate 3).[51] The Prophet's saying regarding the prohibition of persons who eat garlic and onion and who emanate a distinct odour while attending a mosque is used as an indirect reference to support this principle.[52]

The following two conditions are examples of when to disallow or eliminate sources of offensive odour:

1 When a person uses his house as a tannery and his neighbour complains of the offensive odour.
2 When a person constructs a toilet or an uncovered sewer adjacent to his neighbour and when either of these conditions creates an odour offensive to that neighbour. The solution to the latter condition would be to cover it. The former condition is usually solved by ordering the removal of the facility.

Figure 3 Example of a 'solution' ordered by a Kadi to alleviate harm

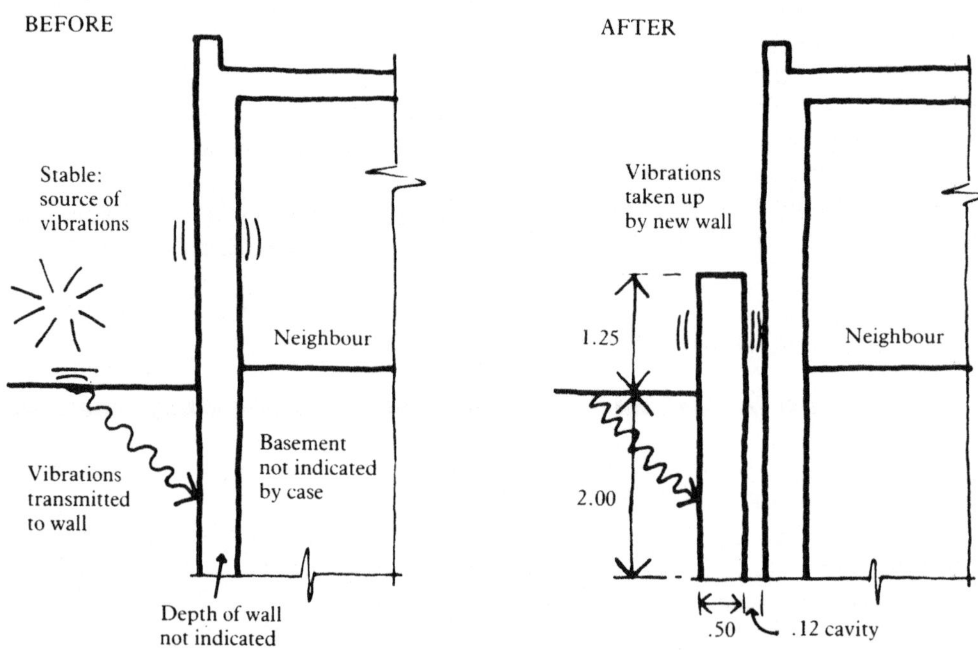

Solution implemented by the order of Kadi Abdul Al-Rafi for preventing the transmittal of vibrations to a neighbour.

Plate 11 (*right*) A portion of the Sur or rampart surrounding the north suburb of Tunis, and located between Burj al-Assel and Bab Khadra. Note the corner is fortified in the form of a small Burj. (Photo: Wisam Hakim, 1975)

Plate 12 (*below*) One of the important city gates (or Bab) of Meknes, Morocco as photographed by the author in 1963. Note the elaborate decoration and scale.

Plate 13 (*left*) A typical busy public thoroughfare flanked by commercial facilities. *Location*: Tunis; Rue Jama'a Zitouna.

Plate 14 (*below left*) A Bat'ha or a public place usually formed at the Y-junction of three streets. *Location*: Tunis, at the junction of Rue el-Methira and Rue el-Arian.

Plate 15 (*below right*) A typical small cemetery. *Location*: Sidi Bou Sa'id, Tunisia. (Photo: James Wright, 1975)

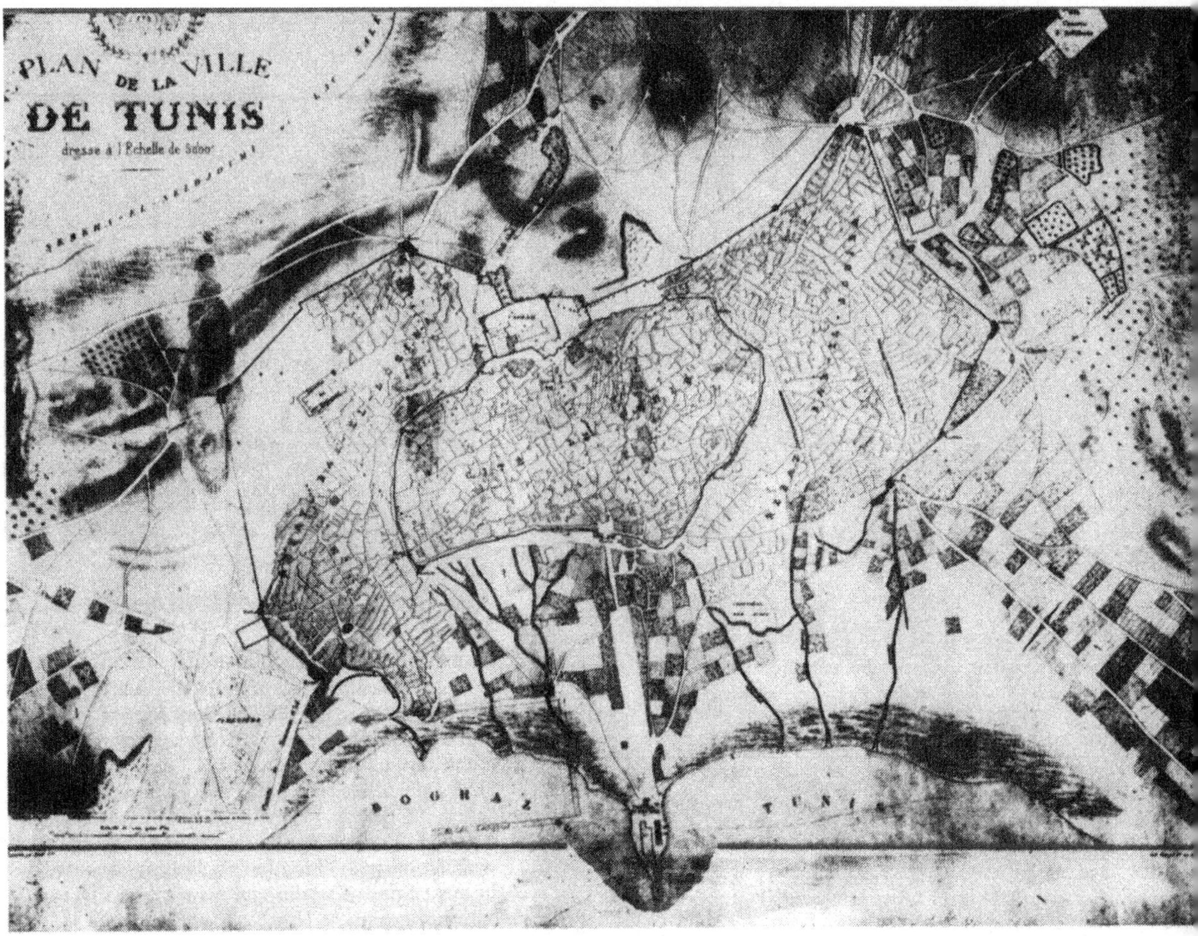

Plate 16 (*above*) The Khandaq or major sewer channels from the city to the lake are clearly drawn by the engineer Colin in this 1860 plan of Tunis. (Reproduced courtesy of the Office de la Topographie et de la Cartographie, Tunis)

Plate 17 (*right*) A Sabat can be short or long. An example of the former is also portrayed in Plate 1. This is an example of a long and continuous Sabat. Note the location of columns used for support. *Location*: Tunis; Rue Ben Mahmoud towards its west end, where a gate is located.

Plate 18 Suq or Bazaar coverage system.
(a) (*left*) Bazaar in Isfahan, Iran as photographed by the author in 1967. The coverage system is of repetitive brick domes with their apex open to allow sunlight and ventilation. These domes are built over a series of buttressing arches. (b) (*above*) A Suq in Fez Morocco. The coverage system is of bamboo matting supported on wooden beams. This type of coverage is popular in most Suqs of traditional Moroccan cities. (Photo: Papini, M.H.A.T., Rabat)

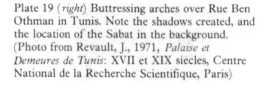

Plate 19 (*right*) Buttressing arches over Rue Ben Othman in Tunis. Note the shadows created, and the location of the Sabat in the background. (Photo from Revault, J., 1971, *Palaise et Demeures de Tunis*: XVII et XIX siecles, Centre National de la Recherche Scientifique, Paris)

Uses that are acoustically offensive

The uses that are frequently mentioned as being acoustically offensive are garment beating and wheat grinding (either hand or by animal). Stables are also considered acoustically offensive. The source of the nuisance from wheat grinders is the vibration caused in neighbours' walls.[53]

Thus, offensive noise can be generated directly or indirectly. The general approach is to disallow or remove the source of noise. In some cases preventive measures are prescribed, and here vibrations were considered harmful only if they exceed a certain limit. In Tunis Kadi Abdul al-Rafi devised a method to establish such a limit.

Ibn al-Rami described a number of cases regarding offensive noise generated by stables. The principle used is to disallow the location of a stable adjacent to a house if its harmful acoustical effects are clear. When there is a physical solution to eliminate the problem, then it is sometimes used. One such solution is described in the following case which occurred in Tunis.[54] A man built a small stable behind his neighbour's rear wall, and the neighbour protested to the Kadi on grounds of the disturbing noise which it created. After inspecting the site Ibn al-Rami confirmed the acoustical harm. The Kadi ordered its removal. The owner of the stable then pleaded with the Kadi on the grounds that the stable is an important source for his income, and he would be willing to implement what is necessary to reduce or eliminate the harm caused to his neighbour. The Kadi agreed and ordered the following solution to be constructed by Ibn al-Rami: a wall to be built with a foundation depth the height of a man (approx. 2 m) in front of the neighbour's wall through which the noise was transmitted. This wall is to be constructed 5 shibers (approx. 1.25 m) above ground level and it should be 2 shibers (approx. 50 cm) thick. There should also be a cavity between the two walls (i.e., between the proposed and the existing walls of the house) of half a shiber (approx. 12 cm) for the full height of the proposed wall (see Figure 3).

Ibn al-Rami reported that this solution did prevent the transmission of noise to the neighbour. As a further precaution the Kadi ordered that it be checked at night at a time when the noise is more discernible by the neighbour.[55]

Overlooking: visual corridors generated by doors, windows, openings and heights

(Relevant illustrations are Figures 4(a) and 4(b) and Plates 4, 5 and 6.)

The Qur'an teaches the virtues and importance of privacy, the right to it, and respect of it.[56] The Prophet is attributed to numerous sayings on this issue.[57] All mediums affecting privacy are included in Muslim teaching, but the visual medium especially is directly affected by urban and building form and is therefore selected for elaboration here, see Figures 4(a) and 4(b).

Within the context of housing, the family is the main concern in visual privacy, particularly the importance of protecting female members from the eyes of male strangers. Accordingly, a context that facilitates visual overlooking is considered harmful and is therefore an offence in Muslim law, and must be avoided. The source of any offence is viewed by Muslim Kadis as correctable and/or removable.

Overlooking: from windows and doors

Windows generating complaints due to overlooking are classified as:

1 *Old* (*Qadim*), that is, they have been in

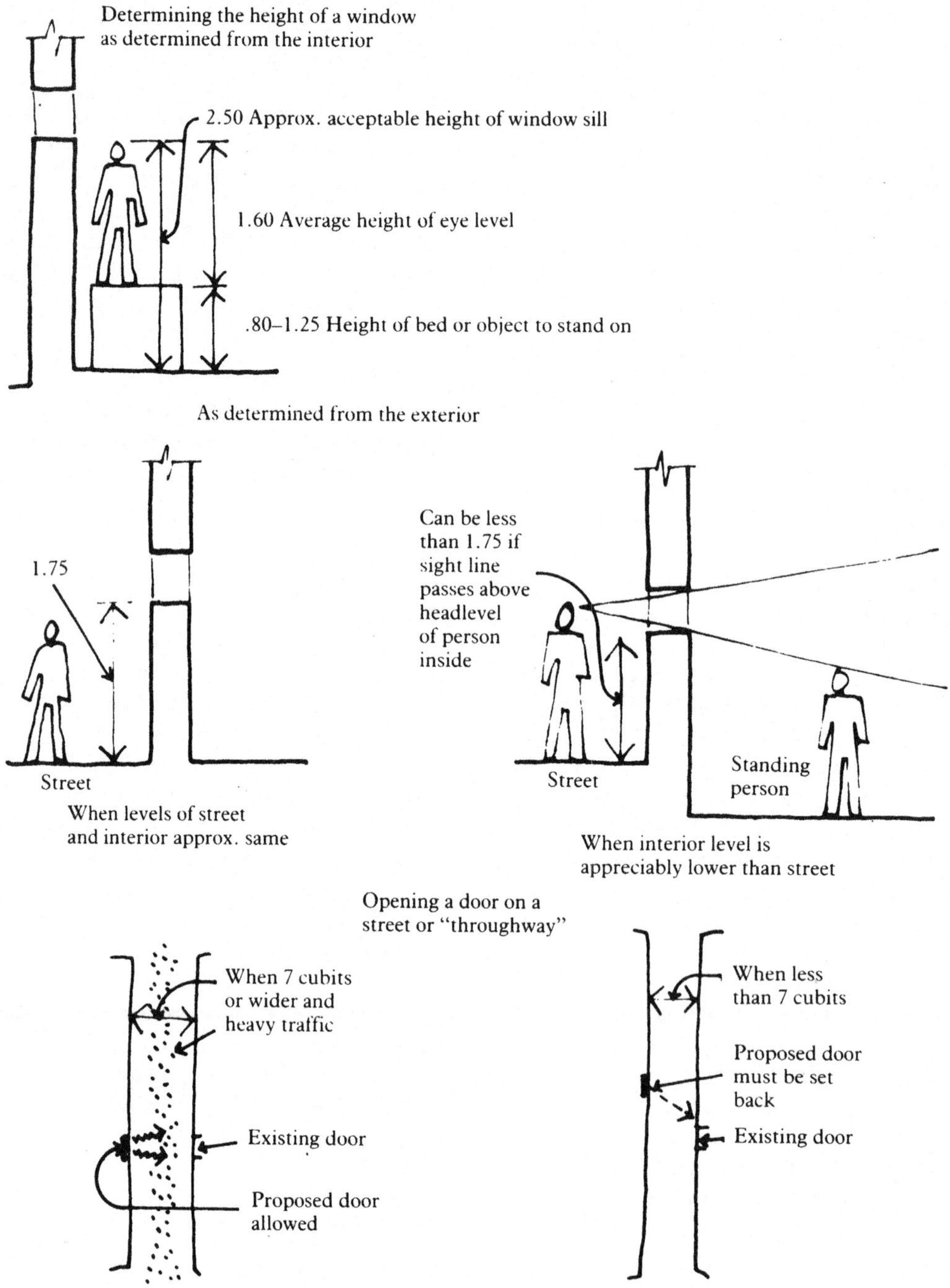

Determining the height of a window
as determined from the interior
2.50 Approx. acceptable height of window sill
1.60 Average height of eye level
.80–1.25 Height of bed or object to stand on
As determined from the exterior
1.75
Street
When levels of street
and interior approx. same
Can be less
than 1.75 if
sight line
passes above
headlevel
of person
inside
Street
Standing
person
When interior level is
appreciably lower than street
Opening a door on a
street or "throughway"
When 7 cubits
or wider and
heavy traffic
Existing door
Proposed door
allowed
When less
than 7 cubits
Proposed door
must be set
back
Existing door

Figure 4(a) Overlooking: visual corridors

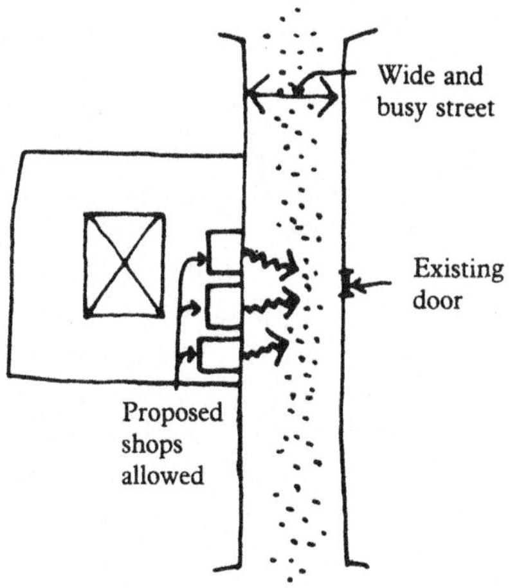

Case 1, page 38

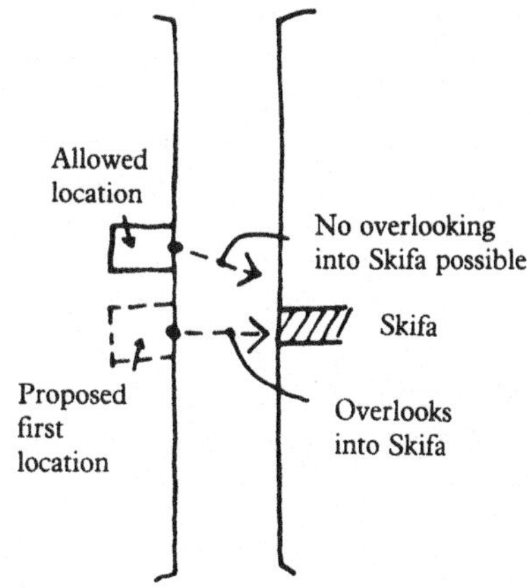

Case 3, page 38

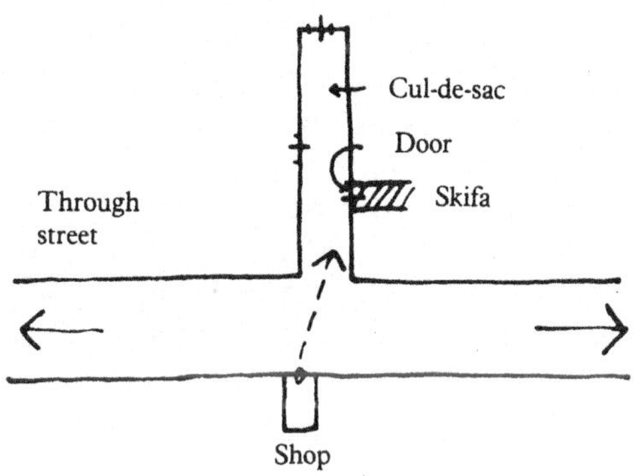

Case 4, page 38

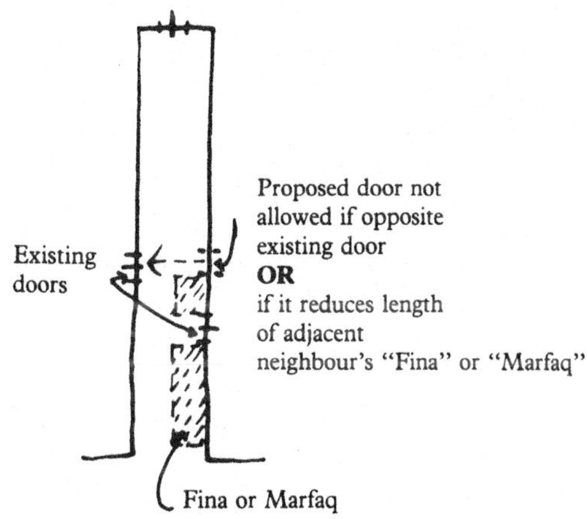

Case 2(iii), page 39

Figure 4(b) Overlooking: further examples of visual corridors

their position for a long time. Keeping them is the more common ruling.

2 *Recent* (*Hadith*), that is they are of recent construction and occurrence. Ordering their owners to shut them permanently is the common ruling.

How high should a window be, to be considered discreetly located, in terms of offering visual protection in a normal situation between neighbours, when there is no intent on the part of a neighbour to overlook the other?

Solution 1

Determined from the interior: narrated by Malik from the solution of Caliph Omar b. al-Khatab:

> A bed is to be placed underneath the window, and if a man standing on it does not see through it, then the window is allowed to remain, otherwise it should be shut.[58]

Note: a bed height is given as between 4 and 5 shibers (i.e., anywhere between 0.80 and 1.25 m). This 'bed height' was also interpreted later as any object in a room which could be used to stand on. Adding 1.60 m to that dimension as an average eye-level height of a man, it would make an acceptable height for a window sill approximately 2.50 m.

Solution 2

Determined from the exterior: acceptability of height determined from the outside (commonly the street). If the window's height is low enough to allow a passer-by to see directly into the interior, then it is considered low and should be raised. The sill should be 7 shibers above ground (i.e., 1.75 m) to be considered of adequate height to prevent a passer-by (with no harmful intention) from overlooking. This condition assumes that the ground level of the interior is approximately the same as that of the exterior. However, when the ground level of the interior is appreciably lower, then the exterior window below 7 shibers is allowed if the sight lines from it are above headlevel of a standing person in the interior.[59]

The case of 'old' window or door overlooking a neighbour

If the window or door is not utilized by its owner and is creating harm, then two opinions prevail. The most common practice is that it should remain if its owner wants to retain it.[60] Some legal scholars would order the window or door shut, even if it is old, if its harm to others is determined greater than its use to its owner. Ibn al-Rami clearly states that the first approach is the most prevalent, and indicates that if the neighbour is truly aggravated by such a situation, then he should be told to build or rectify his building to prevent overlooking by his neighbour.[61]

The case of 'old' openings overlooking adjacent empty plot

Any opening overlooking an adjacent empty plot provides its owner with the rights of first usage. When the empty plot is to be developed, its owner has to plan the building to prevent being overlooked from the existing openings of his neighbour.[62] In other words, no burden or responsibility is placed upon the first neighbour regarding placement of openings relative to an adjacent undeveloped lot. This is a clear case of the importance of the sequence of development upon building decisions and the resulting built form.

The case of 'recent' opening overlooking a neighbour's courtyard

If a window or door is created that would overlook an existing neighbour's courtyard, then it is ordered to be permanently shut.[63] Such a situation usually occurs when a room is added on the roof level. However, if an opening, such as a high-level window, is created which is clearly located so that it cannot be used for overlooking, then it is allowed provided no harm from it can be established.[64]

Ibn al-Rami clearly distinguishes between such a window and a small opening which would allow overlooking yet protect the intruder from being recognized. This type of opening is deemed more harmful and is prevented.[65]

The case of a 'recent' opening towards a neighbour that does not allow overlooking but allows sound penetration
Ibn al-Rami said that this specific condition occurred in Tunis and the normal procedure was to allow the opening, even though some scholars considered sound penetration harmful. This is a clear case of the priority given to the harmful effects of visual penetration.[66]

Stairway landing on roof and case of roof parapets
The exit of the stairway to the roof should not face the neighbours in such a way that when a person exits to the roof he/she would be looking directly toward them. However, there is no requirement for a parapet to screen the person on the roof from his neighbours below. A case occurred in Tunis where the roof exit was screened by a parapet from the neighbours. The parapet fell and the neighbour wanted it to be rebuilt; the Kadi did not order the owner to rebuild it, but warned that he would be punished if he intentionally misused his roof to overlook his neighbour.[67]

The case of a window opening from a room that overlooks a neighbour's roof
Such a window is allowed, even if the neighbours' roof is customarily used to hang clothes and similar purposes.[68]

Building within one's air right even if it excludes air movement and sunlight from a neighbour's window
There seems to be general agreement among the Maliki scholars that a person has the right to build and/or extend a portion of a building within his boundary and vertical airspace. This right is upheld even if the action would exclude air movement and sunlight from an existing neighbour's window/s.

The exclusion of air movement and sunlight is considered a lesser harm than that of preventing alteration or extension within one's boundaries and airspace. Ibn Kenana cited the exception to this norm. He was interested in the intention of a potential change that would create such an obstruction of air movement or sunlight. If the need for a change is clear then it is allowed; however if the change will not benefit its owner and will harm the neighbour, then it should be prevented.

Ibn al-Rami summarizes this condition by quoting from the book of his contemporary Kadi Ibn Abdul-Rafi:

> That all conditions creating harm should be removed, except the obstruction of air movement and sunlight due to the increase in height of an adjacent wall or building. However if such an obstruction was created to inflict harm then it too should be removed.[69]

The case of overlooking from a minaret or roof of a mosque
A *Muezzin* (a man whose duty is to call for prayer) climbs the minaret or roof of a mosque five times a day; he is prohibited from doing so if the mosque is within a short distance of the courtyards of houses allowing direct and clear overlooking.

On a roof a parapet should be constructed to prevent direct overlooking. The use of minarets is allowed when the Muezzin cannot overlook or see people; or if that is impossible then the Muezzin's platform of the minaret must be surrounded by an adequately high parapet.[70]

Opening a door on a street or thoroughfare

When a door is to be located opposite another door across the street, three conditions are identified:[71]

1 If the street is 7 cubits or more wide and is used heavily, then the door can be opened. The reason given is that traffic and the width of the street will help prevent invasion of privacy.
2 The door is not allowed if harm is generated due to direct overlooking so that the *Skifa* (entry room) behind the 'old' opposite door is visible as it is being used.
3 The door should be set aside from the opposite door at an adequate distance to eliminate the harm created by direct overlooking.

Kadi Ibn Abdul-Rafi specifies that a door should be set aside from the one opposite unless the street is wide enough that its activity will obstruct the opposite door. However, Ibn al-Rami specifies setting aside opposite doors particularly on streets narrower than 7 cubits which are not heavily used.

Opening a shop opposite an 'old' existing door of a house on a street (thoroughfare)

The consideration and principles are similar to the problem of opening doors; however, it is clearly acknowledged that the potential harm created by a shop is much greater than that of a door. The following four cases and their solutions clarify the nature of the problem.[72]

Case 1

A man wants to create shop(s) from his house, and the shop(s) would face the door of the opposite house. This condition will be allowed only if the street is wide and busy so that the normal traffic in the street will camouflage the users of the specific door under consideration.

Case 2

The same conditions as Case 1 above, but the following approach to the solution is used: the shop should be set aside from the opposite door if harm is determinable. However, if the configuration of the property of the man who wants to open the shop does not allow setting aside the proposed shop, and if he can prove the necessity for the shop, then he is allowed to build it.

Case 3

A proposed shop opposite an existing door which allowed the person in the shop to see directly into the Skifa (entry hall) of the house opposite. The solution was to order the shop to be set aside by a distance which would not allow the shopkeeper or user to see into the Skifa.

Case 4

According to the sketch which was developed from a detailed description of the case, the owner of the house protested to the Kadi that the shop is creating harm due to its overlooking position. However, the Kadi had a confirmation that the person in the shop could not see into the Skifa of the house, but could only see people as they emerge from or enter the doorway. Accordingly the Kadi ordered that the shop could remain.

Method of determining the harm of a visual corridor through a Skifa

In the above cases a major criteria in determining harm is whether or not the Skifa (entry hall) of a house can be seen from a shop. However, some scholars and Kadis specify exactly what constitutes visual penetration of a Skifa, and the following two conditions do *not* constitute penetration:[73]

1 If a man is standing at the mouth of the Skifa while the door is open, and the space left around him is such that the viewer from the opposite side of the street cannot see behind him, then the Skifa is considered too narrow and small to allow visual penetration.
2 If a man standing near the mouth of the Skifa cannot be seen from the opposite side of the street, because of the size and lighting conditions of the Skifa, then it is considered that the Skifa cannot be visually penetrated.

In both conditions the shop does not create enough harm to justify its prohibition, or to disallow a person to benefit from his property by eliminating the potential income that a shop would generate.

Opening a new or recent door on a cul-de-sac
This is another version of the case discussed on page 26 and here two primary possibilities are identified:[74]

1 If harm to a neighbour is clearly created, then the solution is also clear — it should be ordered shut.[75]
2 When it does not harm a neighbour, three cases are identified:
(i) If all heads of households living in the cul-de-sac agree, then the door can be opened, and this allowance, once given, cannot be rescinded individually or collectively.
(ii) If some agree and others do not, and the ones who agree live at the end of the cul-de-sac and they always by-pass the door under question, two approaches: (a) not allowed unless all agree; (b) allowed if those agree live at the end of the cul-de-sac.
(iii) If all disallowed the door, then three approaches are possible: (a) He should not be allowed if he would be facing directly the opposite neighbour's door, or if the door proposed would be too close to the adjacent neighbour's door and/or decrease the length of his usable Fina (Marfaq).[76] If, however, the door proposed will not create the above specific conditions, then it should be allowed. (b) He should not be allowed if his potential action will force an adjacent neighbour to shift his door to recreate the necessary length of a usuable Fina (Marfaq). (c) He should not be allowed whatever conditions the door will or will not create.

An exception to the above cases is when a man wants to close his original door and replace it with another; he should be allowed if the new door will not create the kind of harm to the neighbour(s) indicated in the previous cases.

Walls between neighbours: rights of ownership and usage

(Relevant illustrations are Figure 5 and Plate 7)

The rights of ownership and usage of party walls were derived from the following three conditions:[77]

1 A wall between two neighbours with each one claiming it.
2 A wall that is owned by one neighbour and provides privacy for the other. In the event that the wall collapses or that its owner wants to take it down, can he be forced to rebuild it?
3 A wall that is jointly owned by two neighbours; can one use the wall without the permission of the other?

The following is a discussion and elaboration of these three conditions (see Figure 5).

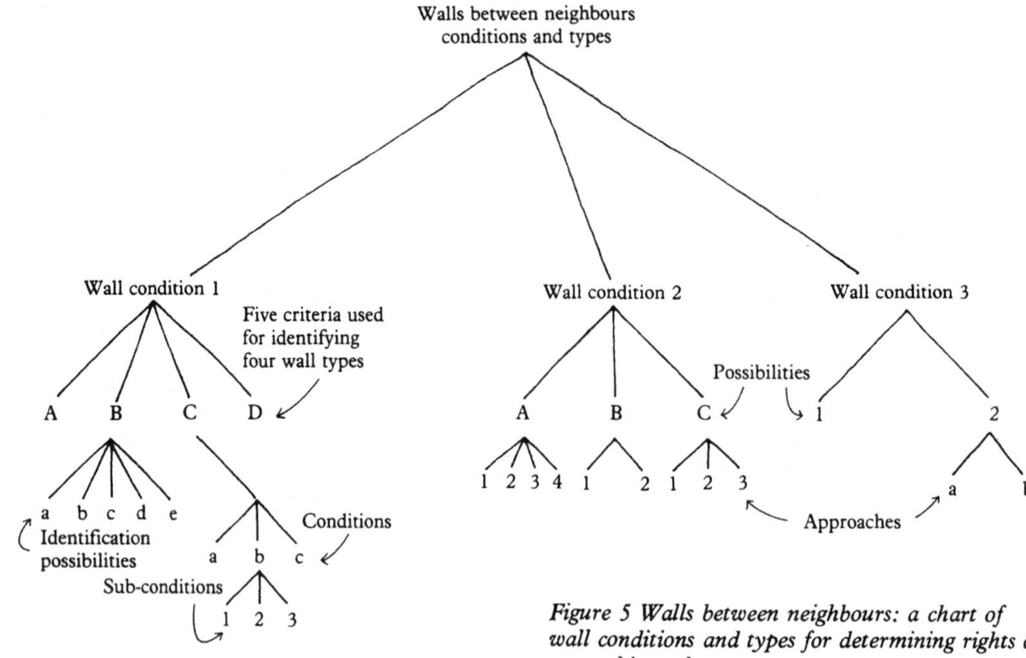

Figure 5 Walls between neighbours: a chart of wall conditions and types for determining rights of ownership and usage

Condition 1: a wall between two neighbours with each one claiming it

According to Ibn al-Rami, the Maliki school of law recognized the wall bond and the following four wall elements (items 2–5 below) as criteria for identifying the ownership of a wall between two neighbours when each claims it to himself:

1 The wall bond.[78]
2 The door in the wall.
3 The recess in the wall (*Taqa*).[79]
4 Wooden beams inserted into wall.
5 Building on top of wall.

These five identifying criteria[80] are applied to each of the following four wall types which cover all aspects for Condition 1:

A: The wall with bond(s) but no other element(s).
B: The wall with element(s) but no bond(s).
C: The wall with element(s) and bond(s).
D: The wall with neither element(s) nor bond(s).

Wall type A: the wall with bond(s) but no other element(s)[81]

If the bonds are related to one of the two houses, and the other house has no elements on the wall, then it is deemed to belong to the house to which it is bonded. In the case of determining ownership of a two-storey wall when the wall bonds for each storey are in reverse, then each level is owned separately. However, if the upper portion is not bonded, then the owner of the lower portion owns the whole wall.[82]

Ibn al-Rami discusses two other cases related to this wall type, but the complexity of the description prevents me from interpreting the exact circumstances. However, two useful items of information emerge: the

Plate 20 (*right*) Oblique aerial photo showing the courtyard of the Zaytuna mosque in the context of its immediate neighbourhood. Note the L-shaped courtyard of the Sidi Ben Arous mosque in the foreground. (Photo: KAHIA, Tunis, taken during the mid-1960s)

Plate 21 (*below*) The major entrance (on the eastern facade) of the Zaytuna mosque. Note the lower level created by the west to east sloping terrain. (Photo: Wisam Hakim, 1975)

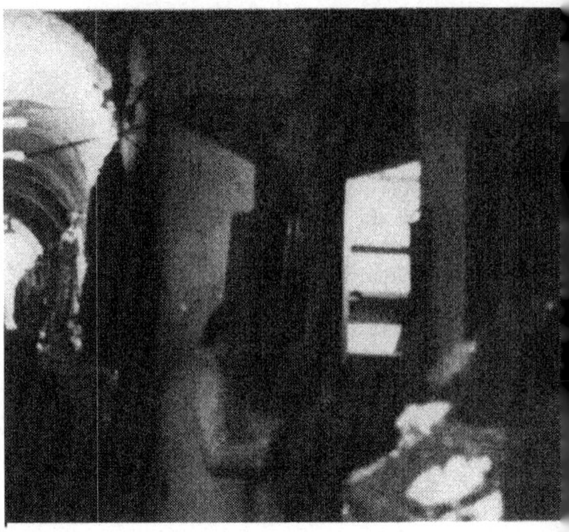

Plate 22 Typical Mesjids. (a) (*above left*) Oblique view of Mesjid Ali Pacha in Tunis showing the facility tucked within Suq des Chachias. Note the very narrow courtyard. The photo was taken from the minaret of Sidi Ben Arous mosque, looking west. (b) (*above right*) The anonymous-looking entrance of Mesjid Nehas (on extreme right of photo) located on the Suq el-Grana, Tunis.

Plate 23 (*left*) The courtyard of a Madrasa in Meknes, Morocco. The fountain is used by the students for ablution. The windows, at the upper level, are of students' rooms. The photo was taken from the main entrance by the author in 1963.

Plate 24 (*below*) The large and spacious courtyard of the famous Madrasa Al-Mustansiriya in Baghdad, Iraq. The photo shows the northern Iwan and parts of the Iwans of the main entrance to the right and the prayer hall on the left. (Photo: Directorate General of Antiquities, Baghdad, after restoration in the 1950s)

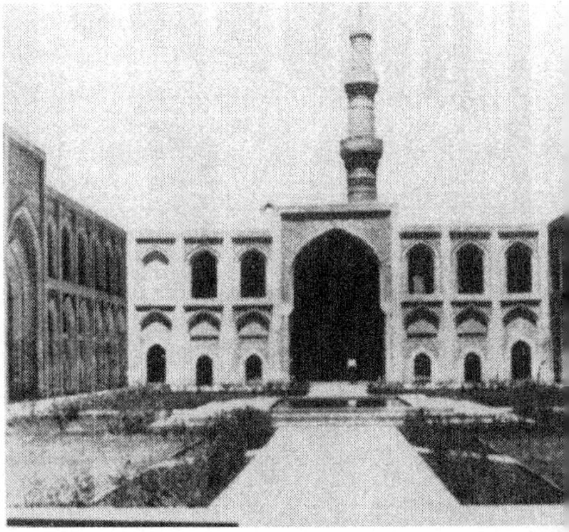

Plate 25 (*right*) A typical Maghribi Marabout structure. This example is located in the village of Sidi Bou Sa'id, Tunisia. (Photo: James Wright, 1975)

Plate 26 (*below left*) An unusual location and type of Marabout. The Marabout Sidi Bou Abdallah is in the form of a large coffin located in the midst of pedestrian traffic in Suq Serrajine, Tunis.

Plate 27 (*below right*) Turba Ali Pasha from the middle courtyard of Madrasa Sulaimaniya in Tunis. Note the Kbu or dome marking the space in which the tombs are located.

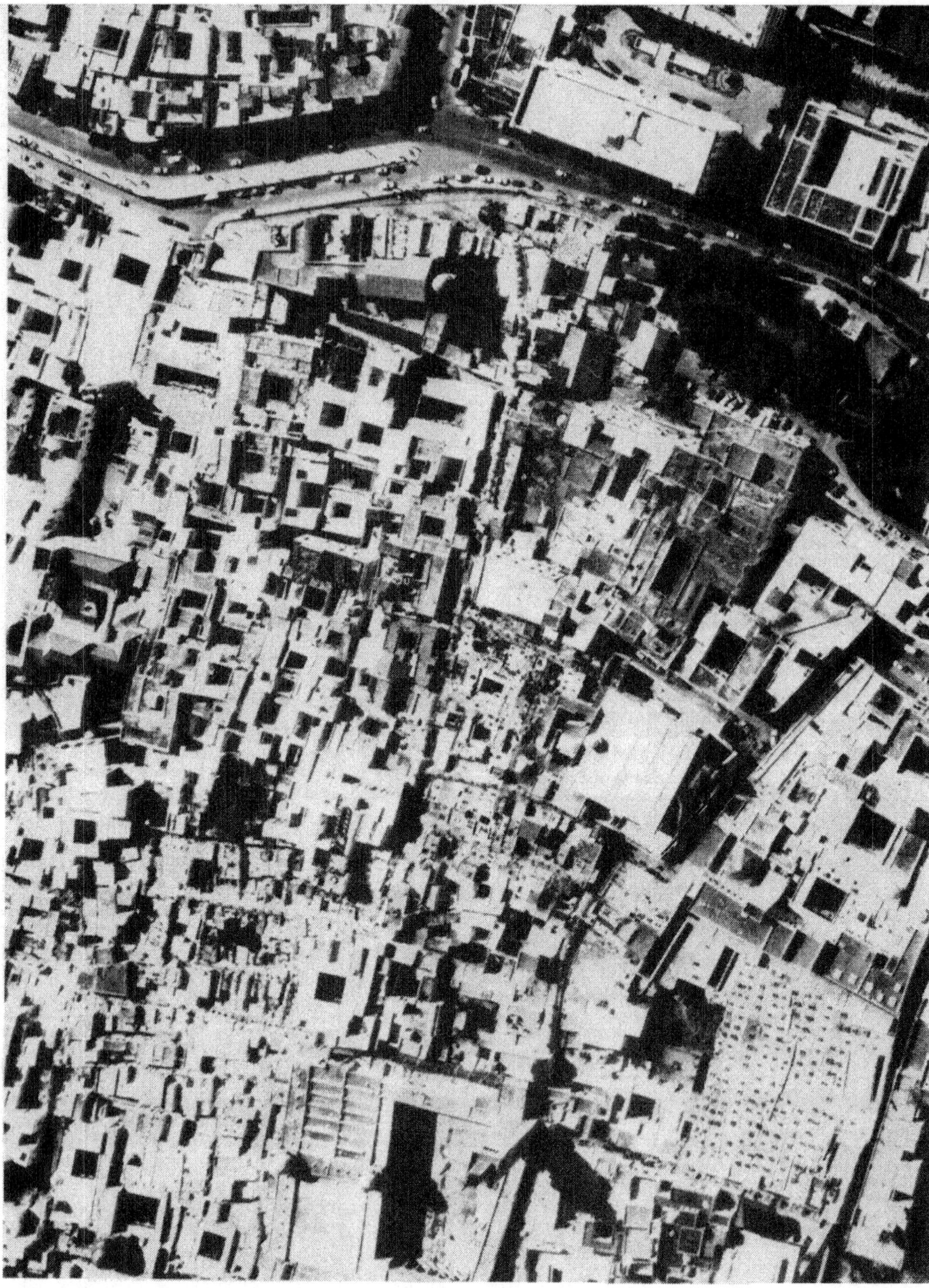

Plate 28 Aerial photo of the west central area of Tunis Medina. Note the small cemetery, south of the spine of Suq Serrajine and east of the ring road, discussed in the text. The small, domed structure within it is a Marabout. The Zaytuna mosque is at the bottom of the photo surrounded by the complex maze of the Suq system. (Photo: Office de la Topographie et de la Cartographie, Tunis, 1972)

first is that in certain cases the wall bond has to be checked at the level of the foundation wall to determine ownership.[83] The second is that many homeowners, in anticipation of future problems of wall ownership identification, established their ownership to a potentially disputed wall at the time of construction in the form of written evidence called *Bayinna.* This written document is accepted by the judge whenever there is a problem of ownership identification in the future. However, in certain complex cases on-site investigation is required in addition to the written evidence.

Wall type B: the wall with element(s) but no bond(s)[84]

Within the Maliki School, ownership is identified by examining wall element(s) and their relationship to the two parties contesting the ownership of the wall. The Hanafi School utilizes only the door and wooden beams as elements for ownership identification. The Shafi'i School prescribes joint ownership for this wall type.

(a) When the door exists as an element only, it is used to identify ownership, and the person recognized as owning the door is identified as the owner of the wall. The Hanafi School applied this principle, and Ali b. Abi Taleb, the Prophet's cousin, also used it. If, however, the door is claimed by both parties, then the wall is identified as being owned by the person who controls the door, usually the side to which the door opens. When there are two doors and each one swings in the opposite direction, that is, when each door is controlled by a different party, then the wall is deemed to be jointly owned. All three schools of law — the Shafi'i, Maliki and Hanafi — agree on this condition.

(b) When a built-in recess exists in a wall, provided it was part of the original wall and not created after, this recess or Taqa, which is primarily used as a cupboard, identifies the ownership of the wall. If there is one on each side of the wall, then the wall is considered jointly owned. The Shafi'i school agree with this too. However, if there is only one recess (Taqa) on one side and there is no other element on the other side, then the wall is considered to be owned by the side with the recess.

(c) When wooden beams are used as the elements for wall ownership identification, and if the wall being examined has beams on one of its sides, then the side with the beams determines ownership. The beams can be used for identification only if they were built as part of the wall, and not inserted at a later date through holes created for that purpose.

(d) When a door and wooden beams are simultaneously used for ownership identification. A wall between two neighbours has a door belonging to one side and used for wooden beams on the other, then the wall is deemed the property of the man with the door, and the other is allowed to use it for his beams. The Hanafi school agrees with this principle, but the Shafi'is considers the wall jointly owned. If such a wall falls, then its owner (the person who controls the door) is obligated to rebuild it, and if the beams were part of the original wall, that is, if they were added during initial construction, then the neighbour can reinsert his beams in the rebuilt wall. However, if the beams were determined to have been inserted in the original wall after construction, then the neighbour cannot claim its re-use for his beams. He could, however, make use of the wall if he contributes in rebuilding it.

(e) When one neighbour uses a wall for loadbearing or spanning and there is no other element for ownership identification, then he is deemed the owner of the wall. However, if both neighbours use the wall for spanning purposes and assuming that they have an equal or near equal number of beams, then they are considered joint owners of the wall. When one of the neighbour's uses, for spanning purposes, is appreciably less than the other's then the Malikis have two ways to determine ownership. Some say the ownership is proportional to the ratio of its use. Others say that regardless of the ratio, the wall should be considered jointly owned. The Shafi'i School holds the latter position.

Wall type C: the wall with element(s) and bond(s)[85]

Ibn al-Rami specifies three possible conditions for this wall type:

(a) One of the neighbours has the bond and element(s) and the other has nothing. The Maliki School clearly identifies ownership of the wall with the former.
(b) Each of the two neighbours has bond(s) and element(s). There is no elaboration on this condition.
(c) One of the neighbours has bond(s) and the other element(s).

This last condition is briefly elaborated by Ibn al-Rami and he cites three sub-conditions:

1 When one neighbour has the bond and the other has a wall recess or a door controlled by his side, then the wall is deemed jointly owned.
2 When one neighbour has the bond and the other has wooden beams resting on the wall, then the neighbour with the bond is deemed owner, and the other has the right to locate beams and to replace a broken beam if necessary.
3 When one neighbour owns the bond at ground level and the wall continues to the second level acting as a party wall between the rooms on the upper storey, then the bond determines ownership of the upper portion of the wall as well. It is owned by the neighbour who owns the bond. However, if there is no bond at the upper level, then the wall belongs to the owner of its lower portion.

Ibn al-Rami describes two interesting cases which add further clarity:

1 A wall between two separate houses or shops supports wooden beams to both sides. The wall continues to the upper level to provide one of the enclosing sides to a room belonging to one of the neighbours. In such a case ownership identification of the lower portion of the wall is determined by the person who owns the bond, and if there is no bond to either side, then it is declared as jointly owned. However, the upper portion is deemed owned by the person who owns the room.
2 The principle of the rights of earlier usage as identified previously in this chapter (p. 20) affects, for example, the location and permanency of wooden beams on a wall, particularly in the case where current users inherited a given situation whose origin is not known. The effect of the principle of the rights of earlier usage is that the owner of the wall cannot remove the beams, and the owner of the beams cannot change their positions, thereby creating a frozen situation. Even if the wall falls, it has to be built to recreate the original location of the beams.

Wall type D: the wall with neither element(s) nor bond(s)[86]

The most usual identification for this wall type is joint ownership. This is sometimes ratified by asking each party to make an oath to its ownership. If both parties jointly make an oath or jointly abstain from the oath then it is deemed jointly owned. However, if one party makes an oath and the others abstain then the wall is deemed owned by the former. This procedure is also used by the Shafi'is.

In the case of a wall that has an identifiable front and back and it has neither element(s) nor bond(s) between the two parties, then it is still considered to be jointly owned, as the Malikis do not attach importance to this distinction in the wall.

Condition 2: a wall that is owned by one neighbour and provides privacy for the other. In the event that the wall collapses or that its owner wants to take it down, can he be forced to rebuild it?[87]

There are three possibilities:

A: If the wall is in good structural condition, but its owner wants to take it down.
B: If the wall is dilapidated, and the owner fears its collapse and wants to take it down.
C: If the wall has collapsed due to an act of God.

Possibility A: If the wall is in good structural condition, but its owner wants to take it down
This is viewed as follows: the intent of the owner in wanting to take the wall down is either to inflict harm or to benefit himself. The owner is not allowed to take the wall down if his intent is to inflict harm. However, if he has taken it down and it is proven that he did it to inflict harm, then he is ordered to rebuild it. In the case where the owner of the wall has taken it down for his own benefit, will he be obligated to rebuild it? Ibn al-Rami specifies four approaches:

1 If he took it down for a good reason and had intended to rebuild it, but for certain circumstances he could not do so or felt that he did not need to, then he is not forced to rebuild it, and the neighbour has to provide for his own privacy if he so desires.
2 He is forced to rebuild it even if he has limited means. The reason given is that the neighbour assumed the wall was permanent when he first built his house adjacent to it.
3 He is forced to rebuild it, but is not rushed to do so, while the neighbour can use a temporary screen to protect his privacy. However, if the neighbour finds it difficult to create a temporary but effective privacy screen, then the owner is forced to rebuild the wall as soon as possible, regardless of his wishes. Ibn al-Rami concurs with this approach.
4 If the owner of the wall can afford to rebuild, then he is forced to do so. However he is not forced to do so if he is of limited means. The latter solution is the one mostly adopted.

Possibility B: If the wall is dilapidated,and the owner fears its collapse and wants to take it down
The Maliki School agrees that the owner should take such a wall down; if he refuses, thereby endangering his neighbour, then he is forced to demolish it regardless of his means.
After the wall is demolished, is the owner forced to rebuild it? There are two approaches:

1 If demolishing was ordered to avoid collapse, then he is not forced to rebuild.

2 He is forced to rebuild it.

However, the popular approach is not to force the owner to rebuild, and the attitude is similar to the first approach of possibility A. That is, if he took it down as a protective measure and had intended to rebuild it, but for certain reasons felt he could not or did not need to anymore, then he is not forced to rebuild it.

This possibility could be advantageous to the neighbour; for example, a wall between two neighbours is dilapidated and leaning; the neighbour who does not own it either asks or is asked to take it down and rebuild it. For the efforts of his labour[88] he will be allowed to use it for spanning purposes by inserting beams into it during its reconstruction. If this arrangement is acceptable then the neighbour's labour is accepted as equity in the reconstructed wall and its owner cannot at any future time revoke its use by asking his neighbour to remove his beams, even if he requires the wall for his own purposes.

Possibility C: If the wall has collapsed due to an act of God

Will its owner be forced to rebuild it? Three approaches are mentioned if the wall collapses:

1 The owner is not obligated to rebuild it, and either neighbour could build a privacy screen if he so desired.
2 The owner is forced to rebuild the collapsed wall.
3 The owner is not forced to rebuild and the other neighbour is told to create a screen for his privacy. However, the owner is obligated to rebuild the wall if the circumstances of the neighbour do not allow him to protect his privacy. Ibn al-Rami mentions that the first approach is the most popular.

Condition 3: a wall which is jointly owned by two neighbours; can one use the wall without the permission of the other? [89]

Ibn al-Rami identifies two possibilities:

1 One of the neighbours wants to benefit from the full width of the wall without his partner's permission. This is not allowed and there is full concurrence within the Maliki School. If the neighbour actually built on the wall without the permission of his partner then he must demolish what he built regardless of its size or magnitude.
2 The neighbour takes half of the wall to build on and leaves the other half to his partner. There are two approaches to this possibility: (a) Neither of the two partners who own a wall jointly can use it to build on or insert beams or any such use without the consent of the other partner. This is the most popular approach. (b) If one of the partners wanted to use the wall for spanning or building on and such action would not preclude the other partner from utilizing the wall in a similar fashion; but if the wall was too weak for the proposed use and he wanted to demolish it and build a stronger wall instead, is he allowed? He is, and his partner cannot prohibit it. After rebuilding the wall the two partners will continue to have the same rights as before. The following three cases clarify other aspects of the rights and usage of a jointly owned wall.

Case 1

A jointly owned wall is load bearing to both sides and has wooden beams inserted into it at two levels. Thus one neighbour has a higher ceiling level than the other and the person with the lower ceiling level wanted to raise his wooden beams to the same level as his neighbour's. The neighbour joint owner cannot prevent him from doing so.

Case 2
A jointly owned wall collapses. Will the two partners be forced to build it? The solution to this situation depends on the nature of the wall before its collapse:

1 If the wall was load bearing, then the Maliki School concurs that both neighbours must collaborate to rebuild it.
2 If the wall was not load bearing and no element was resting on it, then there are three approaches:
(i) Both co-owners must collaborate to rebuild the wall.
(ii) Neither of the two co-owners is forced to do anything.
(iii) Each co-owner is forced to rebuild it with his partner. However, if one of them cannot afford his share, then he is obligated to raise the money even if he must sell part of his house to do so. The other approach in such a situation is to force the person if he is deemed economically able to do so. However, if he is of limited means and cannot afford to rebuild it with his neighbour, then he should not be forced to do so. In this situation both the Malikis and the Hanafis vacillate between forcing and not forcing, whereas the Shafi'is say that neither should be forced to rebuild it. Ibn al-Rami says that the most popular approach is not to force the person.

Case 3
A jointly owned wall collapses, and one of the joint owners rebuilds it and prohibits his partner from utilizing the wall until he pays half the cost of rebuilding. Malik said that the partner who did not collaborate in rebuilding the wall should be told that he cannot utilize the rebuilt wall unless under one of the following conditions: either the wall is demolished and he rebuilds it with his partner, or he pays him half the cost of the wall in its demolished state.

Drainage of rain and waste water

(Relevant illustrations are Figures 6 and 7 and Plate 8.)
The resolution of rainwater drainage and its use/distribution is rooted in values and objectives different from those that govern the discharge of waste water. Among the principles identified earlier in this chapter, the tenth — Excess of water should not be barred from others — is rooted in a number of the Prophet's sayings, and it created the framework for making decisions in situations and conflicts arising from the use and discharge of rainwater.

The discharge of waste water was governed by contrasting values and principles. It was considered a harmful substance and was treated as such in its discharge pattern and in related arising conflicts. Unavoidable maintenance problems were addressed within the framework mentioned, in some instances creating interesting procedures emanating from the principle of sharing a burden on a proportional basis. In essence, therefore, rainwater was regarded as a gift from God to be utilized and shared, whereas waste water was viewed as an unavoidable harmful substance to be dealt with accordingly (see Figure 6).

The following interesting cases from Ibn al-Rami's *Kitab* illuminate the impact of human values on the physical organization and related maintenance procedures devised. I selected and arranged the cases according to the following format:

1 *Drainage of rainwater*
A Principles of rainwater flow between houses.

B Problems and usage arising from rainwater in cul-de-sacs and streets.

2 *Drainage of waste water*

A Construction and usage rights of waste water channels.

B Maintenance rights of waste water channels and cesspools.

Drainage of Rainwater

A: Principles of rainwater flow between houses

The case of rainwater flowing from one neighbour's roof to the other's[90]

According to this case and the citations of Ibn al-Rami, the general attitude toward the flow or spillage of rainwater from one neighbour's roof to the other's is considered harmful. However, in this case the person with the higher roof wanted to divert the rainwater from his neighbour's lower roof. The neighbour protested claiming that he used it for his cistern and that the benefits of the rain flow on his roof exceeded its harm. In this instance the neighbour with the higher roof was prevented from diverting the flow of rainwater.

The case of the rainwater being contested between two neighbours with different roof levels[91]

Two adjacent houses with a portion of one of the houses are at a higher level than the other. The rainwater from this higher portion flows onto the roof of the other property which is then taken to a cistern.

Figure 6 A chart indicating the organization of information presented in the section on drainage of rain and waste water

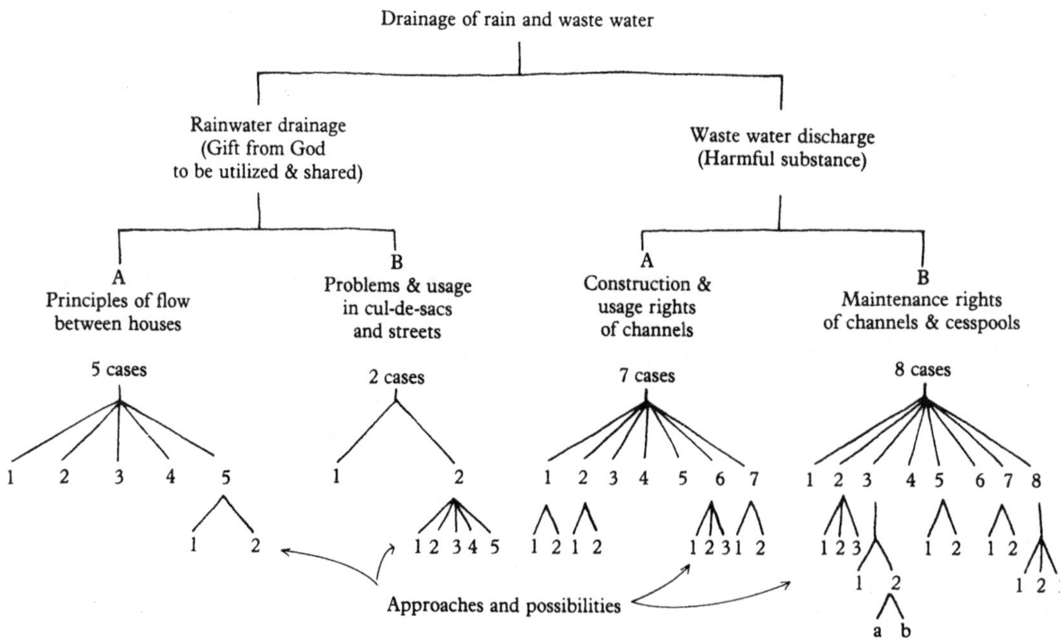

The case was identified when the man with the higher roof wanted to divert the rain flow to within his property, and the neighbour contested it. The following approach ascertained the principle of early usage. If the situation can be determined as 'old' (Qadim), then it is ordered to be maintained as it is. However, if it is determined that the flow to the lower property was 'recent' (Hadith), then the owner of the higher roof is allowed to redivert the rainwater to his property.

The case of rainwater spouts directed onto a neighbours' property[92]

If a situation existed for a long time (i.e., accepted as 'old') of rainwater spouts pouring from one property onto another, then the owner of the property receiving the rainwater cannot change the pattern or direction of the flow without the consent of the owner of the house from which the rainwater originates. A method devised by the receiver of the rainwater must be designed not to harm the other.

Ibn al-Rami cites another example of this case whereby a person has watched his neighbour build an adjacent building and directed the rainwater spouts towards him, without protesting or saying anything. In effect his silence was an approval to his neighbour's actions. He cannot therefore demand after the completion of the project, that his neighbour redivert the rain spouts. It seems clear from this case that any decision-making and/or disagreements have to be resolved just before or during construction.

The case of the increase in the height of a rainwater spout which is directed onto a neighbour's property[93]

A man wanted to build onto his roof from which the rainwater originates and to reconstruct the spout to the same direction from the new roof of the proposed addition. The neighbour protested, and did not accept the proposed new location for the spout and was supported by the Kadi. The principle used was the increase in the level of harm, due to the increased splashing and related nuisances. The solution to the problem was to discharge the water in such a way that it did not create harm or at least did not increase the level of harm previously accepted by the neighbour.

The case of the neighbour who wanted to create a room adjunct to the party wall and discharge the rainwater from its roof to the neighbour's property[94]

Can the person toward whom the proposed rainwater will discharge disallow his neighbour from doing so? Two approaches are put forward:

1 He can disallow it only if he can establish that it will create harm.
2 The person who wants to create the spout must first ask his neighbour's permission, even if he can ascertain no possible harm from it.

However, if the person wanting to build the room decides to take down the party wall (which he owns) and rebuild it within his property at an adequate setback from its original position, thereby creating a channel in its location for the rainwater, will he be allowed to do it? Here there are two approaches:

1 Only if he slopes the new channel so that the rainwater is taken to the outside and does not spill towards his neighbour's property.
2 He is not allowed to solve the problem this way. The reason used is that he will be creating a water channel in place of the wall which is considered harmful to his neighbour, because it is a new element to which he has to adjust.

B: Problems and usage arising from rainwater in cul-de-sacs and streets

Discharging rainwater from a house onto a street or cul-de-sac

If a man builds a house and wants to discharge the rainwater onto a street or cul-de-sac and can prove, if necessary with the aid of expert(s), that there is no other possible outlet, then his neighbour cannot prevent him from doing so.[95] However, the neighbour can influence the method of discharge, whether it be a spout, a down pipe, or a small opening under the main door of the house (see Plate 8).

Ibn al-Rami clarifies that if a spout is used and it will splash the opposite wall if the street is narrow, it constitutes harm which should be prevented. He cites a case in Sousse where a man's spout was creating harm by splashing his neighbour's wall. The local Kadi ordered it removed, but the owner, who had influence, requested the opinion of the Chief Kadi of Tunis. The reply confirmed the decision of the local Kadi.

However, if rainwater is to be discharged by collecting it first within the house and then channelling it through an opening under the main door of the house and onto the surface of the street, then a neighbour cannot prevent it for any reason. It is sometimes necessary to prove — the owner might be asked to produce a sworn statement — that the water is purely from rain and that it is not mixed with any waste water, as the latter is not allowed to be discharged onto the street.[96]

The case of gardens sharing rainwater from streets[97]

Ibn al-Rami mentions five possibilities and considerations:

1 Two gardens abut a street at different levels. The owner of the higher garden has the right to use the rainwater accumulated on the streets up to the level of a man's ankle bone (about 8–10 cm).[98] Water must not be accumulated above this level and should be released to the owner of the lower garden. This must be implemented by the owner of the upper garden whether the water was adequate or not.
2 If the two gardens were on the same level and/or near the source of the rainwater then they should share it equally.
3 When the gardens are at two levels and they have always shared the use of rainwater or another source of unowned water, the owner(s) of the higher garden are not allowed to create a dam or a depression to accumulate and store water. This action is considered harmful to the owner(s) of the lower garden.
4 The age of neighbouring gardens is used as a criteria for establishing priority rights for the usage of rainwater. The older gardens have the priority.
5 When gardens are adjacent to or near other uses which require the utilization of rainwater from the street(s), such as a mill, the garden is always given priority.

Drainage of waste water

A: Construction and usage rights of waste water channels

The case of disposing waste water from washing

A distinction is made between waste water resulting from all kinds of household washing activities and from human excrement, which is collected and discharged separately. Waste water is not

Plate 29 Suq when open and shut. (a) (*above left*) View in Suq el-Trouk, Tunis when open and busy. Note the display of merchandize. (b) (*above right*) View in Suq el-Kouafi, Tunis when shut. Note that very few shops are identified by signs.

Plate 30 (*below*) Typical merchant's Wekala. View in the courtyard of Wekala Ben Ghorbal, Tunis. (Photo: Wisam Hakim, 1975)

Plate 31 (*above left*) **View of the narrow** courtyard from the roof of the two-storey Qishla Sidi Morjani, Tunis. The photo was taken in 1977 when the building was being restored and renovated.

Plate 32 (*above right*) View on the Rue des Libraires, Tunis towards the north. The entrance to Hammam al-Qachachine on the right is under the vaulting. The columns are coloured in green and red separated by a narrow white strip. The colours symbolize the Prophet and Jihad or the struggle for Islam.

Plate 33 (*left*) The entrance to the previous Maristan Aziza Othmana, Tunis, is on the left before the uncovered Suq du Cuivre. The photo is taken under the vaulted portion of the Rue de la Kasba looking east. Note the pattern of light generated by the openings in the vault.

Plate 34 (above) Typical courtyard of a palace in Tunis. Taken in the main courtyard of the restored and renovated Dar Lasram. Note the use of columns and the design of the Burtal or arcade. (Photo: Wisam Hakim, 1975)

Plate 35 (a) (*below left*) A Massassa in the village of Sidi Bou Sa'id, Tunisia. It has two outlets located on the right of the door. Note the dedication plaque over the door. (Photo: James Wright, 1975) (b) (*below right*) A Seqqaya in Fez, Morocco. (Photo: Papini, M.H.A.T., Rabat)

Plate 36 Iranian–Islamic carpet designed according to an abstract plan of a garden. Note water courses, ponds, flowers and trees. This example is from northwestern Iran, c. 1700. Size 6.7 × 2.4 m. (From the collection of the Fogg Art Museum, Harvard University, USA)

allowed to be discharged onto the street surface from the usual location of outlets situated under the door sill, whereas rainwater, as mentioned previously, is allowed.

Ibn al-Rami cites the following two interesting cases:

1 Ibn al-Rami knew of Kairouan's reputation of allowing waste water to be discharged on streets from outlets under the main door sill. He was once visiting that city and confirmed this practice, so he discussed the matter with the local Kadi and advised him that this practice is wrong and should be stopped. The Kadi agreed and ordered a public crier to announce the new order to all citizens and the fact that anybody who did not carry out this order would be punished. Some people did and others did not, so the Kadi walked the streets and found a servant washing the *Skifa* (entry hall) of one of the houses allowing the waste water to pour onto the street surface as he did so. He sent for the owner of the house and ordered that he be lashed thirty times and tied next to his door in the street, so as to make an example of him for others to take the order seriously.[99]
2 A large garden in a suburb of Tunis was sub-divided by its owner and sold to different people who erected houses on their individual plots. The new owner of one of the plots which was adjacent to an 'old' or existing house built a channel which carried his waste and rainwater. The neighbour protested to the Kadi and said that harm was done to him, because until recently the property neighbouring his was a garden, and now there is a waste water channel near his house. The Kadi ordered that the channel be removed, but allowed the new owner to discharge his rainwater onto the street if he wished.

The case of building and connecting a waste water channel in a house which does not have one[100]

If the owner wants to build a channel and connect it to the secondary line in the cul-de-sac, he might face two possible circumstances:

1 The secondary line to which he will need to connect passes through a house on its way to the main line. This secondary line cannot be enlarged or its use increased without the permission and approval of the owner(s) of the house(s) through which it passes.
2 The secondary line to which he needs to connect is within the cul-de-sac and connects to the main line in the street. He can connect to this secondary line only if he pays his pro-rated share of its cost to its co-owners. In turn these co-owners cannot prevent him from connecting into their line unless they can prove, with the attestation of expert(s) that such action will damage their secondary line. In such an event they can prevent him from using it.

The case of relocating a channel from one cul-de-sac to another more conveniently situated[101]

According to the jurist Sahnoun a working channel should not be relocated. He was asked if a person had relocated it, and had used it for the past three or four years, could the owners of the cul-de-sac demand its removal after such a period of time. He said they could because three or four years is considered a short period of time and does not establish the principle of the rights of early usage.

The case of an existing unused channel from a house on a private lane whose owner wants to use it[102]

Among the houses on a private thoroughfare is one that has no door on it but has a cesspool built under the lane and a channel from the house linked to it. Both channel and cesspool were not used for many years, and the owner wanted to use them. The people sharing the lane prohibited him to do so. They were told that they have rights only to the cesspool if they can prove that he does not own it. Failing such proof, the tank can be used by its claimant.

Ibn al-Rami concludes this case by clarifying that anybody who claims a cesspool or a channel must prove its ownership, if necessary by oath, whenever it is contested. If such proof cannot be furnished then the contestant can claim its ownership.

Case of a waste channel passing through someone else's property which needs to be enlarged[103]

If someone whose channel passes through his neighbour's house wants to replace it by a larger one, he cannot do so without the full consent of his neighbour. In relation to this 'solution', a man owned a small and large house adjacent to each other. The waste channel from his small house went through his neighbour's house and he wanted to replace it by a channel from the larger house. The neighbour did not agree and prevented him from doing so, and this action was ratified by the Kadi. Ibn al-Rami explained it thus: the larger channel will carry more effluence than the one from the small house, and it will need more frequent cleaning; both situations will increase the harm to the owner of the house through which the channel is passing through.

The case of a waste channel passing through a neighbour's house which is to be demolished by its owner[104]

If a neighbour wants to demolish his house which, in effect, could demolish his neighbour's waste channel, three approaches are mentioned:

1 He may do so.
2 He cannot do so without the consent of his neighbour who could be harmed by this action.
3 If they can work out an economical solution by relocating the channel through the cul-de-sac then he can demolish his house. However, if the cost is prohibitive, then the owner of the house must protect the channel in the course of demolishing and/or renovating his house.

Ibn al-Rami clarifies the third approach by specifying that the act of demolition in itself is not at issue, but whether or not the channel will be blocked. If the working condition of the channel can be maintained during the course of demolition and/or renovation, then the user of the channel cannot prevent his neighbour from demolishing and/or renovating his house, because that in itself constitutes harm.

The construction or repair of a waste water channel in a cul-de-sac[105]

If a channel is dilapidated or gets demolished and its users want to rebuild it, what implementation procedure should be followed? The following two examples illustrate two approaches to the situation:

1 A shared channel passes under four houses which needed repairs and rebuilding. According to the jurist Sahnoun (d. 240/854) implementation should be shared as follows: the owner of the first house should repair his portion alone, then he should help the owner of the second house repair that portion, then both of them should help the owner of the third house repair that portion, and all three should help the owner of the fourth house repair the last portion of the channel.[106]
2 A shared channel in a cul-de-sac needed repair; some of its users wanted to repair it and the others refused to collaborate.

According to the jurist Ibn al-Qasim (d. 191/806) the people who refuse to collaborate should be forced to help the others on a shift basis. In other words, each person who refuses would have to join the others who will be building the canal on a shift basis. Ibn al-Rami says the most common approach is the one prescribed by Sahnoun in the first example.

B: Maintenance rights of waste water channels and cesspools

The case of cleaning or repairing a cesspool used by two parties at two levels[107]

A cesspool shared by two parties living at two levels is either jointly owned or owned by the man living on the ground level. In both conditions cleaning the cesspool is a joint responsibility, but the task is allocated on a proportional basis to the number of persons in each household. If the cesspool requires repair, and it is jointly owned, then the task is shared. However, if it is owned by the man on the ground level, then it is his responsibility to undertake construction repairs, and the user living on the upper floor is responsible for emptying the cesspool if the job of repairing it requires that.

Owner/tenant responsibilities for cleaning waste water channels and cesspools[108]

General principles

Cesspools and channels are to be cleaned by the tenant when required, provided he is not asked to clean it on terminating his residence. However, in some cities the custom requires the owner to do so. Also, tenants of Funduks are not required to clean cesspools.[109]

Exceptions to above principles

1 If a tenant moves into a house that was not occupied before him, or if his stay is short, then he should be treated as a user of a Funduk and is not required to clean the cesspool or channels.
2 A landlord may stipulate in his contract with the tenant that the waste water channels be cleaned by the tenant. However, this stipulation cannot be applied to cesspools, unless they were cleaned recently or are of recent construction. The reason given is that the extent and potential problems arising from cleaning a cesspool cannot be judged in normal circumstances and that it is unethical to force a potential tenant to agree to such a condition.
3 A tenant can stipulate to a landlord at the time of making up a contract that the latter should be responsible for cleaning and maintaining cesspool(s) and channel(s). This is considered an acceptable request as the landlord will be familar with the extent of the task and has the option to refuse.

The case of a man who rents a house and finds its channel(s) clogged

There are two possibilities here:

1 If it was clogged before contract agreement, the owner has to clean it, and if the house is uninhabitable because of the clogged channel(s) then the owner is obligated, and if necessary be forced, to clean it.
2 If the channels were clogged after the tenant occupied the house, then two solutions are given: (a) the owner has to clean it. (b) the tenant has to clean it, unless other arrangements were made.

Of the two solutions, the usual is to adopt the one customary in the specific city in which the case occurs. The practice for example in Al-Andalus (Moslem Spain) was to allocate the responsibility of cleaning the house to the tenant and the cesspool/channels to the owner. Ibn al-Rami says that Kadi Abdul Rafi preferred the Andalusian practice.

The case of buying/selling out a jointly owned cesspool

If one of the two owners of a jointly owned cesspool wanted to buy his partner's share or sell his own is refused, then the cesspool continues to be jointly owned and will be classified an indivisible element similar to a jointly owned/shared courtyard or Skifa (entrance hall).

The case of cleaning a cesspool of a jointly owned house

One of the following two approaches was used:

1 One based on the equity of each co-owner in the house; here the higher the equity the greater the share in cleaning the cesspool, regardless of the numbers of persons per household.
2 One based proportionally on the number of persons per household, that is the greater the number of persons within a household the larger the share of that household in cleaning the cesspool.

The case of an 'old' (Qadim) channel causing harm to the neighbour[110]

Ibn al-Rami states the following principle which was also clearly stated by the jurist Sahnoun: that an 'old' channel (i.e., one of an earlier establishment) cannot be ordered changed or repaired even if it is causing harm to a neighbour. For example, a house in Tunis had a water well attached to a party wall, with an earlier channel built next to the wall on the other side. The owner of the well noticed that the channel was seeping into his well, and protested the harm being caused to the Kadi. Ibn al-Rami was sent by the Kadi to examine the well and confirmed the seepage and harm it was creating. The Kadi ordered the owner of the well to take whatever protective measures necessary to prevent the seepage and stipulated that the owner of the channel is only required to keep his channel flowing, and was not ordered to undertake any changes to it.

The case of cleaning and maintaining water channels which originate in cul-de-sacs and continue to a street[111]

The assumed context for this case is indicated in Figure 7. An outlet from each house in a cul-de-sac is linked to a secondary channel and in turn feeds into a primary channel in a through street to which other houses on the street link. This primary channel continues to link up to the main sewer line of the city or Khandaq.

Based on this hierarchy one of the two following alternative principles of maintenance apply to the secondary channels in the cul-de-sac:

1 The first alternative is based on the objective of cleaning all the secondary channel system in the cul-de-sac. The first house owner is responsible for cleaning his portion of the channel up to the junction of the second house's outlet, he then joins the owner of the second house to clean to the junction of the third house. They are then joined by the owner of the third house, and so on up to the junction with the primary channel in the through street.
2 The second alternative is based on the objective of cleaning the channel system in the cul-de-sac until the blockage in the system is removed. The procedure starts with the first house owner cleaning his channel outlet up to the junction with the outlet from the second house. The second house owner undertakes the same task, and is followed, if necessary, by the other

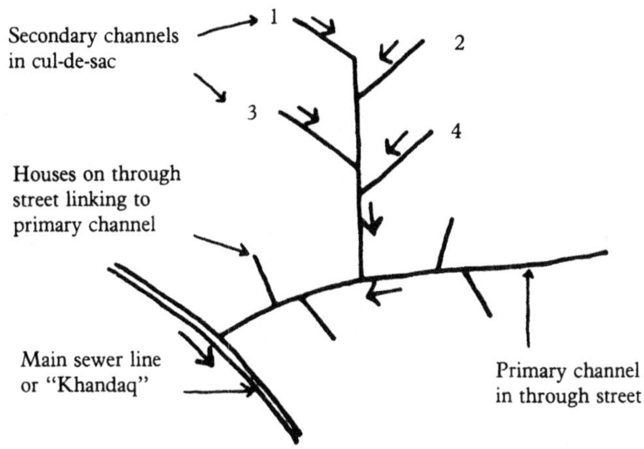

Figure 7 Assumed context for a case of cleaning and maintaining water channels that originate in cul-de-sacs and continue to a street

house owners on the cul-de-sac until the blockage is found and removed.

Cleaning and maintenance of the primary channel in the thoroughfare

The primary channel was regarded as a distinct element in the waste water drainage system. It could be relatively level or of a steep slope, affecting its drainage capability and effectiveness. It was recognized that it could be clogged in one of three possible ways:

1 By sediments clogging the length of the channel.
2 By sediments clogging its upper portion near its junction with a secondary channel from a cul-de-sac.
3 By sediments clogging its lower portion.

Whatever the physical characteristics of the primary channel or the nature of its malfunction, the accepted and most popular principle followed in cleaning and maintaining it was that all users from the cul-de-sac(s) and from the street share on a proportional (persons/household) basis, and not on the number of houses using it.

To conclude this chapter I would like to point out that although Ibn al-Rami's primary sources were works written within the first three centuries of Islam (and his from the eighth/fourteenth century) the same building practice and traditions persisted in Tunis at least to the first quarter of this century.

On a trip to Tunis in early 1977 I had the opportunity to meet with Mr Tahar Ben Lagha, a man in his early sixties who is a master mason and has been working as a consultant to the Tunisian courts on problems arising from traditional building construction. Those problems and others which are rooted in traditional societal customs are considered part of the Urf.[112]

I discussed some material from this chapter with Mr Lagha and compared it with his knowledge of the subject. The similarity was remarkable, not only with specific physical examples he mentioned such as the criteria used for establishing jointly owned walls, the problems associated with window location and privacy, etc. but also in the principles employed, for example the rights of earlier usage. He mentioned that the current Urf in Tunis recognizes about 150 building conditions. Unfortunately I could not acquire more information from him on the subject.

However, I believe that what has been presented in this chapter represents a continuous practice in Tunis, within the Maghribi and Maliki traditions, for at least 750 years, from the Almohads in 556/1160 to the early part of this century.

Chapter 2

A design language: urban and architectural elements

One of the important findings that this research has uncovered is the existence of a vital, yet unconscious, language of physical elements cutting across all scales of the city and making up an agile set of components which are highly versatile in their combination and structuring capabilities.[1] The analogy to a language is evident if we consider the basic building elements such as walls, ceilings, doors, windows and columns, and their possible derivatives as the alphabet. The words that the alphabet creates are the various building types and their respective architectural elements created through time and within the context and values of a culture.

The analogy is reversed when it is viewed in terms of numbers and complexity. An effective building language, such as the one making up the Arabic–Islamic city, is one that is made up of relatively few elements and components, yet provides maximum flexibility and diversity in its powers of combination and structuring.

The strength of a healthy and vital building language which has evolved in a society and which is an integral part of its building and urban development process is that its influence becomes almost subconscious — to an extent that the names of the physical components of all scales of the city become an integral part of the vocabulary and assume a direct interpretation of their usage or function. *The name therefore integrates the form and function of the physical component and its purpose.* Thus, a full set of names operative at each scale in the city, is, in effect, a vocabulary operative at that scale. The combination of these vocabularies, operative at the various scales of the urban environment, constitutes a design language.

With reference to the continuity of the design language across time and place, the Middle East has an established tradition of over 3,000 years of town building and an associated building design language which has been adopted and modified by the Arabs who also added new elements designed to suit the values and social requirements of an Islamic community. Names were given to all physical elements and components and these must have become relatively uniform during the mid-second century of Islam (around 750 AD), during the latter phase of the Umayyad dynasty within a geographic region extending from what is now Spain in the west to Pakistan in the east.[2]

As Islamic culture and civilization developed, however, it began to assimilate and be molded by regional cultural characteristics. The impact of this natural development was also apparent in the vocabulary of building design, so that we find distinct variations within regions of the Islamic world as evidenced by the situation during the latter part of the last century. However, after careful examination we find the following phenomena:

1 The physical components — their form and function — remained relatively unchanged, albeit with slight variations, across centuries of use within most of the Islamic world.

2 The majority of components have names of a similar Arabic origin. Others could have one version of a name in a region and another derivative elsewhere, for example, the term for garden, which is *Jenina* in Tunisia and *Rawda* in Morocco.

3 A minority of names of physical components which have remained relatively unchanged have lost their original connections. They have evolved out of the influence of the local Arabic dialect or of non-Arabic sources, such as the Berber language in North Africa, and Persian in the Middle East.

Later in this chapter I have documented the design language which evolved in Ifrikiya,[3] as known in the latter part of the nineteenth century. In the process of identifying the components of the language and their system of arrangement, I studied the traditional city of Tunis at two different levels:

1 The location arrangement of urban elements within the overall scale, which included the Medina Central and its Rabad — the northern and southern suburbs.

2 Morphological analysis of the core of Medina Central in two parts: (a) the relationship of streets to the land-use pattern and related street coverage; and (b) the location of urban elements/building types to the street system.

Urban elements within the overall Medina and its Rabad (suburbs)

The overall urban complex of a mature and relatively large Arabic–Islamic city (see Figure 8) is made up of the following elements:[4]

1 *Medina* (*also spelled Madina*). It is the Arabic name for an urban settlement. It is used in reference to the whole urban complex, or to its older part if it is physically differentiated from later additions which are usually identified as Rabad (suburbs) or by another name differentiating them from the Medina proper (see Plate 9).

The earliest systematic classification of urban settlements in the Islamic world was undertaken by al-Maqdisi, a Jerusalem-born Arab geographer (d. approx. 380/990). He developed a hierarchy of four settlement types as follows:

(a) *Amsar* (sing. *Misr*), metropolis;
(b) *Qasabat* (sing. *Qasabah*) provincial capitals;
(c) *Mudun* (sing. *Madina*) provincial towns, a main town of a district, or a market town; and
(d) *Qura* (sing. *Qaryah*), villages.[5]

This hierarchy is constructed primarily on administrative criteria. However, specific criteria were applied to define an urban settlement or city regardless of its relevant importance within a hierarchy such as the one created by al-Maqdisi.

A frequently-occurring formula that was used by the Andalusian geographer Abu Obeid al-Bakri (d. 487/1094) says that a given settlement is a large city, or city, or a large town where one finds a Mesjid al-jami — a Khotba mosque — and a Suq (jami wa-aswaq).[6] It is said that Malik, the father of

37 (a) (*above*) Interior view of a Rawda in Marrakech, Morocco. Note that only the walkways are intended for walking. (Photo: Papini, M.H.A.T., Rabat) (b) (*right*) Exterior view of a Jenina of a house in the village of Sidi Bou Sa'id, Tunisia. Note that the overflow of vegetation towards the street is allowed provided it creates no harm to the public right-of-way. (Photo: James Wright, 1975)

Plate 38 (*above*) In the courtyard of the Zaytuna mosque in Tunis, looking towards the main entrance. Note the use of columns in the arcade surrounding the courtyard.

Plate 39 (*below*) Skaf luha or flat ceiling constructed of wood joists. Note the frequency of joists and their decoration. This example from a building in Sidi Bou Sa'id, Tunisia. (Photo: George Guimond, 1975)

Plate 40 (*above*) Two types of dome and a cradle vault combined in one structure. The example is a religious facility in the town of Testour, Tunisia.

Plate 41 (*right*) Example of a thoroughfare with a M'qas junction. The Rue Tourbet el-Bey in Tunis, looking towards Mesjid al-Fateh and the Impasse du Mason to the right.

Plate 42 Example of a cross junction of two major thoroughfares. View from Bat'ha or Place Romdane Bey in Tunis, looking toward the junction of Rue Sidi Ben Arous to the right of the photo, and Rue Saida Ajoula to the left.

Plate 43 (*left*) Example of a cul-de-sac with a buttressing arch and a Sabat. View of Impasse Sidi Gourgi from Rue du Pacha, Tunis. The location of a Sabat on a cul-de-sac is rare.

the Maliki School of Law, recognized a Mesjid al-jami — the mosque in which the Friday noon prayers and Khotba is undertaken — only in those settlements which had a suq.[7] Al-Shafi'i, the founder of the Shafi'i School of Law writes in his *Kitab al-Umm*:

> When there are, all about an important place, secondary centres with inherited connections with this place, and only this place, and when this place has a Suq where the people from these secondary centres go to acquire their provisions, then I cannot allow that any inhabitant of these centres be dispensed from attending Friday prayer in the Mesjid al-Jami of the principle place.[8]

Another more specific requirement of a city, according to religious scholars, is that it should harbour the residence of a governor and a Kadi who can exercise and implement his duties.[9] Abu Hanifa, the founder of the Hanafi School of Law, defines a city as a large settlement which has a system of main through streets, Suqs, and nearly related agricultural units, and a residing governor who is capable of executing his duties as a Kadi to adjudicate the problems arising between people within his jurisdiction.[10]

In essence, therefore a city or Medina should have:

(a) a Mesjid al-jami which is recognized as the Friday mosque where the Friday sermon is given and which should serve the residents of the city and its dependents living outside it;

(b) a governor and/or a Kadi who can execute his duties within the city's area of jurisdiction; and

(c) a Suq serving the needs of the people in the city and the surrounding countryside.

In addition, some Arab authors have mentioned the Hammam (public bath) as another essential feature of the city.[11]

2 *Kasbah* (*also spelled Kasaba*). This term is primarily used in North Africa and also previously in Muslim Spain. It is essentially a citadel which, while being attached to the wall surrounding a fortified town (Medina), remains sufficiently independent to continue the resistance, even after the fall of the city, or to serve as a refuge for the governor if the population revolts against his personal authority or that of the prince that he serves (see Plate 10).

Its position is fixed according to the best strategic situation, and it is sometimes located within an older military establishment. It dominates the town from a hill and may be situated on a water course, a cliff, or a sea front. In Tunis the location of the Kasbah dominates the highest elevation within the urban complex.

A Kasbah usually contained within its walls, in addition to the palace of the sovereign, his confidants and the dwellings of his dependents, one or more mosques, the fiscal services, the guards' barracks, baths, prisons, shops and even markets. It had main squares where people assembled for festivals and the army participated in ceremonies. It also included gardens and private cemeteries. It generally had one gate with a single door which opened on to the town that it defended or from which it held itself aloof. In addition, it frequently had an emergency escape postern, called the Gate of Treason (Bab al-Ghadr) which provided direct outlet to the surrounding countryside. It allowed access for information, reinforcements and provisions, and also the secret evacuation of the Kasbah, to avoid surrender.[12]

3 *Rabad* (*also spelled R'bat*). This refers to the districts or quarters of a town situated outside its central part or Medina. It also means the immediate vicinity of a town. A Rabad usually had a name of its own. In

Figure 8 Urban elements location: Tunis

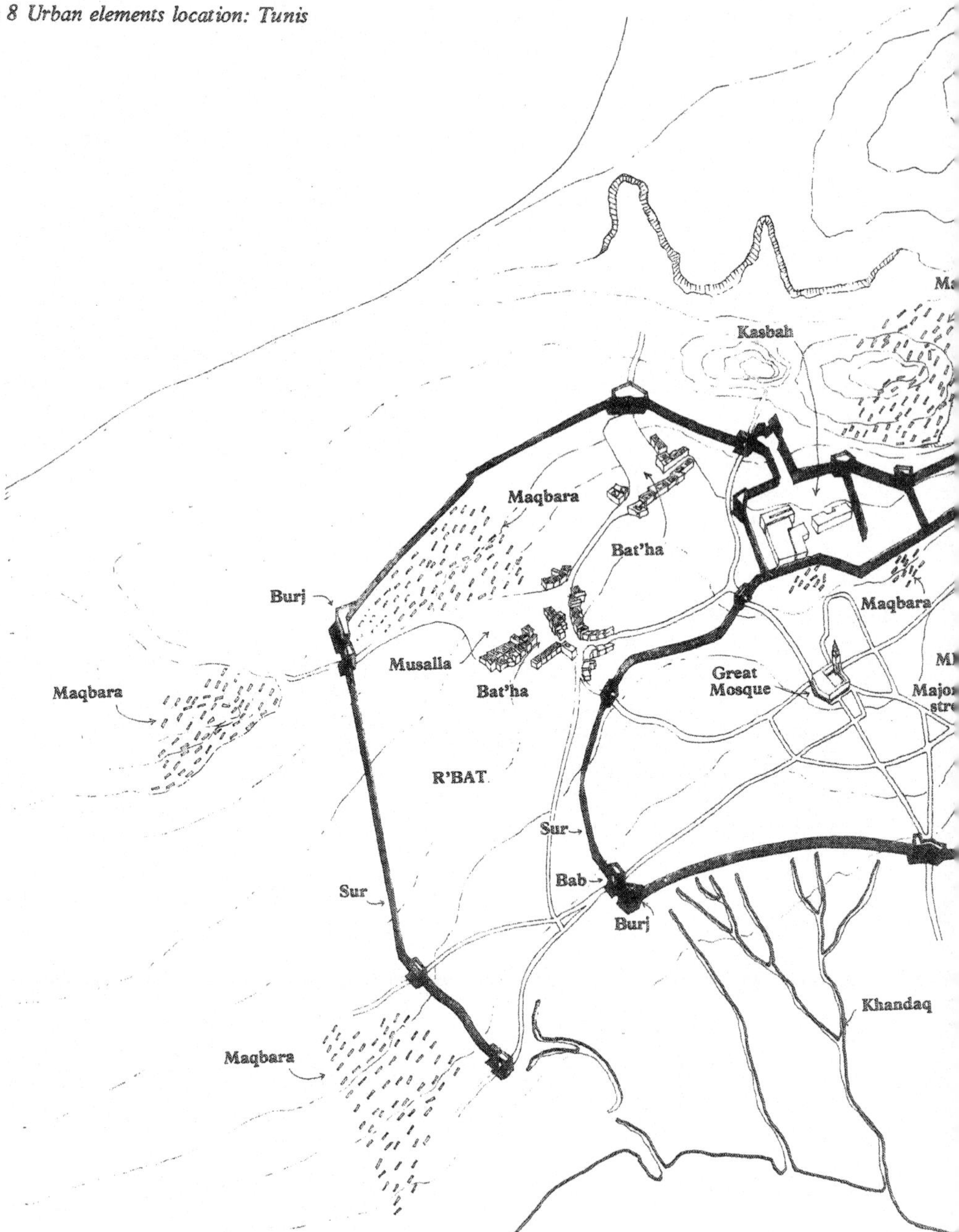

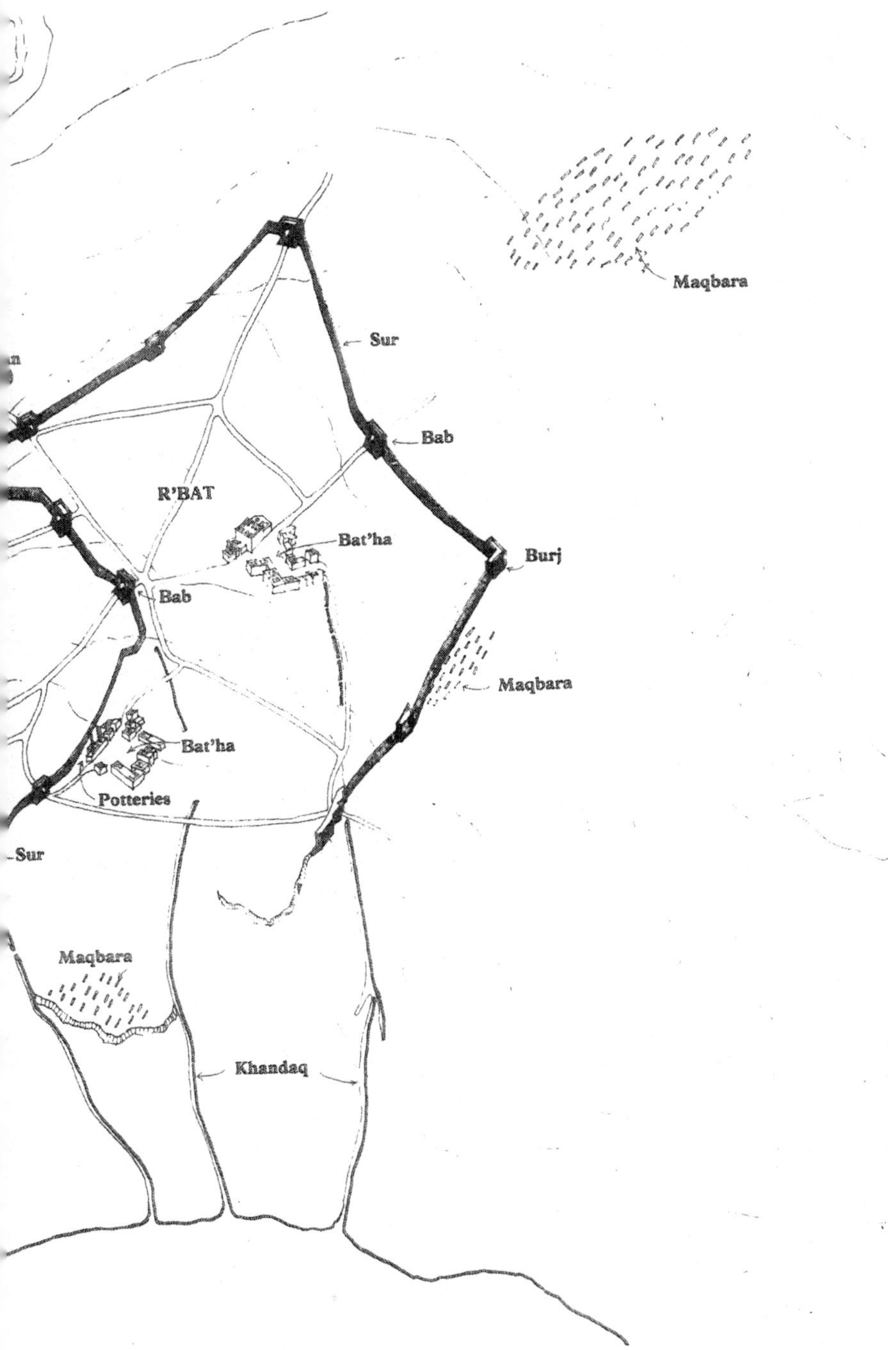
Maqbara
Sur
Bab
R'BAT
Bat'ha
Burj
Bab
Maqbara
Bat'ha
Potteries
Sur
Maqbara
Khandaq

Tunis there are two Rabads, one north of the Medina called Rabad Bab Souika and the other south of the Medina called Rabad Bab Jazira. A defensive wall surrounds both Rabads providing protection to those areas as well as acting as a first line of defence to the Medina which was also surrounded by its own wall (see Plate 9). The term also had other uses; for example, in Muslim Spain the civilian areas below the strictly military castle or fortification were called the Rabad. In addition the word was also used to designate special areas such as the lepers' quarters.[13]

4 *Sur.* The city wall or ramparts surrounding the Medina for defensive purposes. It is made of three elements:

(a) the wall proper which has an average height of 6 m and width of 2 m;
(b) the gates (*Bab*) which are located on the alignment of major streets linking the city to outside destinations; and
(c) the defensive towers (*Burj*) which are strategically located within the perimeter line of the wall overlooking approaches and terrain that might be used by an enemy approaching the city walls (see Plate 11).

In Tunis the Medina, Kasbah and two Rabads are surrounded by Sur (ramparts), thus providing the Medina with a double line of defence. It should be noted that the ramparts surrounding the suburbs on the north, south and west sides converge on the east side close to the *Khandaq* (major sewer lines) thus completing the line of defence to the lake. There is no adequate information available to clarify how the Khandaq was utilized for defence purposes.

5 *Bab.* The term means gate or door. The earliest gateways of Muslim fortified enclosures were simple 'straight-through' entrances defended by a machicoulis and a pair of half-round flanking towers. But as early as the building of Baghdad by al-Mansur in 145–7/762–5 a new type appears — the bent entrance, which was employed for the four gateways of the outer wall.[14]

The Arabic term for a bent entrance is Bashura, as is clear from the passage in which Makrizi describes the Bab Zuwayla of Cairo:

> ... he [Badr al-Djamali] did not make a Bashura, as is the custom for the gates of fortresses. This disposition consists in arranging a bend [*atf*] in the passageway to prevent troops taking it by assault during a siege, and to render impossible the entry *en masse* of cavalry. However, he did place a large slippery stone at the entrance as an anti-cavalry device.[15]

The finest gateways of the fifth/eleventh centuries are the three Fatimid gates of Cairo, the Bab al-Nasr, Bab al-Futuh, and Bab Zuwayla, built by Badr al-Djamali in 480–85/1087–92, but they are 'straight through' and not bent entrances. The Crusades in the two following centuries and the great military experience gained by both sides soon resulted in the bent entrance coming into general use. So great were its advantages that it had reached even the far west of Islam before the end of the sixth/twelfth centuries.[16]

In Tunis both types of gates were used, the straight-through and the bent. Bab Bahr and Bab Saadoon are examples of the straight-through gates, whereas Bab Jdid is an example of a bent entrance. There are seven gates on the inner Medina rampart, and twelve on the outer Rabad ramparts (see Plate 12).

6 *Burj (also spelled Burdj).* These are the fortified towers which are strategically located along the ramparts and form part of the defence system.[17] In Tunis there is one tower located on the inner Medina wall,

three on the wall of the Kasbah, and three on the Rabad outer walls (see Plate 11).

7 *Shar' or Tarik Nafid.* The first term is equivalent to 'street' and the latter to thoroughfare i.e. 'throughway'.[18] An essential component of a mature Arabic–Islamic city is that it should have a system of streets characterized by a network of city-wide thoroughfares connecting the main gates to the core of the city (specifically to the major city mosque and the adjacent Suq complex). They are the main arteries and form an integral part of the network of routes connecting major distant localities to the city (see Plate 13).

The minimum width and height of these streets were determined by the requirement to allow two fully loaded camels to pass without hindrance. These streets were publicly owned and under the jurisdiction of the governor and his representatives.

8 *Bat'ha (also referred as Saha in Tunisia).*[19] This is the term for a public square or a public place. These are usually formed at the Y-junction of three primary streets. Within the Medina this type predominates and is usually where the Mahalla or neighbourhood facilities, such as a Mesjid, bakery, or grocery shop were located. Occasionally in the Medina the Bat'ha is a proportioned and geometrically regulated space in front of a significant building such as the one at the entrance of Dar Hussein which was enlarged by the French during the second quarter of this century. It used to be named Bat'ha al-General, and is now Bat'ha al Ksar (see Plate 14).

In the Rabad (the northern and southern suburbs) Bat'has are also formed at the intersection of main thoroughfares but are usually much larger and more spacious than their counterparts in the Medina, created by their larger dimensions and the visual impact of the relatively lower surrounding buildings. These suburban Bat'has are also used for weekly open markets, such as the Bat'ha al-Ganam (for sheep) and the Bat'ha al-Morkad (for horses).

It is interesting to note Al-Makrizi's definition and perception of a Bat'ha which in fifteenth-century Cairo was called *Rahba.* He defines it as 'a large place' and says that there are many of them in the city:

> They do not change unless they are encroached by building, in which case their name is retained. However, if most of a Rahba's space is taken up by buildings, then it is possible that its name changes and its identity as a location diminishes or disappears. A Rahba is also created by the removal of building(s).[20]

9 *Musalla.* The term means a place where the *Salat* (prayer) is performed. It also refers to a space allocated for this purpose within a public or private building. However, its use at the city scale refers to a large open area outside the Medina walls and within walking distance of it, used primarily for prayers on the occasions of the Eid al-Fitr and Eid al-Adha festivals. The Musalla is usually large enough to accommodate the adult male population of the town and it has a low wall provided with a *Mihrab* to indicate the direction of the Qibla. There might also be a built-in elevated place for the *Khatib* to deliver the sermon.

The concept and use of the Musalla is based on the *Sunna* — the Prophet's practice. It is recorded of the Prophet that during the two Eids he used to go to the Musalla of Banu Salima, which was a specific open space outside the Prophet's city of Medina. He also performed the Salat al-istiska or the prayer for rain at this location. It seems that the schools of law have divergent opinions regarding whether the Eid prayers should be performed in the mosque or Musalla.[21]

In Tunis the Musalla is located within the southern Rabad of Bab Jazira, adjacent to

Maqbara (cemetery) Sidi al-Gorjani, and is a walking distance of 600 m from the Kasbah and Bab el-Manara. The Musalla remained in the form of an open space for Eid prayers from 628/1230 to 1251/1835 when army barracks were built on the site, which was called Caserne Saussier during the French protectorate[22] (see Figure 9).

Ibn Battuta, the Moroccan fourteenth-century traveller narrates the occasion, during his stay in Tunis, when he went with the people of Tunis to their Musalla during Eidal-Fitr:

> While still at Tunis I was overtaken by the feast of the Fast-breaking and I joined the people at the Musalla. The inhabitants had already assembled in large numbers to celebrate their festival and had come out in brave show and in their richest apparel. The sultan Abu Yahya arrived on horseback, accompanied by his relatives and courtiers and guards of his kingdom walking on foot in a magnificent procession. The prayers were recited, the allocation was discharged, and the people returned to their homes.[23]

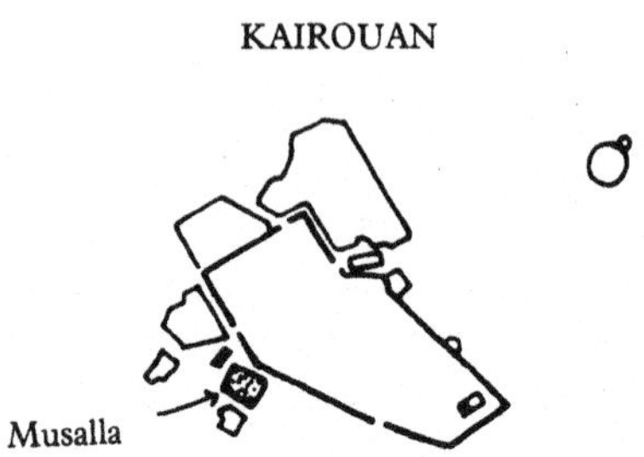

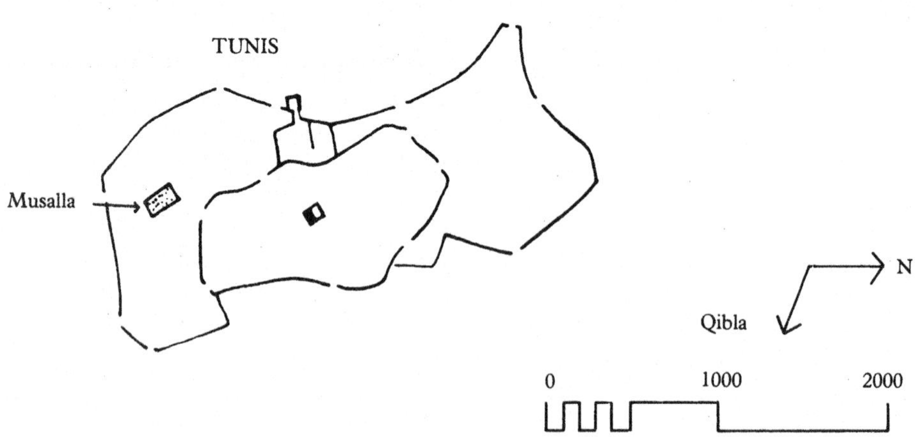

Figure 9 Locational plans of the Tunis and Kairouan 'Musalla' drawn to the same scale and orientation

10 *Maqbara.* The term refers to a public cemetery. In Islamic practice the head of the buried person should be placed facing the *Qibla*, the direction of Mecca. The aggregate impact of this stipulation sometimes created organizational constraints on the utilization of the land within the confines of a crowded cemetery. It is certainly an important consideration for a pre-planned cemetery (see Plate 15).

In Tunis the location and growth of cemeteries accompanied the growth of the city. The earliest cemetery was the Silsila cemetery built on the west side of Jami al-Zaytuna during the period of the early Muslim Foundation (79/698–184/800), and within the walls of what later developed into the Medina. When Tunis reached its mature size in the fifteenth century, additional cemeteries were located in the Rabad and outside the city walls. In most instances cemeteries were walled to provide a sense of place and demarcation to the grounds.

It should be noted that in spite of the reverence and respect which Islamic values and custom bestow on cemetery grounds, we find that throughout several centuries, buildings encroached substantially upon cemetery grounds. A careful examination of the historical development of the city clarifies further this phenomenon.

11 *Khazzan.* The term is used for a water-storage facility. This could be a large public facility such as the one that was located on the west side of the Medina receiving water from the aqueduct and connected via a conduit to the core of the Medina. However, the term also refers to private water cisterns usually located under the courtyard of a house for collecting rainwater, which are commonly known in Tunisia as Majel.

12 *Khandaq.* The term is used to refer to a moat around the city walls, or, as in Tunis, to the main sewer lines that collected the city's sewers and drained them to the lake.[24] A careful examination of the 1860 Colin map of Tunis reveals that the majority of these sewer lines were left uncovered, although portions were covered to provide ground surface continuity between the two sides of a Khandaq, or linked by short foot bridges. The northern and southern Khandaqs must have been wide and deep enough to be used for defence purposes as continuations of the city walls (see Plate 16).

13 *Mahalla.* A final urban element within the scale of the overall Medina, which deserves mention is the Mahalla — the quarters that housed people of a common ethnic or socio-cultural/tribal background. The origin of the word is Mahall which means 'a place', such as a place where one stops to camp.[25] The Mahalla is usually under the administration of an official called Mukhtar in the east or Muharrek in the west, who also acts as representative of the Mahalla to the authorities. In Egypt the Mahallas or quarters of a town were sometimes called *Khitta.* In Tunis the term used is *Homa.* Traditionally the Mahallas in Islamic cities were provided with gates which were locked and guarded at night, particularly at times of insecurity. Owing to the lack of on-site evidence, especially the exact locations of the old Mahalla gates, compounded with the lack of specific descriptive information, I could not establish in Tunis the exact boundaries and configurations on the map of the Mahallas. However a general picture of approximate size and location is provided (see Figure 33 in Chapter 3).[26]

Morphological analysis of Medina core

The second level used for identifying components of the design language and their system of arrangement is by a morphological analysis of the Medina core in two parts. The first follows, and the second is the location of urban elements/building types to the street system.

Relationship of streets to the land-use pattern and related street coverage

(Relevant illustration is Figure 10.)

The street system is first viewed within the overall context of the Medina and its Rabad (suburbs), then highlights of the system within the core are identified:

1 The network of public thoroughfares, which in Arabic have the following four interchangeable terms:[27] *Tarik al-Muslimeen*, *Tarik Nafid*, *Shari'*, and *Nahj*. The first three were used historically; however, the latter two have been widely used since the late nineteenth century in Tunisia. The system of through streets is composed of: (a) First-order streets which make up the backbone of the system and connect all major city gates (Bab) with the core of the Medina where the major city mosque and surrounding Suqs are located. (b) Second-order streets which could be identified as major quarters (Mahalla) streets: these connect between the primary streets and are the main access routes within and between adjacent quarters. They tend to form shortcuts across the first-order streets. (c) Third-order streets which could be identified as minor quarter streets. These provide access and linkages to areas within quarters (Mahallas) which are not serviced by the second-order streets. They tend to be used by people belonging to the quarter or others who require frequent contacts there (see Figure 11).

2 A system of private cul-de-sacs, which in Arabic have the following interchangeable terms:[28] *Sikka ghair Nafida*, *Sikka munsadat àl-asfal*, *Derb ghair Nafid*, *Zuqaq ghair Nafid*, *Zanqa*. The first four terms were used in the past, whereas the last term has been popular in Tunisia at least since the mid-nineteenth century. A cul-de-sac, as discussed in Chapter 1, is private property owned and shared by its users. There is no specific pattern of linkage to the hierarchy of through streets, and they could be connected to any of the three types mentioned above, (see Figure 11). A statistical survey of twenty cul-de-sacs indicates that their length ranges from a maximum of 140 m to a minumum of 9 m, with an average length of 40 m.

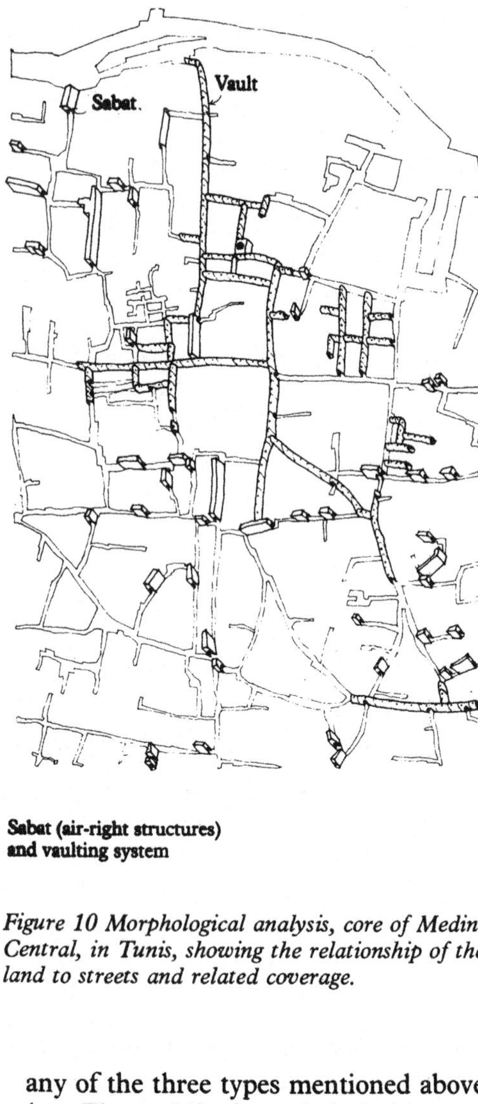

Figure 10 Morphological analysis, core of Medina Central, in Tunis, showing the relationship of the land to streets and related coverage.

The core of the Medina incorporates a good representation of the types of street and cul-de-sac prevalent at the level of the overall Medina. In addition, there is a third type, primarily of a commercial

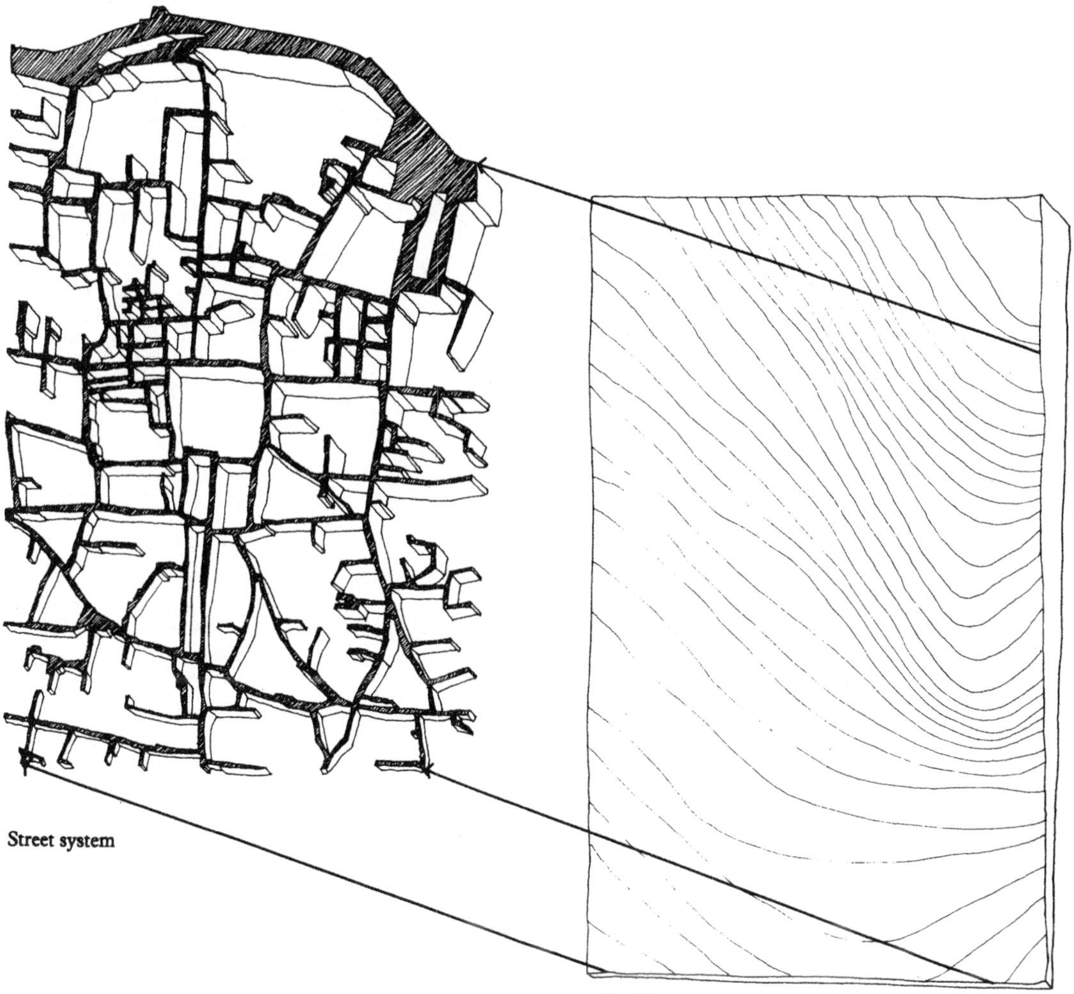

nature. It is part of the morphology of the Suq system, providing versatility, particularly with the aid of gates and can be used partially or wholly to lock up the Suq, or to redirect pedestrian traffic temporarily.

Street coverage system (See Fig. 10)

The core of the Medina is the best location for studying the coverage system utilized in the Arabic–Islamic city. The types of coverage used within the core are representative of all types used at the scale of the Medina and its Rabad. In addition usage in the core illustrates a dynamic of relationships of the different coverage elements which does not occur elsewhere in the Medina or its Rabad. The two predominant types of coverage are the result of opposing requirements: (a) The need for extra space from within buildings, particularly housing, created the Sabat, which is a room spanning the street or occasionally the cul-de-sac. It is usually long enough to create an adequate

Figure 11 Tunis Medina: an example of the street hierarchy and typical linkages to cul-de-sacs

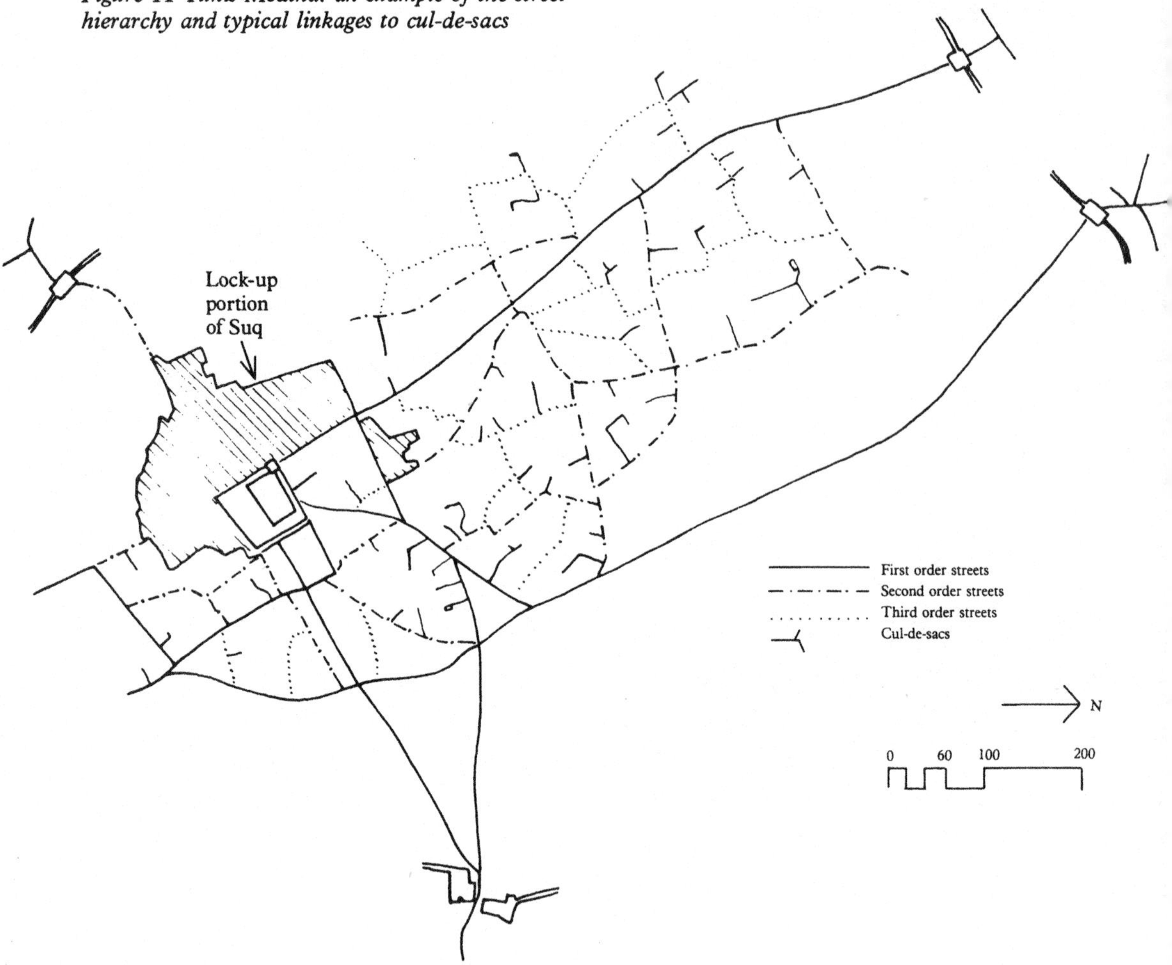

room; however, it could be a succession of rooms creating continuous coverage and a tunnel effect over a street (see Plates 1 and 17).[29] (b) Pedestrian requirement for coverage and protection from the elements, particularly in Suq streets. The most common method used for providing coverage is the vault, which is built with bricks and plastered on both sides,[30] and punctured at regular intervals along its apex providing light and ventilation. Its use is most prevalent in primary Suq streets where the traffic is heaviest. In other Arabic–Islamic cities such as Kairouan and Marakech we also find an alternative method — wooden grills, to provide shade — located on parts of the Suq system (see Plate 18).

The third element that is an integral part of the street coverage system is the flying-buttress arch. It is usually located on narrow streets and cul-de-sacs to provide lateral strength to the opposite walls, and is high enough to allow a fully loaded camel to pass without hindrance. Their repetitiveness in some streets or cul-de-sacs creates a play of sun and shadow which enhances their character (see Plate 19).

Location of urban elements/ building types to the street system

Figure 12 illustrates the location of various urban elements or building types and their relationships within the core of the Medina. For purposes of clarity each urban element is identified once, and in addition, those that have distinct variations due to location and/or configuration are also pointed out. It should be noted here that all the urban elements to be discussed (with a few exceptions which do not apply) have a common organizational feature: they are all organized around a patio open to the sky (in Arabic, the common terms used for patio are *Fina* or *Sahn*). This is one of the fundamental physical features underlying the organization and planning of the traditional Arabic–Islamic city in the Maghrib.

1 *Major city Mosque (Jami).*[31] Its various terms are discussed below. The Prophet's mosque in Medina became a model as a centre for worship and administration during the rapid spread of Islam (see Figure 13). The first building project a Muslim leader would undertake in a new area was to found a mosque as a centre around which to gather, although conditions differed somewhat between a new foundation and an already existing town. Important examples of the first kind are Basra, Kufa in Iraq, and al-Fustat in Egypt. Basra was founded by Ukba b. Nafi as winter quarters for the army in approx. 14/635. The mosque was placed in the centre with the Dar al-Imara, the dwelling of the commander-in-chief with a prison and Diwan, in front of it. It was similar in Kufa which was founded in 17/638 by Sa'd b. Abi Wakkas. In the centre was the mosque and beside it was laid out the Dar al-Imara; later Caliph Omar ordered it combined with the mosque. The plan was an exact reproduction of the mosque in Medina. The importance of the mosque was also expressed in its position, and the commander lived close beside it. There was no difference in al-Fustat; even though there was already an older town there, it was laid out as an entirely new camp. In other cases Muslims established themselves in old towns which were either conquered or surrendered by a treaty, which provided a site for the mosque. However, the distinction between these two situations soon disappeared and the position is, as a rule, not clear.

As late as the reign of Mu'awiya (41/661–61/680) we find a new town, Kairouan, being laid out on the old plan as a military camp with a mosque and Dar al-Imara in the centre. Baladhuri[32] clearly indicated that Muslims, even at a later date, always built a mosque in the centre of a newly conquered town. At first they simply reproduced the mosque of the Prophet in Medina. It was the exception to adapt already existing buildings in towns.

The Friday noon prayer (Salat al-Juma), which should be performed in the mosque, is obligatory for every free male Muslim who has reached the age of discretion. Its importance in the earlier period lay in the fact that all elements of the Muslim camp assembled in the major mosque under the leadership of the general. The major mosque, which for this purpose was particularly large, is given an appropriate name. It is referred to as al-Masdjid al-Azam, al-Masdjid al-Akbar or Masdjid al-Jama'a, Masdjid li'l-jamaa and Masdjid jami, and then as Masdjid al-Jami, with the popular abbreviation of Jami. As the Khutba

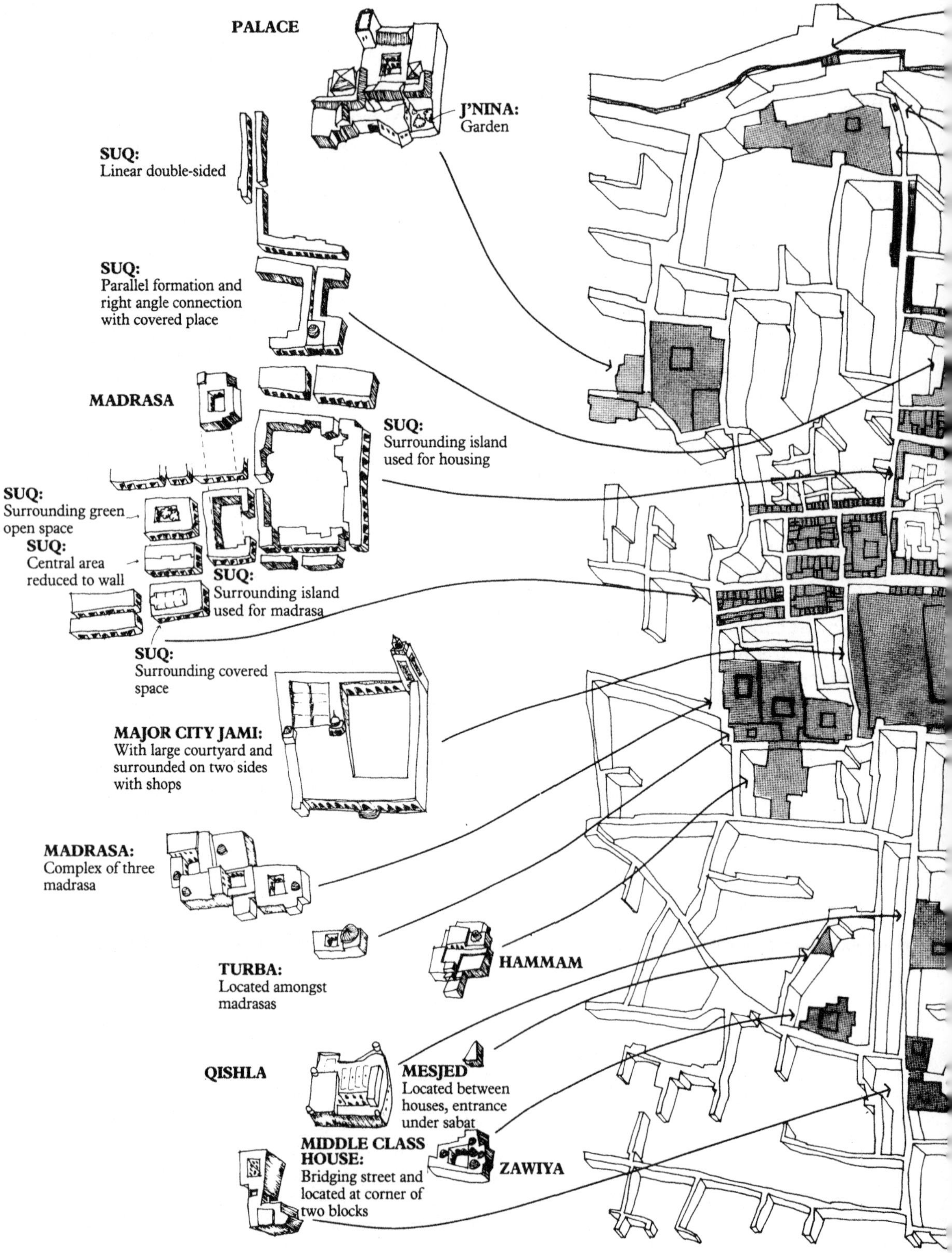

Figure 12 Morphological analysis, core of Medina Central, Tunis: Urban elements location to street system

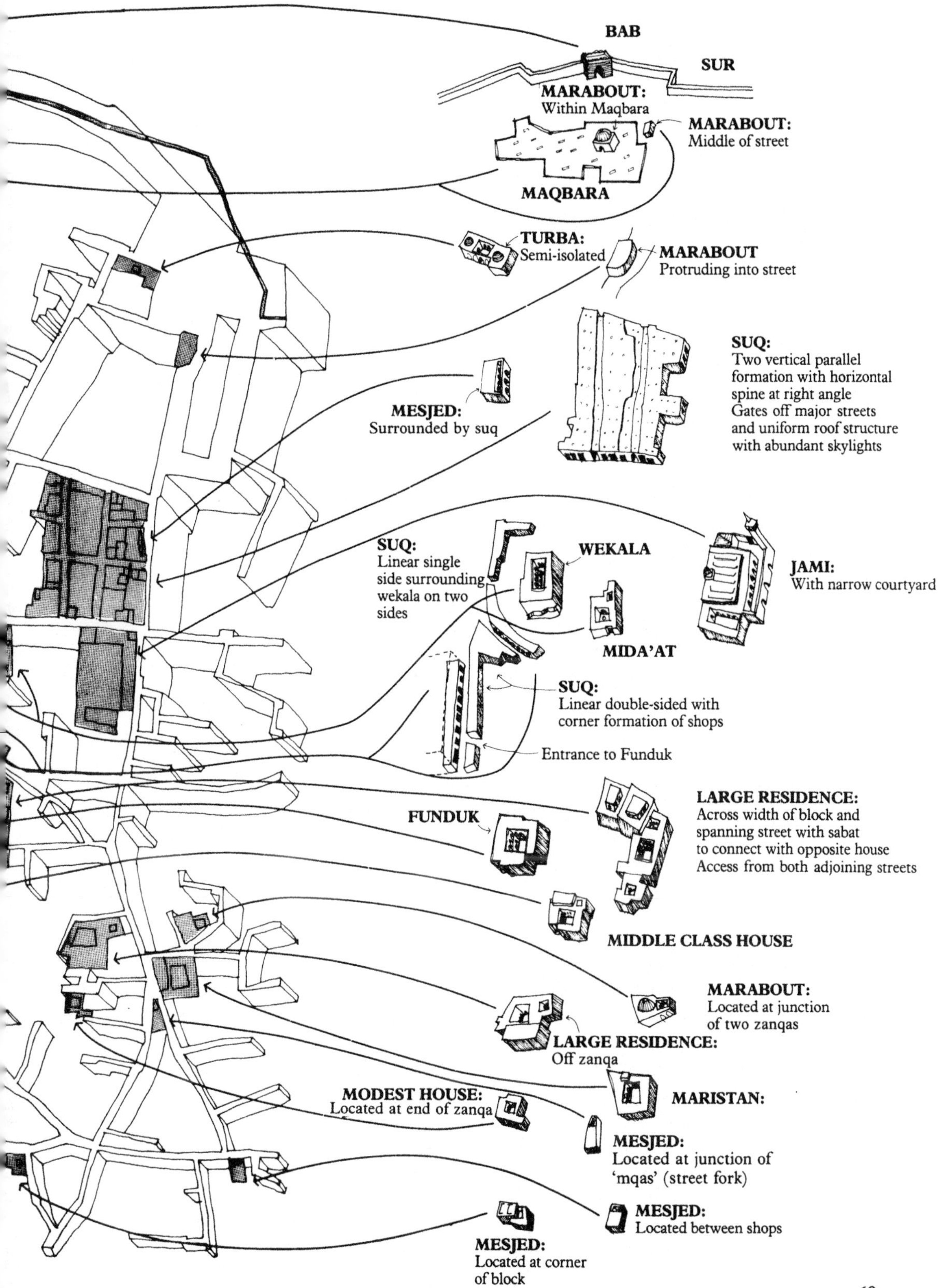
BAB
SUR
MARABOUT:
Within Maqbara
MARABOUT:
Middle of street
MAQBARA
TURBA:
Semi-isolated
MARABOUT
Protruding into street
SUQ:
Two vertical parallel
formation with horizontal
spine at right angle
Gates off major streets
and uniform roof structure
with abundant skylights
MESJED:
Surrounded by suq
SUQ:
Linear single
side surrounding
wekala on two
sides
WEKALA
JAMI:
With narrow courtyard
MIDA'AT
SUQ:
Linear double-sided with
corner formation of shops
Entrance to Funduk
LARGE RESIDENCE:
Across width of block and
spanning street with sabat
to connect with opposite house
Access from both adjoining streets
FUNDUK
MIDDLE CLASS HOUSE
MARABOUT:
Located at junction
of two zanqas
LARGE RESIDENCE:
Off zanqa
MARISTAN:
MODEST HOUSE:
Located at end of zanqa
MESJED:
Located at junction of
'mqas' (street fork)
MESJED:
Located between shops
MESJED:
Located at corner
of block

1. Covered area for prophet's friends
2. Covered prayer area
3. Private rooms
4. Entrance from three sides of building

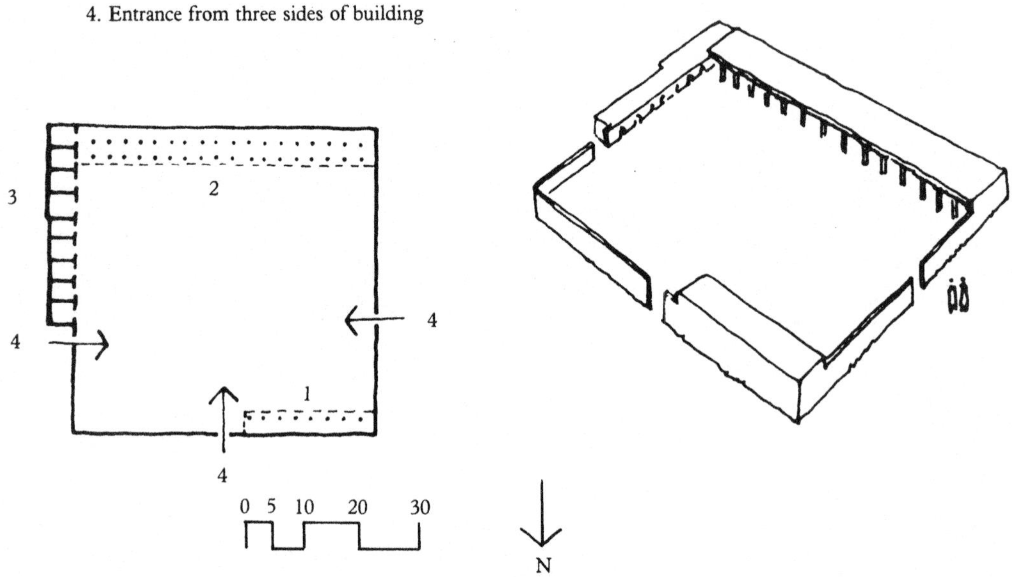

Figure 13 Plan and view of Prophet's mosque/house during the period 2/623–17/638 (after Creswell and Shafi'i).

was the distinguishing feature, we also find Masdjid al-Khutba, Jami al-Khutba and Masdjid al-Minbar (see Figure 14).[33]

Terminology varied somewhat with prevailing conditions. During the time of Caliph Omar it was proper in every town to have only one Masdjid Jami for the Friday service. However, when a community developed out of its military origin and Islam replaced the previous religion of the people, the need for a number of mosques for the Friday service was bound to arise. Thus, mosques for the Friday service were needed in the country and in the villages, and often several were needed within the town.

In Tunis one of the first acts in founding it was Hassan b. Numan al-Ghassani's establishment of Jami al-Zaytuna in 84/703.[34] The layout was inspired by the Prophet's mosque at Medina, as were all other early mosques and it is planned around a courtyard Sahn which is surrounded by cloisters, or *Riwak*. The Riwak at the Qibla side was enlarged to create the roofed prayer area of the mosque. Occasionally when this roofed area is not adequate, the excess number of people use the Sahn. It should be noted that since approximately the late fifteenth century, the Zaytuna mosque Sahn has been the largest open space in the Medina, and consequently provides an impressive and overwhelming sense of space and tranquility in contrast to the adjoining narrow and busy streets (see Figure 15 and Plate 20).

The main entrance facade faces a relatively wide street which forms a T-junction with Rue Jami al-Zaytuna (the

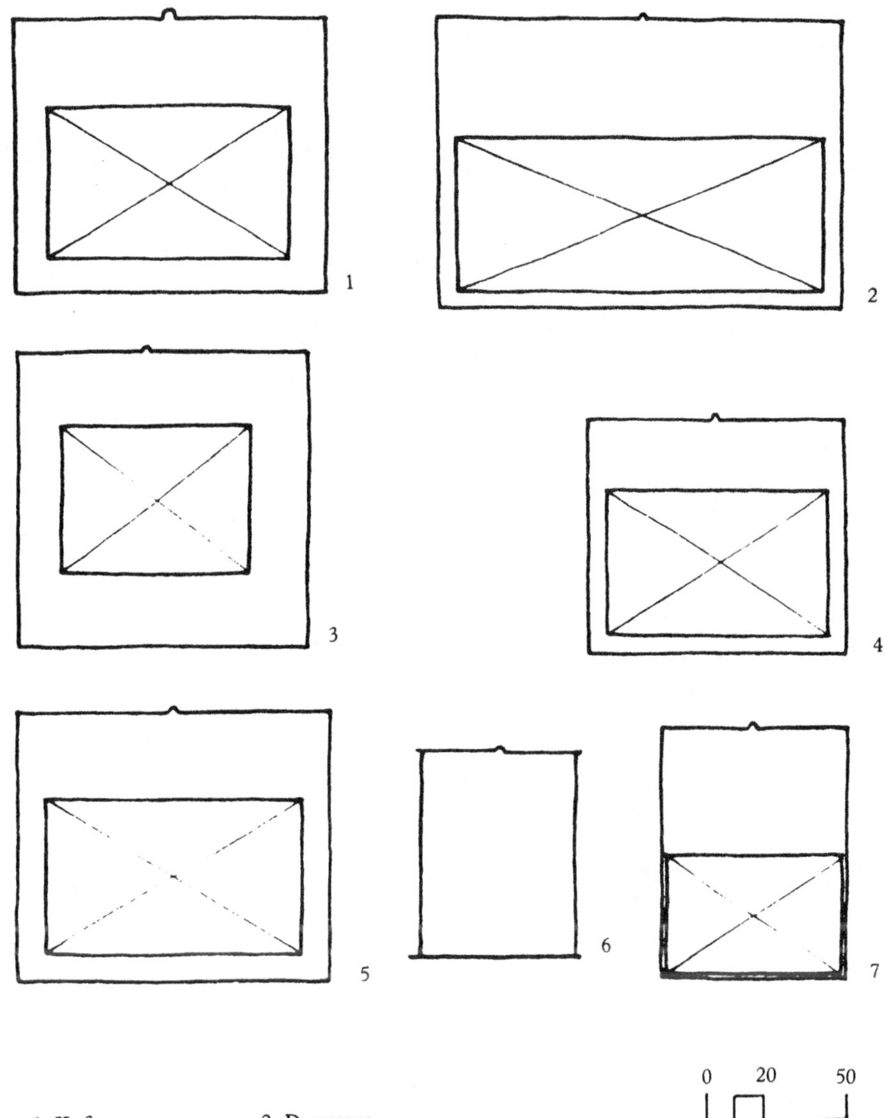

1. Kufa
2. Damascus
3. Medina
4. Aleppo
5. Harran
6. Jerusalem
7. Cordoba

Figure 14 Various major mosques drawn to the same scale and Qibla orientation (after Bianca and Sauvaget)

main street from Bab al-Bahr, the primary eastern gate, to the core of the town). The Suq surrounds the mosque on its three other sides utilizing its structure for support of the vaulting system. The western and southern

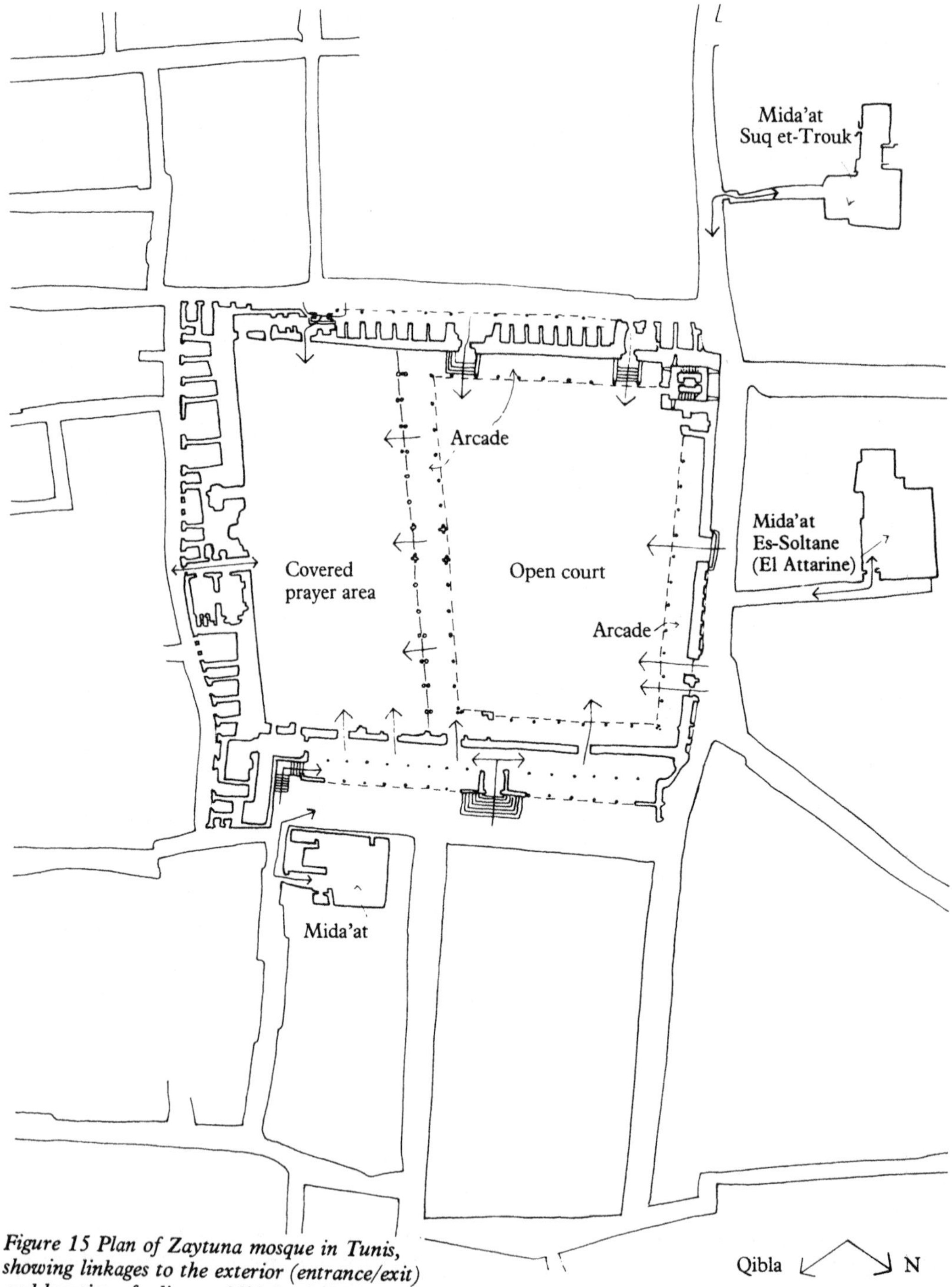

Figure 15 Plan of Zaytuna mosque in Tunis, showing linkages to the exterior (entrance/exit) and location of adjacent Mida'at (ablution facilities)

sides of the mosque are also utilized for rows of shops (see Plates 65 and 69). In addition to the main entrance on the eastern facade, the mosque is provided with nearly anonymous doors on the northern and western facades.

The architectural treatment of the facades is of interest: the eastern facade is the only one treated architecturally, that is, with acceptance of its outward looking posture (see Plate 21). The other three facades are totally anonymous to the extent that a stranger in the town might walk by without realizing the existence of the mosque behind the walls, and this is particularly true of the western and southern facades.

2 *Khutba mosque (Jami)*: As mentioned earlier other Khutba mosques in addition to the major city mosque began to be created primarily in response to population growth. This phenomenon occurred first in the larger eastern Islamic cities such as Baghdad, Samara and Cairo during the second, third, and fourth Islamic centuries (approx. 750–1000 AD).[35]

In Tunis the first such mosque within the Medina was Jami el-Ksar built in 494/1100–522/1128, 410 years after the founding of Jami al-Zaytuna. Other Khutba mosques, within the Medina, which followed were Jami Bey Mohammad in 604/1207–619/1222, Jami al-Kasba, within the Kasbah walls in 631/1233, and others (see Figure 16).

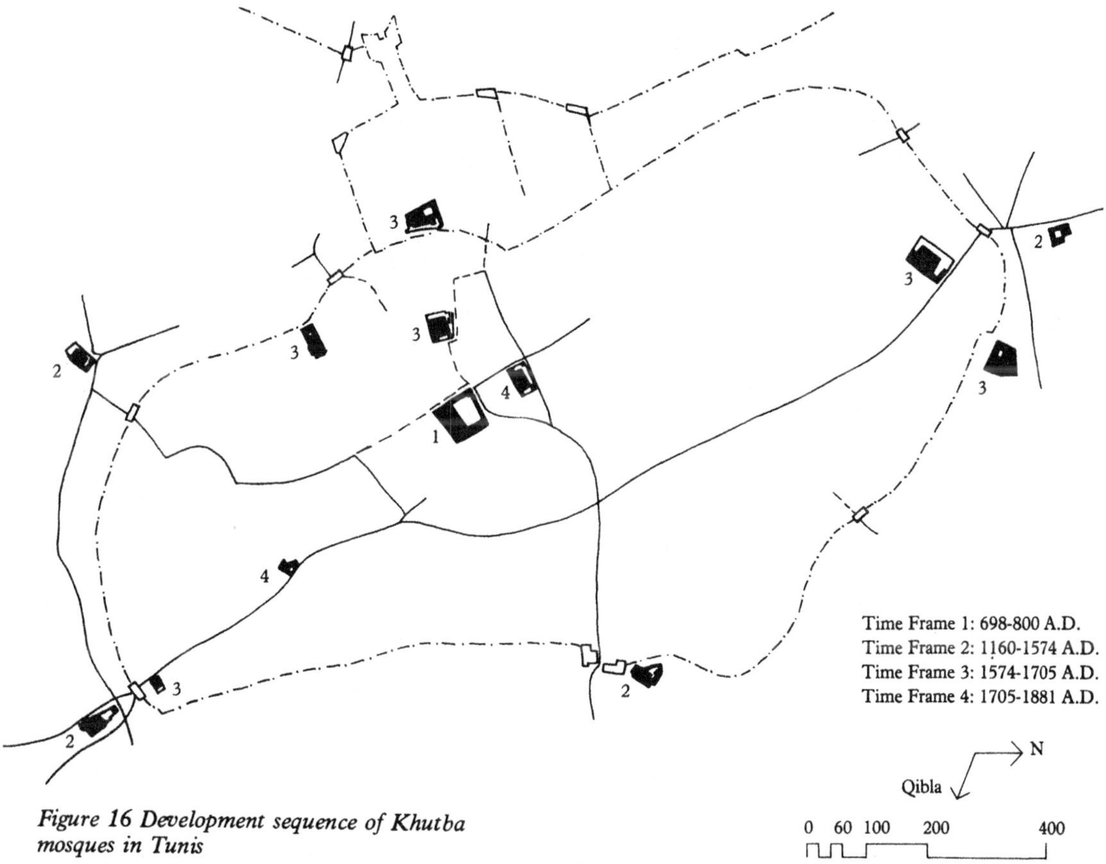

Figure 16 Development sequence of Khutba mosques in Tunis

Mohammad b. al-Khodja says that initially the Malikis allowed, in principle, for three Khutba mosques in Tunis — one in the middle (which is the al-Zaytuna) and two on the sides.[36] However, by the beginning of this century, Tunis and its two Rabads had nineteen Khutba mosques, twelve Maliki and seven Hanafi.[37] An analysis of the ratio of Khutba mosques to population in Tunis from the early sixteenth century to the end of the nineteenth century indicates an average ratio of 1:6,250.[38]

The other core area Khutba jami to note is Jami Sidi Ben Arous (or Jami Hamouda Pasha Moradi), built in 1065/1654 as a Hanafi mosque 922 years after Jami al-Zaytuna. Its features included a narrow U-shaped courtyard wrapping around the enclosed prayer area and proximity to a Turba, Zawiya and Madrasa. It was also located close to Jami al-Zaytuna because of the prestigious location, and to create a rival Hanafi Khutba mosque. This is an excellent example of a Khutba mosque location not determined solely by population increase (see Plate 20).

3 *Local Mesjeds.* These are simple prayer facilities which are conveniently located in large numbers in the Arabic–Islamic city. Their purpose is to provide an easily accessible place for the performance of the five daily prayers, excluding the Friday mid-day prayer and those of the two Eids or festivals. They are usually provided with a water source for ablution and adequate space for a small group of people to pray. Some of them have a small or narrow Sahn (patio) for light and ventilation.

In Tunis, within the 'Medina Central' area, I have managed to locate sixty-six Mesjeds.[39] They range in size from the smallest room-like facility to large facilities which could approximate the size of a Jami, having all its components except the *Minbar* (pulpit). The majority do not have a minaret and do not require the call for the prayer if they are located within hearing distance of a Jami (see Plate 22).

Figure 12 illustrates the physical variety of Mesjed types within the core of the Medina as shaped by their specific locality. Almost all of them are located such that they are not visible or easily distinguishable from their immediate surroundings. Their entrances might indicate the Mesjed if the name is inscribed or if there is a Qur'anic verse on top of the door. Mohammad b. el-Khodja notes the frequency of the Mesjeds by stating that in Tunis the pedestrian is always within 100 Khatwa or paces (approximately 150 m) from any Mesjed or Jami.[40]

4 *Madrasa.* The term means school; however, its traditional usage refers to an institution of higher learning where Islamic sciences and law are studied. It is equivalent to a contemporary college institution.

During the first 400 years of Islam (622–1010 AD) the mosque was the centre of learning. The first Madrasa built as a separate facility for the sole purpose of higher education was in Naisapur during the first half of the fifth century of Islam.[41] There were four particularly famous Madaris in Naisapur: al-Madrasa al-Baihakiya, founded by al-Baihaki (d. 458/1066), when he became a teacher there in 441/1049; al-Sa'idiya founded by the emir Nasr b. Subuktakin (governor of Naisapur in 389/999); one built by Abu Sa'd Ismail al-Astarabadi; and another built for the teacher Abu Ishak al-Isfara'ini. Nizam al-Mulk also built Nizamiya for the Imam al-Haramain al-Djuwaini.[42]

An event of great importance in the early history of the development of the Madrasa was Nizam al-Mulk's (456/1064–485/1092, Vizier of the Saldjuk sultans Alp Arslan and

Malik Shah) founding of the celebrated Nizamiya Madrasa in Baghdad; the building was begun in 457/1065 and consecrated in 459/1067. It was founded for the Shafi'i teacher Abu Ishak al-Shirazi.[43]

Muslim historians are in some doubt as to who should receive the credit for the Madrasa. Nizam al-Mulk seems to receive most of the credit even though others developed the above four Madaris in Naisapur. It seems that his contribution lies in: (a) the enthusiasm and energy which he created for the development of the Madrasa; (b) the scholarships he endowed for the students; and (c) the development of the Madrasa for boarded students, which became the prevalent type after his time.[44]

The prosperity of the Madaris stimulated by Nizam al-Mulk in the fifth Islamic century survived for a long time. In the sixth century Ibn Djubair (580/1184) mentions thirty Madaris in Baghdad, all in the eastern part of the city, the most notable being the Nizamiya, renovated in 504/1110. In 631/1234, the Caliph al-Mustansir founded the magnificent Mustansiriya as a school for the four Sunni schools of law, each with a teacher and seventy-five students, and a teacher for Qur'an, and one for the Hadith, as well as a physician. Attached to it were a library, baths, hospital and kitchens. There was a clock at the entrance and beside it a garden where the Caliph had a pavilion. The Nizamiya and the Mustansiriya survived the destruction of Baghdad by Hulagu, and Ibn Battuta mentioned both at the beginning of the eighth century when he said that the Madaris were still flourishing in the east. The Mustansiriya still exists today and was renovated in the 1940s and 1950s by the Iraqi government.[45]

In Damascus the two rulers Nur al-Din b. Zaugi (541/1146–569/1163) and Salah al-Din (570/1174–589/1193) were as munificent in Madrasa building as their emirs and relatives. This building activity continued into the ninth century; al-Nu'aimi (d. 927/1521) gave the following totals: seven dar al-Qur'an, sixteen dar al-Hadith, three for both Qur'an and Hadith, sixty Shafi'i, fifty-two Hanafi, four Maliki, and ten Hanbali Madaris. There were also three Madaris al-tibb (medical schools), built in the seventh century. The founders were mainly rulers and emirs, but also included merchants, a number of men of learning, and a few women.

Salah al-Din introduced the Madrasa in Jerusalem, and according to Mudjir al-Din (d. 927/1521), there were thirty-one Madaris and monasteries (*Zawiyas*, which were in part used in the same way as Madaris) in direct connection with the Haram area. Next to Nizam al-Mulk, Salah al-Din had the greatest reputation as a builder of Madaris, one which he owes mainly to the fact that his great activity as a builder was in countries that became important in the Muslim world — Syria, Palestine, and Egypt.[46]

In Salah al-Din's time, the Madrasa was also introduced in the Hidjaz. In the year 579/1183 the governor of Aden built in Makkah a Madrasa for the Hanafis and in the following year also founded a Shafi'i Madrasa there. Until the beginning of the ninth century, eleven Madaris are mentioned, but others were also added. Madaris were also built in Madina.[47]

During the period of the Aiyubids and Mamluks the number of Madaris increased to an extraordinary degree. In the street called Bain al-Kasrain in Cairo, there were two long rows of Madaris on the site of the old Fatimid palace. Al-Makrizi (d. 845/1442) mentions seventy-three Madaris, and of those thirteen were founded before 600/1203, twenty in the seventh century, twenty-nine in the eighth, and two after 800/1397.

Tunis acted as the bridge between the two sides of the Mediterranean basin in the transfer and establishment of the Madrasa in the Maghrib. The first Madrasa in Tunis was the Samma'iyya built in 627/1229 by Abou Zakariya Yahya, the founder of the Hafsid dynasty, in the same year that he proclaimed Tunis independent of the Almohad Moroccan Caliph.[48] The first Madrasa built in the extreme west of the Islamic world was the Madrasa al-Saffarin in Fez in the year 684/1285, by the Marinid Abu Yusuf Ya'kub b. Abd al-Hakk. In Andalusia (Muslim Spain), the mosque was the place of learning. However, in 750/1349, the Nasrid Yusuf Abu l'Hadjdjadj founded a large Madrasa in Granada.[49] The complete process of the spread and transfer of the Madrasa from Naisapur to Granada took three hundred years.

Within the Medina Central area of Tunis I have located eighteen Madaris. Mohammad b. al-Khodja lists thirty-seven within the boundary of Tunis and its two Rabads. A breakdown of the latter figure indicates the following: the first eight Madaris were built within the Hafsid era, the following four were built by the Ottomans, the Husaynids built eighteen, and the last seven were built between 1299/1881 and 1357/1938.[50]

The example of a Madrasa, which is extracted from the core of the medina as indicated in Figure 17, is a complex of three Madrasas. The oldest one, named al-Nakhla, is located on the northern side of the block nearest to Jami al-Zaytuna. It replaced a previous Funduk which was located on the site, and was built by Hussain b. Ali in 1126/1714. It had adequate facilities for fourteen boarding students and their teacher, and was reserved for students who came to Tunis from distant places. Their food and upkeep was financed by a Wakf established for that purpose. The second Madrasa in chronological order is al-Sulaimaniya on the southern side of the block founded by Pasha Ali I in 1168/1755 in memory of his son Sulaiman who was killed by his brother. It was allocated for students of the Maliki School of Law. The third Madrasa, Bir al-Hajjar, located between the first two and built two years after the Sulaimaniya in 1170/1757 and was also founded by Pasha Ali I. It too was for students of the Maliki school and had a library facility.[51]

Today the three Madrasas are linked by their courtyards in a north–south direction and are used as one facility (see Figure 17). The buildings are located at separate levels in response to the slope. The southern entrance of the Sulaimaniya Madrasa is used as the main entrance, and as the visitor emerges in the courtyard he is confronted with a pleasant sense of scale. The three Madrasas are single storey structures and each has an arcade (Riwak) surrounding its court. The students rooms, prayer room, and Mida'at surround the courtyard. The primary decoration is in the Skifa (main entrance lobby) and on the arches of the arcades. A fourth, uniquely located Madrasa was in the midst of the Suq and surrounded by shops (see Figures 40 and 42, Example 7). It is the Madrasa Mouradiya built in 1084/1673 by Bey Mourad II. It provides accommodation in single rooms for twenty students from outside Tunis for Maliki studies.[52]

The first three Madrasas are typical of the Tunisian type in terms of proportions, style and architectural treatment. However, they are not typical in being single-storey, as there are a number of two-storey Madrasas in Tunis. In contrast, the Madrasas in Fez or Meknes in Morocco have smaller but highly decorated courtyards, and are usually two-storey structures (see Plate 23).

A typical Tunis Madrasa would therefore consist of students' rooms at two levels located around the courtyard and separated

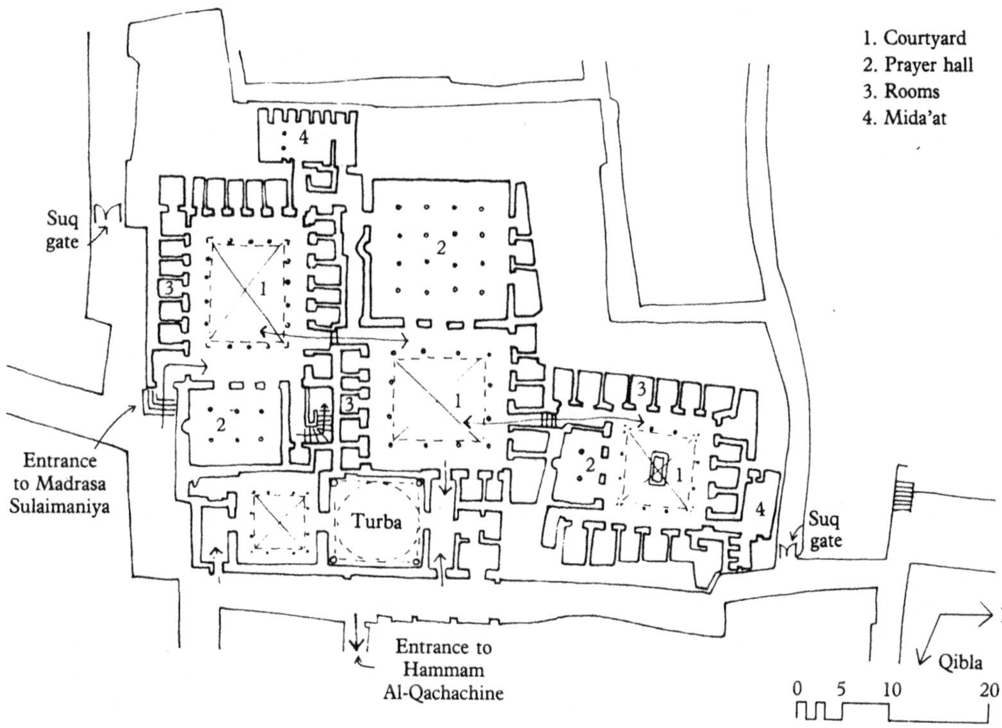

Figure 17 Plan of a three-Madrasa complex and Turba located south of Zaytuna mosque, Tunis

from it by an arcade (Riwak). The prayer room or mosque of the Madrasa is usually prominently located, quite often opposite the main entrance with its Qibla wall facing the direction of Makkah. A Mida'at or ablution area is also provided and that is usually located on one of the sides sometimes tucked behind the rooms.

In the eastern schools the courtyards tended to be large, and the court facades are designed with Iwans, ranging in number from one to four. Design criteria determined their location, and their number was not related to the number of schools of law taught in the Madrasa (see Plate 24.)[53].

5 *Zawiya.* In the Maghrib countries this term is applied to a building, or group of buildings, of a religious nature, which resembles a monastery and a school. The literal meaning of the term is 'corner', and in this context it originated from its meaning as applied to a corner of a building. A common thing for devout men was to live permanently in the mosque, for example within the base of the minaret or in a cell, which was also used for study or meditation.

An excellent definition of the Maghribi Zawiya was given as early as 1847 by Daumas. All or several of the following are found in a Zawiya: a room for prayer with a Mihrab; the mausoleum of a marabout or Sharifan saint, which is surmounted by a dome (Kubba); a room set aside exclusively for the recitation of the Qur'an; a Maktab or Qur'an school; and rooms for the guests of the Zawiya such as pilgrims, travellers and students. The Zawiya is usually adjoined by a cemetery with the tombs of those who have during their lifetime expressed a wish to be buried in it.[54]

In the Maghrib the term *Zawiya* appears around the thirteenth century AD as synonymous with *Rabita*, a hermitage to which a holy man retired and lived surrounded by his pupils and devotees. In Muslim Spain the Rabitas multiplied and their memory is preserved in placenames in the forms Rapita, Ravita, Rabida.[55] The increase of Rabitas in Muslim Spain, and their possible confusion with *Ribats*, is connected with the great movement of mystic piety which, starting in Persia in the fourth century, had brought about the substitution of monasteries — *Khanakah*, *Tekke* or *Dair* in the east or *Zawiya* in the Maghrib, in place of the earlier more military Ribat foundations.[56] However, the term Ribat (plur. *Rubut*) also came to mean Khanakah, a place where Sufis lived together to wage the spiritual *Jihad* (spiritual holy war).[57]

In time the three terms Khanakah, Ribat and Zawiya referred to the same facility, namely a Sufi monastery which was also open for travelling guests, and when they were located at or near a place of pilgrimage, they played an important role as hostels.[58] However, the purpose of these monasteries was to afford Sufis a home and place for their devotional exercises. For example, in the Khanakah of Baibars in Cairo founded in 706/1306, 400 Sufis were maintained, and in Khanakah Siryakus, also in Cairo, 100 were maintained. They were given lodging, food, clothing and money; there were often baths attached to them. The building was arranged for Dhikr exercises and for prayers (Salats).[59]

It should be noted that the development of the monastery (Khanakah, Ribat, Zawiya) was analogous to that of the Madrasa, because learning and manifestation of piety are inseparable in Islam, hence learning was also cultivated in the monasteries. In the eighth and ninth centuries the combination of the two institutions became quite frequent — for example in the Nizamiya in Cairo during 757/1356. During his travels in the eastern regions of the Islamic world, Ibn Battuta found the same relationship, for example in Shiraz and in Kerbela, and this is what he means when he says the Persians call the Zawiya Madrasa.[60]

In Tunis Medina Central I have located thirty-eight Zawiyas, and within the core area illustrated, the Zawiya of Sidi Ali Azouz serves as an example (see Figure 12). It was founded by Ali Bey within the period of his reign (1172/1758–1197/1782).

6 *Marabout-Murabit*. The term *Marabout* is the Europeanized version of the Arabic *Murabit*. In the early period of Islamic expansion the term was used to describe the man who dedicates his life to the *Jihad*, for defending and spreading Islam. He would be attached to one of many Ribats or military fortifications spread across the frontiers of the Islamic world. In the east by approximately the fifth century and in the Maghrib by the seventh, the term was used to describe the man who joins a Sufi group or Rabita for the spiritual Jihad.[61]

In time the term, particularly in the Maghrib, was applied to a saint, or in certain cases to his descendants, an individual who by his own merits or his mystic initiation enjoyed the veneration of those around him.[62] The term *Wali* equivalent to the Christian term saint, was also used for such a person when he was regarded with enough significance.[63] In the whole Maghrib the classical Murabit has given way to the dialectic form *Mrabet* (fem. *Mrabta*, plur. *Mrabtin*).[64]

Since the early part of this century, the term used in Algeria is *Marabet*; in Morocco however, it is less used than its equivalents *Salih*, *Wali*, and particularly *Saiyid*. The term Mrabet is only applied to a member of a marabout family or clan, descendants of an eponymous saint, from whom he has inherited a part of his saintly attributes (*Baraka*).[65]

With respect to a particular building type within the Arabic–Islamic city, it referred to the burial place or tomb of such a person, within a hierarchy of diverse categories, from the venerated patron of a capital or a region to the modest anonymous local saint, whose tomb is only recognizable by a small circular wall (*Hawsh*) around it. The frequency of the whitewashed domes (*Kubba*) which are spread all over the countryside and within villages and cities is a well-known feature, particularly in North Africa. When a certain marabout in the region where he was buried enjoyed a greater esteem than other local saints, his mausoleum could become a node for building activity and settlement, or a Zawiya could grow around it (see Plate 25).

The name of the marabout is always preceded by the title *Sidi* (*Saiyidi*); and sometimes, especially in Morocco, by the term *Mulai* (*Mawlaya*); names of sainted women are always preceded by the Berber title *Lalla*. In the Abadite enclaves of the Maghrib, where saints are also found, the term for a marabout is *Ammi* (which in Arabic literally means 'my uncle').[66]

Within Tunis Medina Central I have located thirty-eight marabouts, and within the core four examples are extracted; they are physically different marabouts in shape and location. The first is marabout Sidi Braham[67] located on the junction of two cul-de-sacs, a structure built around a courtyard with its major interior domed (Kubba). It has a wall with a Mihrab facing the Qibla. It dates from the second half of the eleventh century AH or seventeenth century AD (see Figure 23).

The second is marabout Sidi Bou Krissan which is a typical marabout structure, square in plan, containing the tomb, and roofed with a dome (*Kubba*).[68] It is located within the cemetery walls. The third and fourth types are located in the public right-of-way or protruding into it.

Marabout Sidi Bou Abdallah is a simple grave located in the middle of Suq Serrajine which is one of the major public thoroughfares in the city. The street widens around the grave and it becomes an island around which pedestrian traffic circulates. A lantern hangs from the vault of the Suq on top of it to signify its importance. This is an excellent example of the respect people have for the location of the tomb of a venerated Murabit (see Plate 26).

The fourth example is that of marabout Sidi Cherif which was attached to the corner of Dar al-Bey and protrudes into the formal public square adjoining it. The latter was laid out to respect the position of the marabout. However, the fervour for modernity in the mid-1950s after Tunisia became independent resulted in its removal for the sake of further formalizing the square in front of Dar al-Bey and other government buildings.

7 *Turba*. The term refers to grave, from the Arabic: earth or dust. The term is popular and is used especially in those regions which were under Ottoman rule. In Tunis it refers to private cemeteries, usually of the ruling class. They tend to be part of a building complex including other uses, such as a Madrasa, Jami, or Mesjed. They could also be located within housing areas.

I have located twenty-six Turbas in the Medina Central; the largest is Turba al-Bey, which is the royal tomb of the Husaynid princes who reigned from 1117/1705 to 1377/1957 and is located in the southern portion of the 'Medina Central'. One of the two Turbas (which are extracted from the core area for illustrative purposes) is Turba Las, located on the western edge of the core area and adjoining Mesjed Sidi b. Ziad, sharing with it one party wall. It has a courtyard, and the two opposite covered areas are surmounted by domes. The other is Turba Ali Pasha which has his remains and that of his son. It was built during the same period as the Madrasa Sulaimaniya and Bir Hajjar.[69] It is oblong in shape, sharing two party walls with the two Madrasas, and is planned with a courtyard with the major space roofed by a large dome (Kubba) (see Figure 17 and Plate 27).

8 *Maqbara.* The term refers to public cemetery.[70] In Tunis the Arabic term *Jabbana* is also used. The Maqbara at Rue de Selliers on the western edge of the core area is extracted as an example. It is one of the earliest cemeteries in Tunis and is only a small portion of what was a larger cemetery extending in a north–south axis and dating from the second century AH/seventh century AD. It is walled and irregular in shape, indicating the encroachment from its eastern and southern sides. It has a free-standing marabout within it (see Plate 28).

9 *Suq (plural Aswaq).* The term means the place for goods and necessities (i.e., market) and is used in place names for streets and other localities where there is a market. It usually precedes the market's commodity (e.g., Suq al-Attarine — the perfumers' market).

As discussed earlier in this chapter, the Suq is one of three pre-requisites for an Arabic–Islamic city. Its urban integration, development and characteristics is a unique contribution to the development of the city. A complete set of guidelines for market operation (Ahkam al-Suq) and administration by the Muhtasib developed simultaneously, but this is outside the scope of this discussion.

In Tunis (see Figure 18), it is possible to identify the following Suq types as determined by their location:

(a) The major Suq area around Jami al-Zaytuna, the city's major mosque. These are usually single-storey structures with covered pedestrian streets. They primarily have one single use, that of the Suq and its facilities. The whole area can be locked up by a minimum number of strategic gates. The Suqs (aggregates of many shops) are assembled in numerous combinations.

(b) The linear continuous or semi-continuous Suq. These occur on the major city thoroughfares, particularly those connecting major gates with the core of the city. They are sometimes covered with vaulting. These linear Suqs use the ground floor or street level and are overlapped on upper levels by other uses, particularly housing.

(c) Suqs which occur adjacent to major gates (Bab) of the city. They capitalize on this location because of its function as an activity node. They occur on both sides of the wall and can be viewed as an extension of the linear type from within.

(d) Weekly or seasonal markets using open areas, usually Bat'has which are relatively well located on major thoroughfares. Occasionally they require portable makeshift facilities.

(e) *Suwaiqas*: the term in Arabic implies mini-Suq. These are groups or clusters of neighbourhood shops which are scattered in the city, but which usually occur at places that function as the Mahalla or neighbourhood centre. They usually

Plate 44 Example of Suq vaulting. (a) (*above left*) Suq et Trouk in Tunis, taken from near the base of the minaret of Zaytuna mosque. Note the brick vaulting system and the sequence of structural ribs. (b) (*above right*) View of the same Suq et Trouk sometime during the period 1881–1930. At that time the coverage system was of wood construction. (Photo provided by Paul Vaughan, Tunis)

Plate 45 (*right*) Example of a Sabat supported on two walls. View in the Rue du Tresor, Tunis. Note window levels of the ground floor, and the locational relationship of doors on opposite sides of the street.

Figure 46 (*above left*) Example of Sabat supported on wall and columns. View in the Rue Tourbet el-Bey, Tunis looking south. Note the Sabat in the foreground and background are supported on the right by columns and on the left by the wall.

Plate 47 (*above right*) Example of Sabat supported both sides on columns. View in the Rue du Mufti, the Sabat is located after the junction on the right of Rue Jama'a Ghorbal.

Plate 48 (*left*) Example of a Driba in the village of Sidi Bou Sa'id, Tunisia. The photo is taken just inside the entrance looking towards the closed end of the Driba. This example is 28.5 m long and has Dukkana or built-in seats showing in the foreground of the picture. (Photo: Maria Jones, 1975)

Plate 49 (*above left*) Example of a Skifa. This is the Skifa of Dar Hussein in Tunis, one of the large palaces. The photo is taken within the Skifa looking toward the door leading to the courtyard. Note the elaborate wall and ceiling decoration. (Photo from Revault, J., 1971, *Palais et Demeures de Tunis* (XVII et XIX siecles), Centre National de la Recherche Scientifique, Paris)

Plate 50 (*above right*) Example of a courtyard showing Burtal, a fountain, and a tree. This is the courtyard of a middle-class house somewhere in Morocco. (Photo from *The Timeless Way of Building*, Oxford University Press, 1979, supplied by Christopher Alexander)

Plate 51 (*right*) Example of a Bit trida in a middle-class Tunisian house. Note the roll of decorated cloth on the wall to provide backing for seaters, and the portable Hanut Hajjam located in the alcove of the room. (Photo: Paul Vaughan, Tunis)

Plate 52 (*above left*) Example of a Bit bel-Kbu u Mkasar in Dar Daouletli, Tunis. The central area with the built-in U-shaped seating is the Kbu, and the doors on each side lead to a Maksura (a small private room on each side of the Kbu). (Photo: Revault, J., (1967) *Palais et Demeures de Tunis* (XVI et XVII siecles), Centre National de la Recherche Scientifique, Paris)

Plate 53 (*above right*) Example of a Hanut Hajjam in Dar Bairam, Tunis. Note the tile work on the walls and the elaborate design of the built-in bed alcove. Photo: Revault, J. (1971) *Palais et Demeures de Tunis* (XVII et XIX siècles), Centre National de la Recherche Scientifique, Paris

Plate 54 (*left*) A typical jeweller's shop in the Suq el-Berka, Tunis.

house a bakery, grocery, possibly a nearby Mesjed and occasionally a Hammam. The shops are created from the surrounding housing fabric.

Types (a) and (b) occur within the core of the Medina, and a careful analysis of the morphological formations of the Suq there indicates that complex variations are achieved by using basic elements of the shop, its various grouping possibilities, and the system for covering, which in Tunis is brick vaulting. The resulting physical arrangements are functional and create visual varieties within a simple unified design and organizational framework. Figure 12 and Figures 41, 42 and 43 highlight the varieties of physical relationships and organization that have occurred.

One of the most important features of the Arabic–Islamic Suq system is the division of trades and products sold in group entities and distributed according to a symbolic framework of location in relation to the city's major mosque. It is based on the interpretation of the trade or product in terms of its perceived or symbolic standing, creating at least a three-level hierarchy in terms of acceptable proximity to the Jami.

At the first level of the hierarchy are trades or products encouraged to locate close by the Jami, such as bookshops and perfume products. In contrast the second category should be placed farthest away owing to potentially offensive noise (e.g., copper making) or smells or to their symbolic content (e.g., footwear products). The third category is that of products that do not generate any physical offence and are symbolically neutral. They can be located with relative freedom within the hierarchy, and examples would be clothes, jewellery, and headdress products, see Figure 19.

Another important feature of the Arabic–Islamic Suq is the method of advertising. During business hours each shop advertises its products at the vendor's discretion, sometimes by lavishly displaying them on the front of the shop and occasionally across the width of the Suq street if it is narrow enough. The shopkeeper's courteous manners and his extended invitation to a potential customer is the other method. However, the advertising and invitation are counteracted by the fact that a typical shop is surrounded by many others selling and specializing in the same product since all similar trades and businesses are usually grouped together. The system works however, because of an underlying moral and ethical code, highlighted by the positive human relationships that develop between a vendor and customer which benefits both. It allows the customer to build up a continuing business relationship, and creates more business for the vendor. It also explains the vendor's satisfaction, even in the absence of adequate profit — the result of the Islamic value of dependency on God for one's destiny and fortunes after and above trying one's best.

Because individual shops in the Suq rarely use written placards for advertising, the Suq during business hours is visually very different from when it is closed (see Plate 29). It is sometimes difficult to find one's way in the Suq after business hours even though one is familiar with a particular location owing to the radical change in the visual environment when the Suq is closed. All shop fronts are of similar size with similar wooden gates and uniform colours. Yet this fact reinforces the importance of the products, their display, and the individual vendor's manners — visual and personal bits of information which collectively act as the advertising medium.

Economic activities in the Arabic–Islamic city utilize the above Suq system in addition to other supporting facilities such as the Wekala and Funduk.

Figure 18 Location of Suq types, Funduk and Wekala in Tunis Medina Central and its two Rabad: [location of Funduk(s) and Wekala(s) after Callens (1955)]

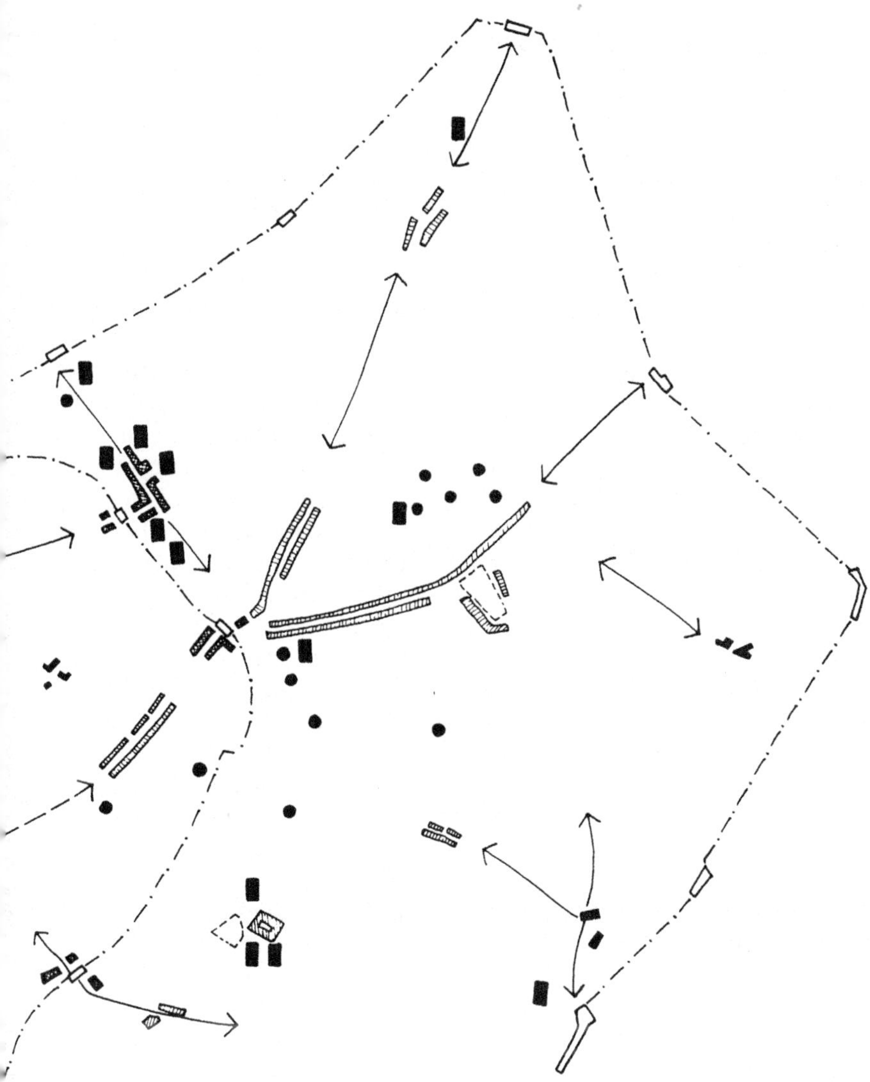

Major Suq around Zaytuna Mosque, which used to be locked up as a total area

Linear Suq (continuous or semi continuous)

Suq adjacent to 'Bab' or city gates

'Bat'ha'-location of weekly or seasonal open markets

'Suwaiqas' or neighbourhood shops

Wekala

Funduk

Location of city walls and gates

10 *Wekala.* The term is a relatively recent version of the much older *Kaysariyya*. It was originally the name of a large system of public buildings laid out in the form of cloisters with shops, workshops, warehouses and frequently rooms for accommodation. According to some historians the Kaysariyya was originally distinguished from the Suq by having covered galleries around an open courtyard, while the Suq consists only of a single gallery. In recent times the term *Kaysariyya* has an identical meaning to the Persian *Karwansaray* or *Caravanserai*, which first came into use in the eastern region of the Islamic world in the tenth century AH/sixteenth century AD.[71]

Of interest is the usage of the word *Kaysariyya* in Egypt, where some historians believe that the concept of this facility originated in Alexandria which was especially rich in covered market places and halls. In Cairo al-Makrizi, in his description of the city, indicates a large number of Kaysariyyas. The term *Wekala*[72] gradually replaced Kaysariyya.

In Tunis Callens identifies two types of Wekalas: the merchant's Wekala and the worker's Wekala:[73]

(a) *The merchant's Wekala* which is usually a two-storey structure planned around a courtyard (see Plate 30). It is designed to accommodate travelling businessmen or merchants, particularly from other Muslim regions, for the export–import business. The ground floor is designed for storerooms for the various products traded. The upper level is planned as a number of spacious and comfortable rooms for the merchants, and often finished with decorative tiles. These buildings are an integral part of the Suq or market system. The main door is left open during business hours for merchants and dealers to walk in freely. These Wekalas are located within the 'Medina Central' and some in the Rabad (suburbs). However, most Wekalas, particularly those in the core area, are physically integrated with the Suq system.

(b) *The worker's Wekala* which is designed to accommodate male immigrant workers from distant towns or villages within the region of Tunisia. They come to the city to seek work or to market a skill they possess. People from the same region and/or of the same trade tend to group together. The buildings are also two-storey structures, but with both floors allocated for rooms. The gate of the building is left shut and unlike the merchant's Wekala, its privacy is valued. Often one finds on top of the main door the sign: 'Nontenants may not enter'. These facilities are not part of the Suq system and are therefore located with no specific relation to the Suq.

Within the core area, I have indicated one Wekala and one Funduk, (see Figure 12), to illustrate their locational relationship to the Suq system and their efficient relationship and proximity owing to the organizational advantages of the courtyard which provides direct and immediate access from the Suq. The examples are Wekala al-Attarine built in 1171/1757, and the Funduk al-Attarine (Example 5 in Figures 40 and 42) specializing in perfumes such as amber, hanna, geranium, jasmine and rose.[74]

11 *Funduk.* This term is particularly used in North Africa to denote a hostelry where foreign — non-Muslim — merchants, would lodge to display and sell their products. The equivalent term of Persian origin, in the eastern regions of the Islamic world, is *Khan*. These hostelries are planned around a courtyard, where the ground floor is generally used to house the animals (camels

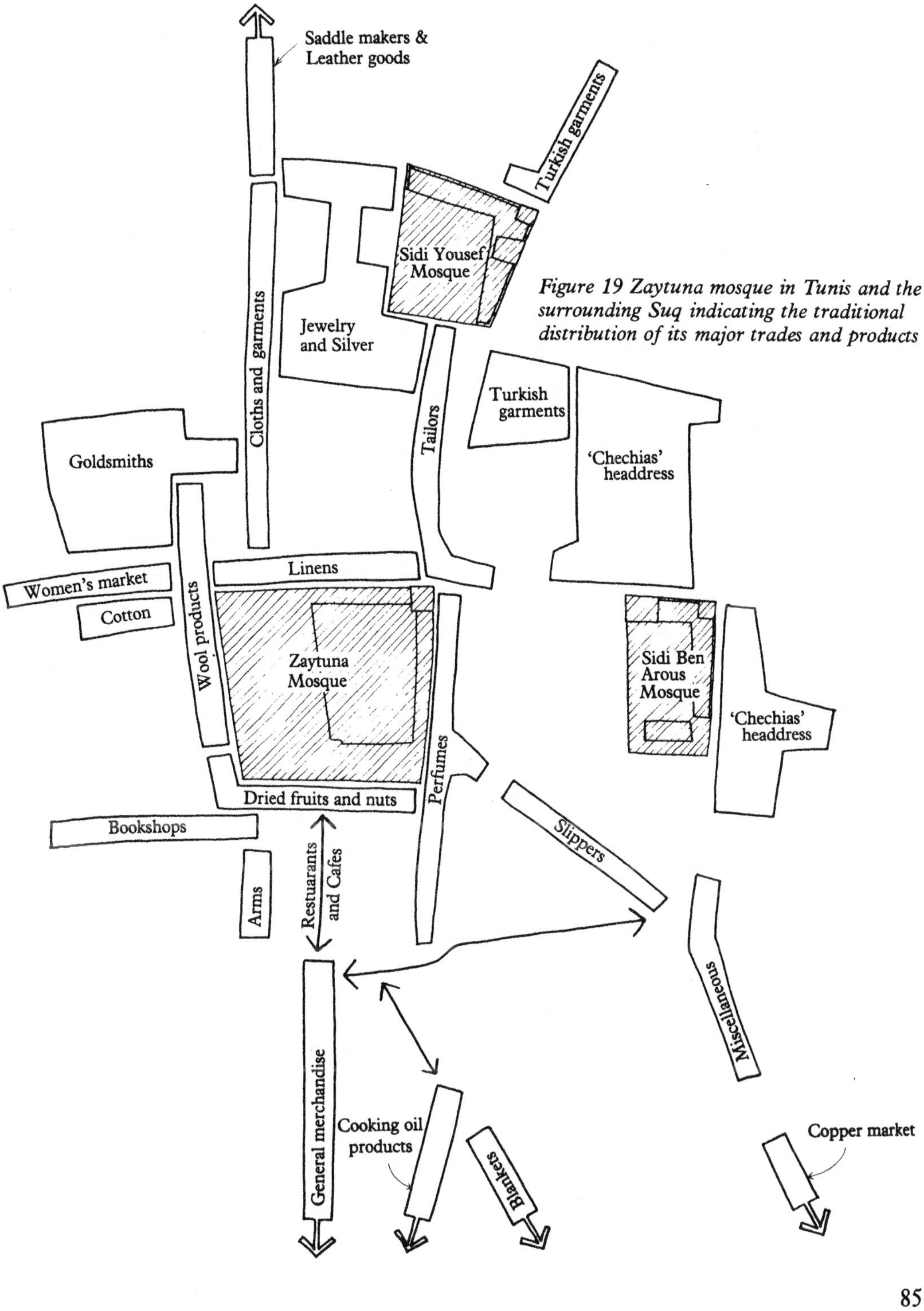

Figure 19 Zaytuna mosque in Tunis and the surrounding Suq indicating the traditional distribution of its major trades and products

and/or horses from the caravan) and when necessary, for storage of merchandise until the consignee takes delivery of it.[75] On the upper floor (usually there is only one), small rooms face a surrounding gallery for access where the merchants are accommodated. The main gate to the building is large enough to allow fully loaded animals to pass through. This, in fact, is a distinguishing exterior feature of the Funduk as compared to the Wekala.

In the middle ages it often occurred that in cities open to international trade, Funduks were placed at the disposal of European merchants on a 'national' basis. For example, in Tunis there was one for the French, in Cairo one for the Venetians, and so on. In general the Funduk belonged to the administration of religious estates (*Hubus* or *Awkaf*) which rented them to various merchants or artisans, or to a concessionaire in the case of a hostelry. Funduks for storage or workshops are found in the industrial or trading quarters, while Funduks functioning as hostelries are usually located near the main gates of the city.[76]

In Tunis Callens identifies two types of Funduks: those for foreign non-Muslim merchants allocated along national lines; and those for rural merchants (see Figure 18):[77]

(a) *The National Funduk* was located near the Frankish (Christian) quarter within or outside of the city wall near Bab Bahr. They were for merchants of French, Italian, or other nationalities, and were usually grouped in separate buildings for each nationality.

(b) *The Rural Funduk* was allocated to rural agricultural merchants who brought their products to the city. It was usually located near the gate that was the terminus of the road from their own region, or alongside the extension of these major thoroughfares within the boundaries of the northern and southern Rabads (suburbs). Others were located near the major open market areas or Bat'has. Most of these Funduks were identified by the products sold there — straw, wheat, coal, spun wool and so on.

Both types of Funduks were designed around a relatively large courtyard with a large gate to allow the entry of loaded animals or wagons. They were also provided with stables on the ground floor. On the upper floor(s) rooms were grouped around a covered access gallery and were small and modest compared to those found in the merchant's Wekala.

12 *Sur and Bab*. These two terms are for wall and gate/door. As urban elements at the scale of the Medina they apply to the city wall or ramparts and city gate(s). Both these terms were discussed earlier in this chapter. On the western edge of the core of the Medina Central, I have indicated a portion of the Sur and Bab al-Manara as examples in this context (see Figure 12).

13 *Qishla*. The term refers to army barracks. It might have been taken from the Turkish term *Qishlaq* which means the place to use in winter.[78] Within the Medina Central I have located six Qishlas, all within the core area. One of those is south of and adjacent to Dar al-Bey, obviously providing immediate protection to it. The other five are all within 100 m of each other, located east of Jami al-Zaytuna and providing ample security for the whole core area. Their location also provides potential control of the major north–south and east–west thoroughfares crossing the Medina Central area. It should be noted that the other major thoroughfares on the western side of Jami al-Zaytuna can be blocked by locking the Suq gates (see Figure 20).

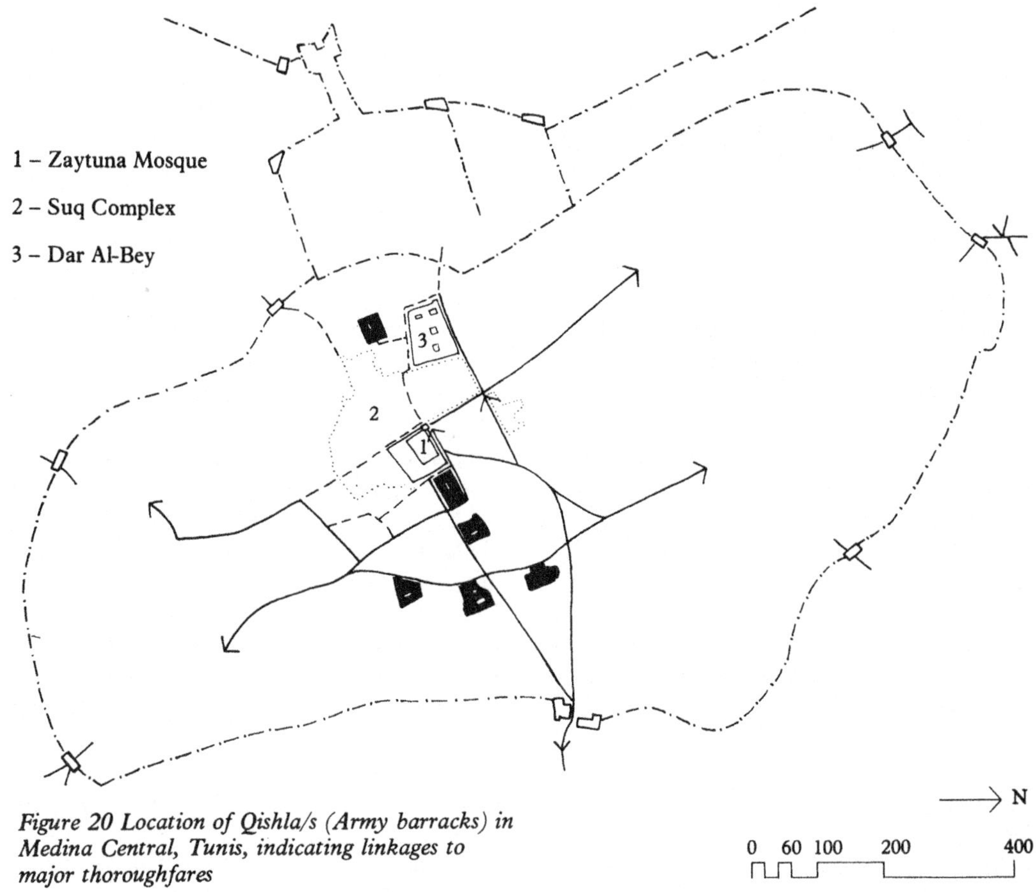

Figure 20 Location of Qishla/s (Army barracks) in Medina Central, Tunis, indicating linkages to major thoroughfares

The selected example, which is extracted from the core, is Qishla Sidi Morjani, built by Hammoud Pasha at the beginning of the nineteenth century for his troops. Later it was used as the centre for the administration of the Habous (Awkaf), and then became the famed Sadikiya College. In 1977 it was being renovated for the extensions of the National Library (see plates 31 and 59).

The building is a two-storey structure planned around an oblong courtyard which is surrounded by arcades at each floor and supported by columns. The building takes up the whole width of the block on which it is situated, and its primary access from rue Jami al-Zaytuna is on the longtitude axis of the courtyard.

14 *Hammam*. The term means a location or place for cleansing oneself. However, in popular use, it denoted a public or private bath with emphasis on the former, because in traditional Arabic–Islamic cities only an extreme minority had Hammams within their houses. In Europe the term denotes a steam bath, still referred to as 'Turkish bath' (and in French as *bain maure*).

Archeological remains reveal its existence as early as the Ummayad period (661–750 AD), and references in texts date their construction to the early years of the first century of Islam, in the towns of Basra in southern Iraq and Fustat in Egypt founded in 14 and 21 AH respectively.[79] Hammams continued at least until the 1950s as one of the important urban institutions in the Arabic–Islamic city.

Some Arab writers have mentioned that the presence of one Hammam or more is an essential component of a complete urban settlement[80] because of its ritual use in the performance of the major ablution. It also became one of the social centres of the Mahalla or quarter: people went to it for relaxation as well as for hygiene. They were numerous in every city (reserved on certain days or at certain hours for men and at others for women), and generated considerable revenue for the private individuals or the authorities who established them. Their popularity led to the installation of private baths in the precincts of palaces, or within larger residences.

There are some reliable early sources of inventories of monuments, such as Ibn Shaddad's on Damascus, citing eighty-five Hammams within the walls and thirty-one in the Rabads for a total of 116. These data seem reasonable when we consider that within the first quarter of this century Damascus had sixty Hammams of various dates, forty-one of which were still in use.[81] Hammams operated within guidelines and moral codes set out and administered by the Muhtasib. The study of a number of *Hisba* manuals will provide detailed examples about the cleanliness of the building as well as the accepted behaviour of the users and attendants.

A great deal of information is available on Umayyad Hammams, successors to the *thermae* of antiquity from which they presumably derived. However, they underwent profound transformations in their layout. Comparing the most important remains of Hammams from this period with earlier buildings indicates that in spite of the striking similarities in the method of construction (e.g., the use of hypocausts and heating pipes in the walls), the layout reveals a new approach. We find, for example, neither the traditional succession of the *apodyterium*, the *frigidarium*, the *tepidarium*, and the *calidarium* nor their relative proportions.[82] The evolution and spread of this new layout — for which there is insufficient data — was in fact dominated by a set procedure for the use of the building, which is apparent in most of the varied interpretations and which reflects an Islamic approach (see Figure 21).

The forty or so Hammams in Tunis Medina and its Rabads differ in the size and comforts they offer to their patrons, yet there are scarcely any variations in the general layout of the buildings and the way in which they work. The area reserved for the users consists of two quite distinct parts: the section for dressing and resting and the bath proper, which includes warm and hot rooms, usually three in all, one leading into the next (see Figure 21).[83]

I have located sixteen Hammams in the Medina Central area which seem to be distributed according to the divisions of Mahallas or quarters. This conclusion depends upon the verification of the exact boundaries of these Mahallas for which there is no available information. Useful statistical figures are the ratio of Hammams to mosques; in Tunis Medina Central the ratio of Hammams to all Jami and Mesjeds is 1:4.75, yet the ratio to Jami only (i.e., Khutba mosques) is 1:0.70. A comparison with other Arabic–Islamic cities should indicate whether the ratio in Tunis is high or low. Hammam al-Qachachine (from the core area) is illustrated in Figure 12. It extends over a narrow block and its entrance is from Rue Des Libraires located under a

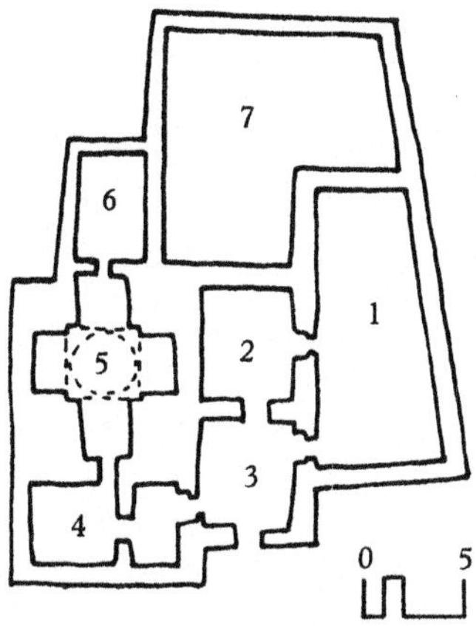

1 & 2 Undressing Rooms
3. Unheated room
4. Hot room
5. Steam room
6. Boiler
7. Service court

(a) Plan of a typical Umayyad Hammam: The Hammam of 'Abda (after J. Sauvaget 'Remarques....' 1939)

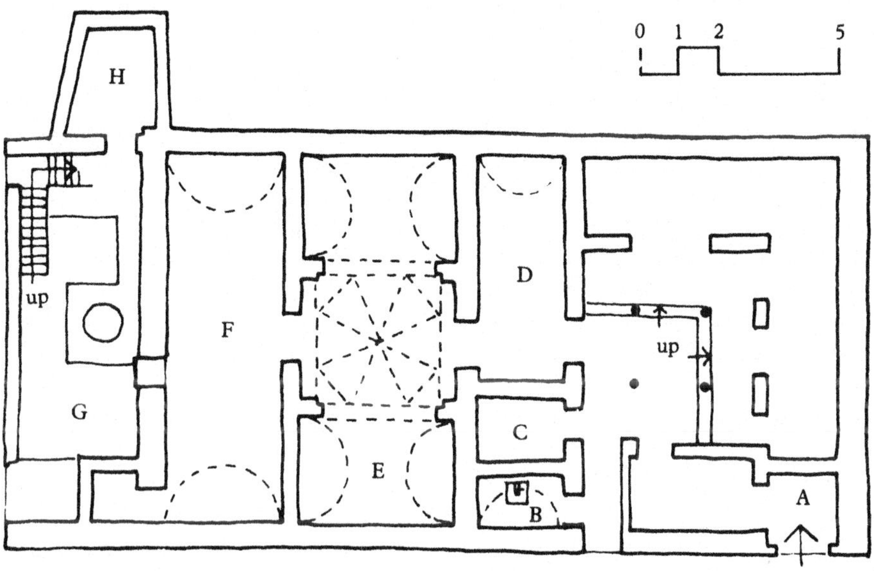

(b) Plan of a typical Maghribi Hammam: The Hammam El-Alou in Rabat, Morocco (after H. Terrasse 'Trois Bains....' 1950)

A. Entrance
B. Latrine
C. Store room
D. Frigidarium
E. Tepidarium
F. Calidarium
G. Furnace
H. Pool

Figure 21 Plans of typical early Islamic and Maghribi Hammams

Sabat. It is the only element of the building visually tangible to the pedestrian and which is appropriately identified and decorated (see Plate 32).

15 *Mida'at.* The term refers to a facility which is used for *Wudu* or ablution as prescribed for Muslims before prayer. One of the Prophet's sayings: 'Idjalu matahirakum ala abwabi masadjidikum' ('Locate your ablution facilities at the door of your mosques') was the general principle in the development and location of the Mida'at.[84] However, it should be noted that drinking water was allowed in the mosques and was usually treated as a separate element.

Following are brief historical notes about the usage of the Mida'at.[85] In Medina, Ibn Djubair mentions rooms for Wudu at the western entrance to the mosque, whereas Ibn Zabala mentions seventeen receptacles for drinking water in the Sahn in the year 199 AH. In Damascus, within the Sahn of the mosque there were facilities for drinking water, and at each entrance to the mosque there was a Mida'at. In Iraq the major mosques always had Mida'at at the entrances. In Palestine during al-Makdisi's time, this was also the case. In San'a, Yemen during the fourth century AH there was water for drinking and for Wudu beside each mosque. In Iran it was the custom to have a *Hawd* (pool) in front of the mosque, and drinking water was provided inside the mosque in jars on a bench. The mosque of Ibn Tulun in Cairo, Egypt had a Mida'at and an apothecary located behind it. Mida'ats were also located in other buildings, such as Madrasas and Maristans.

Within Tunis Medina Central I have located four mida'at facilities, two of which are located adjacent to Jami al-Zaytuna; the older and nearer one to the Jami is Mida'at es-Soltane (indicated in Figures 12, 15 and 22). This was built in the mid-fifteenth century AD and is considered to be a Maliki Mida'at. The other is Mida'at Suq et-Trouk built in the seventeenth century AD for the Hanafis.[86]

The Mida'at es-Soltane is tucked in behind the Wekala al-Attarine and is accessible from the cul-de-sac. The facility is composed of two parts, the ablution area and the lavatories. The former portion is the courtyard of the facility, which is opened for access from one side and provided with a continuous and covered U-shaped ablution trough on the other three sides, and has a fountain in the middle. The lavatories are grouped together and are accessible from the corridor which links the two parts together with the entrance lobby Skifa (see Figure 22).[87]

16 *Maristan.* The term is originally Persian and denotes a house for the sick, or hospital, which was also called *Bimaristan* or *Muristan.* The Arab historians Ibn Djubair and al-Makrizi mention it in relation with the Madrasa, possibly because it usually contained a medical school.[88]

According to al-Makrizi the Umayyad Walid b. Abdul Malik was the first in Islamic history to establish a Maristan in 88/707 in Syria. Ibn Djubair the Andalusian traveller visited Syria in 580/1184 and reported two hospitals in Damascus, one in Nasibin, two in Harran, one in Halab, one in Hama. He refers to a number in Baghdad without particular details, but we know of hospitals there from the third century. In 304 AH Sinan b. Thabit was director of the hospitals in Baghdad, and was also responsible for the foundation of three more. There was also a hospital attached to the great Mustansiriya Madrasa. In Cairo Ibn Tulun built the first Maristan in 259/873.[89]

According to Ibn Abi Usaibi'a the teaching of medicine continued without

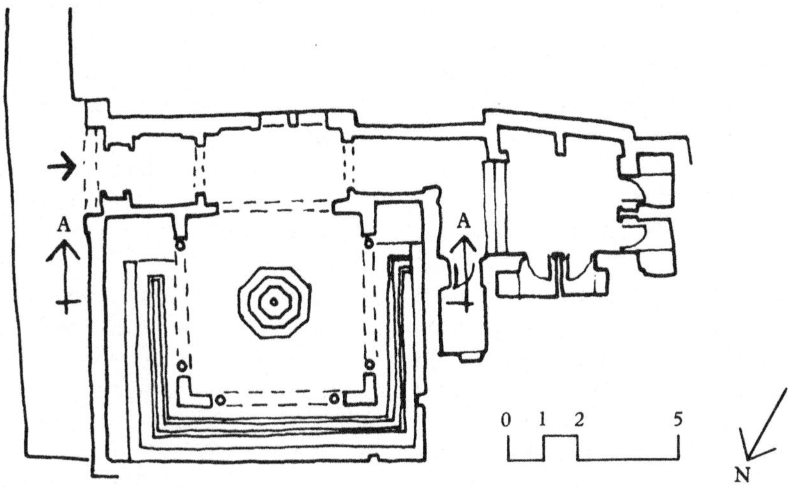

Section A-A

Figure 22 Plan and section/elevation of Mida'at es-Soltane (el-Attarine) in Tunis (after Revault) interruption in the Islamic world; for example he mentions Abd al-Malik b. Abdjar who was in charge of the medical school in Alexandria and who embraced Islam after the conquest. Later the major medical schools were in Antakiya and Harran in Syria, and for a long period most of the physicians were Christians. Teaching was usually done in connection with the hospitals; the head physician had students whom he trained and who assisted him. Lectures on medicine (*Tibb*) were sometimes given in the mosque, but it was for the most part a theoretical science closely connected with philosophy. Tibb was also studied in a Madrasa, and there were special Madaris al-Tibb; thus in the seventh century AH three were built in Damascus. The teachers in them could also be physicians at the hospitals.[90]

According to H.H. Abdul-wahab, the first professional doctor in Tunisia was the Syriac Abu Yohanna Masuwy, who accompanied Amin Yazid b. Hatem Mahlabi from the east to Kairouan in 155/772, and was his personal doctor, although he also served other important persons. He had studied medicine in the famous Bimaristan of Gundeshapur in Iraq.[91]

The first Maristan constructed in Tunisia was in Kairouan by Ziyadat Allah I, between 210/825 and 220/835 in a part of the city called Dimna; it was thereafter called the Dimna. In time this name replaced the term *Maristan* to denote a hospital, in the region then known as Ifriqiya. All later Maristans such as those in Tunis, Sousse, and Sfax[92] followed the model of the Kairouan hospital in layout and organization.

The layout of the typical building was square or rectangular in shape; the patients' rooms around a central courtyard with a surrounding arcade (*Riwak*) which provided covered access to all the rooms. The entrance was approximately on the axis of the courtyard and was through a covered '*Skifa*' flanked by built-in seats for the patient's visitors and by room(s) for the guard(s). Another door from the Skifa led directly to the courtyard. A small prayer room was usually located opposite the entrance on the other side of the court. A link was provided from one of the arcades to an isolated unit with rooms for those who had leprosy.[93]

These hospitals tended to be self-sufficient, and had their own water well and cistern to collect rainwater. The maximum number of rooms in those Maristans were about thirty used by one or two patients, and were approx. 2 by 3 m each. They had full-time nurses and staff. Unfortunately there is no information regarding their budget and income, but we know that they were generously endowed with money and food from private sources and the authorities, particularly during religious festivals.[94] The first Maristan in the city of Tunis was built during the reign of the sixth Aghlabid governor, approximately in 290/903 and was located outside the city walls in the west near the Jewish quarter, which then was outside the walls.

In Tunis Medina Central I have located two such facilities, one is called 'Tekia', built in 1188/1774 as a home for the aged and then was connected to a mental hospital. The other is Maristan Aziza Othmana built by Ali Bey who ruled between 1172/1758 and 1197/1782; today it is referred to as Maristan al-Qdim, or the old Maristan. It is a two-storey structure with its rooms grouped around the central courtyard and its entrance from the major street located on the axis of the court. The ground floor has shops facing the Rue de la Kasba, one of the major Suq streets (see Figure 23 and Plate 33).

17 *Ksar or Palace*. This term applied to very large houses, and until at least the end of the

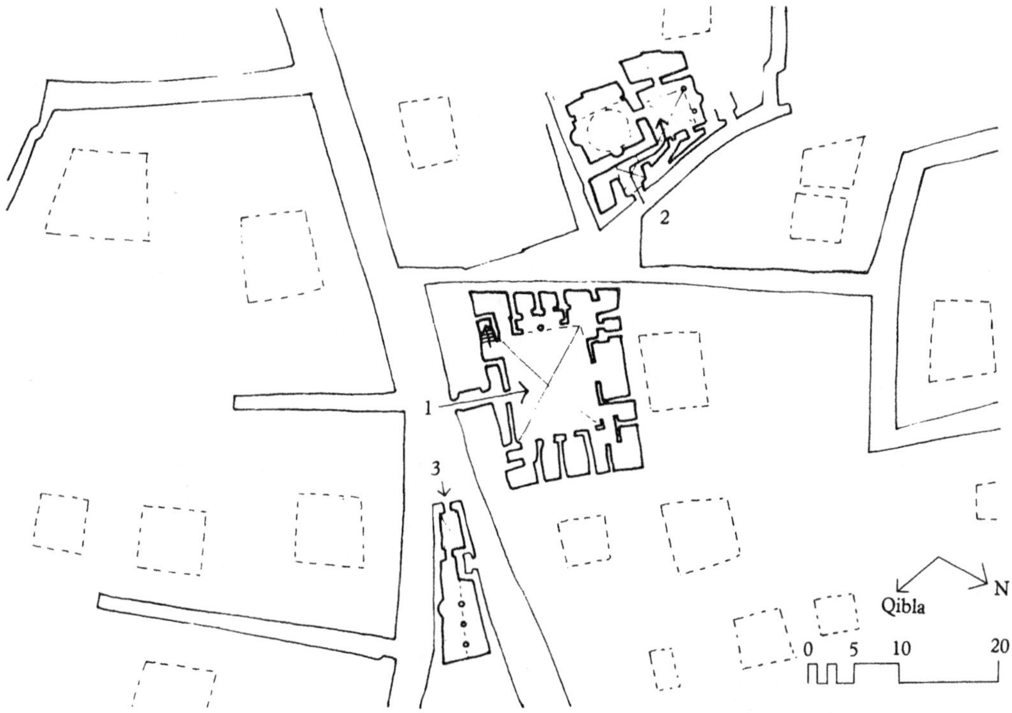

Figure 23 Maristan Aziza Othmana (1), Marabout Sidi Braham (2), Mesjid Al-Fal (3), Tunis

nineteenth century, it also referred to palace, castle or citadel. Earlier on, the term was applied only to the palaces of princes in Ifrikiya. During the Turkish period in Tunisia, these palaces belonged to the ruler — Pasha, Dey or Bey — or else to members of his family, high court officials, and army chiefs — Wazir, Agha, Kahia, Daouletli. They were named by adding the prefix Dar, to the official's name — Dar al-Pasha, Dar al-Bey, and so on. The influence of these palaces can also be seen in the naming of some adjacent streets after them.[95]

Palaces tended to occupy a large area and usually had more than one courtyard; at least one was allocated for service quarters. Occasionally these palaces might also have a walled garden; in addition they are usually richly decorated on the inside, especially the primary courtyard and the major rooms flanking it (see Figure 24).

Because of the resources available to their owners and the generally affluent taste exhibited in the style and decorations, the palaces tended to set trends in architectural design and decoration. This was true even though they were appreciably larger than the average Dar or house which emulated them (see Plate 34).

Within the Medina Central area I have located fourteen palaces with an average area of 2,600 m^2, the largest being 5,300 m^2. The example, extracted from within the core area, is Dar Hussein which has a long history. Yousef Saheb et-Tabaa, favourite minister of Hamouda Pasha, bought it from the Kahia family in 1801. From 1882 it was the headquarters of the French authorities while Tunisia was a protectorate. In May 1957, the newly independent Tunisian government made it the home of the Institut National d'Archeologie et d'Arts, and set aside part of the building as a museum of Islamic art.[96]

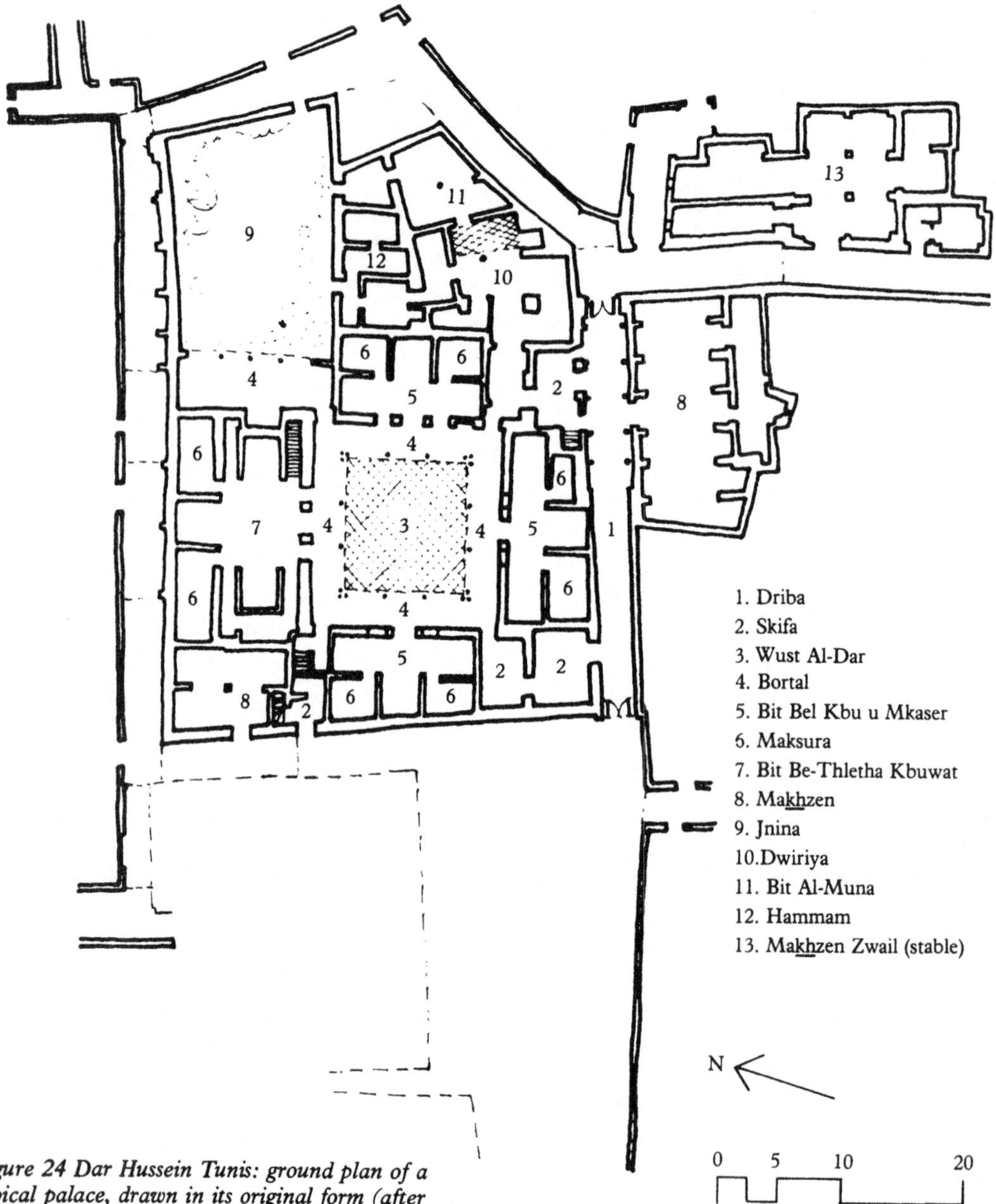

Figure 24 Dar Hussein Tunis: ground plan of a typical palace, drawn in its original form (after Revault)

18 *Dar*. The term denotes a dwelling place or a house. The two most commonly used terms for a dwelling are *Bayt* and *Dar*, which have different roots and meanings. The proper meaning of the term *Bayt* is the covered shelter where one may spend the night. In Tunis, for example, the term commonly means a room. Dar, from *Dara* (to surround) is a space surrounded by walls, buildings, or nomadic tents placed approximately in a circle. In the Maghrib the bedouin encampment is called *Duwwar*.[97]

The concept of a house planned around an open space or courtyard appeared in the Middle East with the earliest cities there; a prime example is the city of Ur in southern Iraq (see Figure 25). Symbolically, however, the first Islamic house is that built by the Prophet Mohammad on his arrival in Medina, as a dwelling place for himself and his family, and as a meeting place for the believers. The courtyard surrounded by walls is its essential feature. A shelter from the sun, to protect the faithful at prayer, runs along the wall facing the Qibla or Mecca. Rooms built along another side were occupied by the Prophet's wives, and their entrances facing the courtyard were fronted by a porch of palm branches which could be screened, if required, by curtains of camel hair. This front annex of rooms, which recalls the Riwak, and the movable screen of the nomadic tent kept the dwelling in touch with the outside world, and served as a vestibule. They soon became essential features of the Arabic–Islamic house (see Figure 13).[98]

In essence the courtyard house and its clustering creates the physical setting that allows the following Islamic social and ethical requirements to be achieved:

(a) *Privacy*. The layout ensures visual privacy from outside or adjacent areas, yet allows members of the household to be in contact with nature via the court; the plan also ensures a high standard of acoustical protection.

(b) *Interdependence*. The organizational consequences of the grouping of courtyard houses necessitates a level of interdependence between neighbours with regard to the use and rights of party walls, maintenance of cul-de-sacs, problems related to rain and waste water (see Chapter 1). This interdependence is compatible with Islamic values as they relate to neighbourly relations.

(c) *Batin vs. Zahir*. One of the essential values in Islam is emphasis on the *Batin* (the inner aspect of self or a thing), and

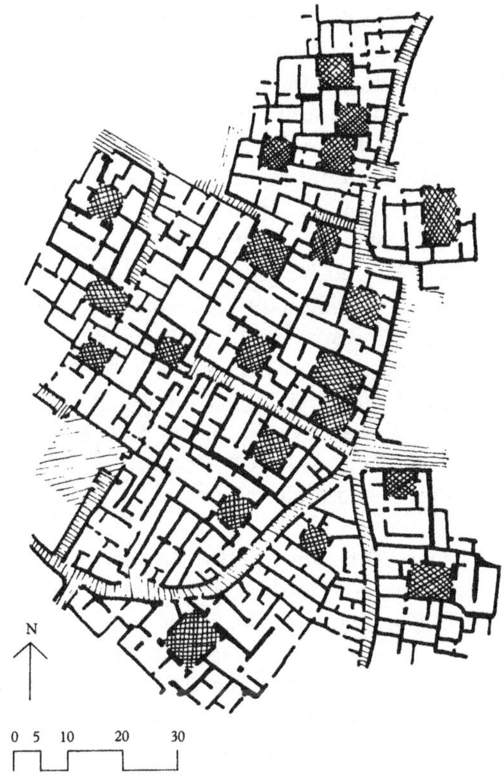

Figure 25 Cluster of courtyard houses, Ur, 2000 BC (after Woolley, 1931)

> subordination of the *Zahir* (the external aspect of self or a thing). For example, internal goodness and well-being are emphasized and arrogance discouraged. The courtyard house and its aggregate organizational pattern is suitable for the application of this principle. Hence we find that the external walls are kept simple and relatively bare with few openings. The courtyard as the central important space is decorated — when the owner can afford it — to a high level of artistic sophistication, despite the fact that it is accessible to and enjoyed only by the occupants, and occasionally their relatives and close friends.

As we have seen in Chapter 1 Islamic law addressed itself to the nature and peculiarities of this form of housing and established a unity within a vast geographic area. This phenomenon was enhanced and underlined by the similarity of climatic conditions within the Islamic provinces (recently countries).

Climatic similarity resulted in the utilization of common design elements, such as the use of waterpools for psychological and functional reasons, the invention and development of the Iwan to provide ventilation and subdued light in major rooms, and so on. We also find regional elements such as the *Serdab* or living room basement for summer use in Iraq and Iran, or the use of large underground water cisterns for rainwater collection in the Maghrib.

Revault, in his excellent study of houses and palaces in Tunis, emphasizes the unity and simple origin of the basic house model — a single-storey structure of rooms surrounding a courtyard with an entrance designed to prevent direct visual access to the courtyard from the exterior. In addition to this type of modest house, Revault classifies the bourgeois type (or middle-class house), the large residence, and the palace.[99] In addition to sharing a common model, all types had to satisfy specific site constraints and were shaped by the use of the same local building materials and methods of construction (see Figure 26).[100]

Revault classifies the user types of these houses as follows: the middle-class house belonged to a master craftsman, a merchant who sells in the Suq, or a teacher in a Madrasa or a Jami. The large residence belonged to a high religious official — Maliki or Hanafi — or to a high official, superior officer, or army captain, or else to a rich craftsman-merchant or to a person from an established Tunisian or Andalusian family.[101] The palace differs from the large residence in its greater size, and in certain parts of the building which are peculiar to its type.

Within the core of the Medina Central, and primarily with the aid of Revault's work, I have indicated the large residences and middle-class houses; the balance of the housing (due to the lack of other sources of information) is assumed to belong to the modest category.[102] In addition to the palace example, I have illustrated five houses from the core area, covering the three categories mentioned above and have indicated graphically their diverse locational and bulk characteristics (see Figure 12).

There are other buildings in the Arabic–Islamic city which were used for specific functions, such as the Diwan (or courthouse), but they were so few in number within the city that their location and specific peculiarities had no appreciable impact on the city plan; there would therefore be no

Figure 26 Four types of houses from Tunis Medina, as classified by Revault (after Revault)

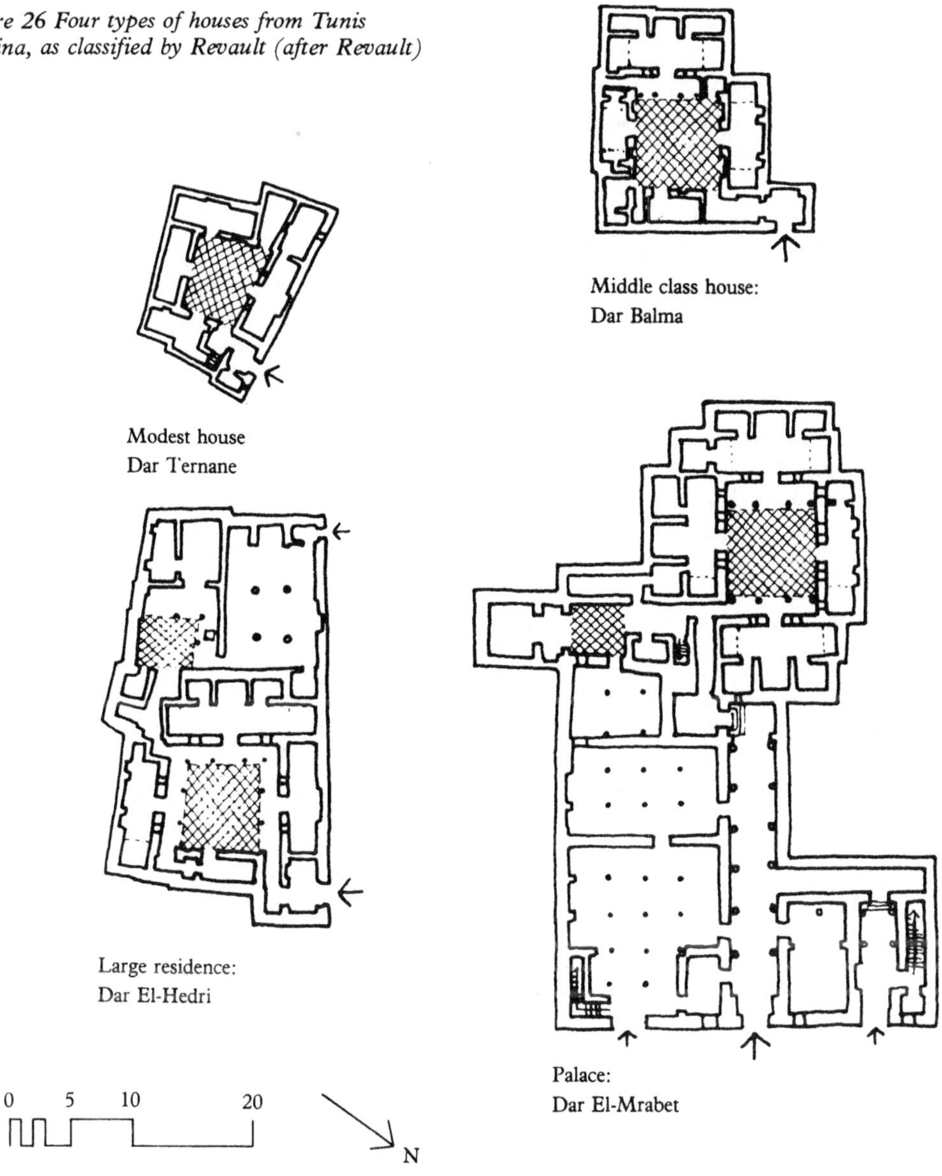

merit in discussing them. However, we should comment briefly on public water fountains and private gardens, termed as *Massassa* and *Jenina* respectively in Tunis.

The Massassa is a water outlet located on the exterior wall of a building on an active street, and is provided with a copper mouthpiece protruding from the decorative tilework on the wall to allow a passer-by to drink water by suction. In other Arabic–Islamic cities and according to the availability and source of water, the accessibility to the pedestrian might differ. The concept is based on charity and is derived from the

Prophet's teachings and directly related to his Sayings 12 and 14 (Appendix 1). These handsomely decorated water outlets are welcoming features along major thoroughfares or within the city's active areas (see Plate 35).

The Jenina or garden is the Tunisian term of the more popular *Rawda* (plural, *Riyad*) and is usually part of large residences or palaces. The style and layout of these gardens originated in Iran and is preserved in some of the designs of Persian carpets — straight pathways, intersecting at right angles and separating square patches of green on which fruit trees and decorative plants abound (see Plate 36). Sometimes canals with flowing water cross the pathways, sometimes their intersections are marked by ornamental fountains.[103]

Despite the high walls that usually surround these gardens, they do provide relief and variety to the pedestrian in the streets due to the visibility of tree tops, occasionally overflowing vegetation, and sometimes the aroma of Yasimin, all of which provide a distinct contrast to the high walls abutting the streets (see Plate 37).

To end this chapter, I have grouped all the elements and building types discussed or mentioned in tabular form indicating their transliterated name, its original Arabic, and the English meaning. These tables thus group together and highlight the components of this simple, yet versatile design language.

Table of urban elements within the overall Medina and its Rabads

	Element		*Brief Definition*
1	Medina	مدينة	Urban complex or city
2	Kasbah	قصبة	Fortified quarters (citadel) of rulers
3	Rabad	ربض	Suburb in immediate vicinity of the older central part of a medina
4	Sur	سور	City wall (ramparts)
5	Bab	باب	City gate
6	Burj	برج	Fortified tower
7	Shar' or	شارع	
	Tarik Nafid	طريق نافذ	Public through street
8	Bat'ha or		Public square or place. These are usually formed by the junction of three streets, called in Tunis M'qas (مقص)
	Saha or	ساحة	
	Rahba	رحبة	
9	Musalla	مصلى	Large open space for Eid prayers adjacent to medina

	Element		Brief Definition
10	Maqbara or	مقبرة	Public cemetery
	Jabbana	جبانة	
11	Khazzan	خزان	Large public water-storage facility
	Majel	ماجل	Private water cistern
12	Khandaq	خندق	Main sewer line or city moat
13	Mahalla or	محلة	City quarter
	Homa or	حومة	Term used in Tunisia
	Khitta	خطة	Term used in Egypt

Note. All Arabic terms are in the singular.

Morphological analysis of the Medina core

Relationship of streets to the land use pattern and related street coverage

	Element		Brief Definition
1	Tarik al-Muslimeen or	طريق المسلمين	Four terms for public through street
	Tarik Nafid or	طريق نافذ	
	Shari'or	شارع	
	Nahj	نهج	
2	Sikka ghair Nafida or	سكة غير نافذة	Five terms for a private cul-de-sac
	Sikka munsadat al-asfal or	سكة منسدة الاسفل	
	Derb ghair Nafid or	درب غير نافذ	
	Zuqaq ghair Nafid or	زقاق غير نافذ	
	Zanqa	زنقة	
3	Sabat	ساباط	Room(s) spanning street
4	Vault (Aqd)	عقد	Coverage for Suq streets

Location of urban elements/building types to street system

	Element		*Brief Definition*
1	Jami or	جامع	Various terms for a mosque which provides the Friday sermon
	Mesjid al-Azam or	المسجد الأعظم	
	Mesjid al-Akbar or	المسجد الاكبر	
	Mesjid al-Jama'a or	مسجد الجماعة	
	Mesjid al-Jami or	مسجد الجامع	
2	Mesjid al-Khutba or	مسجد الخطبة	
	Jami al-Khutba	جامع الخطبة	
3	Mesjid	مسجد	Facility for the daily prayers
4	Madrasa	مدرسة	School: institution of higher learning for Islamic sciences and law
5	Zawiya	زاوية	Term used in the Maghrib for religious facility; functions as a monastery and school
	Khanakah	خانقاه	Three terms used in the east (Mashreq) for monastery
	Tekke	تكية	
	Dair	دير	
	Ribat	رباط	A term which later was used to denote a monastery
6	Murabit (Marabout)	مرابط	
	Wali	ولي	Three terms for a 'saint'; refers to the burial place or tomb of such a person, usually enclosed by a dome (Kubba)
	Saiyid	سيد	
	Kubba	قبة	
7	Turba	تربة	Private cemetery, usually of the ruling class
8	Maqbara or	مقبرة	Public cemetery
	Jabbana	جبانة	
9	Suq	سوق	Market
	Bazaar	بزار	Iranian equivalent term
	Hanout	حانوت	Shop

	Element		Brief Definition
10	Wekala	وكالة	Two-storey structure with shops and stores on ground floor and rooms to accommodate traveling merchants on upper floor
	Caravanserai	كاروانسراي	Iranian equivalent term
11	Funduk	فندق	Hostel for foreign or countryside merchants
	Khan	خان	Iranian equivalent term
12	Sur	سور	City wall
	Bab	باب	City gate
13	Qishla	قشلة	Army barracks
14	Hammam	حمام	Public or private bath
15	Mida'at	ميضاة	Public ablution facility
16	Maristan	مارستان	Hospital
	Dimna	دمنة	Equivalent term popular in Ifrikiya
17	Ksar	قصر	Palace, castle, or citadel
18	Dar	دار	Dwelling place or house
19	Diwan	ديوان	Courthouse
20	Massassa	مصاصة	Public water fountain with copper mouth-piece; functions by suction
	Seqqaya	سقاية	Term used in Morocco The general term for any type of public water facility is Sabbala (سبّالة)
21	Jenina	جنينة	Private garden, term used in Tunisia
	Rawda	روضة	Equivalent term popular in Morocco

Chapter 3

An interpretation of the building process and urban form

This chapter attempts to illustrate and interpret the workings of the building process and its impacts at the city and neighbourhood scales. It also examines the resulting urban form quantitatively and qualitatively. The primary example used for reference is Tunis Medina whose history and urban development was researched for this purpose.[1]

The 'building process' is defined here as those actions, events and decisions which have direct influence on the nature of building activity and the resultant urban form. It includes the impact of decisions by the ruling authority (the public sector) and citizens (the private sector) on the development of the man-made physical environment. The 'urban form' is defined as the three-dimensional state of the city or any of its parts at any given time in history. Although it is dynamic and changing when viewed across a time frame of centuries, the urban form can also be viewed as relatively static within a short period. Reference to the scale of the environment is critical in this regard. I will also try to point out, with examples, the impact of societal values and related building guidelines (the subject of Chapter 1). I will also refer to the use of the design language (see Chapter 2) and its related urban and architectural prototypes. Hence the building process will be discussed with examples according to:

1 decisions and actions by the ruler or governing authority, primarily as affecting the macro environment; and
2 building decisions and activity by citizens, primarily as affecting the micro environment

In discussing these, the following variables will be utilized:

1 the impact of societal values and the controlling influence of related building guidelines; and
2 the use of the local design language and its related components, building types and system of arrangement.

Building process: examples of decisions and actions by the ruler or governing authority

The founding of Tunis, as is true of most other Islamic cities, was permanently affected by the nature and conditions of its site and the location/construction of the first Khutba mosque.[2] Accordingly, the first and most important act by Hassan b. al-Numan after conquering Carthage in 79/698 was the decision to locate his city on an inland location less vulnerable to maritime attack.

The second most important act was the design and construction of the Khutba mosque or Jami. The location of the structure within the site was influenced by the convenience of two existing intersecting roads. These are thought to be the Cardo and Decumanus of a pre-existing Roman network (see Figure 27).

The model and details of a mosque as a building type are discussed in Chapter 2. Here, however, we shall discuss the Qibla wall and its orientation which is a significant issue in the hierarchy of building decisions. Hence the orientation of the Zaytuna mosque Qibla wall influenced that of nearby mosques and other structures containing a prayer area. It should be noted, however, that the aggregate impact of orientation decisions, coupled with the street layout and configuration, created an on-going system of interdependence and influence between these two planning factors. The dominance of one over the other and the impact on the morphology of the city depended on which occurred first.

The Qibla wall direction of the Zaytuna mosque was built at 29° 23′ off the exact direction to the Qibla and was probably influenced by the intersection of the two existing roads on the site (see Figure 28)[3]. After analyzing the Qibla wall orientation of all mosques and Mesjids in the Medina Central area of Tunis (i.e., the older area within the inner walls), I have come to the conclusion that, regardless of when these structures were built, the impact of the Zaytuna mosque coupled with the layout of the major thoroughfares was predominant in influencing the Qibla direction of other religious structures in the vicinity. However, we find some exceptions in major structures built further away from the central core, such as the mosque of Sidi Mahrez and the mosque Bab el-Bahr which were oriented more accurately toward the Qibla.

In Isfahan, Iran, we find a classic example of the impact of the Qibla wall orientation on the urban plan and its form. One of the predominant mosques in that city, the Masjid-i-Shah, was turned away from the formal axis of the Maydan-i-Shah which is an elongated, rectangular open space, thus creating an architectural challenge which was superbly resolved, particularly in the design of the main entrance (see Figure 29).

It is of interest to note that even though the Qibla direction should be accurately implemented whenever possible, we find that once a direction has been established by a major religious structure, its influence far outweighs the realities of geometrical exactness. This, I believe, is due to the respect society accords its major religious facilities. Site and construction constraints are other deterrents discouraging deviation from an established precedent.

Decisions and actions related to the creation of major streets were important and their impact lasted for centuries. Initially when the city was founded, the main thoroughfares were established to emanate from the core and toward the major established destinations. These streets tended to be relatively wide and direct. In Tunis we find this to be true, particularly within the Medina Central area. The development of the suburbs at a later period produced a primary street network within those areas which were adequately integrated, with the main streets emanating from the older central area.

The configurations of the inner and outer city walls in Tunis were influenced by the location of the city gates (Bab) and defence towers (Burj). These were established on the alignments of the major streets. Even the naming of the gates was related to the various destinations of major streets. Figure 30 shows the primary street network of Tunis during the late nineteenth and early

Figure 27 Muslim foundation, 698–800 AD; Tunis in its regional setting

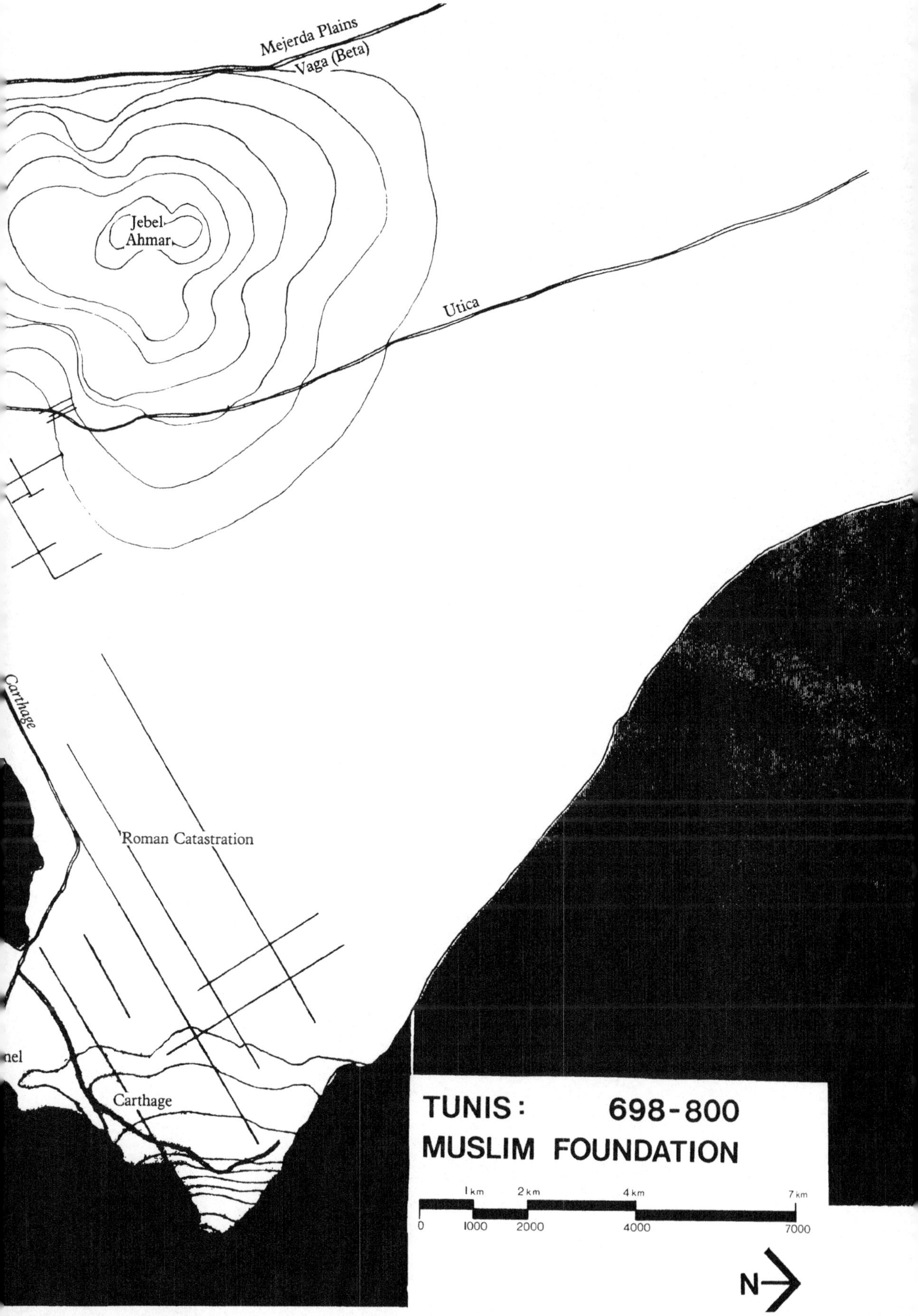

Mejerda Plains
Vaga (Beta)
Jebel Ahmar
Utica
Carthage
Roman Catastration
nel
Carthage
TUNIS: 698-800
MUSLIM FOUNDATION
1 km
2 km
4 km
7 km
0
1000
2000
4000
7000
N

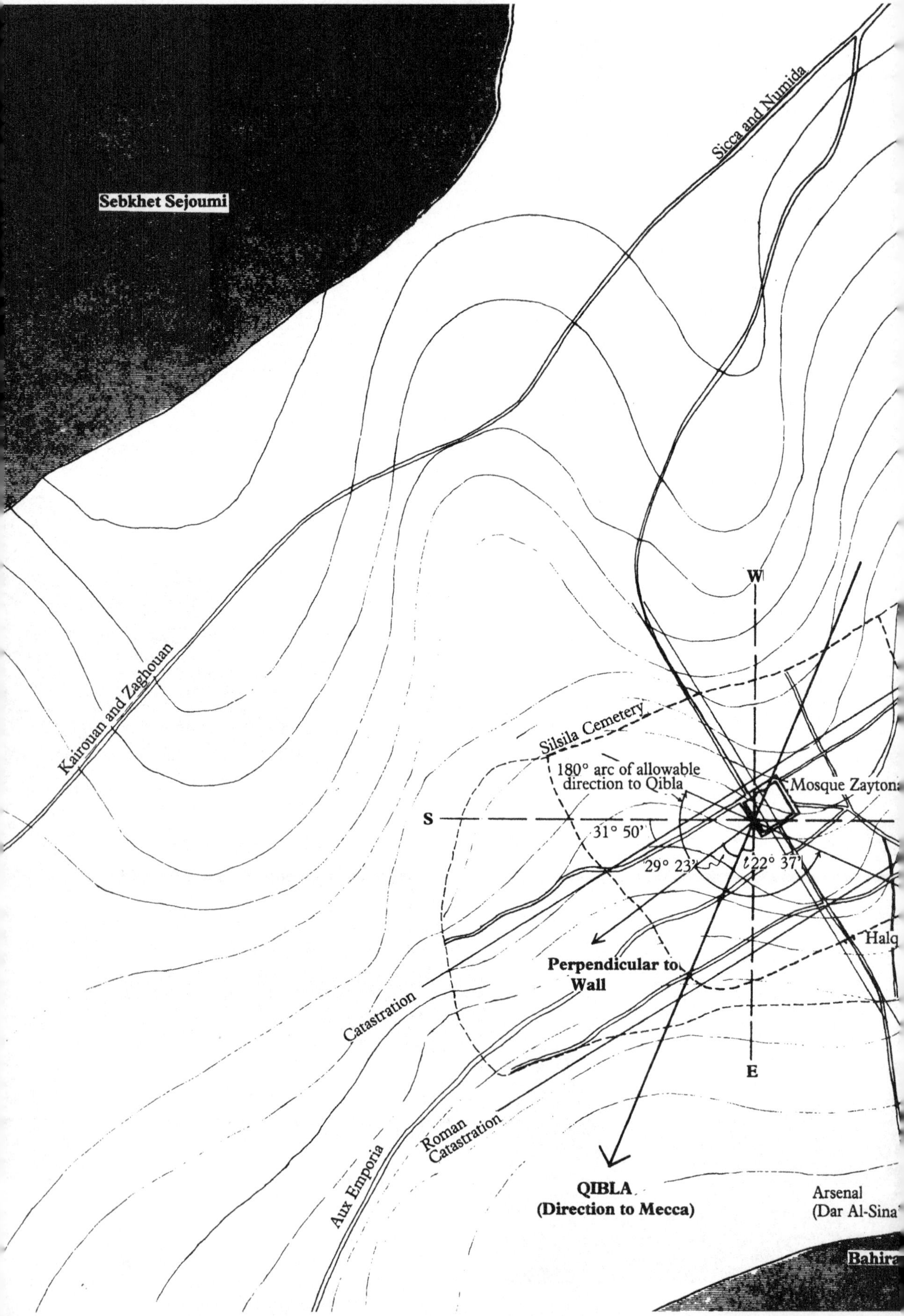
Sebkhet Sejoumi
Sicca and Numida
Kairouan and Zaghouan
Silsila Cemetery
180° arc of allowable direction to Qibla
Mosque Zayton
W
S
E
31° 50'
29° 23'
22° 37'
Perpendicular to Wall
Halq
Catastration
Roman Catastration
Aux Emporia
QIBLA (Direction to Mecca)
Arsenal (Dar Al-Sina
Bahira

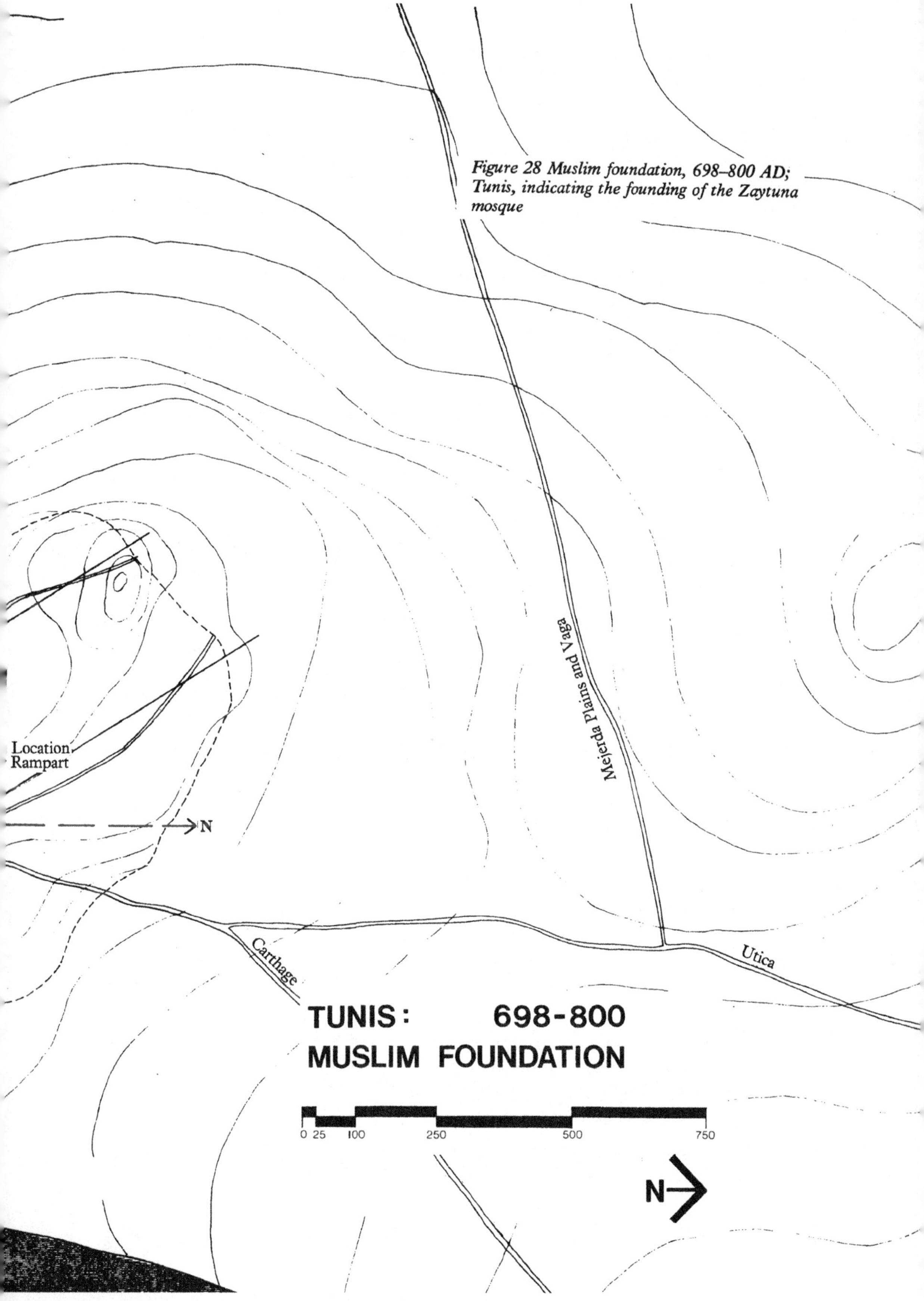

Figure 28 Muslim foundation, 698–800 AD; Tunis, indicating the founding of the Zaytuna mosque

twentieth centuries. Note that when the Suq area is locked from dusk to dawn, the north–south street of Sidi Ben Arous and Tourbet el-Bey is cut off and detour is necessary through the lower eastern north–south street. This did not create a significant problem as all the quarters locked their gates soon after dusk and traffic was minimal. The nature of the access system (streets and cul-de-sacs) and the use of gates for the town, its quarters, and the Suq created a highly secure layout.

The location of the Kasbah[4] within its walls on the high ground west of Tunis Medina core was the ruler's choice for isolating the palace and its compounds from the city proper which was also walled. This system of defensive measures could be viewed as doubling security for the ruling notables and their retinues.

It is interesting to note in this regard Ibn Khaldun's[5] criteria for security and the availability of water:

> For the protection of towns, all the houses should be situated inside a surrounding wall. Furthermore, the town should be situated in an inaccessible place, either upon a rugged hill or surrounded by the sea or by a river, so that it can be reached only by crossing some sort of bridge. Thus, it will be difficult for an enemy to take the town, and its inaccessibility will be increased many times.[6]

and

> In connection with the importation of useful things and conveniences into towns, one must see to a number of matters. There is the water [problem]. The place should be on a river, or near springs with plenty of fresh water. The existence of water will be a general convenience to the inhabitants.[7]

The importance of water and its quality is clearly evident in Tunis. Owing to the nature of the site and prevalent technological practice, three water sources were used:

1 cisterns located under each house which collected water during the rainy winter months for household needs;
2 aqueducts through which water was transported from distant locations to the core of the city for public use; and
3 individual wells for drinking water.

We find, however, that in Tunis the water from individual wells from the western north–south axis of the town, which was on higher ground, was of better quality and known locally as 'sweet water,' whereas the water acquired from the eastern north–south axis of the town was brackish.[8]

The quality of water influenced the authorities' decisions throughout Tunis's history; they allocated areas with sweet water to citizens with preferred tribal or religious affiliations. Those locations and the immediate areas surrounding major mosques[9] tended to be the popular or prestigious locations in the city; this explains the distribution of various quarters during Tunis's long history. Examples are the locations of the more prestigious quarters of the Bani Khurasan, Hafsia, Andalusian, Pashas and Beys. In addition the area surrounding the Zaytuna mosque (excluding the Suq area) always retained its popularity and prestige even though it cut across boundaries of a number of quarters.

Another important and interesting phenomenon in Islamic cities was that of real-estate perpetuity which was made possible by Islamic laws of *Waqf* and inheritance.[10] According to Cattan the Waqf:

> permitted an owner to settle his property to the use of beneficiaries in perpetuity, his intentions as to the devolution of the benefits, the determination of beneficiaries and all other matters relating to the trust being observed and respected in the same manner as a legal enactment.[11]

In the case of a Waqf whose proceeds are assigned to a permanent charitable insti-

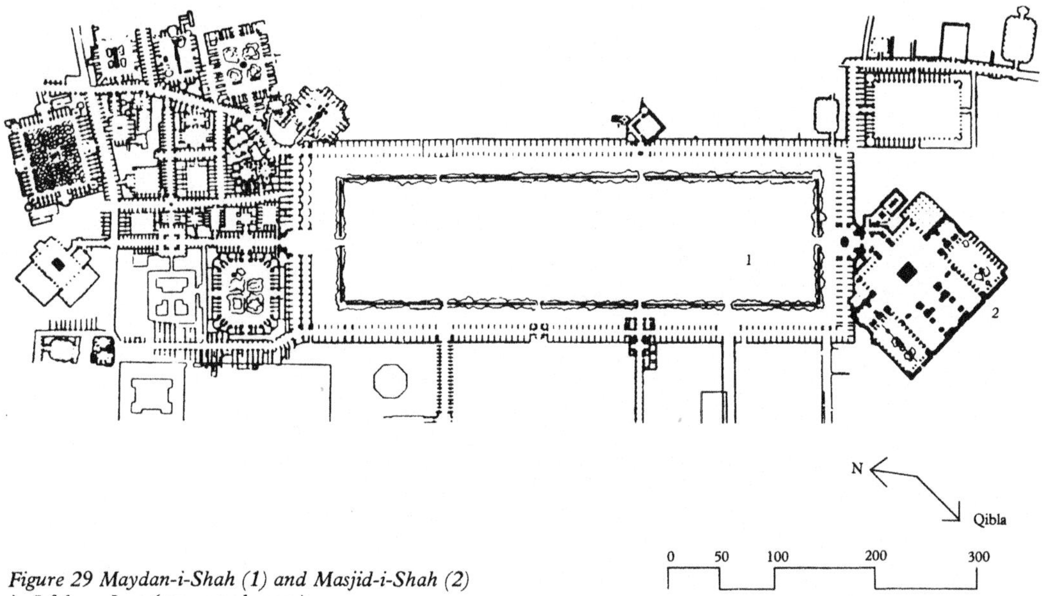

Figure 29 Maydan-i-Shah (1) and Masjid-i-Shah (2) in Isfahan, Iran (source unknown)

tution, such as a mosque or a hospital, it is called a *Waqf Khayri* (charitable Waqf). If they are assigned first to a non-permanent purpose, as when the maker allocated the proceeds to himself during his lifetime and then to his children upon his death, but directed to a charitable purpose after the last beneficiary has died, it is called a *Waqf Dhurri* (descendant's Waqf).[12]

The concept of Waqf originates in the teachings and sayings of the Prophet. In Appendix 1, Saying 18 suggests the concept, and Sayings 19 and 20 indicate a number of virtues among which is the Waqf, which can be attributed to an individual after his death. Hence we find that the Hanafi School of Law defines the Waqf as:

> the detention of the corpus from the ownership of any person and the gift of its income or usufruct either presently or in the future, to some charitable purpose.[13]

Another less-known factor that encouraged perpetuity of property was the location of the burial place of a venerated person, who was occasionally interred on his property or in an adjacent site. Hence a strong attachment to the location is maintained by descendants and relatives of the individual or by others who love and respect his or her memory due to religious or social grounds.

Perpetuity from the above factors outlasted shifting boundaries of quarters or neighbourhoods during centuries of growth and change. Even though the Arabic–Islamic city, like other cities in various cultures, experienced continuous change and growth, the phenomenon of 'spot' perpetuity acted as fixed linkages across time, and tended to perpetuate and maintain building configurations and design.

Finally it should be noted that in attempting to appreciate the dynamics of the building process at the city level, major decisions and building events acting as catalysts for further development and expansion were critical. Examples from Tunis are the founding of new Khutba

Figure 30 Primary street network, Tunis; the plan includes the north and south Rabad(s)

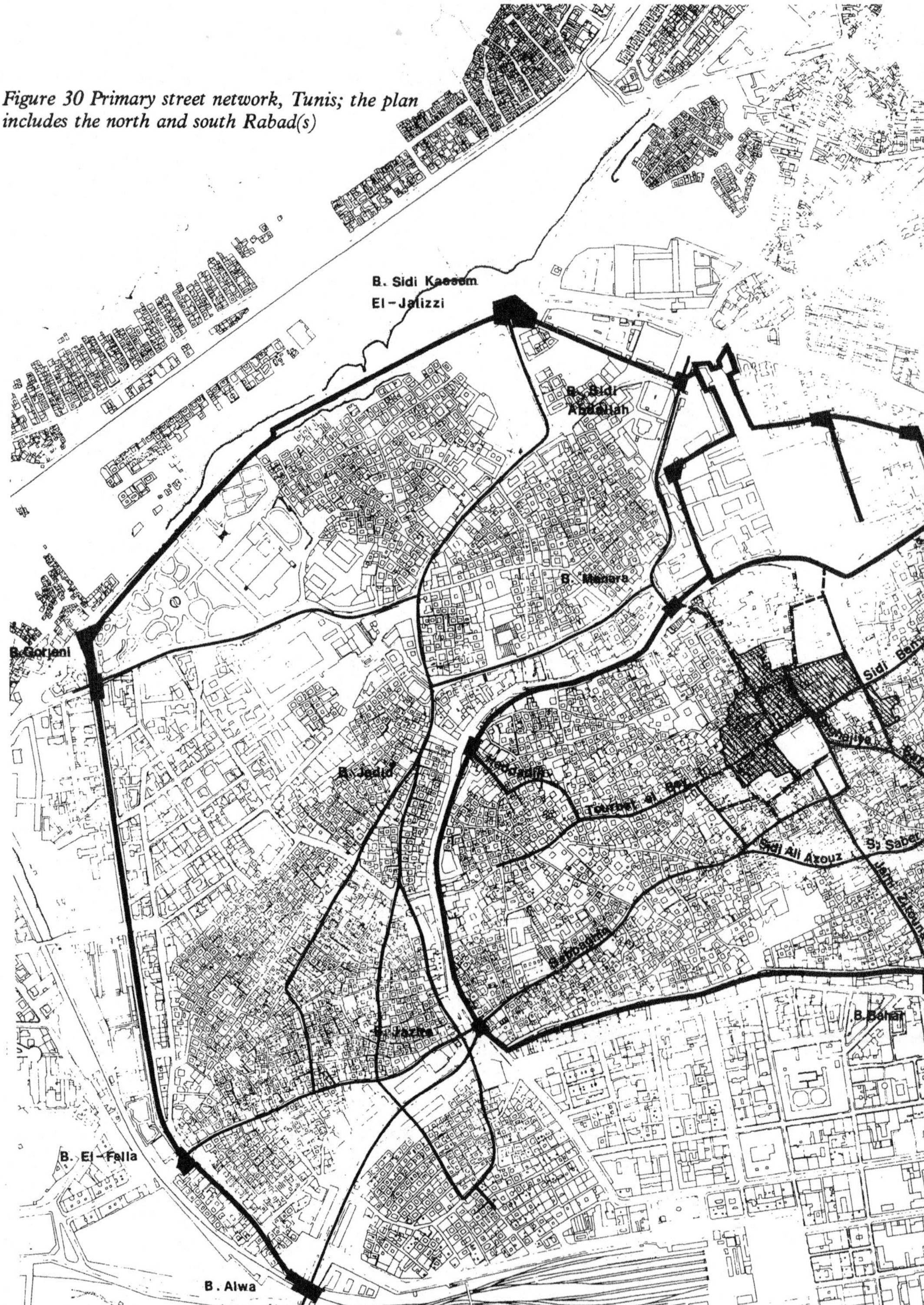

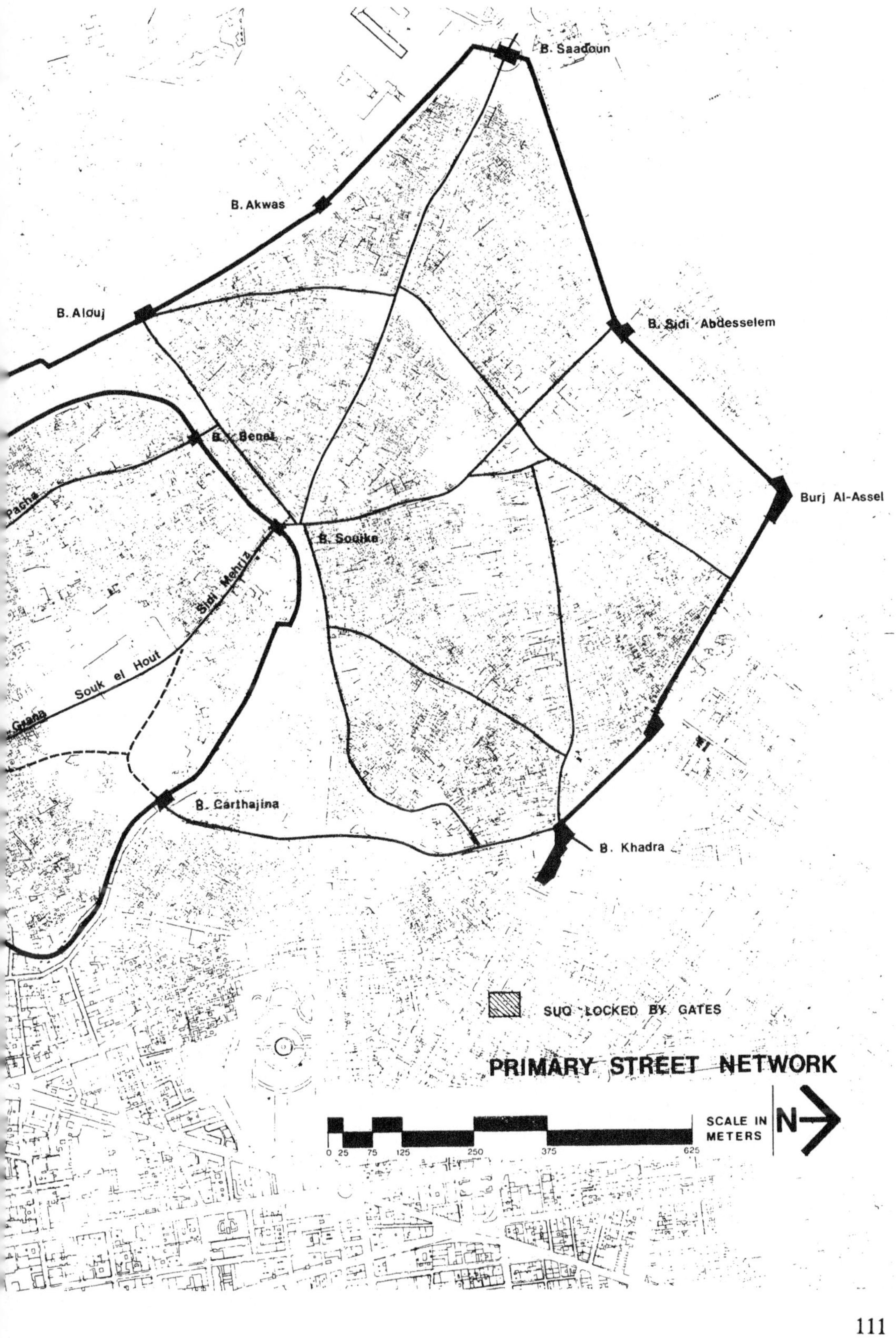
B. Saadoun
B. Akwas
B. Alouj
B. Sidi Abdesselem
B. Benat
Burj Al-Assel
B. Souika
Sidi Mehriz
Souk el Hout
B. Carthajina
B. Khadra
SUQ LOCKED BY GATES
PRIMARY STREET NETWORK
0 25 75 125 250 375 625
SCALE IN METERS
N

mosques after the thirteenth century, and the location of the Musalla in the southern suburb and the building of Madrasas and Zawiyas.[14] Another important example is the creation of the Kasbah by the Almohads in 554/1159, later completed by the Hafsids.[15] Further study of building activity in Tunis during the Almohad and Hafsid era (556/1160–982/1574) will illuminate its influence on the city's formation and growth, which extends to the early years of this century.

Building process: examples of decisions and activity by citizens

So far this chapter has attempted to portray the nature of decisions and actions affecting the macro environment. The following discussion focuses on the nature of building decisions and activity by 'citizens' in typical situations that primarily affect the micro environment. Let us therefore simulate such a typical situation through which I will illustrate one example for each component of the following five-part framework which I devised to represent the physical factors that shaped the traditional Arabic–Islamic city, particularly on the neighbourhood scale. These components are:

1 streets: thoroughfares, cul-de-sacs and related elements;
2 locational restrictions of uses causing harm, such as from smoke, offensive odour and noise;
3 overlooking: visual corridors generated by doors, window openings, and heights;
4 walls between neighbours: the rights of ownership and usage; and
5 drainage of rain and waste water.[16]

This framework encompasses all building activity issues touched on in the Fiqh literature of the Maliki School of Law.

Using Plates 6, 7, 28 and 59 as reference, let us imagine a typical situation where a person wants to build on a vacant lot or to re-use a similar site upon which a dilapidated house stands. If the intention is to rebuild a structure for the same use, then he can proceed; however, if the plan is to build a public bath or bakery, for example then he will more than likely be faced with objections from the neighbours. The reasons given are that such new public buildings will create harm in two ways:

1 by generating additional traffic on the streets providing access to the facility forcing the neighbours to readjust to this new condition, and
2 in both cases, by generating smoke.

After exploring other uses, let us assume the owner of the site decides to build a house. He asks a local builder to construct it, and they will then communicate with each other about the design requirements by using the local design language. This is done by identifying each part by its design language name. To illustrate, let us use examples from the local language in the Tunis region (see p. 127 on housing elements). The owner requires one *Skifa* (entrance lobby with entry doors placed so that no one can see directly into the courtyard from the outside), with two *Dukkana* facing each other (built-in bench provided in Skifa, traditionally used by the male owner or occupant to receive casual visitors or salesmen). He specifies that the *Wust al-dar* (open courtyard in the centre of the house) should have under it a *Majin* (cistern for collecting rainwater from the roofs), and one *Burtal* in front of the main room (a colonnaded gallery off the courtyard giving importance and sometimes sun protection to the room behind). Around the courtyard he asks the builder for three *Bit Trida*

Plate 55 Shops located on a Bat'ha. This example is in the village of Hammamet, Tunisia.

Plate 56 Junction of four Suq segments. View from the enlarged central space of Suq el-Berka in Tunis, looking toward the junction of its two segments and the gate which isolates it from Suq el Kababjiya.

Plate 57 View in the entrance Driba of Wekala Ben Ghorbal off the Suq el-Leffa in Tunis. Note the vaulted ceiling and the tile work on the walls.

Plate 58 Various views of streets surrounding the island in Tunis selected to study Urban Form: Housing. For location of each photo see Figure 40.

(a) (*above left*) Rue des Tamis looking south. The height of the clearance under the Sabat is 5.36 m.

(b) (*above right*) View from the covered portion of Rue de la Kasba toward its junction with Suq du Cuivre on the left. The Mesjid al-Fal is located at this M'qas junction, its entrance partly open facing the camera.

(c) (*below left*) Impasse de la Folie. Note this cul-de-sac begins with a Sabat and also has buttressing arches toward its interior. The width at its mouth measures 2.25 m.

(d) (*facing above left*) Rue de la Kasba looking west. The island selected for study is on the left of the photo.

(e) (*facing above right*) View of the Impasse el Messaoui taken from its mouth. The width at its entrance is only 1.20 m.

(f) (*facing below left*) View of Suq el Ouzar towards the southwest. The clearance height under the Sabat is 4.40 m, the wall to wall width under the Sabat is 1.93 m.

(g) (*facing below right*) View of the Impasse de la Paysanne. The entrance width and height clearance is 1.75 and 2.60 respectively. The width in the cul-de-sac is 2.45, and the clearance of the Sabat is 4.54 m. Note that the end of the cul-de-sac is uncovered.

Plate 59 Aerial photo of the island selected for studying Urban Form: Housing, in the context of its surrounding city fabric. Note the Zaytuna mosque at the top of the photo. (Photo: Office de la Topographie et de la Cartographie, Tunis, 1972)

(simple rooms) and one *Bit bel-kbu u mkasar* (a primary room common in middle- and upper-middle-class houses). It is usually located opposite the entrance to the court, and is divided into:

1 a central alcove called *Kbu* where there is usually built-in seating and elaborate wall and ceiling decorations, and which is used as the primary living area when close relatives or friends are received;
2 two small rooms symmetrically located on each side of the Kbu and called *Maqsura* — they are used as bedrooms;
3 two opposite alcoves used for built-in beds and/or storage. The built-in beds could be on one or both sides, and are usually framed with a decorative wooden structure called *Hanut hajjam*.

And so on, sometimes to the smallest details of decoration and finishes.

If the house is relatively complex, then the builder will more than likely sketch out the plan and any other details primarily for his own use and not as a communicating device with the owner. When the design language is not adequate for both owner and builder to clarify a point, then either one — more than likely the owner — will take the builder to another house to show him what he has in mind.

The builder is expected to know the tradition of building practice and the principles or guidelines that have to be followed and respected. Surprisingly their detailed implications was not common knowledge among the lower ranks of builders. Often reference is made in ancient manuscripts to implemented building decisions which were in violation and were later ordered by the local Kadi to be demolished or corrected in response to a complaint by a neighbour. However, it seems that the more established and older builders with many years of experience who were often called upon by affluent clients had detailed insight in the subject.[17]

Having determined the layout of the site and using the design language for communicating planning requirements, the builder and owner had to examine the likely impact of their decisions on surrounding buildings; for example, if one of the neighbour's walls had a window then its location had to be respected according to the principle of the earlier rights of usage. The layout of the new house would have had to take that into account to avoid creating a direct visual corridor on the private domain, in effect blocking potential overlooking problems.

Furthermore, a neighbour's wall could be used for inserting beams instead of building another adjacent wall for support. However, elaborate guidelines had to be respected for such utilization as well as the associated problems of maintenance rights — for example, the ratio of the wall to be used depended on its ownership. In the case of rebuilding a dilapidated house, correct identification of the ownership of adjacent walls was therefore crucial and was achieved by a careful examination according to a set of criteria which helped to determine whether ownership was single or joint. The most common of those criteria was to determine the nature of the *Aqd* (or wall bond at the corners or junctions of two walls). This was done by examining the materials and mortar to determine if they were built together. This practice, which was sanctioned by the Prophet, is traceable to the decade of 622–632 AD in Medina, and is still followed today for the same purpose in the older parts of Islamic cities under the framework of the *Urf* (local customary law).

The question of drainage of rain and waste water had also to follow certain rules and guidelines. Drainage of rainwater was a particularly delicate problem as it had to respect the principle that excess water should not be withheld from others. Therefore the interdependence of rainwater evacuation from adjacent houses and from the house being built had to be taken into account.

As to the relation of the house to the street(s), let us assume that one side of the house adjoins a through street, and the owner desires additional area; here, he has the option of building a *Sabat* (room bridging the street). The support for the structure on the opposite side had to be resolved, usually by acquiring permission from the owner of the facing building, knowing full well that such a permission was not totally irrevocable. The decision, no doubt, depended on the owner's perception of his future relationship with his opposite neighbour. More than likely the decision would be to use columns for support, which would give the owner independence of his neighbour. The other option was to utilize columns to support both sides, opening up the future possibility of selling the Sabat to the owner of the opposite building, and generally upgrading the marketability of the house (see p. 125 and Figure 36(v)c).

The above was a brief look at issues involved in the process of building in a typical situation to illuminate the fact that the built form was a direct result of the dynamics of decision-making according to the Fiqh guidelines.

We will now address the urban form of the city and its parts. Having already discussed the nature of decision-making by rulers and citizens and their influence at the city and neighbourhood scales, we turn to the organizational, three-dimensional features of the city and its various components. The term 'urban form' is used in this context.

Urban form is best appreciated and understood by quantitative and qualitative evaluation. Again the Medina of Tunis will be the primary source and reference. The historical time frame for this purpose is the Husaynid period (1117/1705–1299/1881). However, most of my map and some other sources were developed during the first fifty years of the period (1299/1881–1375/1956) when Tunisia was a French protectorate.

Urban form: quantitative evaluation and interpretation

Using the detailed maps I developed for Tunis and with the aid of detailed aerial photographs, I measured the whole 'Medina Central' area precisely with a polar planimeter.[18] I know of no other Islamic city measured in this detail and therefore cannot benefit from comparison. However, I will refer to other statistics, available in some sources, for comparison.

This evaluation will start from large-scale issues and proceed to details. In doing so it will touch on various building uses and other attributes of the urban form.

The greater Medina of Tunis (which includes its north and south Rabad or suburbs) is one of the larger Medinas in the Maghrib region. At its peak and just before the French protectorate, the overall area of the Medina Central, its two suburbs, and the Kasbah was 305 ha (hectares). During the first 100 years of its history (79/698–184/800) the area was about 87 ha. In the period 184/800–556/1160 the area grew to 111 ha and then during the Almohad and Hafsid era (556/1160–982/1574) the area covered between 218 and 286 ha. By comparison the sizes of other medinas were: (during the ninth century) 100 ha in Kairouan, 32 ha in Sousse, 24 ha in Sfax; (in the tenth century) 39 ha in Mahdiya; (in the eleventh century) 120 ha in Fatimid Cairo; (during the eleventh and twelfth centuries) 75 ha in Granada; (in the twelfth) 123 ha in Damascus; and (in Morocco) 106 ha in Rabat and 650 ha in Marrakech, including its gardens and cemeteries within the walls.[19]

The following statistics further describe perceptual and qualitative aspects of Tunis:

1. The north and south suburbs are respectively 15 and 14 per cent larger than the Medina Central. In effect, there are almost three equal-sized medinas attached to each other. Traffic between them was through the central area (see Figure 31(a)).
2. Although the perimeter of the Medina Central is 43 per cent of the total perimeter of the urban complex, more than half that length was protected by the two suburbs and Kasbah (see Figure 31(b)).
3. The average width and length of the Medina Central is 632 m and 1496 m respectively. These dimensions were based on five and three width and length locations, the maximum width being 800 m and length 1,550 m. Using the average dimensions and constructing a rectangular shape which is then divided in two by the core (representing the Zaytuna mosque and central Suq), we create two areas with sides of 632 m and 748 m respectively. These areas are well within the tolerable walking distance of 400 m for the average pedestrian (see Figure 31(c)). In other words the size and shape of the Medina Central corresponds to a pedestrian-scaled environment.
4. Open spaces within the Medina Central (excluding streets and cul-de-sacs) constitute only 12.3 per cent of the town's built-up area (see Figure 31(d)). These open spaces include public and private courtyards, gardens and cemeteries. This is an efficient ratio considering that

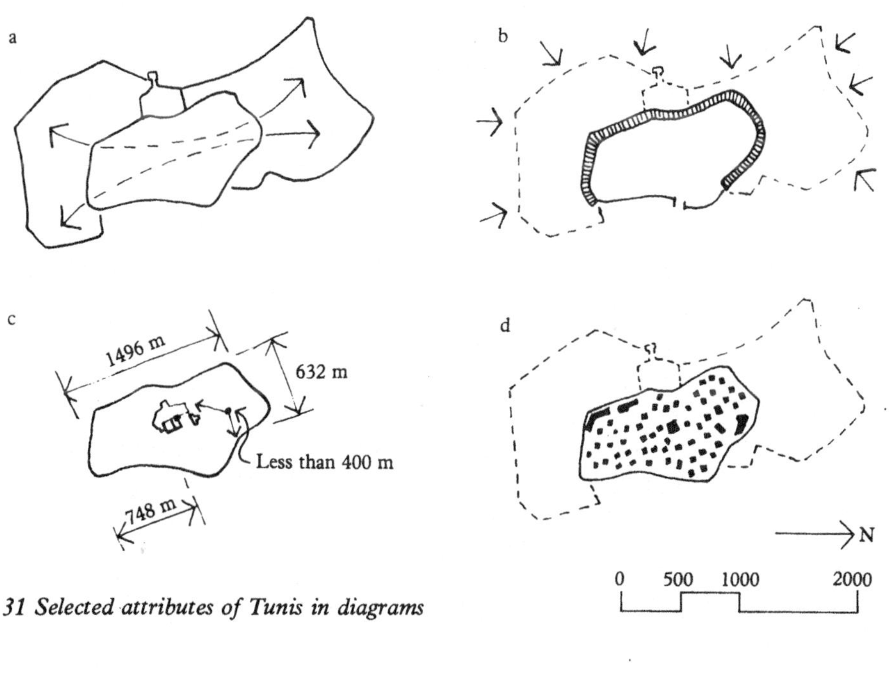

Figure 31 Selected attributes of Tunis in diagrams

every individual house and building has its own courtyard.

5 The percentage of public and private domains in the Medina Central area is 28.5 and 71.5 (see Figure 32). The public domain is defined as the ground coverage of all through streets and public buildings, the private domain as the ground coverage area of all houses and cul-de-sacs. The latter under Islamic law is considered private property belonging to the people who use it for access. However, if the cul-de-sacs are counted as part of the public domain then the percentage changes slightly to 30.2 public and 69.8 private.

6 Ground coverage of various building types and uses are as follows: religious structures 6.9 per cent; economic structures 6.6 per cent; government and defence structures 3.4 per cent; health-facility structures (primarily Hammams or public baths) 1 per cent; housing 69.6 per cent; and all types of streets 12.5 per cent.

7 Because ablution is a requirement before prayer, a number of sources on the Islamic city point out the ratio of Hammams or public baths to mosques and particularly the Khutba mosque. In Tunis Medina Central the ratio of mosques (Khutba mosques plus all mesjids) to Hammams is 4.75:1. However, the ratio of Khutba mosques to Hammams is only .69:1. In Damascus the ratio of mosques to Hammams was 6:1 and in Baghdad 5:1, the latter being similar to Tunis.[20]

8 I have identified nine quarters within the Medina Central area of Tunis (see Figure 33). The percentage of each quarter to the Medina Central area ranges from a minimum of 7.5 per cent to a maximum of 15.4 per cent. The average being 11 per cent which is equivalent to 9.94 ha.

9 Although housing for the rich or poor follows the same concept and pattern, the size of living area, the type of building materials used, and the sophistication of applied decoration distinguish one from the other. Even so, it is difficult to draw a distinct line between types. The following are average areas at ground level only, based on the classification by Revault, using his terms:[21] average 'palace' based on 20 samples — 2,600 m^2; average 'large residence' based on 68 samples — 620 m^2; average 'middle-class' house based on 48 samples — 430 m^2; average 'modest' house based on 2,710 samples — 190 m^2.

10 As mentioned above, the area of all streets is 12.5 per cent of the Medina Central area. Cul-de-sacs constitute only 13.3 per cent of that area, yet provide access to buildings which cover 28.5 per cent of the built-up area. In other words, just under one-third of all buildings in the Medina Central are serviced by only 13.3 per cent of the total access system. Another interesting phenomenon is that 15.5 per cent of the access system is covered by vaults and *Sabat* (room bridging street), and of that 43 per cent is vaulting and 57 per cent Sabat. No cul-de-sacs are covered by vaulting, and of all the access system covered by Sabat, only 15 per cent cover cul-de-sacs. The latter phenomenon can be explained by the fact that it was difficult for a person who wanted to build a Sabat to obtain permission from all owners of the houses serviced by a cul-de-sac. This is due to Islamic law which regards a cul-de-sac private property; any changes within it could be accomplished only with the consensus of all parties, not just a majority. A Sabat over a through street, however, could be built without any of the neighbours' consent

provided it created no harm to any party. Permission from the opposite neighbour had to be sought if structural support was required. The longest and shortest cul-de-sacs I could determine were 140 m and 9 m respectively. The average length of twenty sample cul-de-sacs is 40 m. The average width of through streets and cul-de-sacs based on eight samples is 3.55 m and 2.54 m respectively. The minimum width of a cul-de-sac is approximately 1 m.

11 The area of all open spaces (excluding streets) is 10.8 per cent of the Medina Central's area. It is divided as follows: 72 per cent private courtyards and gardens, 11.4 per cent public courtyards, 4.7 per cent public gardens, and 11.9 per cent cemeteries. If we consider cemeteries as part of the public open space then the per cent of public and private open space is 28 per cent and 72 per cent respectively. These figures are almost identical to the distribution of public and private domains in the city (28.5 per cent and 71.5 per cent). In other words, the allocation of the land in the city between the public and private spheres is identical to the allocation of related open spaces.

12 The percentage distribution of the built-up area within the Medina Central in structures of one to five storeys is as follows: single storey 38 per cent, two storeys 52.7 per cent, three storeys 8.7 per cent, four storeys 0.5 per cent and five storeys 0.1 per cent. The single- and two-storey structures combined constitute 90.7 per cent of all structures, with the majority being two storeys. Although I have not calculated these distributions in the north and south suburbs, I do have one source which indicates that single-storey structures predominate in the suburbs.[22] The factors which have influenced the development of more than single-storey courtyard structures in the various Maghribi Islamic cities would be interesting to determine. For example most of Marrakech is single-storey, whereas most of Fez is two-storeys.

13 An important aspect of a quantitative study is density. People or houses (units) per area are the two most common measures used in referring to density. For our purpose I will indicate population per area based on the following assumed distribution of people/house type: palace: twelve, large residence: nine, middle-class house: six, modest house: six. The gross density would measure 193 persons/ha or seventy-eight persons/acre. Keeping in mind the vast range in size between the palace and the modest house, and based on approximately 2,846 houses the gross density would measure thirty-two houses/ha or thirteen houses/acre. The net density is measured as number of houses divided by the private domain (which is the ground coverage area of all housing plus all cul-de-sacs) and is equal to forty-four houses/ha or eighteen houses/acre. The net population density based on the above distribution of households would be 270 persons/ha or 109 persons/acre.

Before concluding this quantitative review and for the sake of furthering research I would like to indicate discrepancies between my calculations and those of Alexandre Lezine of a number of areas (or islands) which he selected for study in the Medina Central.[23] I believe my calculations are more accurate since they were based on larger and detailed maps. Figure 34 indicates the locations of those islands and the discrepancies are listed in the notes to this chapter.[24]

Figure 32 Public and private domains: Medina Central, Tunis

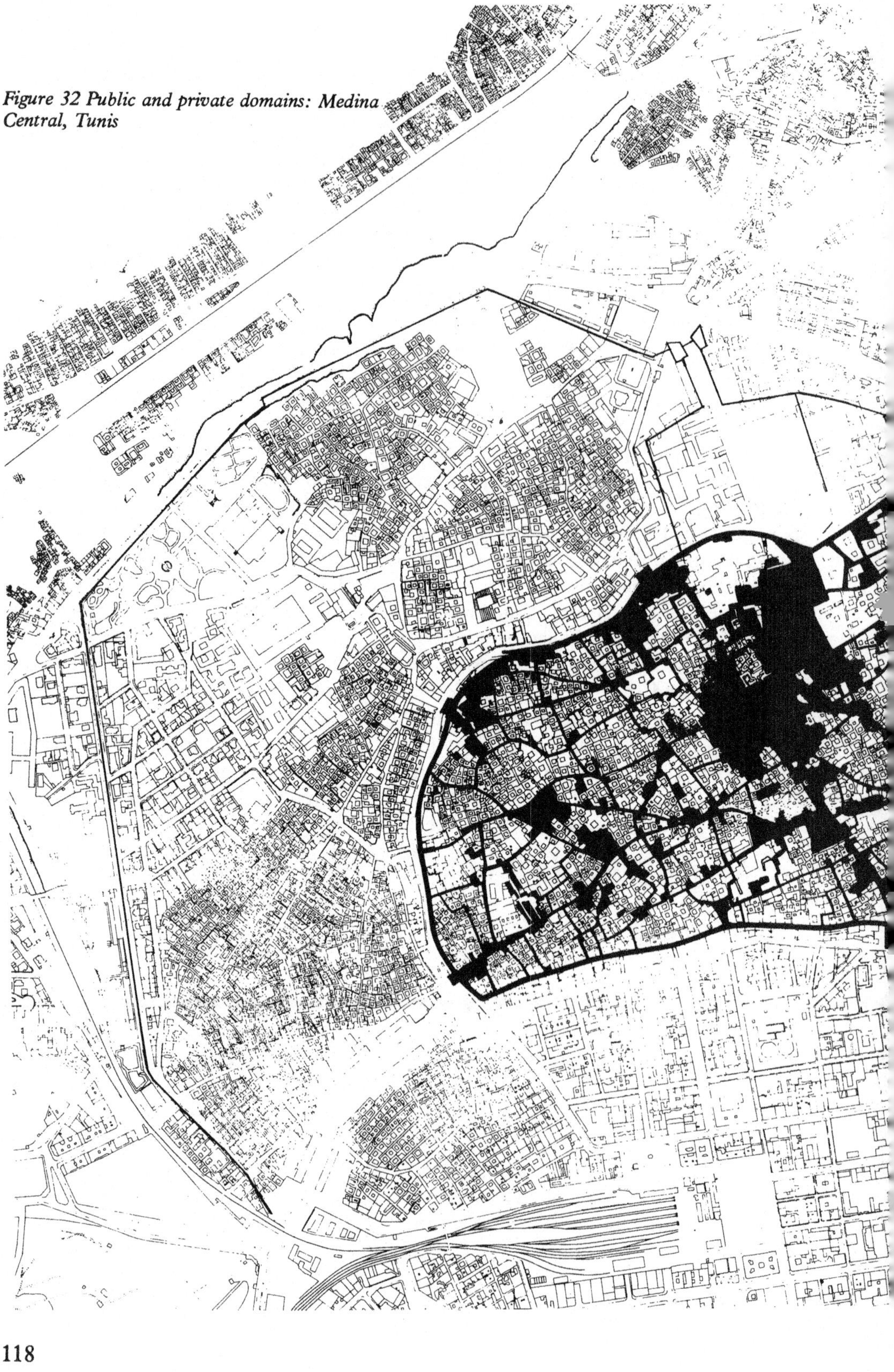

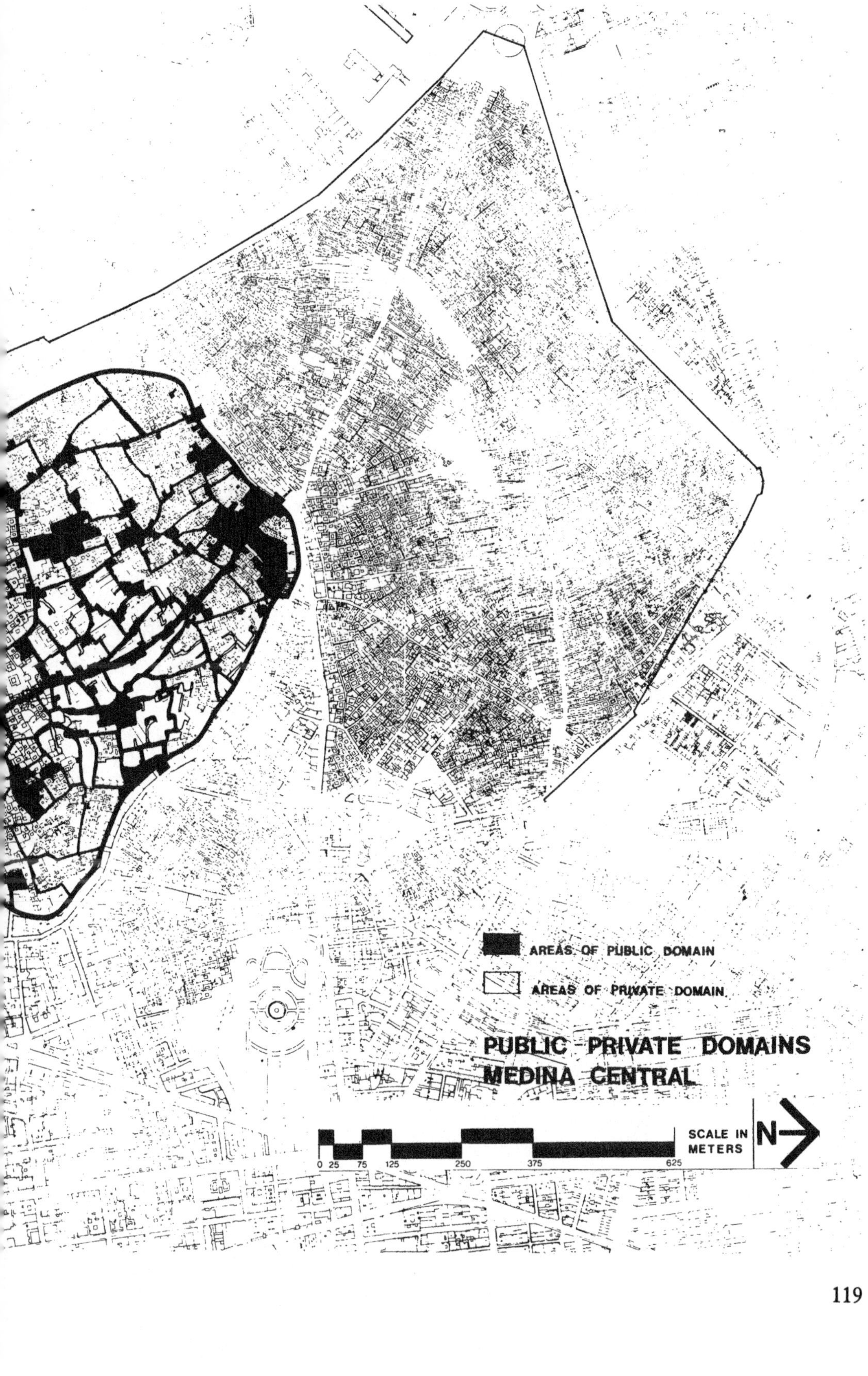
AREAS OF PUBLIC DOMAIN
AREAS OF PRIVATE DOMAIN
PUBLIC-PRIVATE DOMAINS
MEDINA CENTRAL
0 25 75 125 250 375 625
SCALE IN METERS
N

Figure 33 Approximate quarter boundaries: Medina Central, Tunis

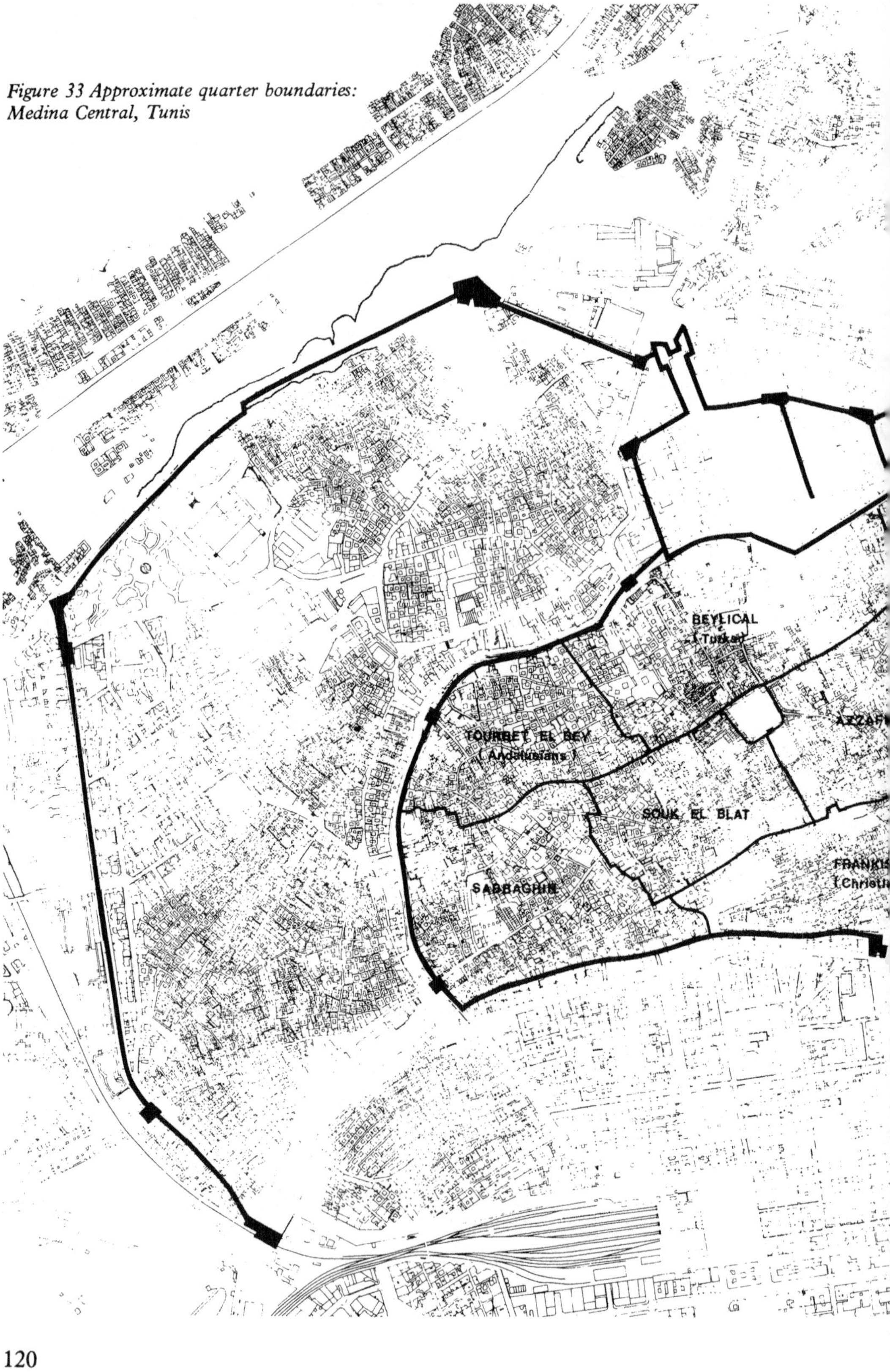

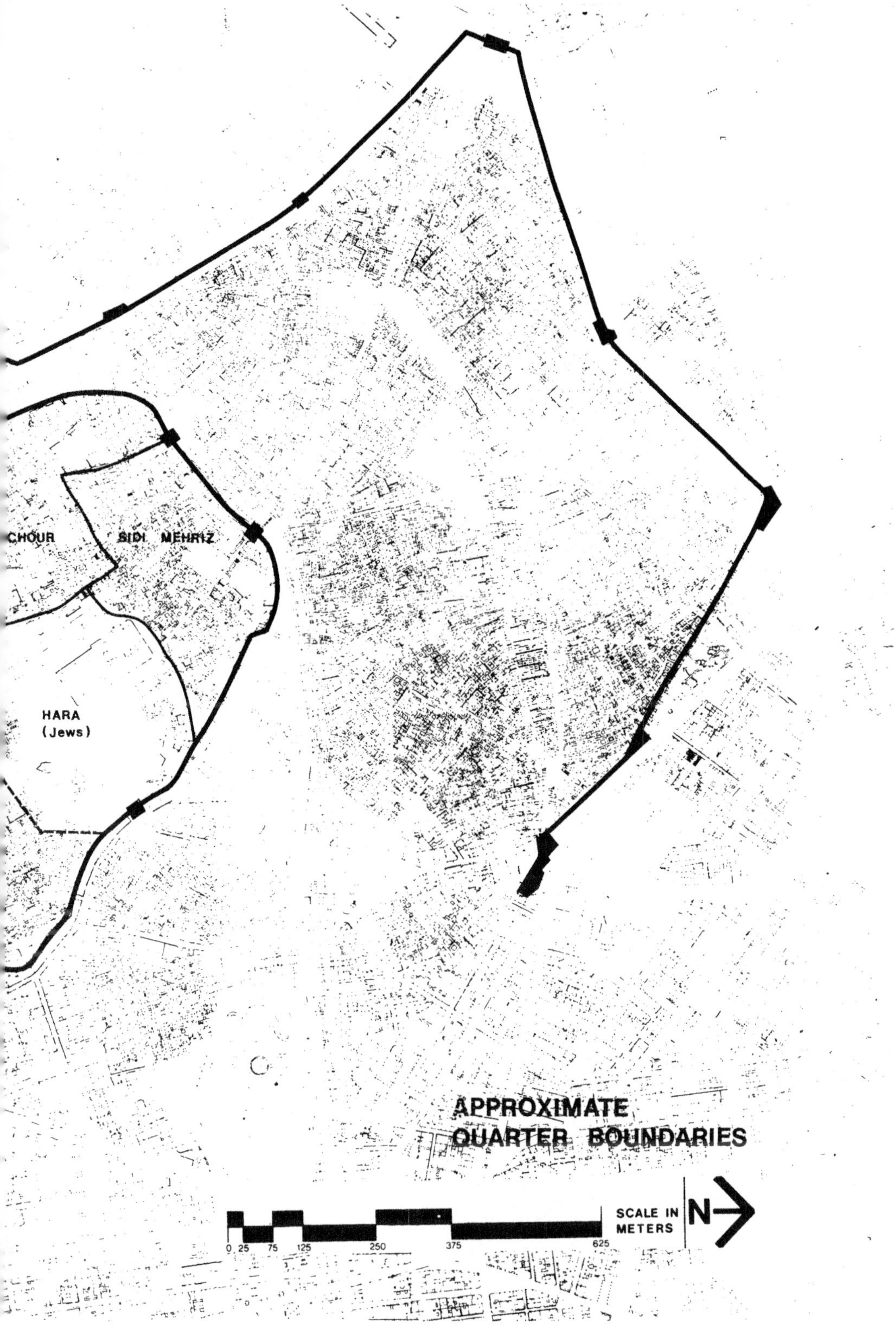
CHOUR
SIDI MEHRIZ
HARA
(Jews)
APPROXIMATE
QUARTER BOUNDARIES
0 25 75 125 250 375 625
SCALE IN
METERS
N

Figure 34 Statistical data references: Tunis

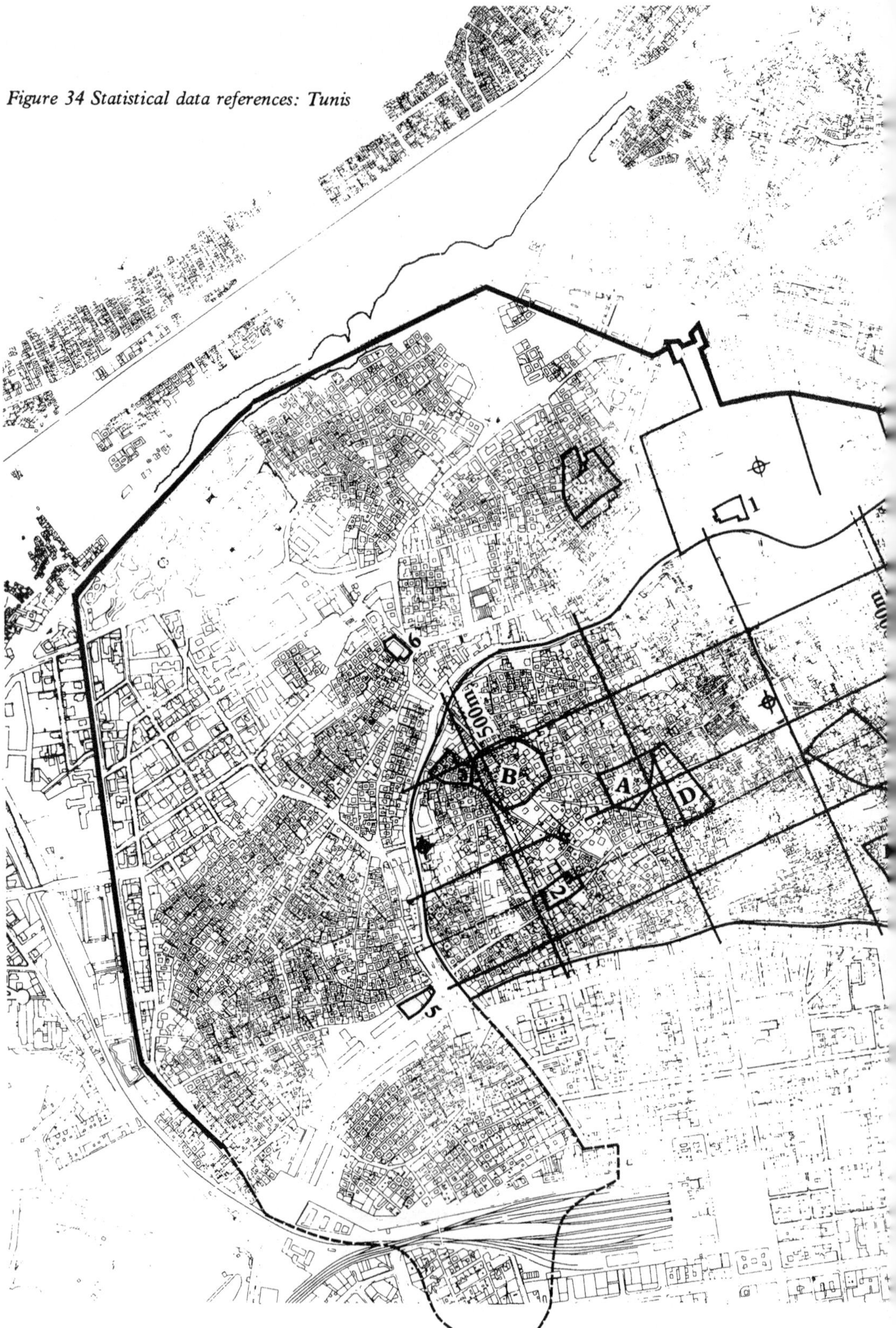

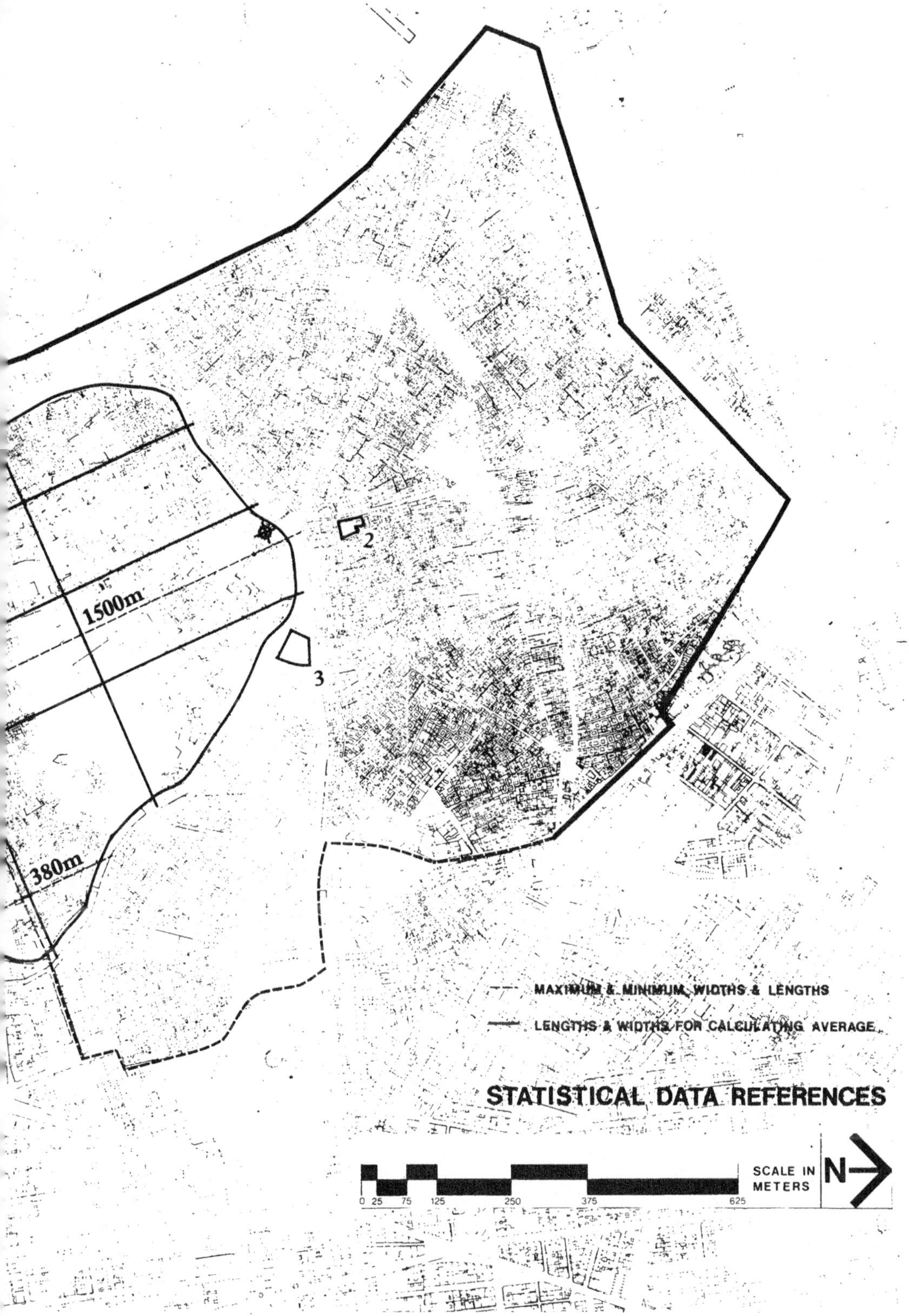
1500m
380m
2
3
MAXIMUM & MINIMUM WIDTHS & LENGTHS
LENGTHS & WIDTHS FOR CALCULATING AVERAGE
STATISTICAL DATA REFERENCES
0 25 75 125 250 375 625
SCALE IN METERS
N

Urban form: qualitative/ organizational nature

This part of the chapter is in many ways an extension of Chapter 2. There I discussed the design language in terms of a morphological analysis of the core of the Medina Central. The sequence used in that presentation was from the large to the small scale.

Here I would like to continue exploring the urban form using the morphological analytical approach by stressing its qualitative and organizational features. The sequence of presentation is the reverse of the one used in Chapter 2. I start with the details and culminate by indicating how they typically come together to shape urban form. In other words I will reduce a complex physical entity to its essential parts and then rebuild it.[25]

The Medina of Tunis will again be used as the primary reference source for this analysis, which is presented according to the following format:

1 Primary building elements as determined by materials and traditional building techniques.
2 Primary organizational/planning/design elements as evident in housing and commercial facilities.
3 Combination of building and organizational elements to achieve urban form.

Primary building elements as determined by materials and traditional building techniques

1 *The wall* (see Figure 35(a)). In addition to its function of delineating and creating space, its mass provided high levels of security and privacy.[26] Most walls were built as load-bearing elements with an average thickness of 1 cubit (approximately 50 cm). The mass also helped provide an acoustical barrier and lag for heat penetration.

2 *The column* (see Figure 35(b)). Used extensively as supports for arcades in courtyards of various building types combining structural and aesthetic attributes (see Plate 38). Marble and stone were the most common materials used for columns, and in some regions brick or timber were also used. The design of columns and their capitals varied according to time and place.

3 *The beam and arch* (see Figure 35(c)). Beams were usually constructed of timber. The span was limited to the properties of the timber used. They were used with flat timber ceilings and as lintels over openings. The beam was exploited for aesthetic purposes by decoration and used as an element of a designed ceiling (see Plate 39). Arches were also used for spanning and providing support when needed. They were often decorated, particularly when used in arcades facing a courtyard.

4 *The roof* (see Figure 35 (d)). Owing to the scarcity of timber, most enclosures were roofed with vaults and occasionally with a dome (see Plate 40). The spanning capability determined room shapes and sizes. Vaults were also used as coverings for the Suq system.

Primary organizational/planning/ design elements as evident in housing and commercial facilities

1 *Streets and related elements.* Streets were discussed in Chapters 1 and 2. In the former they were presented in terms of their legal definition and status, whereas in Chapter 2 streets were defined in terms of their systematic nature and were used as a physical framework for relating various land

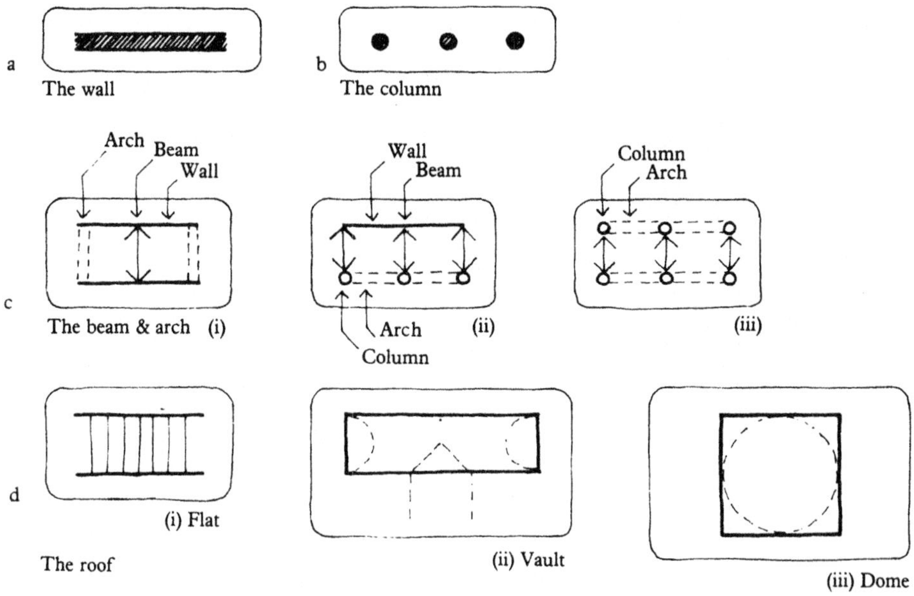

Figure 35 Primary building elements

uses and building types. For the purposes of this chapter I will highlight major organizational elements of streets so that their role is clarified on p. 129-36:

(i) Through open street (see Figure 36(i)). Batha or small plaza occurring at junctions of through streets, usually as: (a) M'qas or fork junction (see Plate 41); and (b) cross junction (see Plate 42).
(ii) Cul-de-sac (see Figure 36(ii)). A cul-de-sac with a gate at its mouth is a Driba servicing a number of houses.
(iii) Buttressing arch: used to support and reinforce opposite walls, particularly if they exceed one storey in height. They are also used to frame quarter (neighbourhood) and Driba gates (see Figure 36(iii) and Plate 43).
(iv) Vaults: primarily used to cover Suq streets (see Figure 36(iv) and Plate 44).
(v) Sabat: room bridging a street (see Figure 36(v)), usually over through

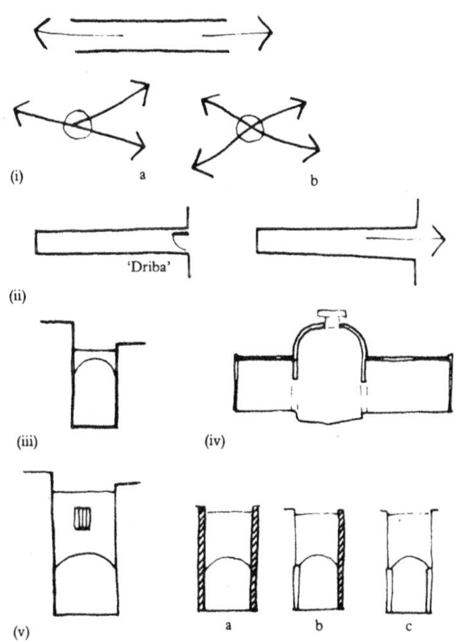

Figure 36 Streets and related elements

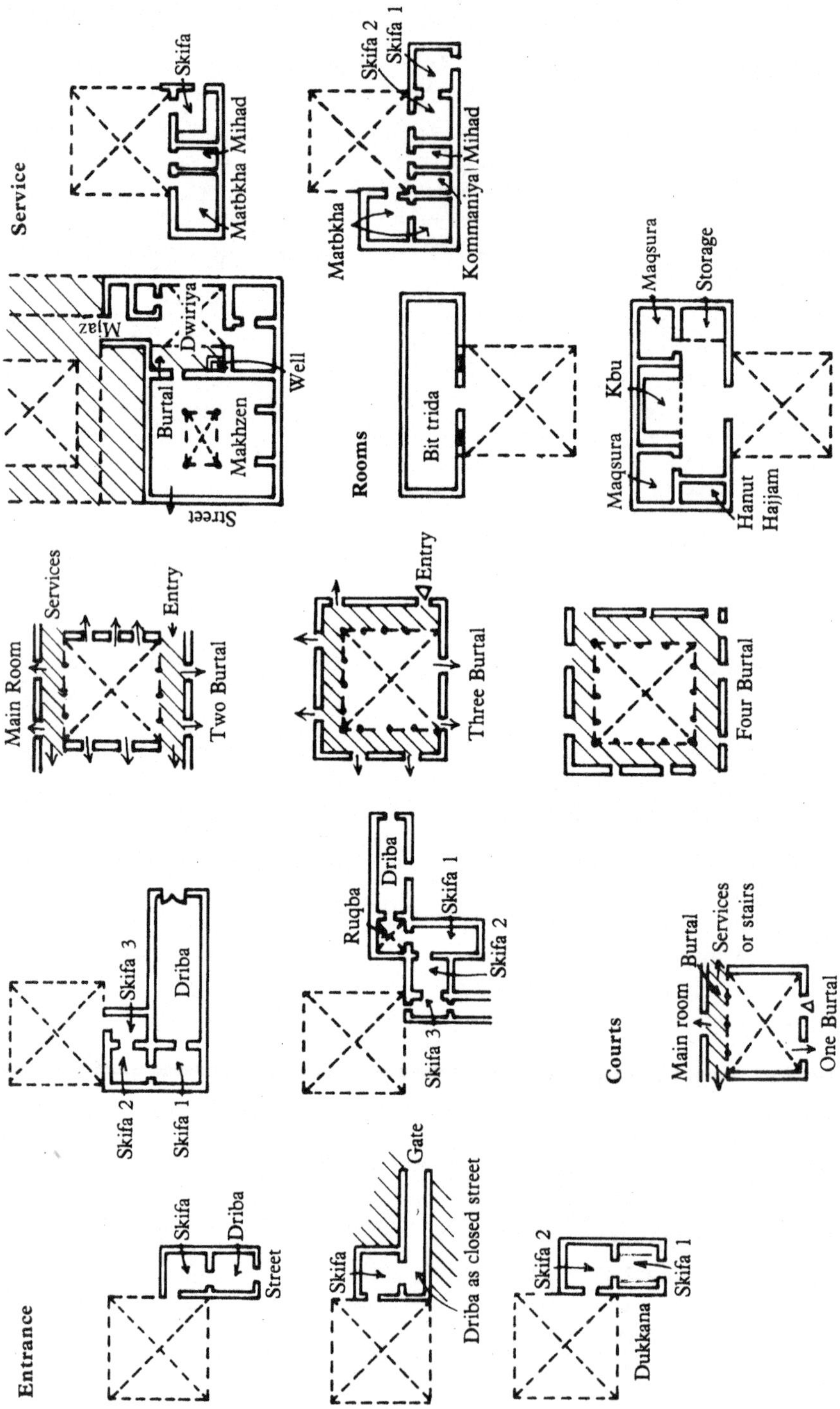

Figure 37 Housing elements; from Hakim, B. (ed.) (1978) Sidi Bou Sa'id – Tunisia

streets, and occasionally over cul-de-sacs. A Sabat uses support in one of three forms: (a) direct support of opposite walls (see Plate 45); (b) support of columns on one side and wall on other (see Plate 46); and (c) support of columns on both sides (see Plate 47).

(vi) Drainage channels in streets: open or covered. They are used to drain rain and waste water, and not sewage, which was collected in septic tanks.

2 *Housing elements*,[27] see Figure 37.

(i) Entrance: (a) *Driba* دريبة : a primary entrance vestibule or private lane which allows Skifa to be further removed from the street (see Plate 48). (b) *Skifa* سقيفة : a secondary entrance corridor or lobby with entry doors placed so that no one can see directly into the courtyard from the outside (see Plate 49). Used in conjunction with a Driba or another Skifa. (c) *Dukkana* دكانة , or built-in bench is usually provided in the first Skifa. Traditionally the male owner or occupant of the house received casual visitors or salesmen in the first Skifa. (d) *Ruqba* رقبة: a small unroofed space occurring at the end of a Driba, at the junction of a Driba and a Skifa or at the junction of two Skifas. Sometimes the location of a well.

(ii) Court: (a) *Wust al-dar* وسط الدار private open courtyard in the centre of the house. It could have a gallery Burtal on one, two, three, or four sides. It sometimes has a small water pool and/or fountain at its centre (see Plate 50). In rich houses a *Majin* ماجن : or cistern is built under the courtyard for collecting rainwater from the roofs. (b) *Burtal* برطال : a colonnaded gallery off of a main courtyard, giving importance and sometimes sun protection to the main room, and/or giving access to services or stairs. (c) *Dwiriya* دويرية : a secondary courtyard in a service area joined to the main courtyard by a corridor. One of its sides is sometimes roofed by a *Burtal Dwiriya* برطال دويرية giving protection to a well. The Dwiriya is sometimes connected to the Makhzen, the major space for storing bulky provisions, which is also accessible from the street.

(iii) Rooms: (a) *Bit trida* بيت طريدة : the most common room type (see Plate 51). It usually has no wall recesses. It occurs in rich and modest houses. (b) *Bit bel-kbu u mkasar* بيت بالقبو ومقاصر : the primary room in a rich or middle-class house (see Plate 52). It is usually located opposite the entrance and could have a colonnaded gallery in front of it. The room is divided into sections: a central alcove called *Kbu* قبو where there is usually built-in seating and elaborated wall and ceiling decorations, and which is used as the primary living area where close relatives or friends are received; and two small rooms symmetrically located on each side of the Kbu and called *Maqsura* (singular) مقصورة used as bedrooms; and two opposite alcoves for built-in beds and/or storage. The built-in beds could occur on one or both sides, and are usually framed with a decorative wooden structure and called *Hanut Hajjam* حانوت حجام literally translated as 'Barber's shop' because they look like the decorative fronts of barber shops found in Tunisia (see Plate 53).

(iv) Service: (a) *Matbkha* مطبخة: kitchen. (b) *Kommaniya* كمانية: pantry. (c) *Mihad* ميحاض : toilet.

3 *Commercial facilities: elements of the Suq*, see Figure 38.

(i) The typical shop varies in size, with the depth usually greater than the frontage width, see Plate 54. The smallest shop in plan tends to be 1½ by 1½ meters (see Figure 38(i)).

(ii) Typical series of shops with or without an arcade usually occurs within a neighbourhood and on a Batha (see Plate 55). They also tend to occur on both sides of major wide thoroughfares (see Figure 38(ii)).

(iii) A typical segment of a Suq system has a vaulted passageway with the potential for communal lock-up gates (see Plate 44). This formation with or without a covered vault tends to occur also on major thoroughfares of the city (see Figure 38(iii)).

(iv) On a large scale the typical intersection of four spines (or elongated segments) encloses within it islands of shop clusters and other uses. The junctions are often utilized for the location of lock-up gates. On a small scale the enclosed space formed by four segments is used typically for a Wekala, Funduk, Madrasa, or a general storage space. Occasionally an uncovered green space is created, (see Figure 38(iv) a and b, and Plate 56 for a special case in Tunis).

(v) The sketch indicates a typical context for a Wekala or Funduk (see Figure 38(v)). It is a corner location with the Suq on both sides. Often it is linked to

Figure 38 Commercial facilities: elements of the Suq

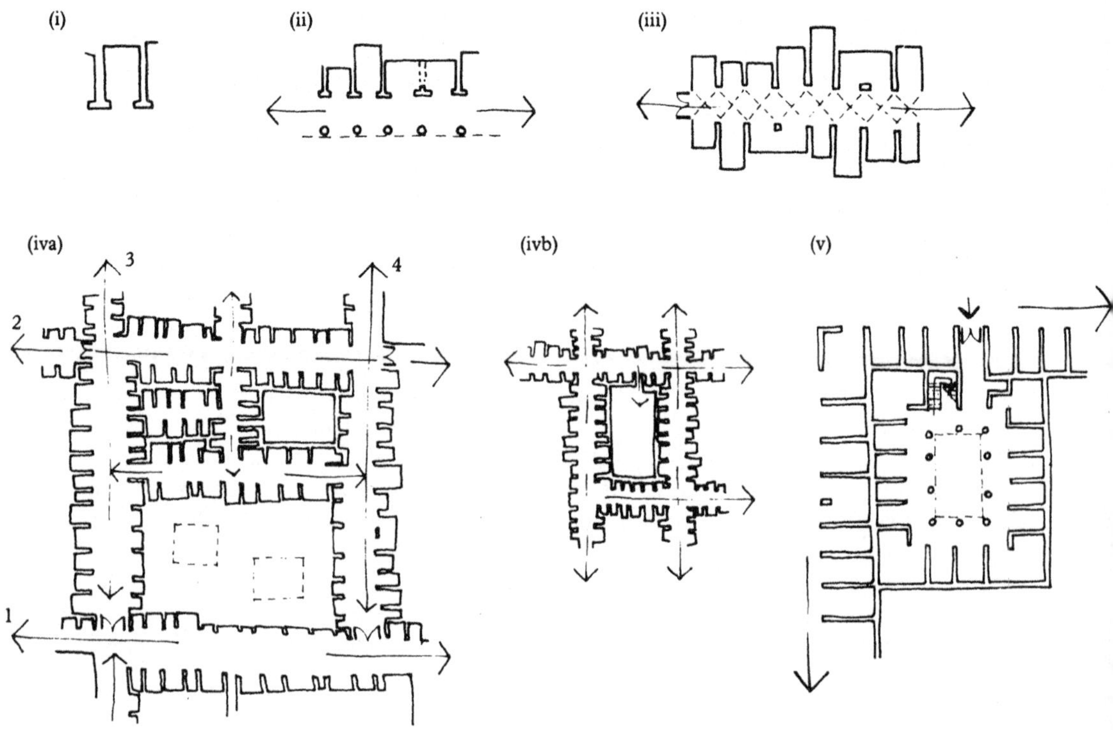

Plate 60 Funduk el Attarine
(a) (*above left*) View through the entrance of Funduk el-Attarine from Suq el-Attarine, Tunis.
(b) (*above right*) View from within the courtyard of Funduk el-Attarine. Note the gallery on the upper level provides access to rooms.

Plate 61 (*right*)Suq des Fammes in Tunis, looking south.

Plate 62 (*above left*) Suq Echaouchia in Tunis, looking south.

Plate 63 (*above right*) Suq el Kouafi in Tunis, looking toward its gate and junction at Suq el Leffa.

Plate 64 (*below left*) Looking toward the Qibla wall of Zaytuna mosque on the Rue de la Laine in Tunis. Note that the dome over the Mihrab is visible from this street.

Plate 65 (*below right*) Within the vaulted portion of Rue de la Laine in Tunis, looking toward its junction with Suq des Fammes. The Qibla wall of the Zaytuna mosque is behind the shops on the right of the photo.

Plate 67 (*above*) Inside the first courtyard of Madrasa Sulaimaniyah in Tunis. The Skifa or entrance is on the right of the photo where the students are standing. The three doors under the Burtal or arcade lead to the same prayer hall space.

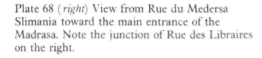

Plate 66 (*above*) Rue du Tamoin in Tunis, looking toward its junction with Suq el Kachachine. Note the Sabat is used in a unique location: between two rows of shops.

Plate 68 (*right*) View from Rue du Medersa Slimania toward the main entrance of the Madrasa. Note the junction of Rue des Libraires on the right.

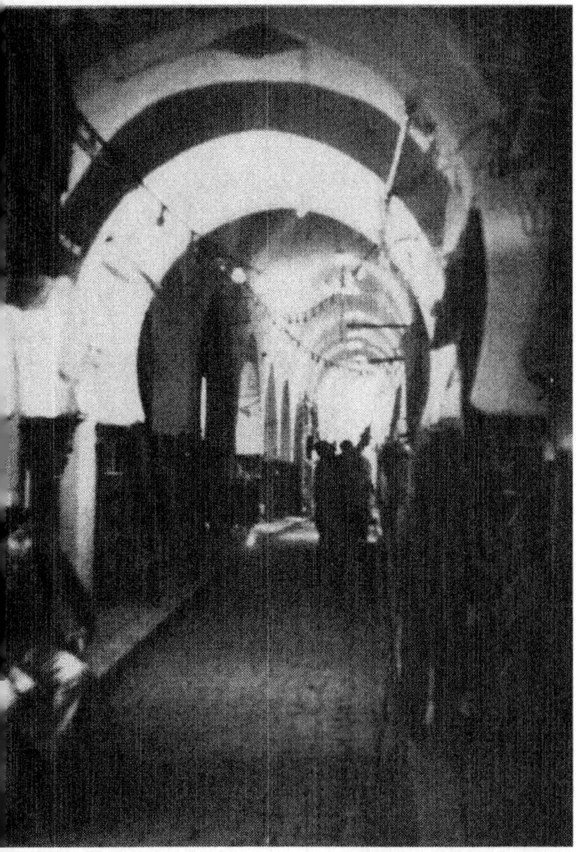

Plate 69 (*above left*) Suq el Qmache in Tunis, located on the western wall of the Zaytuna mosque, where shops are built adjunct to the wall and are fronted by an arcade supported by decorated columns.

Plate 70 (*above right*) Impasse el Oukala off Suq el Bey in Tunis. Note that there are shops on both sides of this cul-de-sac. The gate at its end led to a Wekala, which is now demolished. The minaret of the Zaytuna mosque is visible in the background.

Plate 71 (*left*) Suq el Leffa after its junction with Suq el Koufi and looking toward its junction with Suq el Qmache. This is one of the narrowest Suqs in Tunis. The entrance to Madrasa Mouradiya (also known as Madrasa at-Tawba) is located halfway down on the right.

the Suq from one side (see Plate 57), and surrounded by buildings and uses on the other sides. In a Wekala or Funduk there is usually an upper floor accessible from a gallery. For a detailed discussion of Wekala and Funduk see Chapter 2.

Combination of building and organizational elements to achieve urban form

This section will illustrate the urban form which usually results from the combination of building and organizational elements. The housing and commercial sectors will be used as contexts for examples.

Urban form: Housing

I selected an 'island' of housing surrounded by commercial and other uses for illustration (for location see Figure 40, Plates 58(a)–58(g) and 59). I was fortunate to find adequate information on this island to make a detailed analysis of its morphology and use feasible. In an area of 1.19 ha (2.94 acres) which includes half the width of the perimeter streets, the ground coverage 56 per cent housing, 31 per cent commercial facilities, 4 per cent religious structures, and 9 per cent access. There are no palaces in this island, however the ground coverage used by housing is allocated to the remaining three types as follows: 39 per cent for large residences, 14 per cent middle-class and 47 per cent for modest houses.[28]

Figure 39 shows the island with the boundaries of all houses indicated, and each house identified by a number.[29] The island's housing components are broken down into their four essential uses, namely the entrances, courtyards, rooms and service areas. A series of four examples of each use is indicated representing a succession of simple to complex variations. Each example is identified by the house number from which it was taken.

Of interest is the percentage of distribution of uses at ground level for all the houses. Using the area of all houses (6,717.5 m^2) as a base for the calculation, we find the distribution as follows: entrances 18 per cent; courtyards 25 per cent; rooms 27.5 per cent; and service areas 29.5 per cent. In this regard I would like to point out that the entrance system does take up an appreciable percentage of the total area due to security and privacy purposes, in addition to the nature of the Skifa(s) as entrance room devices. Considering that they were extensively used as outside reception/guest rooms for males, then the percentage is reasonable. Also, the effective living area for most of the year, when the climate is pleasant, is the courtyard plus the rooms, or 52.5 per cent (25 per cent courtyards plus 27.5 per cent rooms). The high percentage of ground use for service areas represents the measures taken to store large amounts of food, the requirements for cooking and washing facilities, and very often space for a home bakery.[30]

Urban form: The Suq

In the previous section the essential five elements of the Suq system were identified. In Figure 12, generalized urban form samples are extracted from their locational context and annotated. Here I elaborate further by illustrating detailed plans of specific clusters and configurations. This should clarify further the versatility of the Suq's organizational elements. Plates 60 to 71 relate to this section and their locations are indicated on Figures 40 and 43.

ENTRANCES

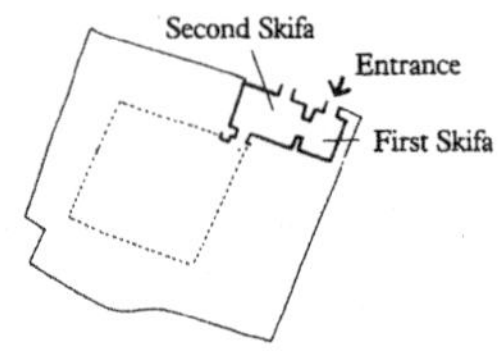

Example from house 28

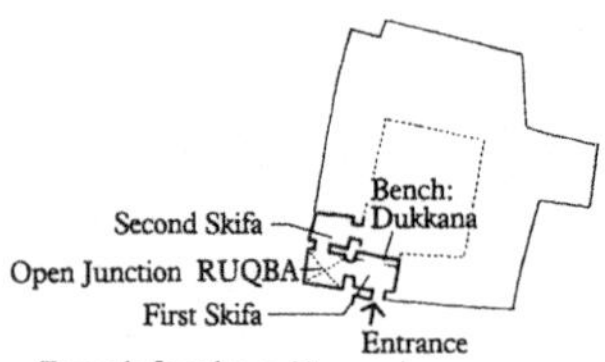

Example from house 11

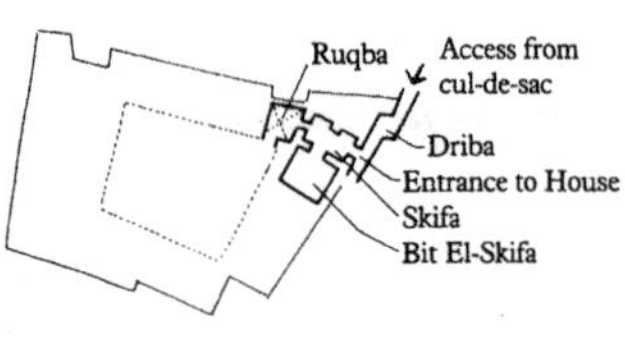

Example from house 13

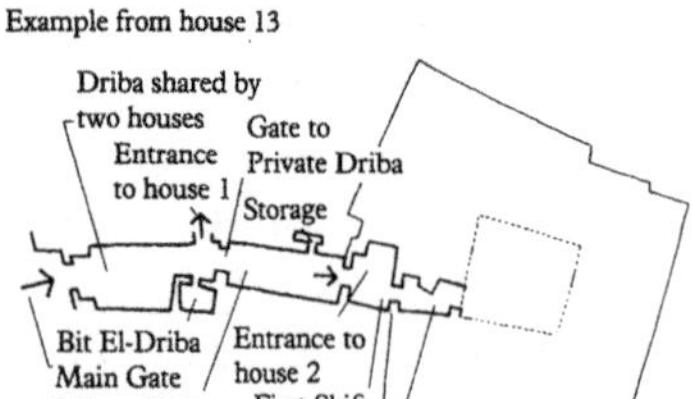

Example from house 14

COURTYARDS

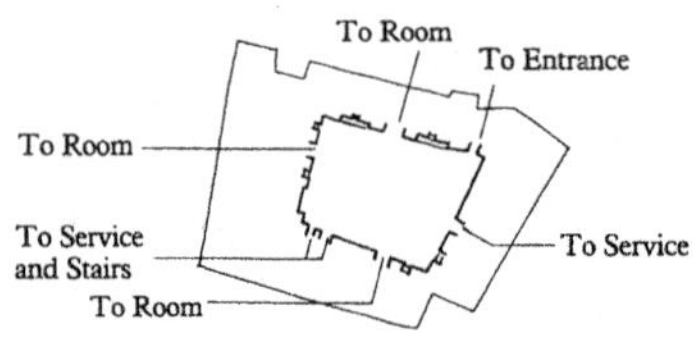

Example from house 13

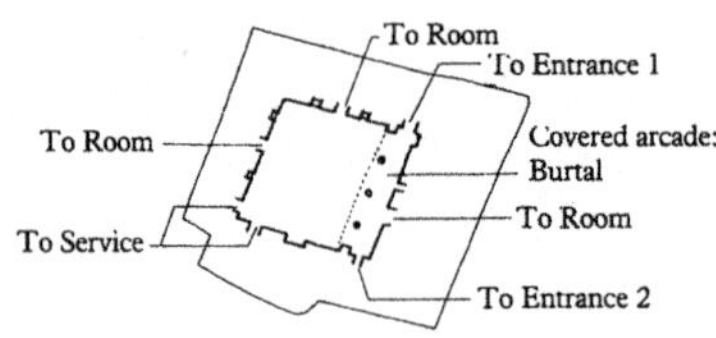

Example from house 28

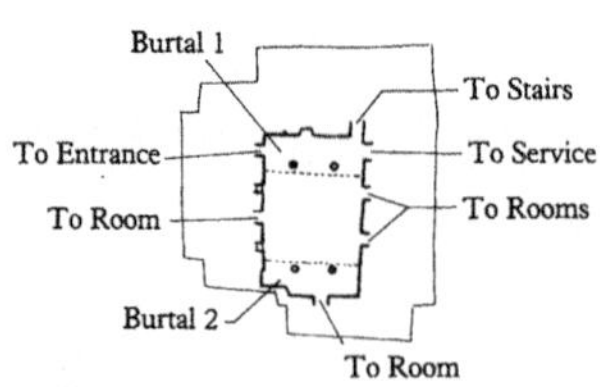

Example from house 3

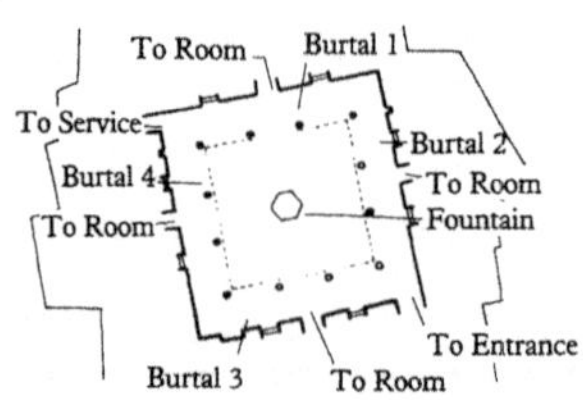

Example from Dar Ben Abd-Allah, Tunis (after Revault)

ROOMS

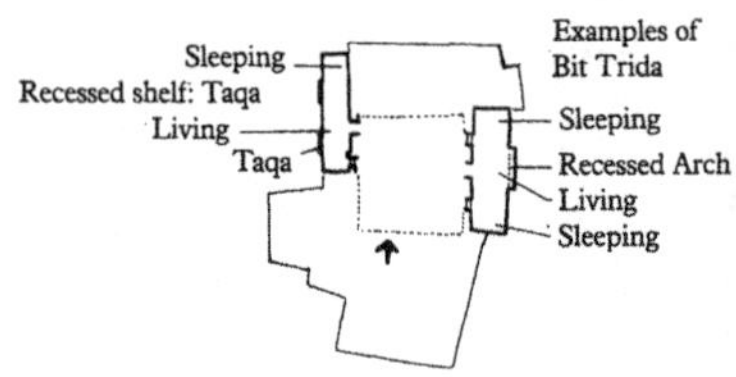

Example from house 21

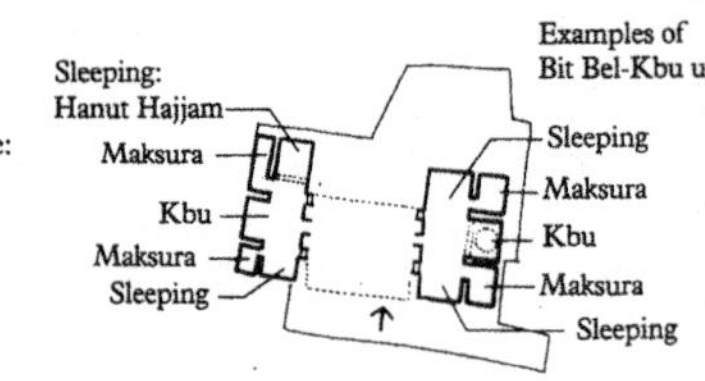

Example from house 19

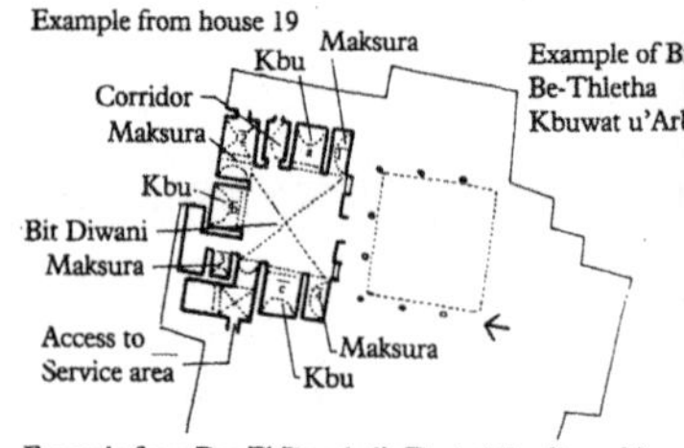

Example from Dar El-Daouletli, Tunis (after Revault)

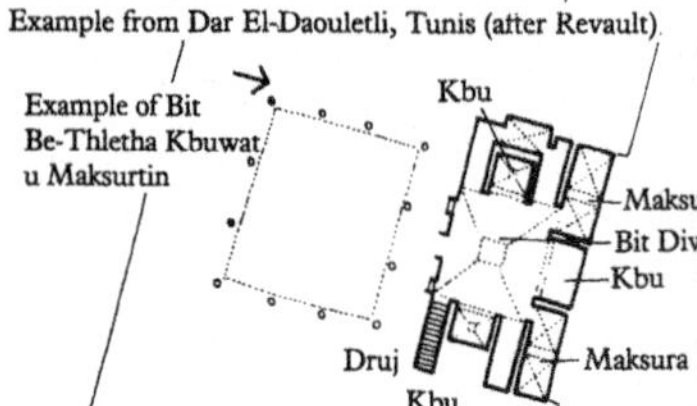

Example from Dar Hussein, Tunis (after Revault)

ERVICES

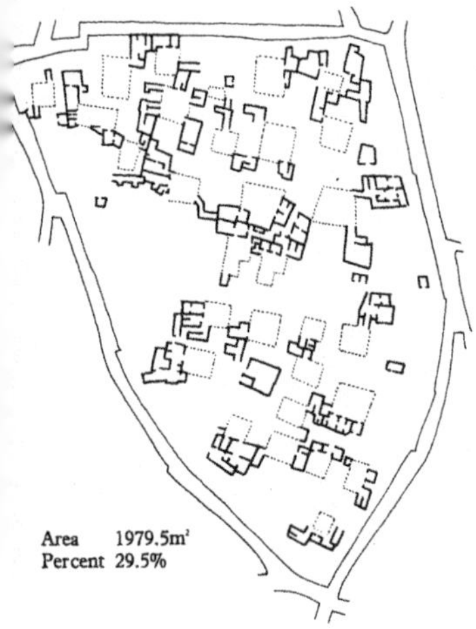

COMPOSITE KEY PLAN

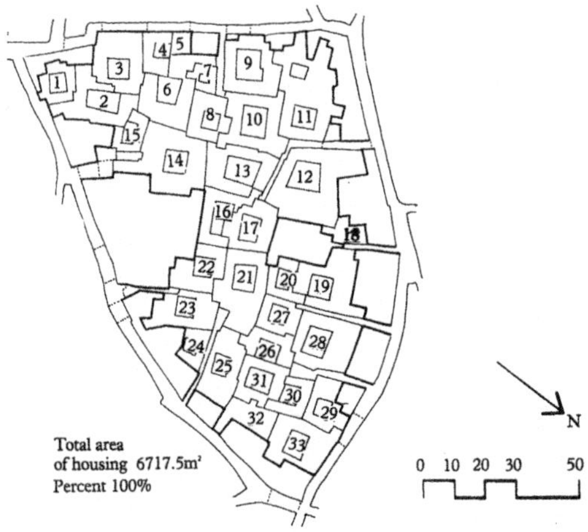

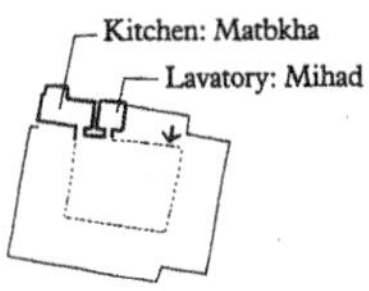

xample from house 27

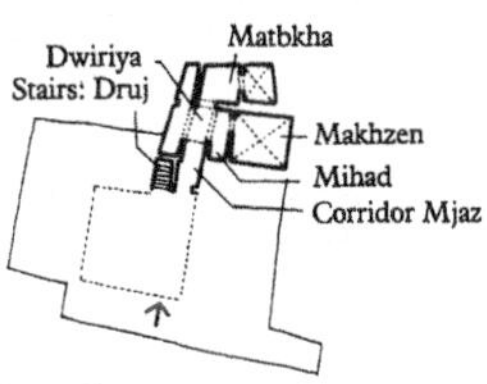

xample from house 19

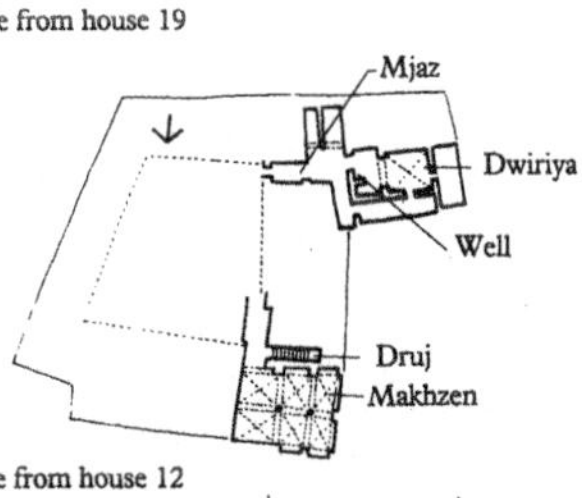

xample from house 12

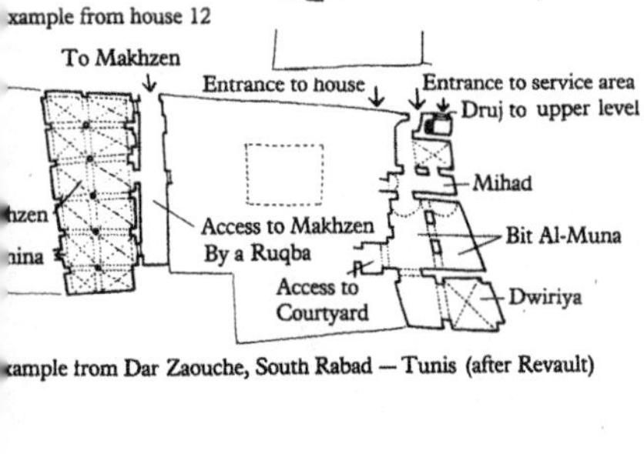

xample from Dar Zaouche, South Rabad — Tunis (after Revault)

Figure 39 Urban form: housing — a morphological analysis of an island in Tunis

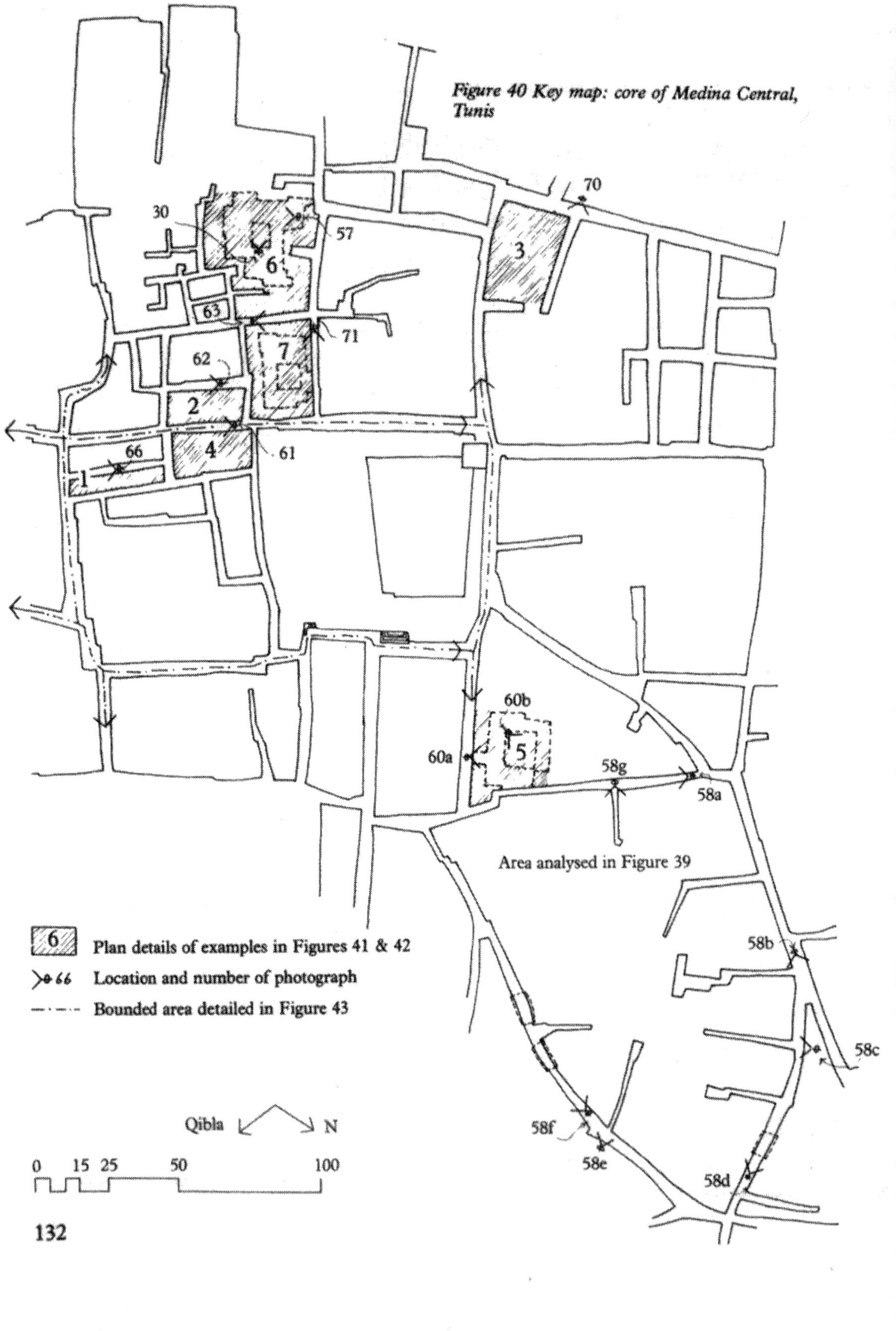

Figure 40 Key map: core of Medina Central, Tunis

Figure 40 is a key map indicating the context and location of specific examples illustrated below:

Cluster of shops back to back along a common party wall, see Figure 41
Example 1: narrow island 5 m wide. Average 2 m clear depth for shops.
Example 2: medium-depth island 11 m wide. Average 4 m clear depth for shops.
Example 3: wide island 22 m in width. Shop depth ranges from 6 to 13 m.

Cluster of shops around an inner space utilized for various purposes, see Figure 42
Example 4: shops surrounding inner covered space used for storage of merchandise. Size of space 5 by 16 m.
Example 5: Funduk al-Attarine, see Plates 60(a) and 60(b), located on a corner and surrounded by shops on the entrance and corner sides. A house attaches itself to its back. Size of Funduk 21 by 25 m.
Example 6: Wekala Ben Ghorbal, surrounded on four sides by shops of various

Figure 41 Urban form: the Suq, showing the clusters of back to back shops

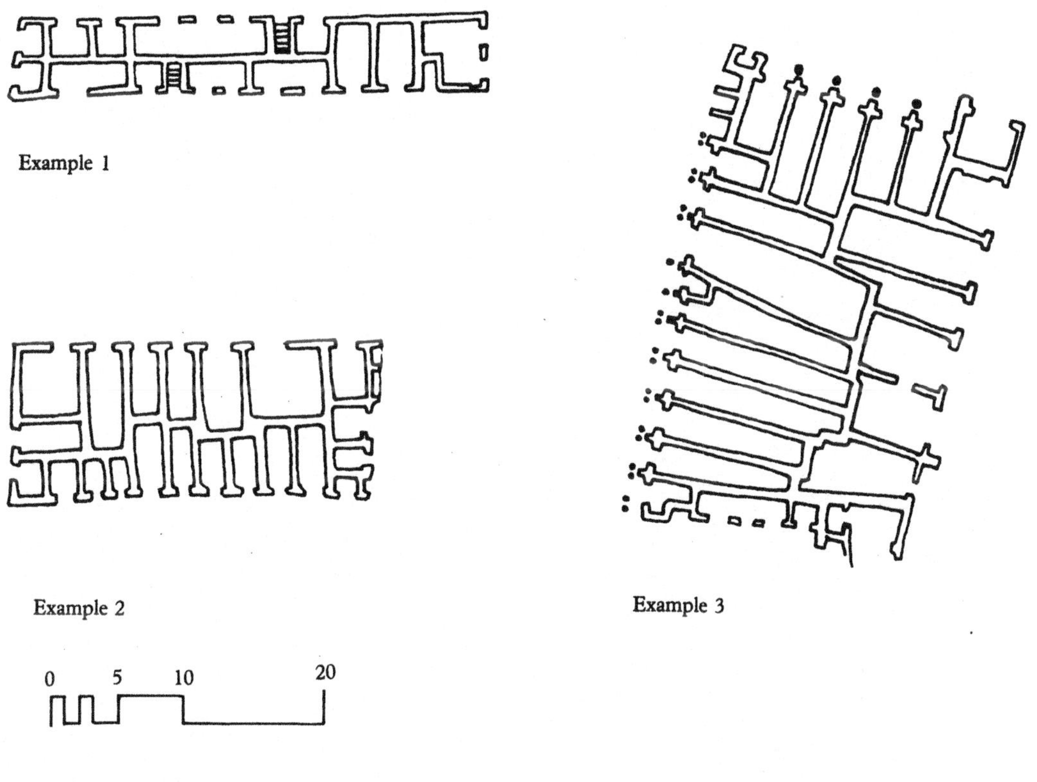

Figure 42 Urban form: the Suq, showing the clusters of shops surrounding buildings for other uses

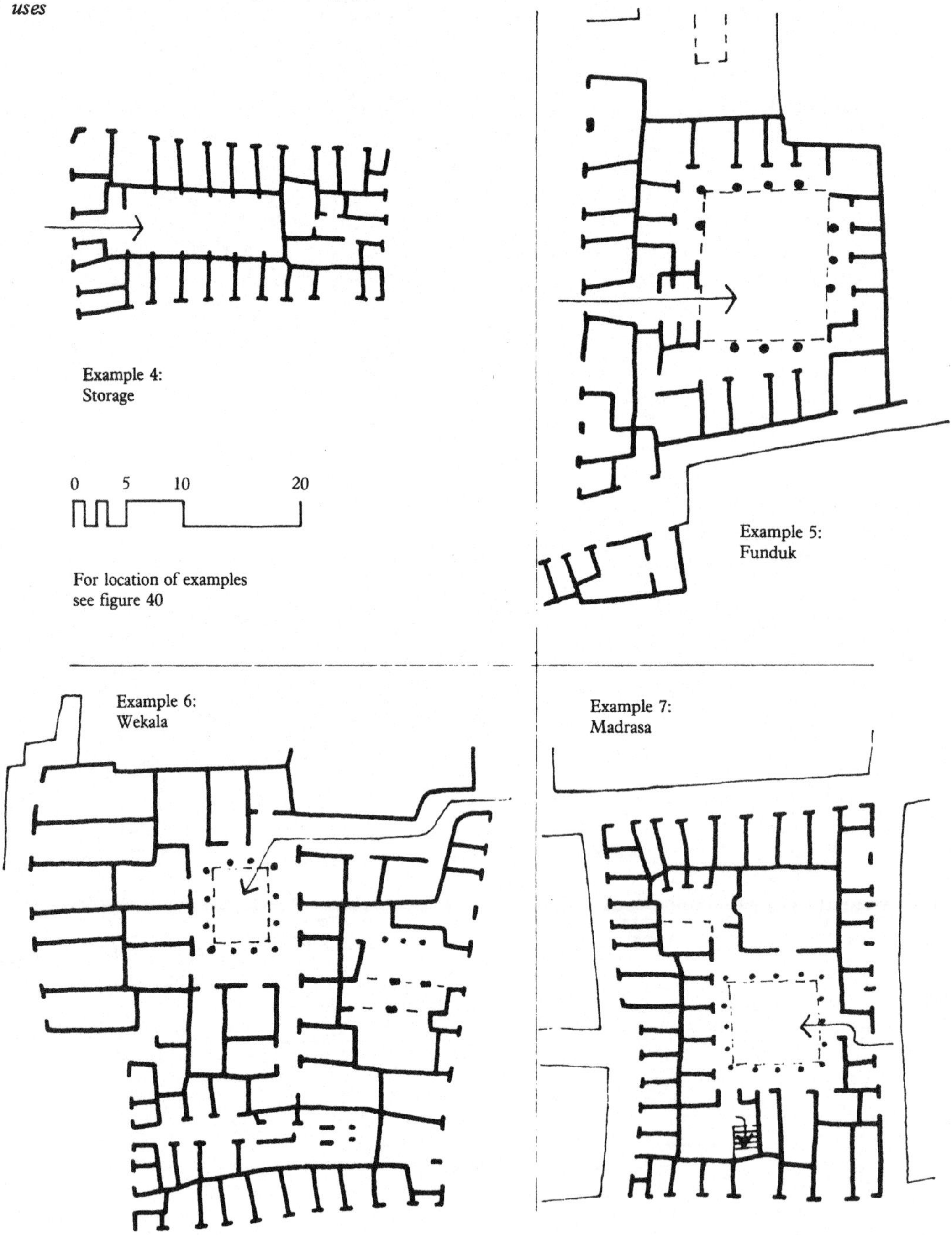

Figure 43 Urban form: the Suq, showing the area of Suq south of Zaytuna Mosque, Tunis

sizes. Access is through a long Driba to the courtyard (see Plates 57 and 30). Width and length of Wekala is 17 by 25 m.
Example 7: Madrasa al-Mouradiya, also known as Madrasa al-Tawba. Surrounded on four sides by shops with access from Suq des Etoffes. Dimensions of Madrasa 15 by 25 m.

Various types of clusters and shop configurations forming a significant area of the Suq

Figure 43 illustrates the Suq area south of Zaytuna mosque, approximately 66 by 80 m including half the perimeter streets. It is bounded on the north by Rue de la Laine, the south by Suq el-Kachachine, the east by Rue des Libraires, and west by Suq des Femmes. Three Madrasas linked together to form a large complex utilize the eastern portion of this large island and take up almost half its area. The diagram indicates the following:

1 The hierarchy of the access system: namely the primary, intermediate, and secondary streets.
2 Location of Suq gates forming a part of an overall lock-up system for the whole Suq.[31]
3 Utilization of mosque and Madrasa exterior walls for shops forming an integral part of the total Suq system. The shops are located on the west and north sides of the Madrasa complex creating a Z-shape formation. The south and west walls of the Zaytuna mosque are used by shops as indicated.
4 Location of covered portions of streets by vaults or Sabats as indicated. They are a portion of the total street coverage system shown in Figure 10.

These examples point out the versatility of the housing and Suq elements and illustrate the organizational/urban form diversity created. Also a major contributing factor in this regard is the nature of the building process which was discussed in Chapter 1. Careful examination and analysis of other parts of Tunis and various Islamic cities will reveal endless organizational samples and their related urban form qualities.

Chapter 4

Conclusions

The Islamic city first became a serious subject of research around the first quarter of this century. Since then various studies have been undertaken and articles written. By the late 1960s distinct approaches and methodologies of study were identified, which could be summarized as the existence of an Islamic city pattern, the precise study of local conditions, and the examination of a specific building type such as the mosque.[1]

The general trend by Western scholars was during the early years of this century, to accept Islam as a basis for the interpretation of the morphological pattern. This basis, however, was narrow and dependent largely on a descriptive analysis of urban form/organization and architectural design. Some scholars within the last fifteen to twenty years have tended to play down the importance of Islam in the interpretation of the city.[2]

This study demonstrates that the earlier reliance on Islam as a basis for analysis was essentially sound. However, the results of their work are somewhat distorted, largely because of their emphasis and methodology. They generally followed a descriptive approach to the physical manifestation of the city without equal emphasis and analysis of the processes of building and urbanization.

To illuminate further the situation as it existed until recently reference is made to a recent study whose intent was to disqualify the attribute 'Islamic' and replace it with 'Oriental', based on the evidence that the urban form and organizational system prevalent in most traditional cities within the Islamic world, particularly in the Middle East, originated in pre-Islamic models.[3] This observation is accurate, and in my brief study of pre-Islamic times, I found that the most predominant organizational pattern of cities in the Islamic world utilized the Mesopotamian model which dates back to about 3,000 years before Islam.

This work reveals that the roots of the structure and the unity prevalent in the numerous cities within the vast Islamic world are primarily attributable to the relationship of parts and the resultant structuring system which is generated and sustained by a set of building principles and guidelines. These are the product of the *Fiqh*: the mechanism interpreting and applying the value system of the *Shari'a* (Islamic divine law) within the processes of building and urban development. Hence all cities in the Arab and Islamic world inhabited predominantly by Muslims share an Islamic identity which is directly due to the application of Shari'a values in the process of city building.

The other revelation concerns the nature and impact of the Fiqh as a mechanism. Its primary sources, the *Qur'an* and the *Sunna* (or traditions of the Prophet), are crucial for the transfer of the value system to design and urban form. An analogy can be made to 'values' and 'goals' in contemporary urban planning practice. In its capacity as a guiding framework for action, it was based on elucidating *intent* and indicating criteria for *performance* for various problems and conditions. It did not rely on prescriptive standards. Therefore its impact on the built form was distinctly different from a mechanism based on numerical standards, as with contemporary Western zoning and subdivision regulations. Its use permitted diversity and complexity within the urban environment, particularly at the neighbourhood scale, and in fact such diversity and complexity occurred.

Unlike current zoning laws which are centrally created and applied at the local level without being responsive to specific micro conditions, the Fiqh mechanism, although linked to a single source — the *Shari'a* — developed various subtle interpretations within regions of the Islamic world. This was due to the interpretations of various Islamic schools of law and the respect that was granted to the *Urf* or local traditions. By its nature, therefore, this mechanism was very responsive to the particular conditions occurring at the neighbourhood scale, and in effect functioned as a guide for participation and decision making in matters of building, particularly among proximate neighbours.

Another important attribute of the Arabic–Islamic city is the unconscious emergence and definition of a vocabulary of terms integrating the form and function of the physical components of buildings and of the urban elements/building types of the city. This vocabulary tended to be operative regionally and understood by users and builders. It acted as an effective communication tool between people involved in the building process.

Both the vocabulary or design language as presented in Chapter 2 and the Fiqh mechanism as elaborated in Chapter 1 tended to perpetuate and sustain urban form and the organizational/planning system. The former also encouraged the re-use and improvement of design elements and planning features. It should also be noted that the interaction between the 'Fiqh' and the design language created a certain tradition of design and three-dimensional features which could be described as 'patterns' in the same sense as put forward in *A Pattern Language.*[4] Few of these patterns had specific terms identifying them, and most were not isolated by terms or recognized as entities.

These attributes explain how local diversity of urban form, building types, and design was achieved within macro organizational and built form systems having astonishing similarities throughout the Islamic world. The spread of the predominant morphological system was initially made possible by the rapid expansion of Islam from Arabia in the seventh and eighth centuries. Its coherence and maturity, at all scales of the built environment, coincided with the maturity of Islamic civilization. The latter phenomenon was the result of communication activities which, considering the conditions of the time, was remarkably intensive. An important outcome of communication and the exchange of knowledge was the spread of the Fiqh literature, including its considerations for building activity. Design approaches and concepts and their related three-dimensional characteristics were also transmitted in the intense exchange of information and ideas. The travels of merchants contributed substantially to this process.

To summarize, this study demonstrates the importance of law through building guidelines as a prime factor which shaped the traditional Arabic–Islamic city. It de-emphasizes the climate as a major determining factor. Even though the similarity of climate contributed to the uniform urban pattern, the Fiqh guidelines and the physical organizational pattern had the primary impact. This conclusion takes into account the subtle difference in approach of the major Islamic schools of law, and the similarities and differences in the availability of building materials, local or regional traditions of building technology, and influences on architectural style.

The study also shows that similarity of technology (particularly the means of transportation) played a crucial role in unifying the Arabic–Islamic city. In this case the camel was the primary means for distant transportation and for carrying heavy loads in the Middle East between the fourth and sixth centuries AD and was an established fact during the seventh century at the time of the Prophet Mohammad.[5] This fact in conjunction with the dynamics of the building process determined the resulting street patterns. These were directly influenced by the size and capabilities of the camel, which explains for example, changes in level and rounding off building corners. All these factors may dispel the interpretations and dogmatic assertions by representatives of disciplines not immediately relevant to the issue at hand.[6]

Finally, the following question must be posed: how can we apply the knowledge gained to contemporary cities and architecture in the Arab and Islamic world, so that they can emerge with the positive attributes of and connection to a great heritage and experience extending back at least ten centuries?

The answer to the above question requires a separate investigation. However, the arguments presented earlier demonstrate that the key lies in the transmission of societal values through a legal mechanism with attributes similar to those of the Fiqh, and through the institution of building processes which are more responsive to that end. This is particularly crucial in light of technological change, availability of a variety of building materials and construction techniques, as well as the whims of fashion and style which, primarily, are imported from other cultures.

Since the contemporary Arab and Islamic worlds are made up largely of independent political entities which do not necessarily share similar priorities, then surely for cultural reasons and as an interim measure, they should address this question and make the necessary modifications in their building processes wihin the specific constraints of each individual country. All can benefit from a common strong heritage. This approach could be pursued while working towards a more unified distant goal in dealing with this and other important cultural issues. In this suggested scenario, schools of architectural and urban planning in the Arab and Islamic countries will play a crucial role.

Suggestions for future research

Many ideas occurred to me during the research and preparation of this work. I will list the primary ideas and/or topics that I feel are important to undertake. These are historical or traditional aspects of the Arabic-Islamic city and studies needed for application today and in the near future. Needless to say, some would require the information and experience provided by studies of the first group, as in this work.

Historical or traditional aspects

1 *Hisba.* The institution, areas of its jurisdiction and responsibilities, impact on urban management. Overlap and/or interaction with Kadi's realm of jurisdiction, etc.
2 *Waqf (Habous).* Impact of physical fixedness of buildings or parts of a building on urban form. Impact on growth and change. What are the lessons for us today, such as in urban development and economics.
3 *Allocation of land.* Its ownership, principles of land taxation and its impact on the city's economy, size, and real-estate transactions.
4 *Surveying and engineering techniques* which were used in building and construction.
5 *Building construction techniques.* Combination of materials, mixtures used, etc. Their attributes and limitations.
6 *Water extraction.* Techniques utilized and experience/knowledge accumulated in locating and transporting water.
7 *Traditional energy-saving practices and techniques*, for example the recycling of building materials, the utilization of water, cooling devices such as wind towers and disposal methods of human and animal excrement.
8 *Symbolic manifestations* exercized in the building process and externalized in the built form.
9 A comparative analysis of 'solutions' and guidelines between the schools of law and their manifestations in physical differences to the same problem.
10 A complete documentation of design languages used within major regions of the Arab and Islamic world, indicating sources of terms, their meaning, and physical interpretation as building and urban elements.
11 An atlas of major building types and cities, drawn to the same scale and presented in plans, elevations and sections for the buildings, and maps drawn in the same format and colours for the cities, supplemented with the necessary aerial photographs.

Studies required for our contemporary context

1 A comparative study of existing building codes and regulations in the Arab and Islamic countries including the identification of their origins, and impacts on development. The information is to be used as a basis for developing model prototype building codes and performance criteria, derived from the traditional Fiqh. It also takes into account the experience of the various countries since the early years of this century.
2 An examination of available contemporary technology, its direct use or adaptation to urban design patterns which are derived from the traditional experience. The objective is to increase comfort and amenity, for example by a retractable roof for the courtyard, fountains and pools which recycle their water or utilize it for other purposes. The filtration and recycling of waste water.
3 Development and integration of passive cooling and heating systems into a physical organizational pattern.
4 Development of detailed prototype designs for various building types, based on the recycling of the traditional experience.
5 Development of a new curriculum for the teaching of architecture and urban design for the specific requirements of the Arab and Islamic countries.

The above are only a few suggetions of what should be undertaken immediately for this field. Long lists of topics such as these could be drawn up for other disciplines. If rich Arab and Islamic countries would spend a fraction of their wealth on such studies and subsequently implement their relevant findings, we could witness a social, economic and total cultural re-orientation within two generations. This would make the Islamic culture an active contributor to contemporary world civilization, just as it was centuries ago. *Wa'Llahu a'lam.*

Appendix 1

Selected Qur'anic verses and Sayings of the Prophet*

*Verses and Sayings in the original Arabic and the translation of their meanings in English were checked for accuracy by the Presidency of Scientific Researches, Ifta, Call and Guidance in Riyadh, Saudi Arabia.

Selected Qur'anic verses

English translations from:
(a) *The Holy Qur'an: Text, Translation and Commentary*, by Abdullah Yusuf Ali. Published in the U.S.A. by Khalil Al-Rawaf, 1946;
(b) *The Meaning of the Glorious Koran*, an explanatory translation by Mohammad Marmaduke Pickthall. New York: New American Library, Inc., no date;
(c) *The Koran Interpreted*, a translation by A.J. Arberry. London: George Allen and Unwin Ltd., 1955.

The translator's name appears after the 'Sura' and verse numbers. The version presented here is closest in rendering to the requirements of Chapter 1.

1 'O mankind! Eat of that which is lawful and wholesome in the earth, and follow not the footsteps of the devil. Lo! he is an open enemy for you.' 2:168 (Pickthall)

« يا ايها الناس كلوا مما في الارض حلالا طيبا ولا تتبعوا خطوات الشيطان انه لكم عدو مبين »

سورة البقرة ٢ : ١٦٨

2 'O ye who believe, eat of the good things that We have provided for you, and be grateful to God if it is Him ye worship.' 2:172 (Ali)

« يا ايها الذين آمنوا كلوا من طيبات ما رزقناكم واشكروا الله إن كنتم اياه تعبدون »

سورة البقرة ٢ : ١٧٢

3 'They will question thee concerning what they should expend. Say: "The abundance".' 2:219 (Arberry)

« يسألونك ماذا ينفقون قل العفو ... »

سورة البقرة ٢ : ٢١٩

4 'O ye who believe! Spend of the good things which ye have earned, and of that which we bring forth from the earth for you, and seek not the bad [with intent] to spend thereof [in charity] when ye would not take it for yourselves save with disdain; and know that Allah is Absolute, Owner of Praise.' 2:267 (Pickthall)

« يا ايها الذين آمنوا انفقوا من طيبات ما
كسبتم ومما اخرجنا لكم من الارض ولا
تيمموا الخبيث منه تنفقون ولستم بآخذيه إلا
أن تغمضوا فيه واعلموا أن الله غني حميد »
سورة البقرة ٢ : ٢٦٧

5 'You are the best nation ever brought forth to men, bidding to honour, and forbidding dishonour, and believing in God. Had the people of the Book believed, it were better for them; some of them are believers, but the most of them are ungodly.' 3:110 (Arberry).

« كنتم خير امة اخرجت للناس تأمرون
بالمعروف وتنهون عن المنكر وتؤمنون بالله
ولو آمن اهل الكتاب لكان خير لهم منهم
المؤمنون واكثرهم الفاسقون »
سورة آل عمران ٣ : ١١٠

6 'O ye who believe, eat not up your property among yourselves in vanities, but let there be amongst you traffic and trade by mutual goodwill. Nor kill [or destroy] yourselves: for verily God hath been to you most Merciful.' 4:29 (Ali)

« يا ايها الذين آمنوا لا تأكلوا أموالكم بينكم
بالباطل إلا أن تكون تجارة عن تراض منكم
ولا تقتلوا انفسكم إن الله كان بكم رحيماً »
سورة النساء ٤ : ٢٩

7 'And serve Allah. Ascribe no thing as partner unto Him. [Show] kindness unto parents, and unto near kindred, and orphans, and the needy, and unto the neighbour who is of kin [unto you] and the neighbour who is not of kin, and the fellow-traveller and the wayfarer and [the slaves] whom your right hands possess. Lo! Allah loveth not such as are proud and boastful.' 4:36 (Pickthall)

« واعبدوا الله ولا تشركوا به شيئاً
وبالوالدين احساناً وبذى القربى واليتامى
والمساكين والجار ذى القربى والجار الجنب
والصاحب بالجنب وابن السبيل وما ملكت
ايمانكم إن الله لا يحب من كان مختالاً
فخوراً »
سورة النساء ٤ : ٣٦

8 'O ye who believe, fulfil [all] obligations. Lawful unto you [for food] are all four-footed animals, with the exceptions named, but animals of the chase are forbidden while ye are in the Sacred Precincts or in pilgrim garb, for God doth command according to His Will and Plan.' 5:1 (Ali)

« يا ايها الذين آمنوا اوفوا بالعقود احلت لكم
بهيمة الانعام إلا ما يتلى عليكم غير محلى
الصيد وانتم حرم إن الله يحكم ما يريد »
سورة المائدة ٥ : ١

9 'There is not an animal [that lives] on the earth, nor a being that flies on its wings, but [forms part of] communities like you. Nothing have we omitted from the Book, and they, [all] shall be gathered to their Lord in the end.' 6:38 (Ali)

« وما من دابة في الارض ولا طائر يطير
بجناحه إلا امم امثالكم ما فرطنا فى الكتاب
من شيء ثم الى ربهم يحشرون »
سورة الانعام ٦ : ٣٨

10 'O children of Adam, wear your beautiful apparel at every time and place of prayer; eat and drink, but waste not by excess, for God loveth not the wasters.' 7:31 (Ali)

« يا بنى آدم خذوا زينتكم عند كل مسجد
وكلوا واشربوا ولا تسرفوا انه لا يحب
المسرفين »
سورة الاعراف ٧ : ٣١

11 'Say: "Who has forbidden the ornament of God which He brought forth for His servants, and the good things of His providing?" Say: "These, on the Day of Resurrection, shall be exclusively for those who were believers during the life of this world. So We distinguish the signs for a people who know".' 7:32 (Arberry)

« قل من حرم زينة الله التى اخرج لعباده
والطيبات من الرزق قل هى للذين آمنوا في
الحياة الدنيا خالصة يوم القيامة كذلك نفصل
الآيات لقوم يعلمون »
سورة الاعراف ٧ : ٣٢

12 'Take the abundance, and bid to what is honourable, and turn away from the ignorant.' 7:199 (Arberry)
Note: The original Arabic refers to the 'Urf' rather than the honourable. So that the exact rendering in view of the contents of Chapter 1 would be '. . ., and bid to what is customary [or accepted by local tradition], . . .'. For a definition of Urf see Note 112 of Chapter 1.

« خذ العَفو وأمر بالعُرفِ وأعرض عن
الجاهلين »
سورة الاعراف ٧ : ١٩٩

13 'And it is God who has appointed a place of rest for you of your houses, and He has appointed for you of the skins of the cattle houses you find light on the day that you journey, and on the day you abide, and of their wool, and of their fur, and of their hair furnishing and an enjoyment for a while.' 16:80 (Arberry)

« والله جعل لكم من بيوتكم سكنا وجعل لكم من جلود الانعام بيوتا تستخفونها يوم ظعنكم ويوم اقامتكم ومن اصوافها واوبارها واشعارها أثاثا ومتاعا إلى حين »
سورة النحل ١٦ : ٨٠

14 'O ye who believe, enter not houses other than your own, until ye have asked permission and saluted those in them: that is best for you, in order that ye may heed.' 24:27 (Ali)

« يا أيها الذين آمنوا لا تدخلوا بيوتا غير بيوتكم حتى تستأنسوا وتسلموا على اهلها ذلكم خير لكم لعلكم تذكرون »
سورة النور ٢٤ : ٢٧

15 'If ye find no one in the house, enter not until permission is given to you; if ye are asked to go back, go back: that makes for greater purity for yourselves, and God knows well all that ye do.' 24:28 (Ali)

« فإن لم تجدوا فيها احدا فلا تدخلوها حتى يؤذن لكم وإن قيل لكم ارجعوا فارجعوا هو أزكى لكم والله بما تعملون عليم »
سورة النور ٢٤ : ٢٨

16 'Say to the believers that they should lower their gaze and guard their modesty, that will make for greater purity for them, and God is well acquainted with all that they do.' 24:30 (Ali)

« قل للمؤمنين يغضوا من ابصارهم ويحفظوا فروجهم ذلك أزكى لهم إن الله خبير بما يصنعون »
سورة النور ٢٤ : ٣٠

17 'And diminish not the goods of the people, and do not mischief in the earth working corruption.' 26:183 (Arberry)

« ولا تبخسوا الناس أشياءهم ولا تعثوا في الارض مفسدين »
سورة الشعراء ٢٦ : ١٨٣

18 'Then watch thou for the day that the sky will bring forth a kind of smoke plainly visible.' 44:10 (Ali)

« فارتقب يوم تأتي السماء بدخان مبين »
سورة الدخان ٤٤ : ١٠

19 'Enveloping the people: this will be a penalty grievous.' 44:11 (Ali)

« يغشى الناس هذا عذاب اليم »
سورة الدخان ٤٤ : ١١

Selected Sayings of the Prophet

All sayings that I have translated to English were extracted from reference numbers 2–10 listed at the end of this Appendix. The original narrator or Hadith source is indicated after each saying, followed in brackets by the number and page of the reference from which the saying is taken. All but eight sayings are linked to the principles and guidelines listed on pp. 19, 20 and 22 of Chapter 1. I have indicated the relevance of Sayings 21, 22, 28, 56, 57, 58, 59 and 60 as they are not linked to specific principles in Chapter 1. The use of terms in the masculine encompass in all instances the feminine gender.

1 'Keep yourselves clean as Islam is clean.' Ibn Habban (Ref. 7, p. 79)

« تنظفوا فان الاسلام نظيف »

ابن حبان

2 'Cleanliness encourages believing, and the believer's place is in Paradise.' al-Tabarani (Ref. 7, p. 79)

« النظافة تـدعو إلى الايـان ، والايمان مـع صاحبه في الجنة »

الطبراني

3 'God be praised is good and He loves goodness, clean and He loves cleanliness, generous and He loves generosity, perfect and He loves perfection, so clean your "fina"...' al-Termedhi (Ref. 7, p. 94). *Note*: For a description of 'Fina' see p. 27, Chapter 1.

« إن الله تعالى طيب يحب الطيب ، نـظيف يحب النظافة ، كريم يحب الكرم ، جواد يحب الجود ، فنظفوا أفنيتكم .... »

الترمذي

4 'If you disagree about the width of a street, make it seven cubits.' Muslim via Abu-Hurairah (Ref. 8 Vol. II, p. 238)

« اذا اختلفتم في الطريق جعل عرضه سبعة أذرع »

مسلم عن ابي هريرة

5 'Avoid sitting on thoroughfares', they said it is difficult to avoid as it is our gathering places where we spend time talking, 'but if you insist then you should respect the rights of thoroughfares'. What are these rights they asked, 'Avoid staring, do not create harm, salute back to those who salute you, bid to honour and forbid dishonour.' Abu Said al-Khadari (Ref. 6, p. 284)

« اياكم والجلوس على الطرقات » فقالوا
مالنا بد انما هي مجالسنا نتحدث فيها « فاذا
أبيتم إلا المجالس فاعطوا الطريق حقها »
قالوا وما حق الطريق « غض البصر وكف
الاذى ورد السلام وامر بالمعروف ونهى عن
المنكر »

أبى سعيد الخدري

6 'If a man is walking in a street and finds a branch of thorns and removes it, then God will thank him and forgive him.' Abu-Hurairah (Ref. 6, p. 285)

« بينما رجل يمشى بطريق وجد غصن شوك
فاخذه فشكر الله له فغفر له »

أبي هريرة

7 'If somebody cuts a tree, God will place his head in fire.' Abu Dawood via Abdullah Ben-Hubaish (Ref. 8 Vol. II, p. 238). This interpretation is provided by the same reference: a tree which provides shade to the traveller and to animals should not be cut for no reason or by a person with no rights to it.

« من قطع سِدرَة صَرَّب الله رأسه في النار »
ابو داود عن عبدالله بن حبيش
المعنى : من قطع سدرة في فلاةٍ يستظل بها ابن
السبيل والبهائم غشما وظلما بغير حق يكون
له فيها ضرب الله رأسه في النار .

8 'Avoid the three accursed: excreting in streams, in thoroughfares and in the shade.' Abu Dawood via Ma'adh (Ref. 5, p. 45)

« اتقوا الملاعين الثلاثة البراز في الموارد
وقارعة الطريق والظل »

ابو داود عن معاذ

9 'Those who have eaten it should not come near our mesjid. If you have to eat it, then cook it first.' Abu Dawood via Qarrah. (Ref. 5, p. 87). This interpretation is provided by the same reference: the Prophet is here referring to onions and garlic.

« من اكلها فلا يقربنَّ مسجدنا . ان كنتم لا
بد اكليها فاميتوهما طبخاً »

ابو داود عن قرة

ان رسول الله (ص) نهى عن شجرتي
البصل والثوم .

10 'He who takes from the land without rights will, on the Day of Resurrection, be submerged to the seventh layer of the earth.' al-Bukhari via Ibn Omar (Ref. 5, p. 307)

« من أخذ من الارض شيئاً بغير حقه خسف به يوم القيامة الى سبع ارضين »
البخاري عن ابن عمر

11 'If the people see a tyrant and do not stop him, they will soon be punished by God.' Mentioned in the Hadith al-Sahih (Ref. 10, p. 106)

« اذا رأى الناس الظالم فلم يأخذوا على يده أوشك ان يعمهم الله بعقاب »
ورد في الحديث الصحيح

12 'On the Day of Resurrection God will not consider [or support], and will make a man face severe torment who had excess water in a thoroughfare and denied it to the passer-by . . .' Abu Hurairah (Ref. 6, p. 265)

« ثلاثه لا ينظر الله اليهم يوم القيامة ولا يزكيهم ولهم عذاب اليم :
رجل كان له فضل ماء بالطريق فمنعه من ابن السبيل .... »
ابي هريرة

13 'If you deny excess water, you will deny the benefits of pasture.' Abu Hurairah (Ref. 8 Vol. II, p. 310)

« لا تمنعوا فضل الماء لتمنعوا به فضل الكلأ »
ابي هريرة (متفق عليه)

14 'Muslims are partners in three things: water, pasture and fire.' Abu Dawood and Ibn Majah via Ibn Abbas (Ref. 8 Vol. II, p. 311)

« المسلمون شركاء في ثلاث في الماء والكلأ والنار »
ابو داود وابن ماجة عن ابن عباس

15 The Prophet decreed that the flow of scarce water be measured to the ankles by the user of the higher ground, then sent to the lower ground. Ibn Majah and Abu Dawood via Omar and Ben-Shu'aib via his father via his grandfather (Ref. 8 Vol. II, p. 312)

قضى رسول الله (ص) في سيل المهزور ان يمسك حتى يبلغ الكعبين ثم يرسل الاعلى إلى الاسفل .
ابن ماجة وابوداود عن عمرو بن شعيب عن ابيه عن جده .

16 'If somebody plants in someone else's land without their consent, then he has no claim to it or to its initial cost.' Rafi' Ben-Khadij (Ref. 3 Vol. III, p. 250)

« من زرع فى ارض قوم بغير اذنهم فليس له من الزرع شىء ولو نفقته »
رافع بن خديج

17 'Somebody who gives life to a dead land can claim it, and no tyrant has rights to it.' Abu Dawood and al-Darqetni via Ben-Zubair (Ref. 3 Vol. III, p. 251)

« من احيا ارضا ميتة فهى له وليس لعرق ظالم حق »
اخراج ابو داود والدارقطني من حديث عروة بن الزبير

18 'If you wish, retain its origin [*habbasta aslaha*] and provide it as charity.' al-Bukhari (Ref. 5, p. 331)

« إن شئت حبست اصلها وتصدقت بها »
البخاري رواه الجماعة

19 'When a person dies, his work terminates except for three things: on-going charity, useful knowledge, or a good son who prays for him.' Muslim, Abu Dawood, al-Termedhi and al-Nisai' (Ref. 3 Vol. III, p. 516)

« اذا مات الانسان انقطع عمله إلا من ثلاثة اشياء : صدقة جارية او علم ينتفع به أو ولد صالح يدعو له »
مسلم وابوداود والترمذي والنسائي

20 'The work and good deeds of a believer that continue after his death are: disseminated knowledge, leaving a good son or a Qur'an for inheritance, a mesjid which he built or a house for travellers, opening a stream, or a charity created from his wealth and which continues after death.' Ibn Majah (Ref. 3 Vol. III, p. 516)

« إن مما يلحق المؤمن من عمله وحسناته بعد موته : علما نشره أو ولدا صالحاً تركه أو مصحفا ورثه أو مسجدا بناه أو بيتا لابن السبيل بناه أو نهراً اجراه أو صدقة اخرجها من ماله في صحته وحياته تلحقه بعد موته »
ابن ماجة

21 'Of happiness: a good wife, a spacious home, a good neighbour, and a good mount.' Ibn Habban (Ref. 7, p. 94)

« اربع من السعادة : المرأة الصالحة والمسكن الواسع والجار الصالح والمركب الهنيء »
ابن حبان في « صحيحه »

22 'God forgive my sins and make my house more spacious and bless my sustenance.' al-Nisai' and Ibn al-Sunair (Ref. 7, p. 94). *Note*: I have included Sayings 21 and 22 because of reference to the 'spacious house' as a positive feature. The attribute of spaciousness, in my view, could be real in area and/or perceived owing to the nature of the design.

« اللهم اغفر لي ذنبي ووسع لي فى داري وبارك لي فى رزقي »
النسائي وابن السنير باسناد صحيح

23 'No person with an atom of arrogance in his heart will enter Paradise.' A man said: 'A person likes to wear good clothes and shoes.' The Prophet answered: 'God is beautiful and He loves beauty.' Muslim (Ref. 7, p. 95)

« لا يدخل الجنة من كان فى قلبه مثقال ذرة من كبر »
فقال رجل : ان الرجل يحب ان يكون ثوبه حسنا ونعله حسنا . فقال (ص) « ان الله جميل يحب الجمال »
مسلم

24 'The angels do not enter a house in which there are statues.' Muslim (Ref. 7, p. 97)

« إن الملائكة لا تدخل بيتاً فيه تماثيل (أو تصاوير) »
متفق عليه واللفظ لمسلم

25 'God did not order us to cover stone or clay.' Muslim via Zaid Ben Khalid al-Juhaini via Abu Talha al-Ansari (Ref. 7, p. 107)

« إن الله لم يأمرنا أن نكسوا الحجارة والطين »
مسلم عن زيد بن خالد الجهني عن أبي طلحة الانصاري

26 'God does not look at your appearances or wealth but looks at your hearts and deeds.' Muslim (Ref. 7, p. 304)

« إن الله لا ينظر الى صوركم ولا اموالكم ولكن ينظر الى قلوبكم واعمالكم »
مسلم

27 Via Aisha [the Prophet's wife] said: 'We had a curtain illustrated with a bird design and visible to whomever enters'; the Prophet said: 'Relocate this, as everytime I enter and see it I remember this world.' Muslim (Ref. 3 Vol. III, p. 503)

عن عائشة قالت : كان لنا ستر فيه تمثال طائر ، وكان الداخل اذا دخل استقبله ، فقال رسول الله (ص) : « حولي هذا ، فاني كلما دخلت فرأيته ذكرت الدنيا »
مسلم

28 'Do not face the qibla when you defecate or urinate, but face east or west.' and 'If you want to defecate, then do not face the qibla or turn your back to it, but face east or west.' Sahih al-Bukhari (Ref. 2, Vol. I, p. 109) *Note*: I have included this saying because of its implications for the location and design of toilets in any building. The reference to east and west has to do with the relationship of the Prophet's city 'Medina' to the Qibla in Makkah.

« لا تستقبلوا القبلة بغائط أو بول ولكن شرقوا أو غربوا »
« اذا أتيتم الغائط فلا تستقبلوا القبلة ولا تستدبروها ولكن شرقوا أو غربوا »
صحيح البخاري

29 'He who looks into a house without the occupants' permission, and they puncture his eye, will have no right to demand a fine or ask for punishment.' Ahmad and al-Nisai' via Abu Hurairah (Ref. 3 Vol. II, p. 576)

« من اطلع في بيت قوم بغير اذنهم ، ففقأوا عينه فلا دية له ، ولا قصاص »
احمد والنسائي عن ابي هريرة

30 'To those who have accepted Islam orally but are not yet believers at heart: do not hurt Muslims, and do not pursue their faults, because he who pursues the faults of his Muslim brother, then his faults will be pursued by God, and if God wants to expose somebody's faults, He will do so even if the person is in his house.' al-Termedhi and Ibn Majah (Ref. 7, p. 307)

« يا معشر من اسلم بلسانه ولم يفض الايمان الى قلبه لا تؤذوا المسلمين ، ولا تتبعوا عوراتهم ، فانه من يتبع عورة أخيه المسلم يتبع الله عورته ، ومن يتبع الله عورته يفضحه ولو في جوف رحله »
الترمذي وابن ماجة بنحوه

31 'On the Day of Resurrection lead will be poured in the ears of anyone who eavesdrops on others who dislike him.' al-Bukhari (Ref. 7, p. 307)

« من استمع الى حديث قوم وهم له كارهون صب في اذنيه الآنك يوم القيامة »
البخاري

32 'If a man pushes aside a curtain and looks inside without permission, he has then reached a point which he is not allowed to reach.' Ahmad and al-Termedhi (Ref. 7, p. 308)

« ايما رجل كشف ستراً فأدخل بصره قبل أن يؤذن له فقد أتى حداً لا يحل له أن ياتيه »
احمد والترمذي

33 'The analogy of a person who undertakes to execute God's disciplinary laws and a person who is subjected to them is similar to that of a group of people in a ship distributed between an upper and lower decks. Those below have to go up for their water supply and they say: If we could make a hole in our deck without causing harm to the group in the upper deck; they will all perish if they are allowed, and will all be saved if they are prevented.' Sahih al-Bukhari (Ref. 9, p. 73)

« مثل القائم على حدود الله والواقع فيها كمثل قوم استهموا في سفينة ، فأصاب بعضهم اعلاها وبعضهم اسفلها ، فكان الذين في اسفلها اذا استقوا مروا على من فوقهم ، فقالوا لو انا خرقنا في نصبنا خرقاً ولم نؤذ من فوقنا ، فان تركوهم وما ارادوا هلكوا ، وإن أخذوا على أيديهم نجا ونجوا جميعاً »
صحيح البخاري

34 'Do not harm others or yourself, and others should not harm you or themselves.' Ahmad and Ibn Majah (Ref. 7, p. 77)

« لا ضرر ولا ضِرار »
احمد وابن ماجة

35 A man had a tree in someone else's land, and the owner of the land was being harmed when the tree owner entered his property, so he complained to the Prophet. The Prophet ordered the owner of the tree to accept an exchange for it or to donate the tree to the property owner. He refused, so the Prophet allowed the property owner to remove the tree and told the tree owner: 'You are a doer of harm.' Ibn Taimeyah (Ref. 9, p. 78)

في السنن ان رجلا كانت له شجرة في ارض غيره وكان صاحب الارض يتضرر بدخول صاحب الشجرة فشكا ذلك الى النبى (ص) فأمره أن يقبل منه بدلها أو يتبرع له بها ، فلم يفعل فاذن لصاحب الارض في قلعها وقال لصاحب الشجرة « انما أنت مضار »
ابن تيمية

36 'He whose neighbour is not safe from his harm and dishonesty, will not enter Paradise.' Muslim via Anas (Ref. 8 Vol. I, p. 249)

« لا يدخل الجنة من لا يأمن جاره بوائقه »
مسلم عن انس

37 'The angel Gabriel kept exhorting me about the neighbour to the point that I thought he would grant him the right of inheritance.' al-Bukhari via Aisha (Ref. 5, p. 383)

« ما زال يوصيني جبريل بالجار حتى ظننت انه سيورّثه »
البخاري عن عائشة

38 'He who believes in God and the Day of Judgment should not hurt his neighbour, and he who believes in God and the Day of Judgment should be hospitable to his guest, and he who believes in God and the Day of Judgment should speak goodness or else not say anything.' Abu Hurairah (Ref. 6, p. 465)

« من كان يؤمن بالله واليوم الآخر فلا يؤذ جاره ، ومن كان يؤمن بـالله واليوم الآخـر فليكرم ضيفه ، ومن كان يؤمن بالله واليـوم الآخر فليقل خيراً او ليصمت »

ابي هريرة

39 'God will not provide security to the person who sleeps with a full stomach while his adjacent neighbour is hungry.' Abu Hurairah (Ref. 9, p. 132)

« والله لا يؤمن من بات شبعان وجاره جائع الى جنبه »

ابي هريرة

40 'To God, the best friends are those who are good to each other and the best neighbours are those who are good to each other.' al-Termedhi via Abdullah Ibn Omar (Ref. 8 Vol. I, p. 249)

« خير الاصحاب عند الله خيرهم لصـاحبه وخير الجيران عند الله خيرهم لجاره »

الترمذي عن عبدالله ابن عمر

41 Via Ibn Mas'ud spoke of a man who said to the Prophet: 'How do I know that I have done good or bad?', and the Prophet said: 'If you hear your neighbours saying that you have done good, then you have done good, and if you hear them saying that you have done bad then you have done bad.' Ibn Majah (Ref. 8 Vol. I, p. 250)

عن ابن مسعود قال قال رجل للنبي (ص) كيف لي ان اعلم اذا احسنت أو اذا اسأت ، فقال النبى (ص) :

« اذا سمعت جيرانك يقولون قـد أحسنت فقد احسنت واذا سمعتهم يقولون قد اسأت فقد اسأت »

ابن ماجة

42 Via Aisha who asked the Prophet: 'O Messenger of God, I have two neighbours, to which one I should give this present?' The Prophet said: 'To the one whose door is nearest to yours.' al-Bukhari (Ref. 8 Vol. I, p. 251)

عن عائشة قالت يارسول الله إن لى جارين فالى ايهما اهدى قال « الى اقربهما منك باباً »

البخاري

43 'In the Day of Resurrection, the first adversaries are two neighbours.' Ahmad via Aqaba Ben Amir (Ref. 8 Vol. I, p. 252)

« أول خصمين يوم القيامة جاران »

احمد عن عقبة بن عامر

44 'Do you know the rights of the neighbour . . . you must not build to exclude the breeze from him, unless you have his permission . . . '. Ibn Adi and al-Kharati (Ref. 8 Vol. I, p. 254)

« اتدرون ما حق الجار .... ولا تستعمل عليه بالبناء فتحجب عنه الريح إلا بأذنه ..... »
ابن عدي في الكامل والخراطي في مكارم الاخلاق عن أمرؤ بن شعيب عن ابيه عن جده

45 'A neighbour should not forbid his neighbour to insert wooden beams in his wall.' Abu Hurairah (Ref. 8 Vol. II, p. 237)

« لا يمنع جارٌ جَارَهُ أن يغرز خشبة في جداره »
ابي هريرة (متفق عليه)

46 'A neighbour has pre-emption rights over his neighbour's property. If they share common access and the neighbour is absent, then the other should wait for his return.' Narrated from a number of sources via Jabir (Ref. 3 Vol. III, p. 221)

« الجار احق بشفعة جاره ، ينتظر بها وان كان غائباً إذا كان طريقهما واحداً »
رواه اصحاب السنن باسناد صحيح عن جابر

47 'The neighbour has rights of proximity' al-Bukhari via Abu Rafi' (Ref. 8 Vol. II, p. 237)

« الجار احق بسقبه »
البخاري عن ابي رافع

48 Al-Bukhari narrated via Jabir Ben Abdullah that the Prophet decreed that anything that is indivisible is subject to the principle of pre-emption, but if boundaries can be set and access delineated, then pre-emption does not apply. (Ref. 3 Vol. III, p. 216)

روى البخاري عن جابر بن عبدالله ان الرسول (ص) قضى في الشفعة فى كل ما لم يقسم ، فاذا وقعت الحدود وصرفت الطرق فلا شفعة .

49 Muslim narrated via Jabir: the Prophet decreed pre-emption for any indivisible joint property such as a house or a garden. Either partner cannot sell without permission of the other, and if one of them sells without permission, then priority is given to the rights of the other partner. (Ref. 3 Vol. III, p. 217)

روى مسلم عن جابر قال : قضى رسول الله (ص) بالشفعة في كل شركة لم تقسم : ربعة (منزل) أو حائط (بستان) ، لا يحل له أن يبيع حتى يؤذن شريكه ، فان شاء اخذ وان شاء ترك ، فاذا باع ولم يؤذنه فهو احق به .

50 'He who is a joint owner in palm tree[s] or a house cannot sell before receiving permission of his partner, if the partner agrees then he can sell; if not, he should not sell.' via Jabir (Ref. 3 Vol. III, p. 217)

« من كان له شرك في نخل أو ربعة فليس له أن يبيع حتى يؤذن شريكه ، فان رضى اخذ وان كره ترك »
عن جابر

51 'A partner has pre-emption rights in everything in which he is a partner.' al-Termedhi via Ibn Abbas (Ref. 8 Vol. II, p. 238)

« الشريك شفيع والشفعة في كل شيء »
الترمذي عن ابن عباس

52 'He who cheats us is not one of us.' Narrated by a group of the Prophet's companions (Ref. 7, p. 89)

« من غشنا فليس منا »
رواه جماعة من الصحابة

53 'Buying and selling should be by mutual consent while in the presence of both parties. The transaction will be blessed if they were truthful and open, and withdrawn if they were dishonest and misinformed each other.' al-Bukhari (Ref. 7, p. 521)

« البيعان بالخيار ما لم يتفرقا ، فان صدقا وبينا بورك لهما في بيعهما ، وان كذبا وكتما محقت بركة بيعهما »
البخاري

54 'Nobody is allowed to sell something unless he clarifies its contents [or condition], and anybody who knows its contents [or condition] is obligated to disclose it.' al-Hakim and al-Baheeqi (Ref. 7, p. 251)

« لا يحل لأحد يبيع بيعاً إلا بيّن ما فيه ، ولا يحل لمن يعلم ذلك إلا بيّنه »
الحاكم والبهيقي

55 'The Muslim is the brother of the Muslim, and a Muslim is not allowed to sell his brother something that has a defect without disclosing it first.' Via Aqaba ben Amir (Ref. 3 Vol. III, p. 112)

« المسلم اخو المسلم ، لا يحل لمسلم باع من اخيه بيعاً وفيه عيب إلا بيّنهُ »
عن عقبة بن عامر

56 'Injury caused by an animal is an act of God.' (Ref. 3 Vol. II, p. 572)

« جرح العجماء جبار »

57 'If one of you was in the shade and soon was partly in the sun and partly in the shade, then he should rise.' Abu Dawood via Abu Hurairah (Ref. 8 Vol. I, p. 584). *Note*: This prescription has implications for the design of facilities with open seating, particularly in a hot climate.

« اذا كان احدكم في الفى فقلص عنه الظل
فصار بعضه في الشمس وبعضه في الظل
فليقم »

ابو داود عن ابي هريرة

58 Via Jabir said that the Prophet prohibited a person from sleeping on an unscreened roof or terrace. al-Termedhi (Ref. 8 Vol. I, p. 589). *Note*: The design implication is that all roofs and terraces used for sleeping should be screened.

عن جابر قال نهى رسول الله (ص) أن ينام
الرجل على سطح ليس بمحجورٍ عليه
الترمذي

59 'A judge who has done his best and hands down a correct decree receives two rewards [from God], and if he does his best and hands down an incorrect decree then he receives one reward.' Via Ibn Hurairah (Ref. 4, p. 204)

« اذا حكم الحاكم فاجتهد ثم اصاب فله
اجران ، واذا حكم فاجتهد فأخطأ فله أجر
واحد »

رواه الجماعة كلهم عن ابي هريرة
إلا الترمذي فعن عمرو بن العاص

60 Ma'adh narrated that when the Prophet sent him to Yemen, he asked him: 'What would you do if you were asked to judge?' Ma'adh replied: 'I judge by what is in God's Book.' The Prophet said: 'What if it is not in God's Book?' He said: 'By referring to the Sunna of the Messenger of God'. The Prophet said: 'What if it is not in the Sunna of the Messenger of God?' He said: 'I will use my reasoning without hesitation'. Ma'adh said: 'The Prophet patted me on the chest and said: "Thank God for providing a messenger to the Messenger of God who is agreeable to the Messenger of God".' Abu Dawood and al-Termedhi (Ref. 4, p. 205) *Note*: Sayings 59 and 60 illuminate the Prophet's attitude about the responsible role of a 'Kadi' or judge.

وفي حديث معاذ ان النبي (ص) لما ارسله الى
اليمن قال له :
« كيف تصنع اذا عرض لك قضاء ؟ » قال
اقضي بما في كتاب الله ، قال : « فان لم يكن
في كتاب الله ؟ » قال فبسنّة رسول الله
(ص) ، قال « فان لم يكن في سنة رسول
الله ؟ » قال : اجتهد رأيِّ لاآلو .
قال معاذ : فضرب رسول الله (ص) صدري
ثم قال :
« الحمد لله الذى وفق رسول رسول الله لما
يرضى رسول الله » .
رواه ابو داود والترمذي
عن طريق الحارث بن عمرو

References:

1 *The Holy Qur'an.*
2 al-Bukhari (n.d.) *Sahih al-Bukhari.* Nine parts in three vols, Kitab al-Sha'ab, Cairo.
3 Sabiq, al-Saiyed (1969/71) *Fiqh al-Sunna*, Vols. II and III,Dar al-Kitab al-Arabi, Beirut.
4 al-Salih, Subhi (1965) *al-Nuzum al-Islamiyah* (Islamic systems: origins and development) Dar al-'Ilm lil-Malayeen, Beirut.
5 Ali, Muhammad (n.d.) *A Manual of Hadith*, Lahore, Pakistan.
6 Amarra, Mustafa Muhammad (n.d.) *Jawahir al-Bukhari wa Sharh al-Qastalani* (Jewels from al-Bukhari and interpretations by al-Qastalani), al-Maktaba al-Tijariyah al-Kubra, Egypt.
7 al-Qardawi, Youssef (1969) *al-Halal wa al-Haram fi al-Islam* (Allowance and Prohibition in Islam). al-Maktab al-Islami, Cairo, 5th rev. edn.
8 Karim, Fazlul (1938/9) *Al-Hadis*: an English translation and commentary of 'Mishkat-ul-Masabih'; Vols I and II, Calcutta, East Pakistan.
9 al-Mubarak, Muhammad (1972) *Nizam al-Islam: al-Iktisad* (The Islamic system: Economics), Dar al-Fikr, Beirut.
10 al-Mubarak, Muhammad (1974) *Nizam al-Islam: al-Hukum wa al-Dawla* (The Islamic system: Government and State), Dar al-Fikr, Beirut.

Appendix 2

Chronological list of the men who spread the teachings of Malik*

* This list represents the primary sources used by Ibn al-Rami in developing his manuscript. Accordingly his writing was used for identifying these men. Subsequently the major reference used for the full name, birth/death dates, and brief biography of each individual is al-Zerekly (1969) *al-A'lam* (Biographical Dictionary) 3rd edn, Beirut.

Imam Malik (born 93 AH/712 AD — died 179 AH/795 AD)

الامام مالك

مالك بن أنس بن مالك الاصبحي الحميري ، أبو عبد الله

Malik Ben Anas Ben Malik al-Asbahi al-Humairi, Abu Abdallah.
One of the four Sunni Imams, and the founder of the Maliki School. Al-Mansour asked him to write a book which could be used as a guideline for social conduct, and in response he prepared the 'al-Muwatta' (الموطأ) Born and died in Medina.

Al-Majshun (died 164/780)

الماجشون

عبد العزيز بن عبد الله بن أبي سلمة التيمي ، مولاهم ، المدني ، ابو عبد الله

Abdelaziz Ben Abdullah Ben Abu Salam al-Taimi, Muwlahum, al-Madeni, Abu Abdullah.
A Feqih, one of the trusted and knowledgeable in the Hadith. He has a number of works. Originally from Isfahan, moved to Medina and was considered one of its well-known Feqih. He later moved to Baghdad, where he eventually died and was buried in the Quraish cemetery. During his funeral Caliph al-Mahdi prayed for him.

Ibn waheb (125/743–197/813)

ابن وهب

عبد الله بن وهب بن مسلم الفهري بالولاء ، المصري ، أبو محمد

Abdullah Ben Waheb Ben Muslim al-Fahri bilwala, al-Masri, Abu Muhammad.
A Feqih and an Imam. An associate of Imam Malik. He was trusted, knowledgeable, and used reasoning in law (*Ijtihad*). He has a number of books, such as in the Hadith: 'al-Jami' (الجامع) and 'al-Muwatta' (الموطأ). Born and died in Egypt.

Ibn al-Kassim (132/750–191/806)

ابن القاسم

عبد الرحمن بن القاسم بن خالد بن جنادة العتقي المصري ، ابو عبد الله

Abdulrahman Ben al-Kassim Ben Khalid Ben Jannada al-Ataqi al-Masri, Abu Abdullah.
Feqih, he learned from Imam Malik and his disciples. He wrote 'al-Mudawana' (المدونة) in sixteen volumes as a narration from Imam Malik, and it is considered one of the best works in the Maliki School. Born and died in Egypt.

Asad Ben al-Furat (142/759–213/828)

أسد بن الفرات

اسد بن الفرات بن سنان مولى بني سليم ،
أبو عبد الله

Asad Ben al-Furat Ben Sannan Muwla Beni Selim, Abu Abdullah.
Kadi of al-Kairouan, and a prominent leader in the Islamic army. Editor of *al-Assadiyah* (الاسدية), a work in the Maliki Fiqh. Originally from Khurasan, born in Harran (or Najran), he was taken by his father to Kairouan when a child. He grew up there and in Tunis. He was the first to conquer Sicily in the year 212 AH/827 AD. He died from wounds while conducting a siege of Zaragosa.

Ashhab al-Qaisi (145/762–204/819)

أشهب القيسي

اشهب بن عبد العزيز بن داود القيسي العامري
الجعدي ، أبو عمرو

Ashhab Ben Abdelaziz Ben Dawood al-Qaisi al-'Ameri al-Ja'adi, Abu Amro.
During his lifetime, he was considered the Feqih of Egypt. He was a friend of Imam Malik. Died in Egypt.

Ibn al-Majshun (died 212/827)

ابن الماجشون

عبد الملك بن عبد العزيز بن عبد الله
التيمي بالولاء ، أبو مروان ، ابن الماجشون

Abdelmelik Ben Abdelaziz Ben Abdullah al-Taimi bilwala, Abu Murwan Ibn al-Majshun.
A good Maliki Feqih, he was regularly consulted for his opinions (*Fatwa*), as was his father before him.

Ibn Dinar (died 212/827)

ابن دينار

عيسى بن دينار بن واقد الغافقي ،
ابو عبد الله

'Isa Ben Dinar Ben Waqid al-Ghafeqi, Abu Abdullah.
An Andalusian Feqih and one of its well-known Ulama or knowledgeable authorities. From Toledo but resided in Cordoba. He undertook a journey in search of knowledge in the Hadith. Died in Toledo.

Ibn Abdelhakam (150/767–214/829)

ابن عبد الحكم

عبد الله بن عبد الحكم بن أعين بن ليث ابن رافع ،
أبو محمد

Abdullah Ben Abdelhakam Ben A'ain Ben Laith Ibn Rafi', Abu Muhammad.
An Egyptian Feqih and one of the Ulama. He was one of Malik's esteemed companions, and the leading authority in Egypt after the death of Ashhab al-Qaisi. He has a number of Fiqh and other works, one of which is 'al-Qada fi al-Bunyan' (القضاء في البنيان) (decrees in building). Born in Alexandria and died in Cairo.

Asbagh Ben al-Faraj (died 225/840)

أصبغ بن الفرج

أصبغ بن الفرج بن سعيد بن نافع

Asbagh Ben al-Faraj Ben Sa'id Ben Nafi'.
An esteemed Maliki Feqih in Egypt. He was Ibn Waheb's scribe. Has a number of works.

Ibn Abu 'Isa (152/769–234/849)

ابن أبي عيسى

يحيى بن يحيى بن أبي عيسى بن وسلاس الليثي ، أبو محمد

Yehya Ben Yehya Ben Abu 'Isa Ben Waslas al-Laithy, Abu Muhammad.
A leading Andalusian 'Alim (knowledgeable authority). From Tangier, he was a Berber from the Masmouda tribe. He studied in Cordoba and journeyed to the East during his youth. He studied the 'Muwatta' under Imam Malik and also learned from knowledgeable authorities in Makkah and Egypt. Returned to al-Andalus where he spread the teachings of Malik. Died in Cordoba.

Sahnoun (160/777–240/854)

سحنون

عبد السلام بن سعيد بن حبيب التنوخي ، الملقب بسحنون

Abdelsalam Ben Sa'id Ben Habib al-Tanukhi, known as Sahnoun.
Kadi and Feqih. He became the leader in knowledge in the Maghrib region. Narrated the 'Mudawana al-Kubra' (المدونة الكبرى) via Ibn al-Kassim. Originally from Hims in Syria, but was born in Kairouan. He was appointed the Kadi of Kairouan in the year 234 AH/848 AD and continued in that post until his death.

Ibn Sahnoun (202/817–256/870)

ابن سحنون

محمد بن عبد السلام (سحنون) بن سعيد ابن حبيب التنوخي ، ابو عبدالله

Muhammad Ben Abdelsalam (Sahnoun) Ben Sa'id Ibn Habib al-Tanukhi, Abu Abdullah. A Maliki Feqih with many works. From Kairouan, where he died.

Ibn Abdous

ابن عبدوس

محمد بن ابراهيم بن عبد الله ، ابن عبدوس

Muhammad Ben Ibrahim Ben Abdullah, Ibn Abdous.
A pious Feqih from Kairouan. He has works in Fiqh and Hadith.

Ibn Abu Zaid (310/922–386/996)

ابن أبي زيد

عبد الله بن عبد الرحمن أبي زيد النفزاوي القيرواني ، أبو محمد

Abdullah Ben Abdulrahman Abu Zaid al-Nafzawi al-Kairouani, Abu Muhammad.
A Feqih and one of Kairouan's great men. He was the Maliki Imam during his time and was described as the leader of the School and as the Small Malik. Of his books the most well known is *al-Risala* (الرسالة) (The Message) which was annotated and explained by many. Born and raised in Kairouan, where he also died.

Ibn Abu Zamnin (324/936–399/1008)

ابن أبي زمنين

محمد بن عبد الله بن عيسى المريّ ، ابو عبد الله ، المعروف بابن أبي زمنين

Muhammad Ben Abdullah Ben 'Isa al-Marri, Abu Abdullah, known as Ibn Abu Zamnin.
A Maliki Feqih from Albira. He resided in Cordoba, but returned to Albira, where he died.

Al-Lakhmi (died 478/1085)

اللخمي

علي بن محمد الربعي ، ابو الحسن ، المعروف باللخمي

Ali Ben Muhammad al-Rab'i, Abulhassan, known as al-Lakhmi.
Maliki Feqih originally from Kairouan. Edited many useful books, and one of his best was a lengthy commentary on Maliki Fiqh entitled *al-Tabsira* (التبصرة). He resided in Sfax, where he died.

Ibn 'At al-Naqari (542/1148–609/1212)

ابن عات النقري

A knowledgeable authority in Hadith and history. Andalusian from Shatiba. He has a number of works. He witnessed the battle of al-'Iqab in which al-Andalus ended. He was lost during that battle and never found.

Ibn Abdulrafi' (637/1239–733/1332)

ابن عبد الرفيع

Chief Kadi, the most knowledgeable during his time. He learned from the Andalusian immigrants who came to Tunis. His book *Mu'in al-Hukkam* (معين الحكام) in two volumes is full of information and of great benefit. He was buried in Tunis.

Ibn al-Rami (died 734/1334)

ابن الرامي

محمد بن ابراهيم اللخمي ، المعروف بابن الرامي

Muhammad Ben Ibrahim al-Lakhmi, known as Ibn al-Rami.
Master-mason from Tunis, where he died. Author of the manuscript: *Kitab al-I'lan bi-Ahkam al-Bunyan* (كتاب الاعلان باحكام البنيان) (*The book for communicating building solutions*).

Appendix 3

Sample literal translation from Ibn al-Rami's manuscript

The manuscript edition of Ibn al-Rami's *Kitab al-I'lan bi-Ahkam al-Bunyan* (The book for communicating building solutions) that I have used was hand-written and printed lithographically in Fes, Morocco in the year 1332 AH/1913 AD. The following literal translation is of page 27 of that edition which is reproduced below. The purpose of reproducing this passage is to provide the reader with a 'feeling' for and an appreciation of my sources for Chapter 1, and in particular the fourteenth-century style of narration used in the Maghrib (western) region of the Islamic world. That style was very representative of previous written work and continued with minor change at least to the late eighteenth century.

Ibn al-Rami writes:

Regarding a vacant lot owned by a man, and his neighbour builds a room with a window overlooking the lot

Master-Mason Muhammad said: According to al-Wadiha, those from Medina disagreed about this in two ways: Ibn Habib said via Ibn Majshun that when a room or a window belongs to a man and he overlooks his neighbour, if it was opened and used before the house which it overlooks was built, then the man is not disallowed and the other should screen himself. However, if the room or window was built later, then its owner is disallowed and should be ordered to screen the room's door or window or to place an adequate screen in front of it. Ibn al-Majshun said that if the door were opened today and it overlooked the neighbour's lot and its owner wanted to disallow it because of the harm it would create when he eventually builds, then he cannot disallow it before he builds and cannot return and disallow it after he builds on his lot, because the day the door was opened there was no overlooking on anybody and no harm created. It was an earlier act of benefit to its owner. Ibn Habib via Mutarif said that the owner of the vacant lot can disallow the opening if he builds, and he will not lose his rights even if he did not protest earlier. These rights, however, do not apply if the room's owner purchased it with an opening as it is; but the lot's owner can disallow it if the opening was created after the room was purchased, and can do so at any time he wishes. Master-mason Muhammad said that Asbagh and Ibn Habib followed Mutarif's approach.

Regarding someone who opens a window and can see his neighbour's courtyard

Master-mason Muhammad said: From the Darar by Ibn 'At a person is disallowed from building a room which overlooks his neighbour's courtyard. Master-mason Muhammad said: From the 'questions' of Kadi Ibn al-Hajj via al-Hindi, someone who builds a balcony to a room and can overlook his neighbour's courtyard or room is disallowed. That opening must be shut by removing its sill and building it up, because if the sill is left and time passes, the owner can use it as evidence of its pre-existence and can open it again. Kadi Abu Abdullah said and Ibn Rushd told me that when someone built an opening too small to put his head into, the knowledgeable used to disagree. Some used to disregard it and others not. Master-mason Muhammad said: It is wrong because a small opening which you cannot place your head into is a cause of greater harm than a larger one. The reason is that a small opening can be used to look out from without being seen or warned, and this is not acceptable unless the small opening is built in a manner without causing harm. However, if the small opening provides the same view as a larger one would, then the harm created by the small opening is greater . . . .

تكون للرجل فيفتح فيها بابا أو يفتح جاره غرفة أو يفتح فيها كوة
يتكشف فيها على عرصة جاره. قال المعلم محمد اختلف العربيون في
ذلك في الواضحة على قولين ابن حبيب قال ابن الماجشون في الغرفة أو الكوة تكون في
دار الرجل يطلع منها على جاره وإن كانت قديمة وادعى قبل بنيان منزل الدار المطلع
عليها أنه يمنع من ذلك ويكون منزله يفتح على قديمه وإن كانت الغرفة أو الكوة من الحديث
منع صاحبها من ذلك وأمر أن يسد باب غرفته وكوته ويجعل أمامها سترا حتى يوارى بها
ما ادعى الماجشون ولو كان منزل يوم فتح باب الغرفة على عرصة جاره قبل بنيانه فيها أراد
صاحب الغرفة منعه لضرر ذلك فيه إن أراد بنيا فليبن له ومنعه قبل أن يبني ولا يعود الناس
منعه بعد بنائه إذا كان يوم فتح لا يطلع على أحد ولا يطلع عليه منه ضرر ومنعه فيه
حائز ملك وبقول ابن حبيب عن مطرف لا يمنعه إذا بنى ولا يكون له وأفعال الدار اليوم
من الذي من عجم لا أن يكون صاحب الغرفة اشترط أما على ذلك فليس لذلك أن يمنعه وإنما
له منعه عند الإضرار بها عند ذلك فيفتحها على الذي فيه شاء أن يمنعه فيجوز ذلك فيهما
وقال المعلم محمد وبقول مطرف أخذ أصبغ وابن حبيب الكلام فيمن أحدث كوة
يرى منها اسطوان جاره. قال المعلم محمد من الحكم لابن عتاب فيمن أحدث غرفة
يطلع منها على اسطوان جاره يمنع منها. قال المعلم محمد ومن مسائل ابن الحاج
قال ابن الهندي ومن أحدث كوة الغرفة يطلع منها على ما في اسطوان دار جاره أو غرفته منع من
ذلك من جهة أن الغرفة يمكن الاطلاع منها متى قصد ولا يكون هذا مثل الإطلال البستان وطلوع
النخلة لأن النخلة إذا رقيت في موضعها وطال الزمان كانت حجة للمحدث للباب يعني
بها ويجعلها متى شاء. قال الفقيه أبو عبد الله وذكر ابن رشد أن اختلاف الشيوخ فيمن
يمنع من إخراج رأسه أن الشيوخ كانوا يختلفون في ذلك فمنهم من كان يرى له ومنهم من
كان لا يراه. قال المعلم محمد ومن أغلط فيما أرى لأن عمل الشرجب أقوى ضررا من إخراج
الرأس والشرجب يكون بنظر فيه ويرى أنه ولا يحترز منه وإذا أخرج رأسه تحرزت منه وليس
لذلك عمل عند الآن يكون إذا عمل الشرجب انقطع به النظر عن جاره فيتم الحفلة
على الغوليثر وأما إذا كان الشرجب يرى منه مثل ما يرى بلا شرجب فالشرجب أقوى ضررا
قال المعلم محمد ومن مسائل علماء بلدنا كلهم وأصحاب الفتوى في رجل أحدث غرفة
وفتح فيها كوة يرى منها ما في سقيفة جاره إذا فتح بابه فقام صاحب الدار فمنع منزله
لما فيه عليه من ذلك وبينهما سكة نافذة للمارة واسعة وقال صاحب الكوة حجة إن بغلق

Appendix 4

Notes on the benefits of the traditional experience

Various historians consider Napoleon's expedition to Egypt in 1213/1798 a historical and symbolic landmark representing the dawn of a new contact between the West and the Islamic world. Unlike previous contact between East and West, this was at a time when the West was undergoing rapid social, economic, political and technological developments accompanied by the energy for expansion and colonialism.

Supremacy in military technology, a by-product of those developments, enabled the Western powers to penetrate Islamic territories and influence their rulers and governments, setting the stage for ultimate colonial occupation by the end of World War I. The process took 120 years, beginning with Napoleon's excursion to Egypt.

Rapid industrial, economic and technological developments in the West during the nineteenth and early twentieth centuries was naturally accompanied by social and other related changes. Some of those events that concern us here are the development of building codes, standards and planning regulations to address the new situation and realities emerging in Western cities.[1] These events were augmented by the introduction and diffusion of radical technological innovations, such as the motor car, reinforced concrete and steel, and eventually the elevator, which made the high-rise structure possible.

The definition and growth of the 'modern movement' in architecture was taking place as a consequence of and simultaneous with the above developments. This movement, whose history and values are rooted in the artistic and stylistic preoccupations of building design, has created during this century an unfortunate one-sided convergence of design and building values. Western architects have just begun to question what happened in an attempt to sort out the confusion; however, as an example of this manifestation we find that most believe that such concepts as design participation, self-help, performance criteria, and so on are unique by-products of the theory and practice of modern architecture. The truth, of course, is that man has always utilized these concepts and techniques, as this study has shown within the context and framework of Arabic–Islamic civilization.

I believe that modern architecture is at last outgrowing the values implanted by its single traditional parent, that is the single building as art object and the related attitudes of the isolated design solution. The movement is realizing that in order to mature, it must identify its roots in the missing parent. Circumstances in Western civilization have so far kept that parent hidden. This other parent is the habitat of man, its processes and related organizational patterns, which represent the bulk of the environment. Modern architecture is at last growing out of its adolescent stage and entering adulthood, a development obvious in the more progressive Western schools of architecture since the early 1970s. This development will no doubt spread and pick up in vigour during the 1980s and beyond.

Meanwhile, after decades of colonization, the emerging countries of the Arab–Islamic world have been adopting, by choice or circumstance, the outward manifestations of modern Western civilization, such as in city planning, architecture, dress, and music. The relationship between the elements of *Zahir* (outward manifestation) and *Batin* (inward reality) which according to Islamic values should be in favour of the latter, has, in fact, shifted drastically to the former. Adoption, therefore, has been going on without a process of sifting and selection.

An area of drastic change has been in building design and city planning. Remarkably, this process and its outward physical phenomenon has been going on in earnest for at least the past fifty years with no protest or alarm, except the lonely cries of few Western and Arab individuals.[2] This development has been particularly unfortunate for the Arab and Islamic world because Western building and planning codes are rooted in patterns diametrically different from those that evolved in the Islamic world. There are also differences in climate and the socio-cultural context.

Yet the current predominant attitude in the Arab and Islamic world has been, and still is, that modernization and technological developments necessitate these radical changes. Nothing, of course, can be further from the truth; careful study will indicate that technological requirements are not incompatible with the essential organizational features provided by the traditional Arabic–Islamic city. The motor car, utility networks, and other technological devices are not incompatible with an evolved version of the traditional building process/techniques and urban tissue/form, if the latter is deemed useful to perpetuate.

The case study of Tunis has provided valuable lessons which can be divided into the lessons derived from the city-building process (as outlined in Chapter 1) and those derived from its physical organization and urban form (as outlined in Chapters 2 and 3). In the following tables I have listed specific building principles/guidelines derived from Islamic values, identified the primary urban form components, and commented on each of those in terms of their appropriateness and potential use for our contemporary needs.

Building process

Traditional	*Contemporary*
(a) Decisions by rulers: Jami, Madrassa, extending a primary road, Gate, Suq	Building responsibility of government: infrastructure, including for Suq, and public buildings
(b) Building principles derived from Islamic values:	
1 Harm: avoidance of creating harm to others or to oneself as a result of the building process	This principle is usable, but can be more precise as to anticipation of what constitutes harmful

Traditional	*Contemporary*
2 Interdependence: between neighbours without causing harm to others or to oneself. Building guidelines were designed to achieve a state of equilibrium within the framework of interdependence	This principle is usable, in addition to predicting and defining where interdependence is unavoidable
3 Privacy, with special attention to the *visual* privacy of the private domain	Could be eased, but minimum requirements can be established, including specific conditions which should be avoided
4 Rights of original (or earlier) usage	Should be incorporated as *limits* to decision-making when building before others in a specific location. Also as *givens* for others to accept when building adjacent to existing structures
5 Rights of building higher within one's air space	Built-in mechanism to allow for maximum benefit of individual air space, including conditions which would not create air and sun obstructions to others
6 Respect for the property of others	This principle can be easily guarded against with contemporary practices of registration, plan documentation and deeds
7 Pre-emption (Shafa'a)	Primarily to adjacent properties when they are announced for sale. Could be a most beneficial practice. Also possibilities for certain walls, open spaces, and rooms.
8 Width of public through streets 7 cubits (3.50 m) wall to wall	A classification of public streets to be devised, and minimum dimensioning necessary based on standard vehicles. How should dimensioning be devised? Curb to curb? Wall to wall? Including minimum sidewalks and setbacks. (Are setbacks necessary?) The impact of adjacent building heights should be considered.
9 No obstruction of public streets	Problem could arise from parking vehicles temporarily or habitually in certain locations. Parking policy should be clear and simple to follow

Traditional	*Contemporary*
10 Excess water should not be denied to those who need it	With the availability of piped water, this principle has lost its significance. However, excess water can be used to irrigate plants and trees in public areas adjacent to private gardens
11 The right of usage of the Fina belongs to its owner.	This concept can be applied to parking spots adjacent to houses. It can be used to create a green strip, to be maintained by the owner for public benefit. It could also be used as a setback, which is to be maintained by its owner.
Maintenance and upkeep of the Fina	Some other incentive, besides guilt and shame, is required.
12 Sources of smell and noise should not be located near major mosques	Can still be directly applicable
13 Sense of public awareness	Good garbage collection and cleaning system is required. Various incentives for people to keep their environment clean and tidy
14 Beauty without arrogance, which resulted in architectural design and decoration being incorporated from within the private domain; the exterior facade was the by-product of that process. Major entrances were an exception. Exposed facades of public buildings were designed and/or decorated	Public education of what constitutes a quality built environment. A positive argument for the continued use of the courtyard house. Other methods of creating beauty and identity as alternatives to current techniques which are based on style and fashion imported from other cultures

Primary urban form components

Traditional	*Contemporary*
(a) The courtyard house: 1 This house type was usually built to utilize all its plot size, so that the ground coverage of the house would equal the plot	The courtyard house is one of the most efficient house forms for space utilization and for its suitability to the hot-dry climate. There are a great deal of documented scientific studies regarding its behaviour in

Traditional	*Contemporary*
2 Families of varied income (who also occasionally represented different social classes) lived next to each other. This integration was reflected in the agglomeration of different-sized houses to make up various dwelling groups and clusters. It should also be noted that house layouts were essentially similar and comprised various architectural elements. Size, variety, and repetition of elements were related to income and social class; the rich family would have the largest house and the modest or poor family the smallest. Stylistic and architectural design influences were transmitted from the largest type of house or palace downward to others	hot-dry climates.[3] Other studies indicate its space utilization capabilities The contemporary planning regulations in use in Arab and Islamic countries today are copied from the West and reflect Western social values. They encourage segregation based on plot size, which invariably means economic and social segregation. In traditional Islamic societies, however, people of different means and incomes lived next to each other, as reflected in the mix of various dwelling sizes in close proximity to each other. This phenomenon should be encouraged so that Islamic values of interdependence and mutual respect for neighbours, regardless of income and status, is maintained and reinforced through practice.
(b) Circulation: Within the city two street systems were utilized: 1 Public thoroughfares (publicly owned) 2 Cul-de-sacs for private use (owned by the building owners served by it) The public thoroughfares were regulated by stipulations for minimum width and height to allow for the two-way passage of the largest loaded camel. The cul-de-sacs usually had minimum width and height to allow the one-way passage of the largest loaded camel. In certain cases they were narrower, but never less than the width of a single door. The exterior Fina was used: On the *ground* as an area for use by the owner of the wall to which it abuts. In the *air* in the form of a room spanning a street or cul-de-sac, called Sabat.	The most important lessons are: organizational, based on the principle of an access system made up of through streets and cul-de-sacs, and on the efficient use of this system to serve the maximum number of houses. This organizational principle is also economical in terms of infrastructure. In addition to the low percentage of all streets (only 12.5 per cent of Tunis Medina Central), the cul-de-sacs are 13 per cent of all streets, but serve over 30 per cent of all buildings. Furthermore, 15 per cent of all streets in Tunis Medina Central are covered, over half of which are covered by Sabats and the rest by vaulting. The interest in 'air-right' structures in North America over the past fifteen years or so demonstrates the versatility and usefulness of this concept in contemporary society. People sharing in the ownership of any cul-de-sac they use, can provide lessons in land tenure within the urban context. The concept of the exterior Fina also offers a useful example. It could

Traditional	*Contemporary*
	influence the way we allocate parking spaces near houses; the idea of plants which can be maintained privately, thereby lessening the responsibility of the municipality, but enhancing the quality of the environment. The Fina in the air, as long as it did not obstruct the highest passer-by, created the various window and enclosed balcony projections so pervasive in most Middle Eastern countries. These projections and Sabats are compatible with the climate of those regions; they provide shade, light, and shadow variations, as well as visual diversity.
(c) Community facilities 1 The mosque: two types: (i) One Khutba mosque existed for every 2,000 to 6,000 people. These mosques serve more than one neighbourhood or mahalla, both for the weekly Friday prayers, and daily usage. (ii) Local mesjed: a large number of mesjeds are scattered within the city, with more than one within each neighbourhood. They are conveniently located for easy pedestrian access for the five daily prayers. The location of mosques and mesjeds preclude certain adjacent uses, especially those which generate smell and noise or those considered offensive.	Mosques: the design, location, and integration of mosques with the rest of the urban fabric provide valuable lessons for contemporary urban design.
2 The Suq: every traditional Arabic–Islamic city has a major Suq area, which serves the whole city and which, with other facilities (esp. surrounding and/or adjacent to the most prominent and oldest Khutba mosque), makes up the core. The Suq is composed of various sectors, each of which specializes in a specific trade or commodity. The location of various Suqs in relation to the major Khutba mosque is in accordance with the	The Suq is one of the primary characteristics and contributions of the Arabic–Islamic city. The built environment of all traditional Suqs are of the most attractive features which draw people from whatever cultural background. The success is due to many factors which can be attributed to built form and space articulation, grouping of similar trades and retail outlets, methods of display, and the bargaining process.

Traditional	*Contemporary*
nature and type of the commodity within a value-inspired hierarchy devised for that purpose. The basic architectural elements of the Suq design are the *shop* (Hanut), the *vaulting* system for covering the linear circulation spaces formed by the various articulation of shops, and the *gates* for locking up sections of the Suq system.	
3 The Hammam: was one of the major health facilities in the Arabic–Islamic city, particularly essential since the majority of houses did not have private bath facilities, except for large residences or palaces. Almost all the population (male and female) had to depend on using the Hammam at least once a week. Hammams were also used for special occasions and rituals, such as the pre-wedding-night preparation parties for the bride and bridegroom, arranged by the respective male and female friends and relatives. The ratio of Hammams to Khutba mosques and Mesjids ranged from 1:4 to 1:6 with an average ratio of 1:5; the average ratio of Hammams to Khutba mosques only was 1:1.	Hammams: Although contemporary housing, however modest, incorporates facilities for personal bathing and hygiene, the Hammam (public bath) is still an important facility today. The interest in Sauna bathing today and in other health equipment can be incorporated with the Hammam to provide a complete health facility at the neighbourhood scale. The social significance of such a facility cannot be underrated.
4 Other facilities include: (i) the Musalla, which was a large enclosed open space for the community Eid prayers twice a year, and which was located on the periphery of the city. (ii) A large public square might have been incorporated adjacent to the governor's palace or the major Khutba mosque. (iii) Small public squares occurred at junctions of major through streets and particularly reinforcing neighbourhood cores. (iv) A large number of public water drinking sources were donated usually by well-to-do	Other facilities, such as a Musalla, various-sized public squares, and drinking water fountains, are all usable elements for the contemporary Arabic–Islamic city.

Traditional	*Contemporary*
private individuals as a charity to the pedestrian. These facilities were usually located on through streets and decorated so as to make them architecturally attractive.	

I have selected for comment the above urban elements because of their continued relevance to contemporary society. Other elements and building types, which have been omitted, have, in my view lost their relevance or become obsolete.

For those readers who are interested in pursuing this aspect of the study, I would like to refer them to the results of recent research I have undertaken, published in the article: "Islamic Architecture" *Encyclopedia of Architecture*, vol 3, edited by Joseph A. Wilkes, John Wiley & Sons, Inc, New York, 1988/89.

Notes

Chapter 1

1 Coulson, N.J. (1964) *A History of Islamic Law*, Edinburgh University Press, Edinburgh, p. 55.
2 *Ibid.*, p. 56.
3 *Ibid.*, p. 60.
4 Schacht, J. (trans) (1950) *The Origins of Muhammadan Jurisprudence*, Oxford University Press, p. 97, from al-Shafi'i's *Treatis IV: K. Jima'al-'Ilm*, p. 261.
5 Coulson, N.J. (1964) *op. cit.*, p. 62.
6 *Ibid.*, p. 64.
7 Schacht, J. (1955) 'The schools of law and later developments of jurisprudence', in Khadduri, M. and Liebesny, H. (eds) *Law in the Middle East*, Middle East Institute, Washington DC, p. 73.
8 A *mufti* is a specialist on law who can give an authoritative opinion on points of doctrine, and his considered legal opinion is called *Fatwa*.
9 All biographical information in Appendix 2, unless otherwise indicated, is taken from Al-Zerekly, *Al-a'lam: Biographical Dictionary* (in Arabic), 13 volumes, third edition, Beirut 1969.
10 As prescribed by Caliph Omar b. al-Khattab (period of rule 13/634–24/644), and as quoted by Asbagh (d. 225/840) and Ibn Habib (d. 256/870). Referred to by Ibn al-Rami on p. 43.
11 Mohammad al-Tahir b. Ashour. *Kashf al-Mughata fi al-Muwatta* (in Arabic) written in 1360/1941 and published in Tunis by STD 1975, p. 309.
12 Barbier, (1900) (trans from Arabic to French). 'Des droits et obligations entre proprietaires d'heritages voisins' in *Revue Algérienne et Tunisienne de Législation & de Jurisprudence*, Vol. XVI (pp. 17 and 18). Isa ben Mousa, also known as Ibn al-Imam, is from Toledo and studied under his uncle Omar ben Yousef who was Kadi of that city. He also studied in Cordoba under Ibn Isa and in Kairouan under Abu Kassim.
13 Mohammad al-Tahir b. Ashour, *op. cit.*, pp. 308–309.
14 The classic example is Rudofsky, B. (1965) *Architecture Without Architects*, Museum of Modern Art, New York. Since then a number of other books and articles have been published on the same theme.
15 Brunschvig, R. (1947) 'Urbanisme Médiéval et Droit Musulman', *Revue des Études Islamiques*, Vol. XV, pp. 127–155.
16 Ibn al-Imam (trans Barbier) 'Des droites et obligations entre propriétaires d'heritages voisins', *Revue Algérienne et Tunisienne de Législation et de Jurisprudence*, Vol. XVI (1900) and XVII (1901).
17 Ibn al-Rami: *Kitab al-I'lan bi-Ahkam al-Bunyan*. Handwritten and printed lithographically, Fes, 1332 AH (1913 AD). The title can be translated as: *The Book for Communicating Building Solutions*.
18 Al-Zerekly, (1969) *Al-a'lam*, *Biographical Dictionary*, third edition, Beirut.
19 Makhluf, M. (n.d.) *Shajarat al-Nur al-Zakiya fi Tabakat al-Malikiya*, Beirut, p. 207.
20 It should be noted that Kadi Abdul-Rafi was a strict and rigorous judge and that his opinions and actions represented those of a well-established and respected judge in the community. This was largely possible by the overall stability of the times.
21 Spies, O. (1927) 'Islamisches Nachbarrecht nach schafiitischer Lehre', *Zeitschrift für Vergleichende Rechtswissenschaft*, Vol. XLII, pp. 393–421. (p. 404). Also mentioned in Brunschvig *Urbanisme Medieval*, p. 134.
22 Ibn al-Rami. *Kitab*, p. 40.

23 *Ibid.*, p. 40.
24 Brunschvig, R. (1947) *op. cit.* pp. 131–132.
25 Ibn al-Rami. *Kitab*, pp. 81, 82.
26 *Ibid.*, p. 131.
27 *Ibid.*, p. 103. Ibn al-Rami mentions that a width of 8 shiber (4 cubits) is adequate for a full load and that 3 cubits is too narrow.
28 Spies, O. (1927) *op. cit.*, pp. 404–405.
29 Ibn al-Rami. *Kitab*, p. 38.
30 *Ibid.*, p. 45.
31 Consensus in reaching agreement was stressed by Kadis when confronted with problems related to commonly shared elements such as a cul-de-sac. It does not necessarily imply that all parties have to agree, but rather that the majority who agree on a course of action must convince or persuade others holding a different view not to oppose them. Consensus is advocated in the Qur'an, particularly in Sura 42:Verse 38. Abdullah Yusuf Ali translates the reference to consensus in that verse as '... who [conduct] their affairs by mutual Consultation'. A.J. Arberry translates the same portion of the Verse as '... their affair being counsel between them'.
32 Ibn al-Rami. *Kitab*, pp. 45–46.
33 *Ibid.*, p. 45.
34 *Ibid.*, p. 43.
35 *Ibid.*, p. 44.
36 *Ibid.*, p. 44.
37 *Ibid.*, p. 42.
38 This would be a camel carrying a Hawdaj (a box seat especially designed for the use of women). It requires a minimum height of 3.23 m but preferably 3.50 m, see Figure 2(a).
39 Brunschvig, R. (1947) *op. cit.*, p. 135.
40 *Ibid.*, p. 136 and Ibn al-Rami, *Kitab*, p. 80.
41 Ibn al-Rami, *Kitab*, p. 81.
42 *Ibid.*, p. 81.
43 *Ibid.*, p. 81.
44 Pellegrin, A. (1951) 'Le vieux Tunis: les noms de rues de la ville Arabe', *Bulletin Economique et Social de la Tunisie*, No. 59, p. 79.
45 Ibn al-Rami, *Kitab*, p. 109.
46 See Verse 5 in Appendix 1.
47 Ibn al-Rami, *Kitab*, pp. 20, 21.
48 See Verse 17 in Appendix 1.
49 Ibn al-Rami, *Kitab*, p. 21.
50 *Ibid.*, p. 22.
51 *Ibid.*, p. 22.
52 See Saying 9 in Appendix 1.
53 Ibn al-Rami, *Kitab*, p. 22.
54 *Ibid.*, p. 24.
55 *Ibid.*, p. 24.
56 See Verses 13, 14, 15 and 16 in Appendix 1.
57 See Sayings 29, 30, 31, 32 in Appendix 1.
58 Ibn al-Rami, *Kitab*, pp. 25–26.
59 *Ibid*, p. 26.
60 Based on principle number 4, p. 20, of the Rights of Original (or earlier) Usage.
61 Ibn al-Rami, *Kitab*, p. 26.
62 *Ibid.*, p. 27.
63 *Ibid.*, pp. 27 and 31. Ibn al-Rami specifies the method of closing an opening permanently: by removing the sill, door or window, and building up the opening with the same building materials bonded in a tongue and groove manner to all sides of the opening. He warns that if the sill still remains, then it might be used in the future as a pretext for an 'old' opening and therefore might be opened again.
64 *Ibid.*, p. 28.
65 *Ibid.*, p. 27. It should be noted that the impact of a 'recent' opening on a tenant is considered as harmful as if parts of the building being rented collapse and become uninhabitable. Ibn al-Rami clearly indicates this on p. 31, in the case of a tenant who asks his landlord to intercede and ask the neighbour to close such a harmful window. If the landlord does not take action, the tenant will have the right to break his rental contract.
66 *Ibid.*, p. 28.
67 *Ibid.*, p. 29. It should be noted that in Tunis where the climate is not severely hot in the summer, people do not use the roof for sleeping, hence they have no need for the parapet. It is only used for drying clothes or similar utilitarian purposes, and its owners expect access to the roof for such a purpose.
68 *Ibid.*, p. 30. It is clear from this and the previous case that windows or doors should not overlook a courtyard, but they can overlook other roofs.
69 *Ibid.*, p. 30.
70 *Ibid.*, p. 33.
71 *Ibid.*, pp. 33– 34.
72 *Ibid.*, pp. 35– 37.
73 *Ibid.*, p. 37.
74 Ibid., pp. 38–39.
75 The desirability of opening an exterior door on a cul-de-sac in a specific location advantageous to the configuration of the house from within and which cannot be implemented due to a ruling by all those sharing the cul-de-sac, is considered a defect of that particular house. It cannot be changed or altered even if the house is sold to another party. According to Islamic transaction law, it is the duty of the vendor to clarify this 'defect' to the buyer, otherwise the latter could rescind the transaction if he perceives the

impossibility of opening a door in that specific desired location as a major defect in the house.

76 This case is confirmed by Sahnoun's (d. 240/854) version of Malik's teaching in his *al-Mudawana al-Kubra*. However, according to Sahnoun's version, these stipulations do not apply in a through or open street. The Marfaq is identified as that part of a person's Fina which starts from the door to a suitable and adequate length sideways to allow the temporary parking of a camel, horse or donkey for loading or unloading purposes. I could not find any indication as to the exact minimum dimension of the Marfaq. This is not surprising because the characteristics of Islamic law as applied to the building process are of a guiding nature, and very much similar in approach to our contemporary concept of performance specification.

77 Ibn al-Rami, *Kitab*, p. 3.

78 The Arabic terms used for the wall bond are *Aqd* and *Qmt*. The dictionary defines Aqd: to make a knot, to tie, also used to denote the process of roofing. Qmt originates from its general usage denoting to swaddle an infant, or to shackle or to bind a wound. Aqd is the more widely used in reference to the wall bond. The wall bond as an identifying work of ownership is related to:
1 the building process, and
2 the materials used
in the following way:
(i) Since the built form was accepted as the result of an incremental building process, and because of principle numbers 4 and 6 (p. 20 of this chapter), identifying the sequence of development (i.e., who built first) is imperative for adjudicating justly. Ibn al-Rami very clearly states (on his p. 4) that the *Urf* (i.e., the established custom and practice of his time), is when the perimeter walls of a house are established to be bonded together, then that house is deemed built at one time by the same owner, and a neighbour cannot claim ownership of any of its walls.
(ii) The technique for identifying the sequence of development depended on the nature of the building materials used. Traditionally in the Arabic–Islamic city, four primary building materials were used, depending on availability within each region: (a) *Tabya: technique of cobwork*. Earth with which chalk and crushed baked earth or broken stones are often mixed, is rammed between two boards kept parallel by beams. The process of identification in this case was to expose the marks left by the boards; ownership by the same person is determined if the board marks are continuous around the corners examined. (b) *Tawb: unbaked brick that sometimes serves as a facing for cobwork*. It is made of earth and cut straw rammed together in a wooden former. Examples from Abbasiyya (south of Kairouan) dating from 184/800 are 42 × 21 × 10.5 cm. The process of identification was to locate the bonded, unbaked bricks at the corners of the walls which are being contested, or to expose the cobwork which might be covered by the Tawb facing. (c) *Adjur: baked brick*. It is used alone or with rubble. In either case, it is always used at the corners of walls. Identification took place at wall corners by the age, size of bricks, and the mortar used. (d) *Hajar: rubble or rough-hewn stone*. The cementing mortar and plaster are of chalk, sand, crushed fragments of tile, and wood charcoal. Identification is possible by the bond between the rubble and with special emphasis on the mortar used, as mixes from different periods are easily identifiable. Ashlar was also used in large religious and military structures and therefore was seldom encountered in these situations. According to Tahar Ben Lagha, a master mason in Tunis expert in traditional building techniques with whom I talked in 1977, identification between walls — if difficult to ascertain at ground level — would be undertaken by exposing part of the foundation to determine the periods of the walls being disputed. (The four definitions of building materials are from Marçais, G. (1960-) 'Bina', in *Encyclopaedia of Islam* (EI henceforth), (1960-), New Edition, Leiden and London.

79 Taqa is a term that denotes a recess in the wall usually the size of a window and located at approximately the same height. It is usually provided on the perimeter walls of the house due to the adequate thickness available there. A Taqa is designed for storage and/or display purposes, and people sometimes install one or more shelves for better utilization.

80 According to Ibn al-Rami, these five criteria are recognized by the Maliki School of Law, and are not utilized by the Shafi'is. However, the Hanafi School recognizes the following three: the wall bond, the door in the wall and an *adequate* number of wooden beams inserted into a wall.

81 Ibn al-Rami. *Kitab*, pp. 3–6.

82 *Ibid.*, p. 10.

83 See last paragraph of Note 78 above.

84 Ibn al-Rami. *Kitab*, pp. 7–9.

85 *Ibid.*, pp. 10–11.

86 *Ibid.*, p. 11.
87 *Ibid.*, pp. 12–13.
88 The building material is provided by recycling it from the demolished wall, and any additional new material is provided by the owner of the wall.
89 Ibn al-Rami. *Kitab*, pp. 13–14.
90 *Ibid.*, p. 74.
91 *Ibid.*, p. 74.
92 *Ibid.*, pp. 72–73.
93 *Ibid.*, p. 72.
94 *Ibid.*, p. 73.
95 *Ibid.*, p. 71.
96 *Ibid.*, p. 79.
97 *Ibid.*, p. 77.
98 This stipulation is directly based on the principle that excess water should not be barred from others, which in turn is based on the Prophet's sayings and actions. See especially Saying 15 in Appendix 1.
99 Ibn al-Rami, *Kitab*, p. 78. This case illuminates the esteem in which Ibn al-Rami must have been held. For a master mason from Tunis to visit the second most important city in the country and influence the Kadi, he must have been renowned enough to be known outside his urban community.
100 *Ibid.*, pp. 70–71.
101 *Ibid.*, p. 71.
102 *Ibid.*, p. 76.
103 *Ibid.*, p. 71
104 *Ibid.*, p. 77.
105 *Ibid.*, p. 70.
106 The prescribed method is a symbolic externalization of the actual sequence of the flow of waste water and its inherent implicit harm or burden for each of the four users. The first man's channel portion carries only his waste, the second man's channel portion carries his own waste and that of the first house, and so on.
107 Ibn al-Rami. *Kitab*, pp. 65–66.
108 *Ibid.*, pp. 66–67.
109 For a full definition and discussion of Funduk, refer to Chapter 2, pp. 84, 86.
110 Ibn al-Rami. *Kitab*, p. 71.
111 *Ibid.*, pp. 67–69.
112 Levy, R. (1913/34) 'Urf', in EI Leiden and London, 1913–34, 1st edn. The following definition of Urf is by al-Jurjani (740/1340–816/1413) from his book Ta'rifat:

> Action or belief in which persons persist with the concurrence of the reasoning powers and which their natural dispositions agree to accept as right.

In Tunis today there is an Urf Court, under the jurisdiction of the Ministry of Justice, which specializes in Urf cases.

Chapter 2

1 Though the findings were derived from research on the Arabic–Islamic city, the author feels quite confident in predicting that most other cultures would have a similar traditional building language as a basis of their building process.
2 This is an assumption which I have based on an interpretation of my research findings, the rationale being that the rulers, chief builders, and other major figures involved in establishing cities or recycling existing ones would be Arabs. Therefore, they must have used an Arabic vocabulary of names and terms which they must have brought with them, or developed within a relatively short period of time. I found no other evidence on this issue within that period other than the similarity of building design terms used by the various *Fuqaha* (legal scholars) whose works were studied in preparing Chaper 2.
3 An area which used to make up what is today Tunisia, western Libya and part of eastern Algeria.
4 Though the example of Tunis is typically representative, it should not be viewed as a rigid model. There are obviously variations in many cities regarding the manner in which urban elements have manifested their relationships. Occasionally some elements are not utilized or they might be related and located differently within the urban fabric.
5 Al-Maqdisi, (1906) *Ahsan al-taqasim fi ma'rifat al-aqalim*, Leiden, p. 47.
6 Marçais, W. (1928) 'L'Islamisme et la vie urbaine', in *Comptes Rendus des Séances de l'Académie des Inscriptions et Belles-Lettres.* Reprinted in Marçais, W. (1961) *Articles et Conférences*, Publication de l'Institut d'Etudes Orientales, Faculté des Lettres d'Alger XXI, p. 65.
7 *Ibid.*, p. 65
8 *Ibid.*, p. 65
9 Mohammad ben al-Khodja (1939) *Tarikh M'alim al-Tawhid fi al-Qadim wa fi al-Jadid*, Tunis, p. 7.
10 *Ibid.*, p. 7.
11 Marçais, W. (1928) *op. cit.* (n. 6), p. 65. Here Marçais also cites E. Doutté, a traveller in Morocco, about an exchange he had with a peasant guide which proves the continuity of the

definition of the city to this century. Doutté enquired from his guide the name of what he thought was a village in the distance, and the reply was 'That is not a village, it is a city that has a jami and a suq.'

12 Most of the information is derived from the article Deverdun, G. (1960) 'Kasaba' *EI*, new edn, Leiden and London, 1960–.

13 Partially based on Lévi-Provençal, E. (1913–34) 'Rabad' *EI*, 1st edn, Leiden and London.

14 From Creswell, K.A.C. (1960–) 'Bab' *EI*, new edn, Leiden and London.

15 Al-Makrizi (d. 845/1441) *Al-Mawa'iz Wa'l-I'tibar fi Dhikr Al-Khitat Wa'l-Athar.* Vol. I, p. 380.

16 *Ibid.*, Note 15.

17 A detailed study of the Burdj and its development in major regions of the Islamic world is available in Sourdel-Thomine, J., Terrasse, H. and Burton-Page, J. (1960–) 'Burdj', in *EI*, new edn, Leiden and London.

18 See Chapter 1, pp. 24.

19 Pellegrin, A. (1951) 'Le vieux Tunis, les noms de rues de la ville Arabe', in *Bulletin Economique et Social de la Tunisie.* No. 59, p. 78.

20 *Ibid.*, Note 16, Vol. II, p. 47.

21 Based on Pedersen, (1913–34) 'Masdjid' (section 6B)and Wensinck. (1913–34) 'Musalla' in *EI*, 1st edn, Leiden and London.

22 Gibb, H.A.R. (1958) *The Travels of Ibn Battuta* Vol. I, Cambridge University Press p. 14, Note 27.

23 *Ibid.*, pp. 14–15. It is of interest to note that during Ibn Battuta's stay at Tunis, the sultan was Abu Yahya, the great grandson of Abu Zakariah who took office in 718/1318. So Ibn Battuta must have arrived at Tunis after that date, possibly a few years before his departure, which was in 726/1325, seven years before the death of Kadi Abou Ishaq ben Abdul-Rafi (whom he refers to as a preacher) and nine years before the death of Ibn al-Rami. This description of the use of the Musalla coincides with the life of Ibn al-Rami, who is used as the basic source of our information in Chapter 1. Another interesting and useful observation of Ibn Battuta was the way *Fatwas* (a considered opinion on some point of law, which may be issued by any qualified jurist, but can be given executive force only by a Kadi) were discharged by the eminent jurist of Tunis Abu Omar b. Ali b. Qaddah al-Hawari (d. 737/1336):

> It was a custom of his, every Friday after the service of the day, to seat himself with his back against one of the columns of the principal mosque, known as the mosque of the Olive, while the people came to ask him to give a decision on various questions. When he had stated his opinion on forty questions he ended that session.

24 The sewers carried primarily waste water from washing and other such activities from households, public buildings, suqs and streets. Human excrement was collected locally in cesspools. Refer to Chapter 1, p. 51-53.

25 Partial information from Kramers, J.H. (1913–34) 'Mahalla', in *EI*, 1st edn, Leiden and London.

26 See Figure 33 in Chapter 2.

27 Spies, O. (1927) 'Islamisches Nachbarrecht nach Schafiitischer Lehre', *Zeitschrift Für Vergleichende Rechtswissenschaft*, XLIV, p. 401, points out that the terms Tarik Nafid and Shari are interchangeable. The term *Tarik al-Muslimeen* emphasizes its public usage and its underlying intent and meaning are synonymous with the term *people's right of way.* The term *Shari* is used often by Ibn al-Rami. *Nahj* is a term which is currently used in Tunisia, and I found no reference to it in very early sources.

28 The second and third terms are pointed out by Spies (*Ibid.* Note 27, p. 404). The fourth term is used very often by Ibn al-Rami in his book.

29 A good example is the long Sabat over Rue Ben Mahmoud in the western part of the Medina near Suq et-Serrajine.

30 The usual treatment in the eastern regions of the Islamic world is to utilize the brickwork from inside of the tunnel to create decorative patterns harmonious with structural requirements; the exterior is plastered, however. Good examples can be found in Iraq, Iran and Afghanistan.

31 Most of the information derived and adpated from the article 'Masdjid' by Pedersen, J. (1913–34) *op. cit* (n.21).

32 Baladhuri (d. 279/892), *Futuh al-Buldan*, Leiden 1866.

33 The Khutba is the Friday midday sermon given by the Khatib or Imam from the Minbar (pulpit). Arab historians used the term *Minbar* frequently for describing a Khutba mosque. One of two essential requirements to make any type of settlement a complete urban entity is to have a mosque with a Minbar and a Suq, which usually surrounds or is adjacent to it. The specific meaning of the term Minbar is rooted in the Arabic 'nbr' which means 'high' and also means 'seat or chair'. When the Khutba became purely

a divine service and the ruler was no longer the Khatib, the Minbar became the pulpit of the spiritual preacher, and every mosque in which the Friday service was celebrated was given a Minbar, so that in time the Minbar as an object and a term signified the Khutba.

34 See Figure 27 for the general location of Tunis Medina indicated by the dotted lines, and the location of the Zaytuna mosque which occurred at the junctions of the intersecting lines, within the inner dotted lines. Refer to p. 103-106.

35 Grabar, O. (1969) 'The architecture of the Middle Eastern city from past to present: the case of the mosque', in Lapidus, I. (ed.) *Middle Eastern Cities*, p. 36.

36 Mohammad b. al-Khodja (1939) *op. cit.*, p. 7. This could be clearly interpreted as the utilization of population criteria for creating Khutba mosques appropriately located within the city.

37 The Ottoman Turks introduced to Tunis the Hanafi School of Law after 982/1574. However, the Maliki School maintains its popularity and numerical superiority to this day.

38 A ratio of 1:12,000 was recently suggested in Hussain, A. (1976) in 'Masjid (mosque) planning', *Journal of the Urban Planning and Development Division, Proceedings of the ASCE*, Vol. 102, No. UP1, p. 172. A comparative analysis of population structure and mosque sizes in Tunis with contemporary population structure and expected percentage attendance should reveal some of the reason for this discrepancy in ratio.

39 Mohammad b. al-Khodja (1939) *op. cit.*, pp. 3, 4 and 147 mentions 256 Maliki and Hanafi Mesjids within Tunis Medina and its Rabads (suburbs) in the year 1358/1939. He says that ninety-two of those, mostly in the Jewish and European quarters, were not being used since the year 1318/1900 or earlier due to the decreasing population of Muslims in those quarters and dilapidation and the lack of *Wakf* funds to maintain them

40 *Ibid.*, p. 3. Many of those Mesjids were also used between prayer hours as Kottab, a school for teaching children the Qur'an and the basics of the Arabic language. Kottab were also located in Zawiyas and occasionally in Sabats over cul-de-sacs.

41 Located west of the city of Mashhad in northeast Iran.

42 Pedersen, J. (1965) in 'Madrasa', Gibb, H.A.R. and Kramers, J.H. (eds) Shorter *EI* (*SEI* henceforth), p. 303.

43 *Ibid.*, p. 303. Also mentioned in Al-Makrizi *Al-Mawaiz Wa'l-Itibar*, Vol. 2, p. 363.

44 *Ibid.*, p. 303.

45 Directorate General of Antiquities (1960) *The Mustansiriya College, Its History and Architecture*, Baghdad, Iraq.

46 Pedersen, J. (1965) *op. cit.* (n. 42), p. 303.

47 *Ibid.*, p. 304.

48 In those times Tunis was in many ways the cultural link between the eastern and western regions of the Islamic world.

49 Pedersen, J. (1965) *op. cit.*, (n. 42) p. 304.

50 Mohammad b. al-Khodja (1939) *op. cit.*, pp. 171–175.

51 *Ibid.*, pp. 194–197, 206–207.

52 *Ibid.*, pp. 188–190.

53 Naji Ma'rouf (1966) *Origin and Development of Colleges in Islam* (in Arabic), Baghdad, pp. 9–10.

54 Levi-Provençal, E. (1913-34) 'Zawiya' *EI*, 1st edn, Leiden.

55 Marçais, G. (1913-34-'Ribat'. in *EI*, '1st edn, Leiden.

56 Pedersen, J. (1965) *op. cit.* (n 42), indicates that in the fourth century ascetics and Sufis, especially the Karramiya, had a large number of monasteries (Khawanik, plural of Khanakah) in Farghana, Marw al-Rudh, Samarkand, Djurdjan, Tabaristan, etc. The Karramiya also had monasteries in Jerusalem and in Egypt.

57 Al-Makrizi, *Al-Mawa'iz Wa'l-Itibar*, Vol. 2, p. 427, defines Ribat (plur. Rubut) as a house for Sufis, which as a group are called Murabitun (sing. Murabit), who are together because they have a common goal and purpose. He suggests that the idea of the Ribat was inspired by the Sunna of the Prophet because he provided an area of his mosque in Madina for those of his companions who were poor and who had no families. They were called 'Ahl al-safa'.

58 Pedersen, J. (1965) *op. cit.* (n. 42), indicates that Ibn Battuta on his travels usually stayed in them (he calls them Zawaya, plur. of Zawiya), but he also lodged in Madaris, which were generally also used as hospices. Some of these institutions were convents for single women.

59 Al-Makrizi, *Al-Mawa'iz Wa'l-Itibar*, Vol. 2, pp. 416–418 and 422, 423.

60 Pedersen, J. (1965) *op. cit.* (n. 42), pp. 305–306.

61 Refer to the description and discussion of the term *Zawiya*, and to Note 57.

62 Marçais, G. (1913–34) *op. cit.* (n. 55).

63 A detailed discussion of this term is available in Carra De Vaux, B. (1913–34) 'Wali', in *EI*, 1st edn, Leiden.
64 Lévi-Provençal, E. (1965) 'Marabout' SEI, Leiden, pp. 325-326.
65 *Ibid.*, p. 325.
66 *Ibid.*, p. 326.
67 This is one of two Marabouts in the Medina Central which is classified as a Zawiya by the Association Sauvegarde de la Medina, Tunis. I find no contradiction in this, since a number of Marabouts did, in fact, develop into Zawiyas.
68 The Arabic term *Kubba*, literally dome, is also used in Tunis in reference to the Marabout (e.g., Kubba Sidi Bou Krissan).
69 Refer to urban element 4, Madrasa, in this chapter.
70 Maqbara was discussed earlier as part of urban elements within the scale of the overall Medina and its Rabads on p. 62. It is reintroduced here as an urban element within the core area of the Medina Central.
71 Streck, M. (1960–) 'Kaysariyya', in *EI*, new edn, Leiden and London.
72 *Ibid.* The author indicates that the use and meaning of the term *Kaysariyya* in other regions, such as in Fez-Morocco, refers to the central market (for cloth, carpets, jewels, etc) shut off by gates and walls from the other parts of the town, and at night occupied only by watchmen. The word is currently used in Morocco to denote the courtyards, whether covered or not, surrounded by shops whose main commodity is cloth. In Muslim Spain, as in Morocco, it referred to the centre for trade in luxury articles and cloth. In Syria and Lebanon, there is evidence of the use of the term as the 'name of the shops of the wholesale dealers,' as in Beirut, Damascus, and Aleppo.
73 Callens, M. (1955) 'L'hébergement a Tunis, Fondouks et Oukalas', in *I.B.L.A.* No. 70, 2e trim. pp. 260–261.
74 I encountered difficulty in finding adequate and reliable information to locate as many Wekalas and Funduks as possible. This lack of information is substantiated by Callens (1955) *op. cit.* (n. 73), p. 265.
75 Le Tourneau, R. (1960–) in 'Funduk' in *EI*, new edn, Leiden and London.
76 *Ibid.* The author also indicates a subtle difference in the use of facilities named as Funduk in Morocco, where a group of merchants use it to store their goods. The courtyard is shared, and each participant rents one or more rooms. There are no stables for animals in this type of Funduk. Groups of artisans, often of the same trade, sometimes rent the various rooms and use them as a collective workshop, each member remaining fully independent.
77 Callens, M. (1955) *op. cit.*, (n. 73) pp. 260–263.
78 *Al-Munjid al-Abjady* (Arabic dictionary), Beirut, Lebanon 1967.
79 Sourdel-Thomine, J. (1960–) 'Hammam', in *EI*, new edn, Leiden and London. The specific dates for the founding of Basra and Fustat are from Naji Ma'rouf (1964) *Urubat al-Mudun al-Islamiyah*, (in Arabic), Baghdad.
80 Marçais, W. (1928) *op. cit.* (n. 6), pp. 65–66.
81 Sourdel-Thomine, J. (1960–) 'Hammam', *op. cit.* (n. 79).
82 *Ibid.*
83 *Ibid.*, continuation by Louis, A. (1960-) 'Hammam'.
84 Pedersen, J. (1913–34) *op. cit.* (n. 21) 'Masjid' (Section D2j). The author of the article extracted this Hadith from Ibn al-Hadjdj in his book *Madkhal*, Vol. II, p. 58.
85 *Ibid.*, pp. 345–346.
86 Revault, J. (1973) 'Deux mid'as Tunisoises' *Revue de l'Occident Musulman et de la Mediterranée*, 15–16, pp 275-290.
87 For details of both Mida'at, refer to the above article (n.86) which also has various illustrations, including a plan of Mida'at es-Soltane.
88 Pedersen, J. (1913-34) *op. cit.* (n.21), 'Masjid' (Section F 4C).
89 *Ibid.*
90 *Ibid.*
91 Hassan Husni Abdul-Wahab (1972) 'Warakat' *Etudes sur certains aspects de la civilisation Arabe en Ifrikia* (in Arabic) Vol. I, Tunis 1972, pp. 270–271.
92 *Ibid.*, pp. 274, 285.
93 *Ibid.*, pp. 275–276.
94 *Ibid.*, pp. 276–80.
95 Revault, J. (1967) *Palais et Demeures de Tunis (XVI and XVII siècles)*, Paris, p. 69.
96 Revault, J. (1971) *Palais et Demeures de Tunis (XVIII and XIX siècles)* Paris, pp. 230 and 232. More details, including plans and cross sections of this building, are available in this reference on pp. 228–261.
97 Marçais, G. (1960–) 'Dar' in *EI*, new edn, Leiden and London.
98 *Ibid.*
99 Revault, J. (1967) *op. cit.* (n. 95), p. 55.
100 *Ibid.*, p. 75.
101 *Ibid.*, pp. 55 and 58.

102 This assumption should be corrected if and when more information becomes available.

103 Marçais, G. (1960–) 'Bustan, Part I: Gardens in Islam', in *EI*, new edn, Leiden and London. In addition to this useful source, there are other references available on the design and landscaping concepts of Islamic gardens, some of which I have included in the Bibliography.

Chapter 3

1 Hakim, Besim S. (n.d.) *Tunis Medina: An Urban Catalogue of an Islamic City*. Unpublished manuscript with numerous supporting maps, illustrations, and photographs.

2 See discussions in Chapter 2 of 'major city mosque', p. 67 and 'Khutba mosque', p. 73.

3 This deviation is within the traditional accepted range of up to 25 per cent or 45° from either side of the true direction.

4 See discussion in Chapter 2 of 'Kasbah' p. 57.

5 Ibn Khaldun's brief biography follows:

> Abd-ar-Rahman... Ibn Khaldun, statesman, jurist, historian, and scholar, was born in Tunis on May 27, 1332. He was the descendant of an aristocratic family, who for several centuries enjoyed great prominence in the political leadership of Moorish Spain, finally crossing over to North-West Africa a few years before the fall of Sevilla into the hands of the Christians in 1248.

From Ibn Khaldun, *The Muqaddima: An Introduction to History*, edited and abridged by Dawood, N.J. (1967) Princeton University Press. Second paperback printing 1970.

6 *Ibid.*, p. 267.

7 *Ibid.*, p. 268.

8 Revault, J. (1967) *Palais et Demeures de Tunis* (XVI et XVII siècles), Editions du Centre National de la Recherche Scientifique, Paris, p. 75.

9 The wish to hear clearly the call to prayer from the proximity of important mosques made those areas particularly desirable.

10 A useful analysis of the impacts of inheritance laws on the phenomenon of partnerships in houses is presented in Goitein, S.D. (1969) 'Cairo: an Islamic city in the light of the Geniza documents', in Lapidus, I.M. (ed.) *Middle Eastern Cities* University of California Press, Berkeley, pp. 80–96. The complexity in resolving conflicting interests among partners of real estate property contributed also, in my view, to the phenomenon of perpetuity.

11 Cattan, H. (1955) 'The law of waqf', in Khadduri, M. and Liebesny, H.J. (eds) *Law in the Middle East* The Middle East Institute, Washington DC, p. 203.

12 *Ibid.*, p. 204.

13 *Ibid.*, p. 203. In the same source, Cattan mentions that according to the Maliki School, a Waqf may be limited as to time or as to a life or series of lives. After the expiration of the time or the extinction of the life or lives specified, it reverts in full ownership to the Waqif or his heirs. (The waqif is the person who creates the waqf.)

14 See discussion in Chapter 2 of 'Zawiya' on p.77.

15 Lezine, A. (1971) *Deux villes d'Ifriqiya: Sousse, Tunis*, Paul Geuthner, Paris pp. 147 and 148. Of interest is that as a consequence of the ruler leaving the inner city and moving to the Kasbah area, was the gradual disappearance of a large square and street which linked the ruler's previous palace to the Khutba mosque. That street was used for processions and other events. The area was soon allowed to be developed for the Suq and some housing, and Tunis lost forever its Maydan or formal, public ceremonial open space.

16 This framework was used as the basis for structuring the material on cases in Chapter 1.

17 Such as the Tunisian master mason Ibn al-Rami, whose book proved so crucial in writing Chapter 1 of this work.

18 The Medina Central is the older section of the (traditional) city of Tunis which was bounded by the inner city walls. The other areas abutting it are the north and south suburbs or Rabad which were enclosed by their own outer defensive wall.

19 I calculated all data on Tunis. Other data from Lezine, A. (1971) *op. cit.* (n. 15).

20 *Ibid.*, p. 149.

21 Revault, J. (1967) *op. cit.* (n. 8), p. 56.

22 Association Sauvegarde de la Medina (1970) *Medina Oukalisation* (mimeographed) A.S.M., Tunis.

23 Lezine, A. (1971) *op. cit.* (n. 15). See also Figure 31 p. 137 and Figure 39 pp 162–163.

24 *Ibid.* p. 162. The following are the differences between Lezine's figures and mine. Note that the number of houses in both cases are the same for islands A-D and 1-3.

Lezine		*Hakim*
Surface area of island A	5153 m²	5040
Average area of houses in island A	162.50 m²	160
Surface area of island B	9739 m²	9960
Average area of houses in island B	182 m²	190
Average area of houses in island 1	130 m²	170
Average area of houses in island 2	150 m²	180
Average area of houses in island 3	130 m²	150
Average area of 160 houses measured in islands A–D and 1–3	165 m²	185
Houses of western suburb often a square of 14 m on each side corresponding to an area of 196 m². See Figure 39, p. 163 in Lezine's book.	Since the boundary of Figure 39 is not clear, I assumed two boundaries containing 40 and 49 houses respectively. In both cases the average area of the houses was equal to 160 m²	

25 Most children exhibit this tendency when breaking or disassembling their toys and then trying to rebuild them.

26 See Note 78 of Chapter 1 for a brief description of materials and construction commonly used in building walls.

27 The housing elements presented here first appeared in Hakim, B. (ed.) (1978) *Sidi Bou Said, Tunisia: A Study in Structure and Form*, Nova Scotia Technical College, Halifax, Canada.

28 I managed to identify large residences and middle-class houses from information provided by various sources, and particularly by Revault's work. The balance of the houses were assumed to be of the modest type. However, further research might indicate otherwise.

29 For the purpose of facilitating research and cross-referencing, I have identified the houses by the same numbers as used by Lezine, A. (1971) *op. cit.* (n. 15), Figure 37 (opposite p. 160). Houses numbered 3, 9, 10, 11, 12, 13, 14, 19, 20, 21, 27 and 28 are described and discussed in Revault, J. (1967) *op. cit.* (n. 8), pp. 306–323 and Plates LXVIII (p. 304) and LXIX (p. 317).

30 Contemporary courtyard houses can be designed to achieve efficient distribution of uses in favour of living areas by reducing substantially the traditional percentage allocation to entrance and service areas.

31 See Figure 30, p. 110, which illustrates the primary street network in the Medina of Tunis. The streets crossing the island under discussion are indicated, as well as the area of the central Suq which can be locked and isolated by gates. The figure indicates by dotted lines primary streets, which will not be used when the Suq is locked.

Chapter 4

1 These are identified in Grabar, O. (1969) 'The architecture of the Middle Eastern city from past to present: the case of the mosque' in Lapidus, I.M. (ed.) *Middle Eastern Cities*, University of California Press, pp. 26–27.

2 The most vocal exponents of this view have been Claude Cahen since the late 1950s and Ira M. Lapidus since the mid-1960s.

3 Wirth, E. (1975) 'Die orientalische Stadt', *Saeculum* No. 26 pp. 45–94. The author should also be credited for his insight in concluding his article with the following important observation:

> How does it happen that pecularities, pointed out by us, of the oriental city in the course of a few centuries of the Middle Ages have spread out from the relatively delimited area of dissemination in the heartland of the Near East over the whole Islamic world, from middle Asia and the Indus area to Morocco and the Islamic area of Spain? (c.f. L. Torres Balbas 1942–47). Have here certain fundamentals of Islamic law (for example difference between thoroughfare and cul-de-sac, protection of the private sphere of the house) or of traditional social organizations, functioned as a generally acknowledged canon in the Islamic world with a standardizing and assimilating effect? It would still be thinkable that Islam as a religion indeed has not essentially formed the oriental city, that the legal and social order united with it however contributed decisively to the spreading of the apparent forms of the city, as they have been built in the old Orient, in the whole of that part of the world ruled by Islam.

4 The Center for Environmental Structure, Berkeley, California, headed by Dr Christopher Alexander, whose work since the late 1960s has resulted in a two-volume study entitled: *The*

Timeless Way of Building, 1979 and *A Pattern Language*, 1977, both published by Oxford University Press, New York.

5 Bulliet, R.W. (1975) *The Camel and the Wheel*, Harvard University Press. Cambridge, Mass, pp. 14–16 and 27.

6 The most quoted person is Xavier de Planhol, whose views are typical. The following quotes from pp. 1 and 22 of his book *The World of Islam*, 1957 (English translation first published 1959 by Cornell University Press) are illustrative:

> There is a special look to an Islamic city, composed of a tangle of blocks badly ventilated by a labyrinth of twisted alleys and dark courts, the low houses endlessly broken up along their little courtyards.

and

> . . ., irregularity and anarchy seem to be the most striking qualities of Islamic cities.

Appendix 4

1 In the *Habitat Bill of Right*, by the Ministry of Housing and Urban Development, Tehran-Iran, p. 5 indicates that:

> A great number of codes and regulations written to establish minimum standards for housing, community design and urban planning have been formulated in the last 100 years. Building codes, fire codes, health and safety regulations, minimum space standards, and zoning ordinances have all been compiled and enacted into law in many countries. Yet for all their elaborate detail and good intentions, the codes and regulations seem to have had very little impact on the quality of the built environment — on the quality of habitat — and consequently, on the quality of man's life.

2 Such as the Egyptian architect Hassan Fathy and the Swiss Islamic historian Titus Burckhardt.

3 Dunham, D. (1960) 'The Courtyard house as a temperature regulator', *The New Scientist*, September 1960, pp. 663–666. More recently Koenigsberger, O.H. *et al* (1973) *Manual of Tropical Housing and Building (Part I: Climatic Design)*, Longman, London, many parts of which are devoted to building in hot-dry regions.

Bibliography

Abdulah, Samir and Pinon, Pierre, 'Maisons en pays islamiques', *L'Architecture d'Aujourd'hui* Vol. 169 (Sept./Oct. 1973), pp. 6–15.

Abdul-Baqi, Mohammad Fuad, *al-Mu'jam al-Mufahras li-alfaz al-Quran al-Karim* (Dictionary of Quranic terms), 1945, Cairo. Dar al-Sha'ab Press, n.d.

Abdul-Wahab, Hasan Husni, *Khulaset Tarikh Tunis* (Summary of Tunisia's History), 4th rev. edn, al-Dar al-Tunisiyah lil-Neshir, Tunis, 1968.

Abdul-Wahab, Hasan Husni, *Warakat: Etudes sur certains aspects de la civilisation arabe en Ifrikia*, (3 vols in Arabic) Librairie al-Manar, Tunis, 1972.

Alam, Manzoor, 'Ibn Khaldun's concept of the origin, growth and decay of cities', *Islamic Culture*, Vol. 34 (1960), pp. 90–106.

Alexander, Christopher, Ishikawa, Sara and Silverstein, Murray with others, *A Pattern Language: Towns, Buildings, Construction*. Oxford University Press, New York, 1977.

Alexander, Christopher, *The Timeless Way of Building*, Oxford University Press, New York, 1979.

Allen, Edward, *Stone Shelters*, MIT Press, Cambridge, Mass, 1969.

Architectural Association Quarterly Vol. 8 No. 1. A special issue entitled Islamic Investigations. London, 1976.

Ardalan, Nader and Bakhtiar, Laleh, *The Sense of Unity: The Sufi Tradition in Persian Architecture*, University of Chicago Press, 1973.

al-Ash'ab, Khalis, 'Asalet al-Medina al-Arabiyah wa al-Ma'ayeer al Mu'asira Li'takhtitiha' (The Arabic city: traditional and contemporary criteria for its planning), *Afaq Arabiyah* (Baghdad), Vol. 3 No. 1 (Sept. 1977), pp. 34–43.

Association Sauvegarde de la medina, 'Dar Lasram: restauration et amenagement d'un palais dans la medina de Tunis' (mimeographed), A.S.M., Tunis, 1972.

al-Azzawi, Subhi H., 'A comparative study of traditional courtyard houses and modern non-courtyard houses in Baghdad'. PhD dissertation, School of Environmental Studies, University College London, 1984.

Badawy, Alexander, 'Architectural provision against heat in the orient', *Journal of Near Eastern Studies*, Vol. 17 No. 2 (April 1958), pp. 122–128.

al-Baladhuri (d. 892 AD), *Futuh al-Buldan* (Liber Expugnationis Regionum). Edited by de Goeje. E.J. Brill, Leiden, 1866.

Beazley, E., 'The pigeon towers of Isfahan', *Iran* Vol. 4 (1966) pp. 105–109.

al-Bekri, Abou-Obeid (d. 1094 AD), *al-Maghreb fi Dhikir Bilad Ifriqiya wa al-Maghreb* (Description de L'Afrique Septentrionale), Imprimerie du Gouvernement, Alger 1857.

Berardi, Roberto, 'Lecture d'une ville: La médina de Tunis' *L'Architecture d'Aujourd'hui* Vol. 153 (Dec. 1970/Jan. 1971), pp. 38–43.

Berger, Morroe (ed.), *Takhtit al-Mudun fi al-Alam al-Arabi* (City Planning in the Arab world), International Association for Cultural Freedom and the Egyptian Society of Engineers, Cairo, 1964.

Bertaud, Alain C., 'Tradition serving progress', *Human Settlements*, United Nations. Vol. 2 No. 2 (April 1972), pp. 1–12.

Bianca, Stefano, *Architektur und Lebensform im islamischen Stadtwesen*, Verlag für Architektur Artemis, Zurich, 1975.

Binder, Leonard (ed.), *The Study of the Middle East: Research and Scholarship in the Humanities and the Social Sciences*, John Wiley, New York, 1976.

Binous, Jamila, 'La medina de Tunis des origines a la veille du protectorat' (mimeographed),

Association Sauvegarde de la Medina, Tunis, 1970.

Bonine, Michael E., 'Urban studies in the Middle East', *Middle East Studies Association Bulletin* Vol. 10 (Oct. 1976), pp. 1–37.

Bonine, Michael E., 'From Uruk to Casablanca: perspectives on the urban experience of the Middle East', *Journal of Urban History*, Vol. 3 (Feb. 1977), pp. 141–180.

Branch, Daniel Paulk, *Folk Architecture of the East Mediterranean*, Columbia University Press, New York, 1966.

Brockelmann, C., *Geschichte der arabischen Literatur*, 2 vols. and 3 supplementary vols, E.J. Brill, Leiden, 1937-49.

Brown, L. Carl (ed.), *From Madina to Metropolis: Heritage and Change in the Near Eastern City*, The Darwin Press, Princeton, 1973.

Brunschvig, Robert, *La Berbérie Orientale sous Les Hafsides: Des origines a la fin du XV siècle*, 2 vols, Adrien-Maisonneuve, Paris, 1940, 1947.

Brunschvig, Robert, 'Urbanisme médiéval et droit musulman', *Revue des Études Islamiques*, Vol. XV (1947), pp. 127–155.

Buchanan, Colin, and Partners for the National Housing Corporation, Libya, *Housing Design Manual*, 4vols, London, 1975.

al-Bukhari (d. 870 AD), *Sahih al-Bukhari*, 9 parts in 3 vols, Kitab al-Sha'ab, Cairo, n.d.

Bulliet, Richard W., *The Camel and the Wheel*, Harvard University Press, Cambridge, Mass, 1975.

Burckhardt, Titus, *Art of Islam: Language and Meaning*, World of Islam Festival Publishing Co. Ltd., London, 1976.

Cahen, Claude, 'Zur Geschichte der Städtischen Gesellschaft im islamischen Orient des Mittelalters', *Saeculum*, Vol. 9 (1958), pp. 59–76.

Cain, Allan, Afshar, Farroukh and Norton, John, 'Indigenous building and the Third World', *Architectural Design*, Vol. XLV (April 1975), pp. 207–224.

Callens, M., 'L'hébergement á Tunis, Fondouks et Oukalas', *Institut des Belles Lettres Arabes*, Tunis, Vol. 70 (1955), pp. 257–271.

Cantacuzino, Sherban and Browne, Kenneth, 'Isfahan', *The Architectural Review*, May 1976 (special issue).

Cantelli, Maria-Luisa, 'Essai de typologie de l'habitat' (mimeographed), Association Sauvegarde de la Medina, Tunis, 1969.

Chalmeta Pedro, 'La hisba en Ifriqiya et al-Andalus: Étude comparative', *Les Cahiers de Tunisie*, Vol. 69–70 (1970), pp. 87–105.

Coulson, N.J., *A History of Islamic Law*, Edinburgh University Press, 1964.

Cousins, Andréa; Dethier, Jean *et al.*, *L'esprit d'un habitat: architecture et urbanisme traditionnels d'Algérie et de Tunisie*, La Galerie de la Madeleine, Brussels, 1966.

Creswell, Keppell Archibald Cameron, *Early Muslim Architecture: Umayyads, early Abbasids and Tulunids*, 2 vols. The Clarendon Press, Oxford, 1932–40.

Creswell, Keppell Archibald Cameron, 'A bibliography of Muslim archiecture in North Africa (excluding Egypt)', Supplement to *Hesperis*, Vol. XLI Librairie Larose, Paris, 1954.

Creswell, Keppell Archibald Cameron, *A Bibliography of The Architecture, Arts and Crafts of Islam: to 1st Jan. 1960.* The American University Press, Cairo, 1961.

Creswell, Keppell Archibald Cameron, *A Bibliography of The Architecture, Arts and Crafts of Islam: Supplement Jan. 1960 to Jan. 1972*, The American University Press, Cairo, 1973.

Daoulatli, Abdelaziz, *Tunis sous les Hafsides: Evolution urbaine et activite architectural*, Institut National d'Archeologie et d'Art, Tunis, 1976.

Delaval, Bernard, 'Urban communities of the Algerian Sahara', *Ekistics*, Vol. 38 No. 227 (Oct. 1974), pp. 252–258.

Department of Antiquities, Tripoli-Libya, *Some Islamic Sites in Libya: Tripoli, Ajabiyah and Ujlah*, Art and Archeology Research Papers, London, 1976.

Despois, Jean, *La Tunisie Orientale: Sahel et Basse Steppe*, Presses Universitaires de France, Paris, 1955.

Dunham, Daniel, 'The courtyard house as a temperature regulator', *The New Scientist*, Vol. 8 (Sept. 1960), pp. 663–666.

Ecochard, Michel and Le Coeur, Claude, *Les Bains de Damas: monographies architecturales*, 2 vols, Institut Français de Damas, Beirut, 1942–43.

Eichel, Marijean H., 'Ottoman Urbanism in the Balkans: A Tentative View', *The East Lakes Geographer*, Vol. 10 (1975), pp. 45–54.

d'Emilia, A., 'Roman law and Muslim law: a comparative outline', *East and West*, Vol. 4 (1953), pp. 73–80.

Encyclopaedia of Islam, The, First edn, 4 vols and supplement, E.J. Brill, Leiden, 1913–42. New edn, 3 vols and continuing. E.J. Brill, Leiden and London, 1960–.

English, Paul Ward, *City and Village in Iran: Settlement and Economy in the Kirman Basin*,

University of Wisconsin Press, Madison, 1966.

al-Farabi (d. 950 AD), *Der Musterstaat* (Risala fi ara' ahl al-madina al-fadila). Edited by F. Dieterici, 1895. Reprint, E.J. Brill, Leiden, 1964.

Fathy, Hassan, *Architecture for the Poor: an experiment in rural Egypt*, 1969 University of Chicago Press, 1973.

Fathy, Hassan, *The Arab House in the Urban Setting: Past, Present and Future*, Fourth Carreras Arab Lecture at the University of Essex, 3 November 1970. Longman, London, 1972.

Fleury, V. 'Poids et Mesures Tunisiens' *Revue Tunisienne*, Vol. III (1895), pp. 235–245.

Flores, Carlos, *Arquitectura popular Española*, 4 vols, Aguilar S.A., Madrid, 1974–.

Fradier, Georges, 'Tunis — a jewel of Islam', *Unesco Courier*, December 1970, pp. 34–41.

Frankfort, H., 'Town planning in ancient Mesopotamia', *The Town Planning Review*, Vol. XXI, No. 2 (July 1950), pp. 98–115.

Gallotti, Jean, *Le Jardin et la Maison Arabes au Maroc*, 2 vols, Editions Albert Levy, Paris, 1926.

Ghaidan, Usam, *Lamu: a study of the Swahili town*, East African Literature Bureau, Nairobi, 1975.

al-Ghazali (d. 1111 AD), *Ihya' Ulum al-Din* (The Revivification of Religious Sapiences), 16 parts, Kitab al-Sha'ab, Cairo n.d.

Gibb, H.A.R. and Kramers, J.H. (ed.) *Shorter Encyclopaedia of Islam*, 1953. Reprint, E.J. Brill, Leiden, 1969.

Goitein, S.D., 'The Cairo Geniza as a source for the History of Muslim Civilization', *Studia Islamica* Vol. III (1955), pp. 75–91.

Golvin, Lucien, *La Mosquée: Ses origines-Sa morphologie, Ses diverses fonctions, Son rôle dans la vie muslumane, plus spécialement en Afrique du Nord.* Institut d'Etudes Supérieures Islamiques, Alger, 1960.

Gomaa, Ibrahim, *A Historical Chart of the Muslim World*, E.J. Brill, Leiden, 1972.

Grabar, Oleg, *The Formation of Islamic Art.* Yale University Press, New Haven, Conn., 1973.

von Grunebaum, Gustave E., *Medieval Islam: A Study in Cultural Orientation*, 1946, 2nd edn, University of Chicago Press, 1953.

von Grunebaum, Gustave E., *Islam: Essays in the Nature and Growth of a Cultural Tradition.* Routledge and Kegan Paul, London, 1955.

Hakim, Besim S., 'Co-op housing, Baghdad: an evaluation and recommendations', *Ekistics*, March 1972, pp. 166–172.

Hakim, Besim S. (ed.), *Sidi Bou Sa'id-Tunisia: A Study in Structure and Form*, School of Architecture, Nova Scotia Technical College, Halifax, Canada, 1978.

Hakim, Besim S. 'Arab–Islamic Urban Structure', *The Arabian Journal for Science and Engineering*, Vol. 7, No. 2, 1982, pp, 69–79.

Hakim, Besim S. and Rowe, Peter G. 'The Representation of Values in Traditional and Contemporary Islamic Cities'. Two separate papers by the authors combined in one article. *Journal of Architectural Education*, Vol. 36, No. 4, Summer 1983, pp. 22–28.

Hitti, Philip K., *History of the Arabs*, 10th edn, Macmillan, London, 1970.

Hourani, A.H. and Stern, S.M. (eds), *The Islamic City*, Bruno Cassirer, Oxford, 1970.

Husaini, Sayyid Waqar Ahmed, *Islamic Environmental Systems Engineering*, Macmillan, London, 1980.

Hussain, Altaf, 'Masjid [Mosque] planning' and 'Masjid [Mosque] designing', *Journal of the Urban Planning and Development Division, Proceedings of the American Society of Civil Engineers*, Vol. 102 (August 1976), pp. 171–185.

Ibn al-Imam (d. 996 AD), 'Des droits et obligations entre propriétaires d'héritages voisins' (translated from Arabic to French by Barbier), *Revue Algerienne et Tunisienne de Législation et de Jurisprudence*, Vols XVI (1900) and XVII (1901).

Ibn Khaldun (d. 1406 AD), *The Muqaddimah: An Introduction to History*, (translated from the Arabic by Franz Rosenthal, abridged and edited by N.J. Dawood), Bollingen Series, Princeton University Press, 1967.

Ibn al-Rami (d. 1334 AD), *Kitab al-I'lan bi-Ahkam al-Bunyan* (The book for communicating building solutions). Handwritten and printed lithographically in Fes, 1332 AH/1913 AD.

Ismail, Abdel-Fattah, 'Origin, ideology and physical patterns of Arab urbanization', Dr.-Ing. dissertation, Faculty of Architecture, University of Karlsruhe, 1969.

Jordan, Borimir and Perlin, John, 'Solar energy used and litigation in ancient times', *Solar Law Reporter*, Vol. I No. 3, Sept./Oct. 1979, pp. 583–594.

Julien, Charles-André, *History of North Africa: Tunisia, Algeria, Morocco, from the Arab Conquest to 1830*, edited and revised by R. Le Tourneau, Praeger, New York, 1970.

al-Karaji (d. 1020 AD?). *Kitab Inbat al-Miyah al-Khafiyah* (The extraction of hidden -underground-water). Da'irat al-Ma'arif al-Othmaniyah, Hayderabad 1940.

Karpat, Kemal H., 'The background of Ottoman concept of city and urbanity', *Structures Sociales et Developpement Culturel des Villes Sud-Est Europeenes et Adriateques*, Bucharest (1975), pp. 323–340.

Karro, al-Hadi, *Usul al-Tashri' al-Islami* (Sources of Islamic law), al-Dar al-Arabiyah Lil-Kitab, Tripoli, Tunis, 1976.

Kelly, Kathleen and Schnadelbach, R.T., *Landscaping the Saudi Arabian Desert*, The Delancey Press, Philadelphia, 1976.

Kemal al-Din, Husain, 'Isqat al-Kura al-Ardiyah bil-nisba li-Makka al Mukarama wa ta'in Itijah al-Qibla' (Global projections related to Makka and establishing the directions to the Qibla), *Majallat al-Buhuth al-Islamiyah*, Riyadh Vol. I No. 2 (1975–76), pp. 734–776.

Khadduri, Majid and Liebesny, Herbert (eds), *Law in the Middle East: Origin and Development of Islamic Law, Middle East Institute, Washington, DC, 1955.*

al-Khodja, Mohammad b., *Tarikh M'alim al-Tawhid fi al-Qadim wa fi al-Jadid* (History of ancient and recent edifices of unity), al-Tunisiyah Press, Tunis, 1939.

Koenigsberger, O.H., Ingersoll, T.G., Mayhew, Alan and Szokolay, S.V., *Manual of Tropical Housing and Building: Part 1, Climatic Design*, Longman, London, 1974.

Kostof, Spiro, *Caves of God: the Monastic Environment of Byzantine Cappadocia*, M.I.T. Press, Cambridge, Mass, 1972.

Kowsar, Mehdi, 'Temporary or contemporary?', *Ekistics*, March 1977, pp. 144–148.

Lane, Edward William, *An Account of the Manners and Customs of the Modern Egyptians*, 1860 Reprint, Dover Publications Inc., New York, 1973.

Lapidus, Ira M., 'The muslim city in Mamluk times', 2 vols, PhD dissertation, Harvard University, 1964.

Lapidus, Ira M., *Muslim cities in the later Middle Ages*, Harvard University Press, Cambridge, Mass, 1967.

Lapidus, Ira M., (ed.) *Middle Eastern Cities*, University of California Press, Berkeley, Calif., 1969.

Latham, John D., 'Towards a study of Andalusian immigration and its place in Tunisian history', *Les Cahiers de Tunisie*, Vols 19–20 (1957), pp. 203–244.

Latham, John D., 'Towns and cities of Barbary: the Andalusian influence', *Islamic Quarterly*, Vol. 16 (1972), pp. 189–204.

Lawless, Richard I. and Blake, Gerald H., *Tlemcen: Continuity and Change in an Algerian Islamic Town*, Bowker, Epping, 1976.

Legendre, Marcel, *Survivance des Mesures Traditionnelles en Tunisie*. Publications de l'Institut des Hautes Etudes de Tunis, Presses Universitaires de France, Paris, 1958.

Leo Africanus (d. approx 1555 AD), *Description de l'Afrique*, 2 vols, edited by A. Epaulard, Paris, 1956.

Lerup, Lars, 'The dissection of three housing situations: another view of the same old thing', *Journal of Architectural Education*, Vol. XXIX, No. 4 (April 1976), pp. 5–13.

Le Tourneau, Roger, *Fes avant le Protectorat: Etude economique et sociale d'une ville de l'Occident Musulman*, Institut des hautes études Marocaines, Société Marocaine de librairie et d'edition, Casablanca, 1949.

Le Tourneau, Roger, *Les villes musulmanes de l'Afrique du Nord*, Bibliothéque de l'Institut d'études supérieures Islamiques d'Alger 11, Maison des livres, Alger, 1957.

Lévi-Provençal, E. (ed.), 'Le traité d'Ibn 'Abdun: un document sur la vie urbaine et les corps de métiers a Séville au début du XII siècle', *Journal Asiatique*, Vol. CCXXIV (April–June 1934), pp. 177–299.

Lévi-Provençal, E. (ed.), *Thalath Rasa'il Andalusiyah fi Adab al-Hisba wa al-Muhtasib* (Three Andalusian treatises for the conduct of the Hisba and the Muhtasib), Institut Français d'Archéologie Orientale, Cairo, 1955.

Lévi-Provençal, E., *al-Islam fi al-Maghreb wa al-Andalus*, translation of *Islam d'Occident*, by Mahmoud Salim and Mohammad Hilmi, Maktabat Nahdat Mesir, Cairo, 1956.

Lezine, Alexandre, 'Notes d'Archéologie Ifriqiyenne', *Revue des Études Islamiques* (1967) pp. 53–101.

Lezine, Alexandre, *Deux Villes d'Ifriqiya: Sousse, Tunis*, Librairie Orientaliste Paul Geuthner, Paris, 1971.

Luqbal, Mousa, *al-Hisba al-Madhhabiyah fi bilad al-Maghreb al-Arabi: Nashatuha wa tatawuruha* (The Hisba in the Arab Maghreb: origins and development), al-sharika al-wataniyah lil-neshir wa al-tawazi', Algiers, 1971.

Macdougall, Elisabeth B. and Ettinghausen, Richard (eds), *The Islamic Garden*, Dumbarton Oaks Colloquium on the History of Landscape Architecture IV, Trustees for Harvard University, Washington, DC, 1976.

al-Makrizi (d. 1441 AD), *al-Mawa'iz wa'l-I'tibar fi Dhikr al-Khitat wa'l-Athar* (Lessons and considerations from the history of settlements and monuments), New reprint by offset, al-Muthanna Bookshop, Baghdad, n.d.

Maktari, A.M.A., *Water Rights and Irrigation Practices in Lahj: a study of the application of Customary and Shari'ah law in South-West Arabia*, Cambridge University Press, London, 1971.

Malik b. Anas (d. 795 AD), *al-Muwatta wa-Sharhiha lil-Siyooti* (al-Muwatta and its interpretation by al-Siyooti), Dar Ihya al-Kutub al-Arabiyah, Cairo, n.d.

al-Maqdisi (d. 990 AD), *Ahsan al-Taqasim fi Ma'rifat al-Aqalim* (The best classification for knowing the regions), 2nd edn, E.J. Brill, Leiden, 1906.

Marçais, Georges, *Tunis et Kairouan*. Coll. les villes d'art célébres 82. Laurens, Paris, 1937.

Marçais, Georges, 'L'urbanisme musulman', *Cinquième Congres de la Federation des Sociétés savantes de l'Afrique du Nord, Alger*, (1940), pp. 13–34.

Marçais, Georges, 'La Conception des villes dans l'Islam' *La Revue d'Alger* Vol II (1945), pp. 517–533.

Marçais, Georges, *L'Architecture Musulman d'Occident: Tunisie, Algérie, Maroc, Espange et Sicile*, Arts et Metiers Graphiques, Paris, 1955.

Marçais, Georges, *L'Art Musulman*, Presses Universitaires de France, Paris, 1962.

Marçais, Georges, 'Les origines de la maison nord-africaine', *Cahiers des Arts et Techniques d'Afrique du Nord*, Vol. 7 (1973–74), pp. 43–62.

Marçais, William, 'L'islamisme et la vie urbaine' *Comptes Rendus des séances de l'Académie des Inscriptions et Belles-Lettres* (1928), pp. 86–100.

Ma'rouf, Naji, *Urubat al-Mudun al-Islamiyah* (Islamic cities founded by the Arabs) al-Any Press, Baghdad, 1964.

Massignon, L., 'Explication du Plan de Kufa-Irak', *Mémoires de l'Institut Français d'Archéologie Orientale du Caire*, Vol. LXVIII (1940), pp. 337–360.

al-Mawurdi (d. 1058 AD), *al-Ahkam al-Sultaniyah wa al-Wilayat al-Diniyah* (Rulers' judgements in religious states), Mustafa al-Babi al-Halabi and Sons Press, Cairo, 1973.

Mayer, L.A., *Islamic Architects and Their Works*, Albert Kundig, Geneva, 1956.

Mez, Adam, *Die Renaissance des Islams*, translated to Arabic by Muhammed Abu Ryda in two volumes, Cairo 1948.

Ministry of Housing and Urban Development, Iran, *Habitat Bill of Rights*, Hamdami Foundation, Tehran, 1976.

Miquel, André, 'Jerusalem Arabe: notes de topographie historique', *Bulletin d'Études Orientales*, Vol. XVI (1958–60), pp. 7–13.

Miquel, André, *L'Islam et sa Civilisation VII–XX siécle* Librarie Armand Colin, Paris, 1968.

Naji, Abdul-Jabbar. 'Al-medina al-Arabiyah fi al-dirasat al-ajnabiyah' (The Arabic–Islamic city in foreign studies). *Al-Mawrid*, Vol. 9, No. 4, 1981, pp. 136–170.

Nasr, Seyyed Hossein, *Ideals and Realities of Islam*, George Allen and Unwin, London 1966.

Nasr, Seyyed Hossein, *Science and Civilization in Islam*, Harvard University Press, Cambridge, Mass, 1968.

Nasr, Seyyed Hossein, *Islamic Science: An Illustrated study*, World of Islam Festival Publishing Company Ltd., London, 1976.

Nijst, A.L.M.T., Priemus, H., Swets, H.L. and Van Ijzeren, J.J., *Living on the Edge of the Sahara: A Study of Traditional Forms of Habitation and Types of Settlement in Morocco*, Government Publishing Office, The Hague, 1973.

Oliver, Paul (ed.) *Shelter and Society*, Barrie and Rockliff, London, 1969.

Pauty, Edmond, *Les palais et les maisons de l'Egypte Musulmane*, Institute Français du Caire, Cairo, 1933.

Pauty, Edmond, 'Villes spontanées et villes créées en islam', *Annales de l'Institut d'Études Orientales*, Vol. IX (1951), pp. 52–75.

Pearson, J.D. and Walsh, Ann, *Index Islamicus: A Catalog of Articles on Islamic Subjects in Periodicals and Other Collective Publications*, Mansell Information/Publishing Ltd., London, 1906–continuing.

Pellegrin, Arthur, 'Tunis sous la domination turque', *Bulletin Economique et Social de la Tunisie*, Vol. 48 (January 1951), pp. 64–75.

Pellegrin, Arthur, 'Le vieux Tunis: les noms de rues de la ville arabe', 6 articles in *Bulletin Economique et Social de la Tunisie*, Vol. 59 (December 1951) to Vol. 64 (May 1952).

Pellegrin, Arthur, *Histoire Illustrée de Tunis et de sa Banlieue*, Editions Saliba, Tunis, 1955.

Project Tunis-Carthage, Republique Tunisienne, *Sauvegarde et mise en valeur de la Medina de Tunis*, 8 parts in 5 vols, Unesco, PNUD TUN 71-532, INAA, ASM, Tunis, 1974.

al-Qardawi, Youssef, *al-Halal wa al-Haram fi al-Islam* (Allowance and prohibition in Islam), 5th rev. edn, al-Maktab al-Islami, 1969.

Qur'an, The Holy, Text, translation and commentary by Abdullah Yusuf Ali. United States: Khalil al-Rawaf, 1946.

Ragette, Friedrich, *Architecture in Lebanon*, Syracuse University Press, 1974.

Rapoport, Amos, *House Form and Culture*, Prentice-Hall, Englewood Cliffs, 1969.

Rapoport, Amos, *Human Aspects of Urban Form: Towards a Man-Environment Approach to Urban Form and Design*. Urban and Regional Planning Series, Vol. 15, Pergamon Press, Oxford, 1977.

Reuther, Oscar, *Das Wohnhans in Baghdad und anderen Städten des Irak*, Verlag von Ernst Wasmuth A.G., Berlin, 1910.

Revault, Jacques, *Palais et demeures de Tunis (XVI et XVII siècles)*, Editions du Centre National de la Recherche Scientifique, Paris, 1967.

Revault, Jacques, *Palais et demeures de Tunis (XVIII et XIX siècles)*, Editions du Centre National de la Recherche Scientifique, Paris, 1971.

Roche, Manuelle, *Le M'zab: Architecture Ibadite en Algérie*, B. Arthaud, Paris, 1970.

Rudofsky, Bernard, *Architecture Without Architects*, Museum of Modern Art, New York, 1965.

Rudofsky, Bernard, *The Prodigious Builders*, Harcourt Brace Jovanovich, New York, 1977.

Sahnoun (ed.) (d. 854 AD), *al-Mudawwana al-Kubra* (The large Documentary) 16 vols, narrated by Sahnoun and based on Ibn al-Qasim's (d. 806 AD) interpretations of the views of Malik b. Anas (d. 795 AD) al-Sa'ada Press, Cairo, 1905.

Saini, Balwant Singh, *Building Environment: An Illustrated Analysis of Problems in Hot-Dry Lands*, Angus and Robertson, Sydney, 1973.

al-Salih, Subhi, *al-Nuzum al-Islamiyah* (Islamic systems: origins and development) Dar al-'Ilm lil-Malayeen, Beirut 1965.

al-Salih, Subhi, *Ulum al-Hadith wa Mustalahahu* (The knowledge and discipline of the Hadith), 4th edn, Dar al-'Ilm lil-Malayeen, Beirut, 1966.

Sarkis, Youssef Ilyan, *Mu'jam al-Matbu'at al-Arabiyah wa al-Mu'araba ila sanat 1339 H.* (Dictionary of Arabic and Arabized publications to the year 1919 AD), Maktabat Yousef Ilyan Sarkis and Sons, Cairo, 1928.

Sauvaget, Jean, 'Esquisse d'une Histoire de la ville de Damas', *Revue des Études Islamiques* Vol. VIII, No. 4 (1934), pp. 421–480.

Sauvaget, Jean, *ALEP: Essai sur le developpement d'une grande ville Syrienne des origins au milieu du XIX siècle*, 2 vols, Geuthner, Paris, 1941.

Sauvaget, Jean, *Introduction to the History of the Muslim East: A Bibliographical Guide*, edited by Claude Cahen, University of California Press, Berkeley, Calif., 1965.

Schacht, Joseph, *An Introduction to Islamic Law*, The Clarendon Press, Oxford, 1964.

Schacht, Joseph, *The Origins of Muhammadan Jurisprudence*. 1950, 4th edn, The Clarendon Press, Oxford, 1967.

Schacht, Joseph, and Bosworth, C.E. (ed.), *The Legacy of Islam*, 2nd edn, The Clarendon Press, Oxford, 1974.

Sebag, Paul, *La hara de Tunis: l'evolution d'un ghetto Nord-Africain*, Presses Universitaires de France, Paris, 1959.

al-Shafi'i (d. 819 AD), *al-Risala*, Bulaq, 1903, edited by Sheikh Ahmad Muhammad Shakir, Cairo, 1940.

Solignac, J.M., 'Travaux hydrauliques Hafsides de Tunis', *Revue Africaine*, Vol. 79 (1936), pp. 517–580.

Solignac, J.M., 'Recherches sur les installations hydrauliques de Kairouan et des steppes tunisiennes du VII au XI siècle' *Annales de l'Institut d'Études Orientales*, Vol. X (1952), pp. 5–273 and Vol. XI (1953), pp. 60–170.

Sourdel, D. and J., *La Civilisation de l'Islam Classique*, Arthaud, Paris, 1968.

Spies, Otto, 'Islamisches Nachbarrecht nach schafiitischer Lehre', *Zeitschrift Für Vergleichende Rechtswissenshaft*, Vol. XLII (1927), pp. 393–421.

Stephens, Suzanne and Bloom, Janet, 'Before the Virgin met the Dynamo', *The Architectural Forum*, July/August 1973, pp. 77–87.

Tash Kebri Zada (d. 1560 AD), *Muftah al-Sa'ada wa Mesbah al-Siyada fi Maudu'at al-Ulum* (Key to happiness and light to sovereignty in the disciplines of knowledge), Dar al-Kutub al-Haditha, Cairo, n.d.

Thoumin, R. *La Maison Syrienne*, Institute Français de Damas. Librairie Ernest Leroux, Paris, 1932.

Torres Balbas, L. *Ciudades Hispano-Musulmanes*, 2 vols, Ministerio de Asuntos Exteriores, Direction General de Relaciones Culturales, Instituto Hispano-Arabe de Cultura, n.d.

Torres Balbas, L., 'Les villes musulmanes d'Espagne et leur urbanisation', *Annales de l'Institut des Études Orientales*, Vol. 6 (1942–47), pp. 5–30.

Ünsal, Behçet, *Turkish Islamic Architecture: in Seljuk and Ottoman times 1071–1923*, Alec Tiranti, London, 1959.

van Veen, René, 'Three years of building in

Tunisia', 2 special issues of *Forum*, Vol. XXV No. 5 (June 1976) and No. 6 (July/August 1976).
Violich, Francis, 'Evolution of the Spanish city', *Journal of the American Institute of Planners*, Vol. 28, No. 3 (August 1962), pp. 170–179.
al-Wansharisi (d. 1508 AD), *al-Mi'yar al-Mu'arab wa al-Jami' al-Maghreb 'an Fatawi ahl Ifrikiyah wa al-Andalus wa al-Mahgreb* (The Collection of Arabic-Maghribi Criteria based on Fatawi from Ifrikiya, Andalusia and Morocco), 12 vols. Handwritten and printed lithographically, in Fes 1314 AH/1896 AD.
Wensinck, A.J. and Mensing, J.P. (eds) *Concordance et indices de la tradition musulmane* (al-Mu'djam al-mufahras li-alfaz al-hadith al-nabawi), 8 vols, E.J. Brill, Leiden, 1936–1969.
Wheatley, Paul, 'Levels of space awareness in the traditional Islamic city', *Ekistics*, December 1976, pp. 354–366.
Wilbur, Donald N., *Persian Gardens and Garden Pavilions*, Charles E. Tuttle, Tokyo, 1962.
Wirth, Eugen, 'Zum Problem des Bazars (suq, çarşi)', *Der Islam*, Vol. 51 (1974), pp. 203–260 and Vol. 52 (1975), pp. 6–46.
Wirth, Eugen, 'Die orientalische Stadt: Ein Überblick aufgrund jüngerer Forschungen zur materiellen Kultur', *Saeculum*, Vol. 26 (1975), pp. 45–94.
Witmer, John, 'Etude sur l'amenagement de la ville ancienne de Damas par l'assainissement de l'existant', *Annales Archéologiques de Syrie: Revue d'Archéologie et d'Histoire Syriennes*, Vols 11–12 (1961–62), pp. 19–44.
Woolley, C. Leonard, 'Cities of about 2000 B.C.', *Antiquaries Journal*, Vol. VII, No. 4 (Oct. 1927) and Vol. XI, No. 4 (Oct. 1931).
Wulff, Hans E., *The Traditional Crafts of Persia: Their Development, Technology and Influence on Eastern and Western Civilizations*, M.I.T. Press, Cambridge, Mass, 1966.
Yaqut (d. 1228 AD), *Mu'jam al-Buldan* (Dictionary of Settlements/Regions), 5 vols, Dar Sadir/Dar Beirut, Beirut, 1955.
Yeha Ben Omar (d. 901 AD), *Ahkam al-Suq* (Rules for the market), checked by H.H. Abdul-Wahab, al-Sharika al-Tunisiyah lil-tawzi', Tunis, 1975.
Zaydan, Jurji, *Tarikh al-Tamadun al-Islami* (History of Islamic civilization), 5 vols, 1902–1906. Revised edition by Husain Mu'nis, Dar al-Hilal, Cairo, 1958.
Zbiss, Slimane Mustafa, 'La Grande Mosquée (Zitouna) a Tunis', *Comptes rendus des séances (Academi des inscriptions et belles lettres)*, 13 December 1953, pp. 443–452.
Zbiss, Slimane Mustafa, *Monuments Musulmanes d'Epoque Husseynite en Tunisie*, Sabi Press, Tunis, 1955.
Zbiss, Slimane Mustafa, *Bayna al-Athar al-Islamiyah fi Tunis* (A Travers Les Monuments Musulmans de Tunisie). Maison de la Culture, Tunis, 1963.
Zbiss, Slimane Mustafa, *Les Monuments de Tunis*. Société Tunisienne de Diffusion, Tunis, 1971.
Zeki, Abdul-Rahman, 'Al-medina al-Arabiya fi shimal Afriqiya' (The Arabic city in North Africa), *Proceedings of the Sixth Arab Archeological Conference*, Tripoli, Libya, 18–27 September 1971, Arab Educational, Scientific and Cultural Organization, Cairo, 1973, pp. 587-624.
al-Zerekly, Khair al-Din, *al-A'lam*: Biographical Dictionary. 3rd edn, 13 vols in Arabic, Beirut, 1969.
Ziyadah, Niqula, *Urban life in Syria under the early Mamlukes*, American University in Beirut, 1953.
Ziyadah, Niqula, *al-Hisba wa al-Muhtasib fi al-Islam* (The Hisba and the Muhtasib in Islam), Catholic Press, Beirut, 1963.
Ziyadah, Niqula, *Mudun Arabiyah*, (Arabic cities). Dar al Tali'ah, Beirut, 1965.

Index

(Numbers in **bold** refer to Figures in text.)

Postscript

Since completing the research and writing for this book in 1979, a number of dissertations have appeared on various aspects of this area of study, in addition to several books and articles. I am happy to report the present work was instrumental in influencing the direction of some of those studies.[1] Reviews of this book have appeared in numerous languages, and several authors have made extensive use of material from the book. A Japanese and Farsi translation were published.[2] Yet only few of those works have addressed the processes and the system of rules that were followed in making decisions affecting various levels of the built environment. One of the reasons for the rarity of such studies might be the difficulty in finding reliable original sources; the language barrier and difficulties in reading handwritten manuscripts might be another. Yet without employing such sources and meticulous research, nothing of significance can be achieved. Happily more original manuscripts are being verified, edited, and published in their original Arabic, which should make it much easier for future researchers to use this material.[3]

One of the objectives of my work, mentioned in the Introduction, is the challenge of recycling and testing traditional principles in contemporary and future urban design and architecture. This is an issue of cultural continuity in the built environment. I took this matter up again in early 1981 and have continued to examine it since then in a number of published studies.[4]

I have used the essential material and core arguments presented here in a number of articles.[5] Other aspects of this field of study were not covered in the book; I have subsequently published complementary material, such as the role of customary practices (*Urf*) and their impact on the identity of towns and cities.[6] Other important aspects of research related to the Islamic city await study; I have published an annotated list of studies needed to develop a comprehensive theory of urban form in traditional Islamic cultures.[7]

As my research has progressed in this field, it has become increasingly evident that the *processes* underlying the traditional system are the level from which to draw meaningful and practical insights. We should not place undue priority on typologies of the traditional system, as most people involved in the field of architecture and urban design tend to do, since those are in turn controlled and configured by the process and rule system governing decisions in space design and building activities. Thus if we recycle the essence of the process, we can apply it to any typological system and achieve the high quality results associated with the traditional system.[8] For example, the typology utilized in the Hadramaut region in southern Yemen, as well as in the northern part of the country (as at San'a) and in the architecture found in the major Hijazi cities of western Saudi Arabia, is dramatically different from the predominant typology found in most other parts of the Islamic world, as illustrated by the examples in this book. Yet in all these locations the underlying process and its mechanisms were similar, resulting in the same high quality and sophistication found elsewhere. In other words the process is flexible and dynamic and not tied to a specific typology.[9]

During the mid-1990s I allocated time to uncover the rule system related to the built environment in the early centuries of the Byzantine era, so as to provide an intelligent basis for studying the built environment of Greece before independence in the early nineteenth century, and other non-Islamic Mediterranean countries.[10] The knowledge gained from such an investigation will assist in the further formulation of theory, because the case of Greece, Italy, and Spain represents high-quality achievement in the traditional built environment. The similarities and differences between cultures will sharpen our tools for constructing theory and for developing techniques for maintaining the cultural continuity of built environments, with lessons useful for other cultures. The world will be a much richer place for it.

Besim S. Hakim
Jumada al-Thani 1429 / June 2008

1. My lectures and personal interaction with academics and their students during the period 1977-1986 have influenced the content and outcome of a number of Ph.D. dissertations. The earliest that I am aware of, which cited a 1977 draft of chapter one, is by Mahmoud Daza dated 1982 from the University of Pennsylvania. A brief history of events associated with the research and preparation of this book was published in the Saudi engineer's magazine *al-Muhandis*, no. 8, (Dhu al-Hijja 1408/ July 1988): 67. Additional details can be found in the "Communication" published in *MESA Bulletin*, 26/1 (1992): 150-52.

2. Some of the reviews in English were published in the following journals: *Housing and Planning Review*, 41/4 (1986); *Mimar 22* (1986); *Third World Planning Review*, 8/4 (1986); *Progressive Architecture*, 68/1 (1987); *The Geographical Review*, 77/2 (1987); *Cities*, 4/2 (1987); *MESA Bulletin*, 21/1 (1987); *Journal of Architectural Education*, 41/2 (1988); and *Journal of Architectural and Planning Research*, 6/1 (1989). At least two books that I am aware of have used extensive material from the present work:A.E.J. Morris, *History of Urban Form*, 3rd Edition,1994,

and G. Broadbent, *Emerging Concepts in Urban Space Design*, 1990. A Japanese edition was published in Tokyo, December 1990. A Farsi translation was published in Tehran, 2002.

3. For example: Ibn al-Rami's manuscript was not available in published form when I worked with it. The first unverified edition was published in Morocco by *Majallat al-Fiqh al-Maliki wa al-Turath al-Qada'i bil-Maghrib*, 2/ 2,3,4 (1982): 259-490. This was followed by a reliable scholarly verified edition by Abdul-Rahman al-Atram in 2 volumes, *al-Ilan bi Ahkam al-Bunyan* (Riyadh, 1995). A more recent edition using the same title was published by Ferid ben Slimane (Tunis, 1999). Another important manuscript by Ibn al-Imam, Isa ben Mousa al-Tutaili (mentioned on p. 23), was verified and published in Saudi Arabia by Ibrahim ben Mohammad al-Fayez, *Kitab al-Jidar*, (Riyadh,1996). It was also verified by Muhammad al-Numainij and published by ISESCO, (Rabat, 1999). Four years later by Ferid ben Slimane and al-Mukhtar al-Tulaili (Tunis, 2003).

4. A framework suggesting how to learn from the past was first published in *the Proceedings of the conference on the Preservation of Architectural Heritage of Islamic Cities*, Istanbul, Turkey, 1985, published in Riyadh, 1988, pp. 305-17. It was further developed and published in *Al-Muhandis* (Ibid., note 1, pp. 2-6, in English), and then further refined and presented at the *Second International Conference on Urbanism in Islam*, November 1990, Tokyo, Japan, available in the proceedings volume (1994), pp. 377-84. Its final form was published in *Cities*, 8/4 (1991): 274-77, which also includes detailed citations of my other published work in this field. The components of the framework were further elaborated with examples in the encyclopedia article cited in note 5 below, and on page 171 of this book. The rules and design guidelines that were developed for the Muslim community in Abiquiu, New Mexico, in early 1981 were published in *Proceedings of the 74th Annual Meeting of the Association of Collegiate Schools of Architecture*, New Orleans, March 1986, pp. 109-19. An expanded version followed in *Review 86*, UPM, Dhahran, Saudi Arabia, November 1986, pp. 11-28. That project represented an attempt to recycle the rules and know-how of the traditional system and adapt it to contemporary conditions on location in Abiquiu, New Mexico. In early 2006 I was hired by the United Nations Development Program and the Bahraini Ministry of Municipalities and Agricultural Affairs to work on a project for revitalizing the historic districts of Muharraq and Manama in Bahrain. I developed the Control, Management, and Coding aspects of a generative program. Parts of that work was published: "Generative processes for revitalizing historic towns or heritage districts", *Urban Design International*, 12/2-3 (2007): 87-99. I have drawn on the insight of the traditional experience in developing the proposals for that project.

5. "Arab-Islamic urban structure," *The Arabian Journal of Science and Engineering*, 7/2 (1982): 69-79; "The representation of values in traditional and contemporary Islamic cities" *Journal of Architectural Education*, 36/4 (1983):22-28; and the article "Islamic Architecture and Urbanism," *Encyclopedia of Architecture,* vol.3 (New York,1989): 86-103. The case study of Saudi Arabia is used in this encyclopedia article to analyze the changes that occurred due to the abandonment of the system that created the traditional built environment and the consequent adoption of imported Western values and techniques to create new settlements and cities in that country. This was followed by "Rule systems: Islamic," *Encyclopedia of Vernacular Architecture of the World*, vol. 1 (Cambridge, UK, 1997): 566-68. All of these articles summarize and/or elaborate on the essential findings in this book and also address contemporary and future issues of cities in the Arab and wider Islamic worlds.

6. The results of my research on the *Urf* were first published in the *Proceedings of the International Conference on Urbanism in Islam*, Tokyo, Japan, October, 1989, vol. 2 (Tokyo,

Japan), pp. 113-38. A revised version was subsequently published as chapter 7 of the book *Islam and Public Law*, ed. by C. Mallat (London, 1993). A further revised, expanded, and illustrated version was published in *Journal of Architectural and Planning Research,* 11/2 (1994):108-27. Due to the importance of this topic it should be viewed as an extension of this work, and I have attached it at the end of the book.

7. See B. S. Hakim "Urban form in traditional Islamic cultures: further studies needed for formulating theory," *Cities*, 16/1 (1999): 51-55. Of the fifteen topics, there are three that I would like to see investigated very soon. They all deal with the processes of land demarcation and subdivision in the early formation of Islamic cities: the study of the principles and workings of land allotment (*Iqta*), the revivification of land (*Ihya*) within and on the fringes of settlements, and the processes of territorialisation of land (*Ikhtitat*), particularly at the neighborhood and building cluster levels. For my views on the state of scholarship concerning the Islamic city and its architecture to the early 1980s, see my review essay in *Third World Planning Review*, 12/1 (1990): 75-89.

8. For suggestions on how the traditional rule system can be revived and used as a mechanism to revitalize and preserve the character of the traditional sectors of towns and cities in the Maghrib countries of Libya, Tunisia, Algeria, and Morocco, see my article: "Reviving the Rule System: An approach for revitalizing traditional towns in Maghrib," *Cities*, 18/2 (2001): 87-92. The substance of this article was first presented in Tangiers, Morocco, June 1996, at the conference entitled: "The Living Medina: The walled Arab city in architecture, literature, and history," sponsored by the American Institute of Maghribi Studies. The same approach suggested there could be used in other regional / cultural contexts.

9. This is corroborated by the findings of a recent study I undertook with Zubair Ahmed of the traditional rules and their manifestation in the unique neighborhood clusters found in Northern Nigeria and illustrated by examples from Zaria. The results of our work titled "Rules for the built environment in 19th century Northern Nigeria" was published in *Journal of Architectural and Planning Research*, 23/1 (2006): 1-26.

10. See my article "Julian of Ascalon's treatise of construction and design rules from sixth-century Palestine," *Journal of the Society of Architectural Historians*, 60/1 (2001): 4-25. For a comparison of the treatises of Julian of Ascalon and Ibn al-Imam Isa ben Mousa al-Tutaili and the significance of generative processes see my: "Mediterranean urban and building codes: origins, content, impact, and lessons", *Urban Design International*, 13/1 (2008): 21-40.

Besim S. Hakim

"The "Urf" and its role in diversifying the architecture of traditional Islamic cities"

Journal of Architectural and Planning Research
Volume 11, Number 2, Summer, 1994, pages 108 – 127.

Re-printed according to a Special Provisions article in the Agreement between the Publisher and Author, dated December 1991.

Journal of Architectural and Planning Research
11:2 (Summer, 1994) 108

THE "URF" AND ITS ROLE IN DIVERSIFYING THE ARCHITECTURE OF TRADITIONAL ISLAMIC CITIES

Besim S. Hakim

The 'Urf', or customs, in various Muslim societies had a very important role in establishing a framework of accepted norms of behavior operational in its own terms at the level of the community. As a result, each region of the Muslim world, sometimes comprising a number of distinct communities, developed a local distinctiveness in the way certain societal activities are conducted, including building activity. A primary reason why local customs thrived was the recognition by Muslim legal scholars of the importance of the Urf as a mechanism of societal behavior, and was thus accepted as one of the sources for the law. This was a basis for its institutionalization in each community. This paper explains the Urf from the vantage point of Islamic jurisprudence, then discusses its implications on building practice. This is supported by illustrative examples to convey the impacts on architecture at the local level. It also attempts to put forward a theoretical basis for the phenomenon of unity and diversity prevalent in the architecture of traditional Muslim societies. The paper also addresses lessons from this insight for contemporary building and urban design, and suggests areas for further research associated with this topic.

INTRODUCTION

What is the 'Urf'? The following are definitions put forward by a number of Muslim scholars:

- What is accepted by people and is compatible to their way of thinking and is normally adopted by those considered to be of good character — Al-Ghazali (d.1111 A.D.).[1]

- Action or belief in which persons persist with the concurrence of the reasoning powers and which their natural dispositions agree to accept as right — Al-Jurjani (d.1413 A.D.).[2]

- A habit or a way of doing things that is constantly repeated, and which settles well and is accepted by people considered of good character — Ali Haider (d.?).[3]

- What is customary to a people and which they follow in their sayings, acts and in what they reject — Abdul-Wahab Al-Khallaf (d. 1956 A.D.).[4]

- The habit (or custom) of a people in their sayings or acts — Mustafa Al-Zarka (born 1904 A.D.).[5]

- What is customary to a people and which they follow in their living pattern — Abdulaziz Al-Khayyat (born 1923).[6]

As evident in the latter three definitions the trend is for more open-endedness on the part of contemporary scholars. One reason for this is the fact that writing on the Urf as a distinct topic and theory is a recent phenomenon. One of the early treatises which is often cited by contemporary scholars is that by Ibn Abdin — who completed his treatise on Urf in late 1827. This is a very recent date considering the long history of Islamic jurisprudence. The later scholars realized that the Urf's status within the Fiqh (Islamic jurisprudence), is as complex as other areas in jurisprudence. As a result their definitions are guarded and open-ended.

The authors of the four well-known and extensive studies on Urf are listed chronologically:

- Mohammad Amin Effendi known as "Ibn Abdin," treatise dated 1827.[7]

- Ahmad Fahmi Abu-Sanah, treatise published 1949.[8]

- Mustafa Ahmad Al-Zarka, treatise as part of a book, published 1945, revised 3rd edition, 1952 includes comments on item 2.[9]

- Abdulaziz Al-Khayyat, treatise completed and published 1977.[10]

The first treatise written in the early 19th century and the latter three from mid to the start of the fourth quarter of the 20th century — a span of only 150 years.[11] The first section of this paper owes much to Al-Zarka and Al-Khayyat's treatises.

The second section of this paper discusses the implication of the Urf on building practice in the traditional Islamic city, and how the Urf contributed to the distinctiveness and character of each city through the details of its built form and architectonics. To the knowledge of the author this is the first attempt to do this, and because of it, this paper should be viewed as exploratory in nature. The ideas presented can, no doubt, be further scrutinized and developed.

Finally, in brief passages, lessons from the traditional Islamic city in terms of the workings of the Urf are presented. Those observations should be of interest and benefit to those involved in contemporary city planning and urban design in other cultures. The paper concludes with suggestions for further research.

URF IN ISLAMIC JURISPRUDENCE (FIQH)

Some scholars refer to the verse 7:199 in the Quran as the basis for sanctioning the Urf. The translation of the meaning of this verse is best rendered by this author as: *Take things at their face value, and bid to what is customary [or accepted by local tradition], and turn away from the ignorant.*[12] Thus the Fuqaha saw in this Quranic verse a clear sanction for accepting the Urf, and it constituted the seed for a tree of knowledge which was later developed by them as one of the pillars for interpreting and developing the law.

The main points and observations which are extracted from the literature are intended for their relevancy to building activity. Thus what is discussed below should be primarily viewed in light of the purposes of this paper.

The origin of a habit (Ada) is initiated at the individual level. For every act there must be an impetus or reason. This impetus could be external to the individual, or it could emanate from within. So if the person feels content with his act in response to the impetus (whether it is external or internal), and if it is repeated, then it becomes a habit (Ada). If others find this habit agreeable and repeat it by imitation and it spreads in the community, then it becomes a custom or Urf, i.e. the habit of the group or community. Therefore every Urf is a habit (Ada), but not every habit (Ada) is Urf.[13]

As with a habit or act in response to an impetus, we find the same applies in language. A group of people who share a common activity such as in the trades or professions develop a language composed of a vocabulary of terms to ease communication between members of that group. In some instances these specialized terms become known to that part of the larger community who are interested or involved in aspects of that group's activities or concerns. The terms then become part of the local Urf.[14]

The Urf can be initiated by order of the local authority or by its encouragement.[15] Or it can be inherited from previous generations, as occurred with the perpetuation of certain pre-Islamic customs. Or it can evolve locally in response to certain conditions or changes in the milieu of the environment.

Habits (Adat: plural of Ada) and Customs (A'raf: plural of Urf) get embedded in people and become part of their being and culture. The Fuqaha recognized that to require people to abandon their customs is a very difficult and anguishing process.[16] Thus we find that an aspect of the human trait is resistance to changes in habits and customs.

It was recognized early on in Islam that not all habits and customs were good. Many would be offensive to Islamic values and teachings. Thus the necessity emerged in the eyes of the Fuqaha (plural of Faqih: a specialist in Fiqh or Islamic jurisprudence) to develop a theory or reasoning to deal with this situation, i.e. how to distinguish by logic and reason between acceptable habits and customs and those which needed to be rejected because of incompatibility with Islam. The ultimate purpose for the Fuqaha was to develop the necessary framework to help in formulating rational decisions and judgments when faced with questionable habits and customs.[17]

Essentially the Urf is viewed by the Fuqaha as related to:

Linguistic
and
Practical (a way of doing something). And it can be designated as Public (A'm) Urf or Private (Khas) Urf. The former is that which is commonly followed by an established large community or by many communities. Whereas the latter is that which is followed locally by a small community or a specific group of people belonging to a trade or profession within a community.[18] These designations can be shown to interrelate as in Figure 1.

The legitimacy of the Urf — The Urf is viewed by the Shari'a (Islamic Law) as an important basis for rulings and judgments, particularly decisions and judgments based on the knowledge and understanding of a locality.

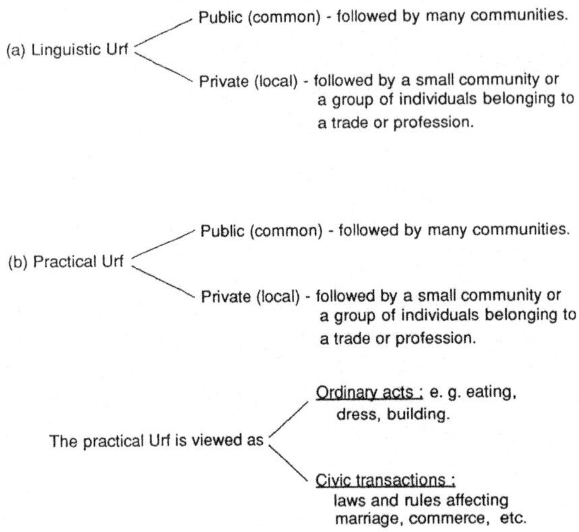

The above can be designated in chart form, thus :

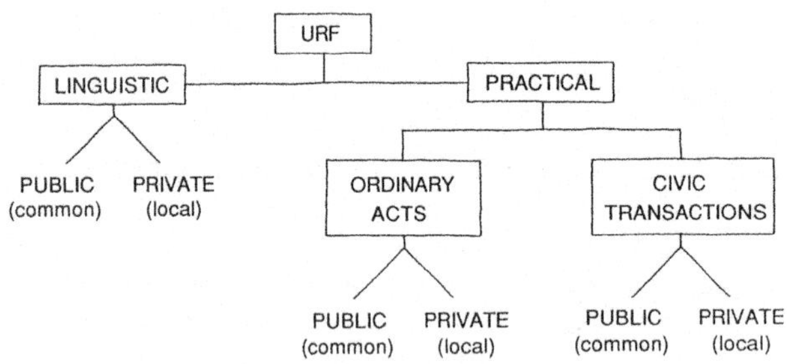

FIGURE 1. Designation of the Urf according to Fiqh scholars.

Legitimacy of the Linguistic Urf. It is accepted that the localized language and its vocabulary should be used as a basis for rulings, judgments and/or disputes. This is so even if certain Urf terms have different meanings in classical Arabic (from which some of the terms might be derived). Thus the Fuqaha acknowledge the Fiqh principle that: *The basis for truth is the proof of custom.*[19] This posture by the Shari'a has encouraged the legitimization of the local dialect or "slang" in adjudicating disputes and resolving conflict. In this way there was no reason to impose, for instance, the spoken classical Arabic in the courts of various regions of the Islamic world. This also meant that judges (qadis) had to be well versed in the nuance of the local language and the people's customs as a whole.

Legitimacy of the Practical Urf. The opinions and writings of Fuqaha clearly demonstrate that both branches of the practical urf (i.e. ordinary acts and civic transactions) are used as a basis for decisions, rulings and judgments, provided that the particular Urf (which is used for such a basis) does not contravene any stipulation of the Shari'a. There is a well known Fiqh principle attributed to Sarkhasi: *That which is established by Urf is like that which is established by the texts.* Article 45 from the Majallat al-Ahkam al-Adliyah stipulates the principle: *Stipulating by the Urf is like stipulating by the texts.*[20]

The nature of a ruling which is based on the Urf can change if the Urf changes with time. Thus rulings must reflect the Urf as practiced and understood in a specific time and place. Therefore, a judgment based on a specific localized Urf is only implemented in that particular locality and cannot be emulated by another community with different customary conditions.[21]

For the Urf to have legitimacy it has to meet the requirements of all of the following conditions[22]:

- The Urf has to be popular and consistently followed by the majority in a community.
- The Urf has to be currently alive, and if it changes then it cannot be used for justifying or unjustifying previous decisions or acts. In other words the legitimacy of an Urf is constrained by its currency.
- When the Urf is used as a condition or as a basis for a judgment or a decision, it must not contravene a pre-existing stipulation or agreement, as this can void its legitimacy.
- The Urf must not by its use abolish or cancel a ruling from the texts or a principle of the Shari'a. This could occur in one of three situations:
- (a) It could collide with a specific Shari'a ruling from the Quran or Sunna.
- (b) It could contravene a general ruling from the texts (All written sources of the Shari'a).
- (c) It could differ with an opinion(s) derived by Ijtihad (Independent Reasoning).

For each of these three situations the Fuqaha have developed guidelines for determining the legitimacy of any kind of Urf — be it linguistic or practical and whether it is common or local.

The preceding text briefly explains how the Urf was viewed by the Fuqaha and its place in the Science of Fiqh. Implicitly it also indicates how it used to be implemented.[23]

IMPLICATIONS ON BUILDING PRACTICE

The implication of the above observations on building practice in the traditional Islamic city was direct and its manifestations evident in any city, particularly if viewed comparatively to other Islamic cities across space and time. Elsewhere this author has alluded to the Urf[24] but in this paper he will elaborate more on the implications and address its manifestation in built form. But first there are a number of observations and issues which need to be addressed before examples are presented.

At which scale of the built environment can we look for the manifestations of the Urf? On the whole the smaller the scale the more evident is the impact. Although in some instances we also find the effect on the larger scale. See the examples in Figures 3, 5, 6,7, and 8.

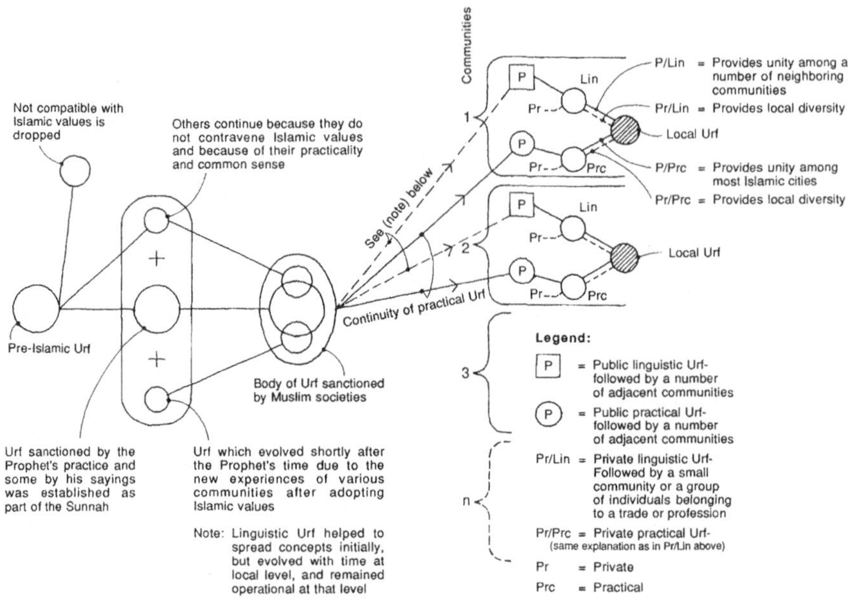

FIGURE 2. A conceptual diagram of the Urf's contribution to the phenomenon of unity and diversity in the built environment of traditional Islamic cities.

Related to the first observation, the evidence indicates more prominence at a scale where individuals' decisions and building craftsmanship occurs. This is especially true in housing areas at the scale of the cluster and progressing down from that scale to more details.[25] Refer to Figures 3, 5, 6, 7, and 8.

The Urf is dynamic, i.e. it changes with time, but because of the conservative nature of people relative to their habits, the rate of change tended to be slow. In the traditional city the relative unchanging nature of building materials and technology converged with conservatism to minimize change in the Urf of building practice. Such as the persistent Urf of curving the corners of buildings to facilitate the movement of animals carrying a load. The use of pack animals continued until the advent of the car (see Figure 6).

Although there was much contact between urban centers in the ancient Islamic world which resulted in the transfer of ideas, such influences were manifest in private works of the wealthy classes and in public buildings controlled by individual patrons or the authority. Where Islamic law was operational on a day to day basis, such as in housing areas and the market places, influences from the outside, if any, were moderate. This was largely due to the respect accorded to the localized Urf.

The phenomenon of diversity within unity so apparent in traditional Islamic cities can be interpreted thus:

Unity was achieved by the initial concept of urban formation which the Arabs brought with them from Arabia to the various geographic regions whose people embraced Islam. This concept had a very ancient history in the Near East region, and from the sketchy evidence available the same system with some modifications was followed during the Prophet's last ten years in Medina. His sayings regarding a number of issues which related to building activity reflected a process of

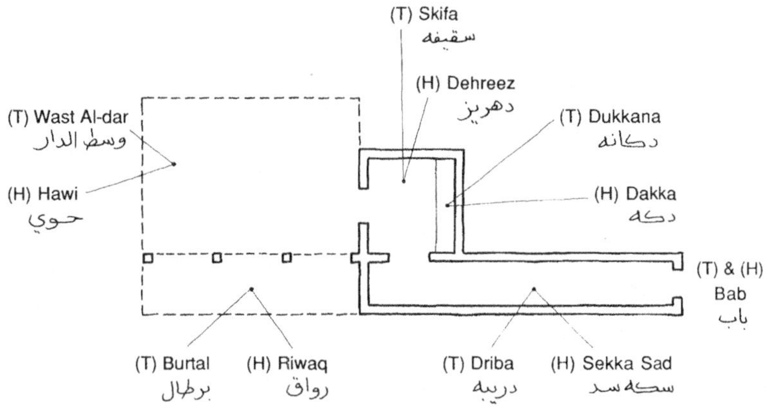

(T) = Tunis region, Tunisia

(H) = Hofuf region, Saudi Arabia

Driba Sekka Sad	A primary entrance vestibule or private lane owned by one house or shared by two or more houses. Occasionally a gate (Bab) is found at the entrance.
Skifa Dehreez	A secondary entrance lobby with entry doors placed so that no one can see directly into the courtyard.
Dukkana Dakka	Built-in bench. Traditionally the male owner or occupant of the house received casual visitors or salesmen.
Wast Al-dar Hawi	Private courtyard open to the sky in the center of the house.
Burtal Riwaq	A colonnaded gallery off the main courtyard, giving importance and sun-protection to the room behind it. This gallery could be on one, two, three, or four sides of the courtyard.

FIGURE 3. The linguistic Urf of two regions distant from each other. The vocabulary is different but they are for the same spatial/organizational elements. However, the style and architectonics of these elements are distinct to each region. Thus we find the unity in the concepts of space and organization and the diversity in the linguistic and practical Urf which produce the specific characteristics of the region's architecture and built form.

reinforcing certain pre-Islamic building practices which were accepted as part of the localized Urf in Medina.[26] But because some of those customs were traced directly to the Prophet's sayings and deeds, they became enshrined as part of the Shari'a texts. They were thus legitimized on two levels: (a) they were part of the Sunnah (the Prophet's sayings and deeds), and (b) they were also localized Urf. It is at the level of their legitimacy as part of the Sunnah that they spread across the Islamic world and contributed to the process of unifying the character of Islamic cities[27] (see Figure 2).

Diversity was achieved due to the recognition by Islamic law of the localized Urf in both its forms: the linguistic and practical. The Shari'a recognized and protected the local vocabulary developed by those in the building trades. The terms which evolved locally had an influence in sustaining the continuity of specific local building practices and their peculiar characteristics. This was because a term from such a vocabulary tended to integrate the form and function of the physical component and its purpose as utilized in that specific locality.[28] This continuity was also sustained by the conservative nature of traditional Islamic society (see Figure 3).

FIGURES 4A, 4B, 4C. The distinct physical organization of Islamic cities — the initial formation of these cities followed a common concept of territorial allocation and land utilization supported by a unique system of distribution of responsibilities among all the actors involved in the decision-making process affecting building activities. This concept was spread to the far reaches of the Islamic world during the early centuries of Islam. The resulting distinct physical characteristics maintained itself despite the processes of growth and change across the centuries. This concept and its system of implementation is a prime factor which produced the phenomenon of unity among the multitude of cities in the Islamic world. A phenomenon which persisted to the early decades of this century.

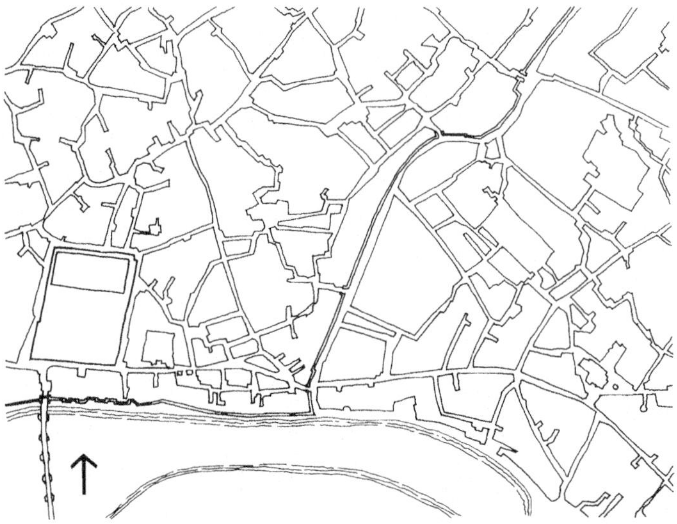

FIGURE 4A. The southern part of Cordoba in southern Spain showing the river to the south and the great mosque at the lower left corner of the sketch. After a map dated 1811 reproduced in E.A. Gutkind's *International History of City Development: Vol III, Urban Development in Southern Europe: Spain and Portugal,* The Free Press, N.Y., 1967.

As for the practical Urf, Islamic law recognized the local peculiarity and ways of doing things of a group of individuals belonging to a specific trade or profession, as in the building trades. Thus the Urf of that trade in a particular locality was respected by the Shari'a. This occurred through the legitimization of decisions resulting from the Urf in cases of disputes or litigation. This state of affairs tended to perpetuate and guard the distinctiveness of local building practices and by extension the resulting built form.

Further amplification to the observations in the preceding paragraphs above is related to the issue of the relationship of Meta-principles and guidelines to localized Urf practices. Elsewhere this author has elaborated on principles and behavioral guidelines which affected the shape of the traditional Islamic city.[29] Those were general principles and could also be viewed as common Urf guidelines, i.e. Urf practice which is common to most communities and regions. They were followed in most Islamic cities and tended to generate the similarities we find common amongst those cities. Whereas localized Urf practices were distinct to a specific urban center or to a group of settlements within one region. Those localized practices helped to produce the distinctiveness and thus micro characteristics of each city or settlement.

An important observation can now be stated: that the *nature* of Islamic law when considered with its interface with the Urf and its framework for decisions — which has resulted from that interface — show the flexibility of this system of law. It is very sensitive to local conditions. It

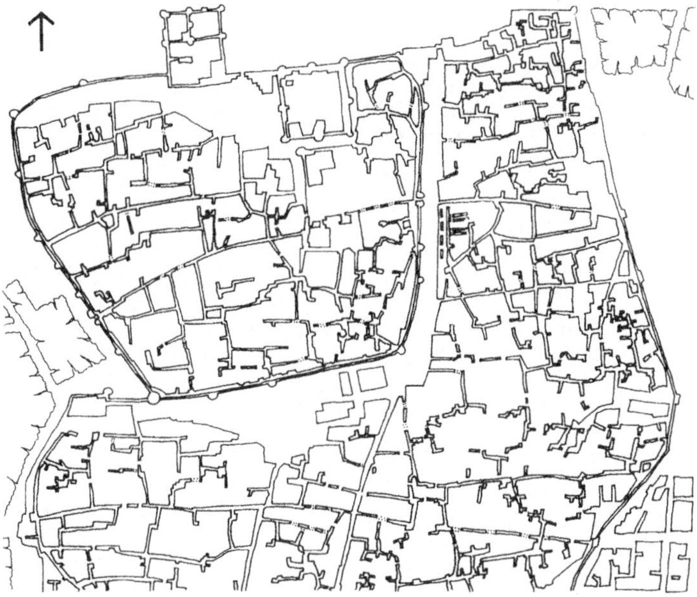

FIGURE 4B. A partial map of Hofuf in eastern Saudi Arabia based on an aerial photograph dated 1935. The Al-Kut district surrounded by its own wall is shown on the upper left of the sketch. After a map by C.P. Winterhalter in his dissertation titled: *Indigenous Housing Patterns and Design Principles in the Eastern Province of Saudi Arabia,* Swiss Federal Institute of Technology, Zurich, 1981.

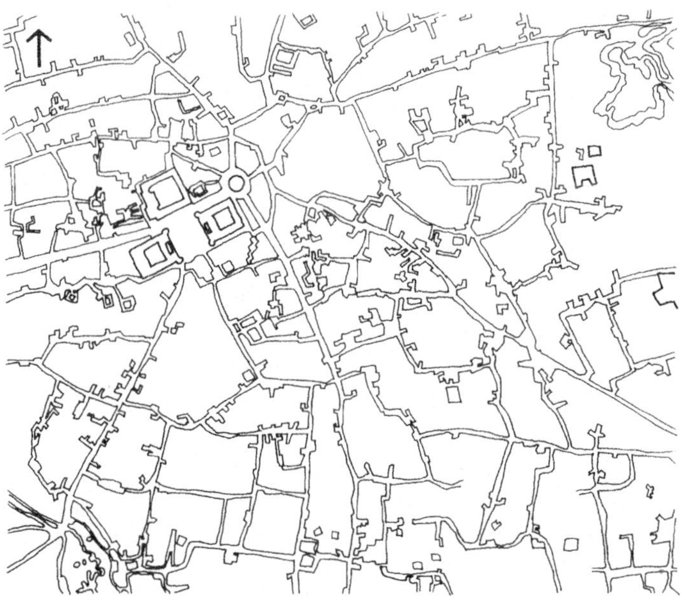

FIGURE 4C. The central part of Samarkand according to a geodesic survey of 1868, the year the city was incorporated into the Russian Empire. After the map reproduced in E.A. Gutkind's *International Histroy of City Development; Vol. VIII, Urban Development in Eastern Europe: Bulgeria, Romania, and the U.S.S.R.,* The Free Press, N.Y., 1972.

FIGURES 5A, 5B. The Sabat — an air-right structure bridging a public-right-of-way is a concept designed to provide additional space for the building to which it is attached. Islamic law recognizes this concept and there are specific guidelines governing its implementation. It is used in most Islamic cities, acting as an element of unity. The local Urf in each city shapes its architectonics and thus contributes to the phenomenon of diversity.

FIGURE 5A. View of a Sabat in Tunis. The columns supporting the structure on the left indicate that it belongs to the building on the right of the sketch. After a photograph by the author taken in the mid-1970's and published in his book *Arabic-Islamic Cities: Building & Planning Principles*, KPI, London (79) 1986.

FIGURE 5B. A Sabat in Hofuf, Saudi Arabia. Palm tree trunks are used as the main structure for support, distinctly different from the structure and building materials used in Tunis. The treatment of windows is also different. After a photograph taken by the author in early 1986.

accords legitimization and protection to a locality's customs and practices and thus contributes substantially to the identity of a place through the individuality of its place-making process and its resulting built form (see Figure 2). Elsewhere the writer discussed another facet of Islamic law which further contributed to distinctiveness of place making. It is that guidelines for building activity and decisions emanating from this system of law are performance/intent oriented and proscriptive in nature. The ramification of this attribute alone is enormous on the quality of the built environment.[30]

FIGURES 6A, 6B. Curving the corner of buildings which are located on public streets — a convention practiced universally in Islamic cities, towns and villages. It might have roots in pre-Islamic periods. A curved corner allows easier negotiation when turning by the rider of beast which is carrying a load, such as a camel, horse or donkey. This element contributed to the phenomenon of unity. However, its specific design and architectural treatment was governed by the local or regional Urf, contributing to diversity.

FIGURE 6A. A corner of a building in the village of Sidi Bou Sa'id north of Tunis. This example shows the enhancement of this practice by decoration, in this case with black and white inter-locking tiles. After a photograph taken in 1975 and published in *Sidi Bou Sa'id, Tunisia: A Study in Structure and Form,* edited by B. Hakim, Technical University of Nova Scotia, Hailfax, 1978.

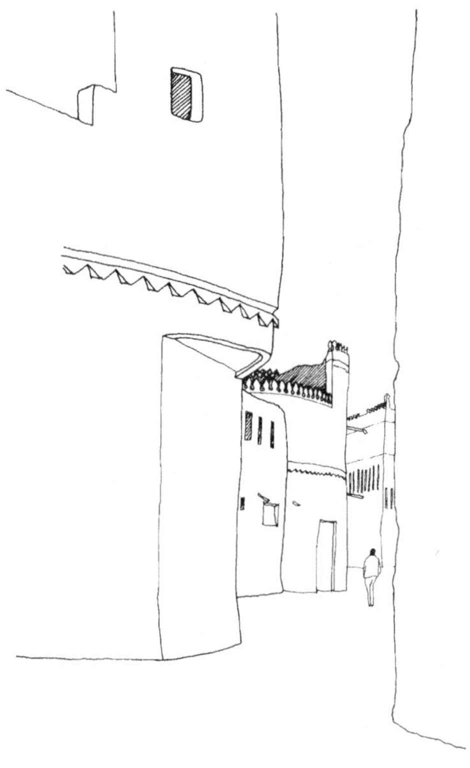

FIGURE 6B. The corner of this building in Riyadh, Saudi Arabia is treated in a more pragmatic manner, "slicing" the building to the required height and even allowing the decoration to continue around the corner. After a photograph by John Amarantides estimated to be taken in the 1970s.

SOME LESSONS FOR CONTEMPORARY URBANISM AND URBAN DESIGN

Due to the dreary sameness which resulted in our cities worldwide under the banner of "progress" and "modernism" during this century — particularly spreading after WW II, we find now that a backlash has resulted within a time frame of one generation, in just over 30 years. This is manifested under different slogans depending on the culture and country. In the Islamic countries we recognize it under the banner of demanding an "Islamic" identity in architecture and urban design.[31] Some of the Arab countries call the same thing under the banner "Arab Architecture."[32] In the West, particularly in the United States, the term "Critical Regionalism" is used for

FIGURES 7A, 7B. Design enhancement of main doors — one of the important concepts applied universally in Islamic cities is the design enhancement of the main doors of buildings, often supplemented by elaborate decoration if the owner could afford it. The main door was the primary element of the building's elevation where intentional design is applied. A clear element of unity, whereas the local Urf created the diversity, where each region developed specific design approaches and decorative motifs.

FIGURE 7A. A main door to a house in the village of Sidi Bou Sa'id, Tunisia. People in this village practiced the Urf which was predominant in the city of Tunis and its environs. The decoration is achieved by nails of two types: (i) large nails holding the door's structure together, and (ii) small nails for surface decoration of various motifs. After a photograph taken in 1975 and published in Hakim, B. (ed.) *Sidi Bou Sa'id,* 1978.

FIGURE 7B. A main door to a house in Al-Kut district in Hofuf, Saudi Arabia. The elegant gypsum decoration above the door is typical of this region's Urf. Structural nails are commonly exposed and form part of the door's visual character. After a photograph by Mashary Al-Naim taken in 1990.

this purpose.[33] This is particularly significant because this backlash and strong feeling against sameness is occurring in a large country with a strong culture and embedded institutions, aided by the mass media and powerful advertising capabilities.

If regional identity and character is accepted as an important attribute for cities, habitat and architecture, then the strategies and methods to achieve that become an important concern. Here the careful study of the experience of other cultures, particularly in history, can be very valuable.[34] The workings of the traditional Islamic city can provide us with needed insight.

FIGURES 8A, 8B. Decoration of internal walls — the concept of decorating the walls of primary rooms is common in many Islamic cities. The type and nature of the decoration however was distinct to each region and sometimes to a specific town. This concept contributed to the phenomenon of unity and diversity.

FIGURE 8A. The central room of a house in the oasis town of Ghadames, Libya decorated for the occasion of marriage. The hatched areas of the sketch represent the original red color used traditionally for wedding decorations. After a photograph by Professor Intisar Azzouz of Al-Fateh University in Tripoli, Libya, as published in the illustrated presentation "Mimar Gallery" in *MIMAR 1*, 1981, pp. 17-23.

FIGURE 8B. A wall mural of a fruit tree with birds perched on the branches. This particular design was found in a house in Hofuf, Saudi Arabia and is a symmetrical design of an orange tree with two birds. It is approximately five feet tall. The trunk, branches and leaves are painted dark green and the oranges are in a mustard-yellow color. It is possible that this design was inspired by the Quran which mentions the abundance of fruit trees in Paradise. After a photograph taken in the 1970's, from King Faisal University's slide collection. Photographer unknown.

It has been over five years, from the mid-1980s, since Kenneth Frampton published ideas for designing architecture at the local level with qualities that "resist" the hegemony of what he calls 'universal civilization.' Although his suggestions are, in the view of this author, far from being comprehensive, they are nevertheless in the right direction and need to be taken seriously.[35] If we consider the last observation (in the first paragraph of this section) as addressing the 'what' of the problem and implicitly 'why' it occurred, then this note on 'Resistance' should be viewed as the basis for developing a framework for working out 'how' appropriate alternative(s) may be achieved. Again the experience of the traditional Islamic city can offer us insight into an alterna-

FIGURES 9A, 9B, 9C, 9D. The persistence of the Urf in contemporary times — examples from Dammam, Saudi Arabia. After photographs taken by the author in June 1989 in the "District 37" housing area, with the exception of photograph 9A taken in early 1986. This district was developed in the 1980s. The basis for development of this and similar housing areas in Saudi Arabia is descibed thus: municipal planners subdivide the land, the plots are then allocated to individuals who are then responsible for building their houses according to municipal regulations and requirements of the Real Estate Development Fund which loans the funds, interest free, to the owners. The system of subdivision which was earlier imposed by the govenrment divides the land into plots of approximately square shapes averaging in area of 580 square meters with a requirement of setbacks from all sides and a maximum allowable footprint area of 60% of the plot. Almost all of the house designs are based on the use of exterior windows which has resulted in overlooking problems. People have responded by developing counter measures which have evolved into contemporary customs (Urf).

FIGURE 9A. A corner of a house which shows the use of five reccent customs: (i) conversion of the garage into a shop. This is a popular Urf especially if the location is suitable; (ii) the use of the bench (dakka) near the shop for visits; (iii) the use of high perimeter walls for privacy and security; (iv) the use of colored glass panels located on top of fence and balcony walls for additional privacy protection from opposite neighbors; and (v) the use of arch motifs, in this case in the balcony, to express allegiance to Islamic culture. A prevalent linkage in the minds of the popular sector.

tive framework, including the specifics of its mechanisms that was operational for over one thousand (1000) years. The following briefly addresses some of those lessons.

One of the key lessons is in the framework of the distribution of responsibilities among all actors involved in the creation, maintenance and changes in the built environment. This might be called the System of Production, or for short 'the System,' which involves the following questions: How is land distributed; how is space allocated; what is considered public and what is private; how do the public/private spheres interrelate; who is responsible for what? In cases of disputes, what is the mechanism of control and authority in resolving conflicts; who is responsible for land subdivision — and in design decisions: what is the role of the community and the user in the process?[36] These are the type of questions which need to be carefully studied in terms of what is occurring now and how it used to occur in the traditional Islamic city. It is only after careful analysis and understanding of the two systems that any fresh strategies can be formulated. The experience of cities in other cultures where a high level of quality in the built environment was achieved, need to be scrutinized for comparison so as to increase the sampling from which we can draw inspiration and specific lessons.[37]

FIGURE 9B. The persistence of the Urf enhancing the front door to the house with a special design (see Figure 7). Since the front door has become part of the perimeter fence wall in the contemporary situation, people have shifted their attention to the front gate for special treatment. This has now become a strong Urf in most of Saudi Arabia, and a great variety of approaches and designs have evolved.

FIGURE 9C. This example shows that the owner has responded to the visual corridors of opposite neighbors by increasing the height of his fence wall only in those locations where it is necessary. Most people however respond by increasing the height uniformly.

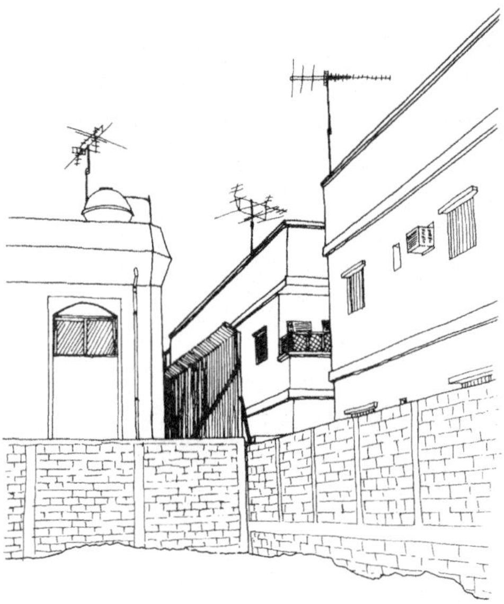

FIGURE 9D. With the requirement of setbacks from all sides and the necessity of opening windows for light and ventilation, people have responded by erecting light-weight walls, mainly of corrugated metal, to prevent overlooking. This is now a common Urf widely used in Saudi Arabia.

As to the nature of the tools and mechanisms which directly affect the contemporary built environment — it is absolutely essential to evaluate those carefully and not take for granted their various stipulations. Sometimes it is in the details (or fine print) of these controls that the root of many of our problems reside. Elsewhere this writer has discussed the differences between contemporary Western zoning and planning tools with those that were operational in the traditional Islamic city. The impacts on the quality of the built environment of these two very different types of systems is enormous. The lessons of the Islamic city is particularly critical in this regard.[38]

The following question needs to be briefly addressed: How does the Urf apply in the case of new building types, new materials and new urban functions? The case of contemporary Saudi Arabia might illuminate the answer. Here deeply rooted social customs such as the concern for privacy persists and manifests itself in new solutions in response to the new practices of land subdivision and built form configurations resulting from imported regulations, such as the setback requirements for individual houses from plot boundaries. The illustrations in Figure 9 clearly show the ramifications — these have in turn generated new customs (Urf) in dealing with the recent changes in land use and building materials. It should be noted that the "new Urf" is primarily the invention of the users in the face of changes.

Unfortunately the public sector's performance is dismal in dealing with the changes brought about by new building types, materials and urban functions. It responds with negative practices and methods, facilitating the degradation of the quality of the built environment. This is primarily due to the clash resulting from imported ideas and associated regulations (dictated by the central government on the local level), with embedded deep rooted customs. Users deal with this problem on a day to day practical basis resulting in adaptations which might or might not be ideal. Whereas the public sector, comprised of appointed municipal officials with little or no experience or training, deal with such problems at a distance and in a superficial manner.

AREAS FOR FURTHER RESEARCH

This paper should be viewed as a first draft in dealing with the Urf as an important factor in shaping the traditional Islamic city. It has covered the basic concepts of the Urf within the Fiqh and the ramification of that status on its legitimacy in the day to day decision making process as affecting building practice. The importance of both the 'linguistic' and 'practical' Urf is stressed, and how each type reinforced the other in building, thus helping to perpetuate a local system across long spans of time.

In view of the issues which the paper has covered, three important areas of research need to be undertaken so that understanding of this topic is further enhanced.

Research of traditional cases based on the Urf, both in the records of local qadis (judges) and in the writing of muftis (specialists on law). This is primarily a literature search. Urf courts were operational in North African countries during the French occupation. The records of those courts need to be carefully examined for cases related to building disputes. Some of these courts, such as in Tunis, continue to function. What is interesting to establish is the nature of the Urf rulings. How deviant, if at all, were they from the principles of the Shari'a and what was their impact on built form and the manner local identity was perpetuated? This type of research is particularly important, since the records of, say the last two hundred (200) years, will coincide closely with the on-ground situation of the built form as it stands now. Assuming that can be physically examined — without resorting to elaborate archaeological techniques — then the results will reflect very closely to what occurred within the time-frame indicated, even though some foundation outlines may date back to very early configurations. The use of successive aerial photos since the early decades of this century is an important tool for such a study.

Field research of selected and representative traditional Islamic cities is essential. These field studies could document the design language (linguistic Urf) which was operational, and the actual physical configuration and arrangements which the vocabulary of the local design language referred to. The results will provide us with a good sampling of the local linguistic Urf which was operational in a specific time and place. As mentioned earlier in this paper, the local design language was used by the community at large and was recognized by the Shari'a in resolving local conflicts arising from building activity. Comparative study of the results of surveys of a number of cities from different regions of the Islamic World would enhance our understanding and appreciation of the built form qualities of those cities. The results of this type of research will also illuminate the design decision-making process underlying the built form and the changes that have occurred over time.

Changes brought about by increasing modernizations due to new building types, new materials, and new urban functions in contemporary times, and the impacts these changes have had on the traditional Urf, be it practical or linguistic, need to be the concern of serious study in numerous Islamic cities. Such research should address among other things, the phenomenon of the clash resulting from imported and imposed (by central authoritarian governments) land use techniques and associated regulations with embedded local practices and systems of decision-making on the culture of the people and the resulting quality of the built environment. It should also address means of modifying or changing regulations to make them sensitive to local conditions and the values shared by the population. A careful study of people's responses to modernization and contemporary changes is essential. This will illuminate the culture's priorities in the face of imposed and/or desired changes in the built environment.

If this paper has opened a new window on the workings of the traditional Islamic city and has broadened our general understanding of the processes of urbanism and urban design, then it has achieved its purpose.

NOTES

1. Abu Hamid Muhammad bin Mohammad Al-Ghazali (d. 505 A.H./1111 A.D.), *Al-Mustasfa min'lm Al-Usul*, 2 Volumes. First printed by al-Amiriyah Press, Cairo 1322 A.H./1904 A.D.

2. Al-Jurjani (d. 816 A.H./1413 A.D.) *Al-Ta'rifat*. The translation from the Arabic is by R. Levy from the article 'Urf' in *Encyclopedia of Islam*, 1st ed., Leiden and London, 1913-1934.

3. Ali Haider (d. * ?) *Durar Al-Hukkam: Sharh Majallat Al-Ahkam*. (written in 1875), translated from Turkish to Arabic by Fahmi Al-Husaini, Dar Al-Kutub Al-Ilmiyah, Beirut, First Printing 1991. (*) Year of death could not be located, but if he had written this book in his 50s, then the latest date of death would be within the first decade of this 20th century.

4. Abdul-Wahab Al-Khallaf (d. 1956 A.D.) *lm Usul Al-Fiqh*. 1st ed. 1942, Dar Al-Qalam, Kuwait, 15th Printing, 1983.

5. Mustafa Ahmed Al-Zarka (1945) *Al-Madkhal Al-Fiqhi Al-Am*. 2 Volumes, 3rd revised ed. 1952 - 10th Printing 1968 by Tarbin Press, Damascus.

6. Abdul Aziz Al-Khayyat (1977) *Nadariyat Al-Urf*. Maktabat Al-Aqsa, Amman.

7. Mohammad Amin Abdin, known as "Ibn Abdin," (d. 1836 A.D.), "Nashr al-Urf fi bina bad al-Ahkam 'la al-Urf," in *Majmu't Rasa'l Ibn Abdin*. 2 volumes, Printed by Dar Ihya al-Turath al-Arabi, Beirut, n.d.

8. Ahmad Fahmi Abu-Sanah, *Al-Urf wa al-'Ada fi Ra'y al-Fuqaha*. Al-Azhar Press, Cairo, 1949.

9. Part five of Volume 2 entitled "Nadariyat al-Urf" in the reference cited in note 5 above.

10. Reference cited in note 6 above.

11. The author has come across other sources of interest: an article "Urf and Law in Islam" by Farhat J. Ziadeh, pp. 60-67 in *The World of Islam*, edited by James Kritzeck and R. Bayly Winder, Macmillan & Co. Ltd., London 1959. It is short and useful for clarifying the semantic history of the term. There is a short section on the Urf, pp. 110-118 by Mohammad Faruq Al-Nabhan in his book *Abhath Islamiyah*, published by Mu'asasat Al-Risalah, Beirut 1986. This is particularly illuminating for the working of the Urf in North Africa. That area's Fiqh and Urf traditions is fully covered by Abdulaziz Binabdullah in *Mu'alimat al-Fiqh al-Maliki*, published by Dar al-Gharb al-Islami, Beirut 1983.

12. This verse and many others and numerous sayings of the Prophet are fully documented as Appendix 1 in this author's book: Besim S. Hakim, *Arabic-Islamic Cities: Building & Planning Principles*, Kegan Paul International, London [1979] 1986, 2nd hardback edition 1988. Verse 7:199 appears on page 144.

13. Although the writer has benefited from a number of sources in developing the first section of this paper, he has for the sake of being brief only made specific reference to M. Al-Zarka's book cited in note 5 above. The material in that book is divided into sequentially numbered paragraphs. Cited below are the number of paragraphs rather than the page numbers, as those differ by edition.

14. Al-Zarka (cited in note 5), paragraph 477.

15. For a discussion of the contrast between Urf as people's customs and Urf as dictatorial top down rulings, see F.J. Ziadah "Urf and Law in Islam," cited in note 11.

16. Al-Zarka (cited in note 5), paragraph 479.

17. Ibid., Paragraphs 480 and 508 to 533.

18. Ibid., Paragraphs 484 and 486 to 490.

19. Ibid., Paragraphs 493 to 495.

20. Ibid., Paragraph 496.

21. Ibid., Paragraph 502.

22. Ibid., Paragraphs 503 to 509.

23. The presentation in the first section is adequate for the purposes of this paper. For a fuller discussion the author refers the reader to the treatises — all in Arabic — of Ibn Abdin (cited in note 7), Abu-Sanah (cited in note 8), Al-Zarka (cited in note 5) and Al-Khayyat (cited in note 6).

24. See Hakim, *Arabic-Islamic Cities* (cited in note 12) and the article by this author "Islamic Architecture and Urbanism" in *Encyclopedia of Architecture*, Vol. 3, pp. 86-103, John Wiley & Sons, Inc., New York, 1989.

25. See Hakim, *Arabic-Islamic Cities*, pp. 126 & 127, and B. Hakim (ed.) *Sidi Bou Sa'id, Tunisia: A Study in Structure and Form*, Technical University of Nova Scotia, Canada, 1978. Available now from Books on Demand, University Microfilms International, Ann Arbor, Michigan, U.S.A.

26. For a complete discussion of the principles and behavioral guidelines which helped to unify the character of Islamic cities, see Hakim, *Arabic-Islamic Cities*, pp. 18-22. Two illustrative examples are cited here: (1) the Prophet's stipulation of 7 cubits (3.20 meters) as a minimum Right-of-Way for through public streets to allow two fully loaded camels to pass — is due to the fact that it was an implicit Urf because the camel had become the primary mode of transport about 300 years before the Prophet's time; (2) the Aqd or wall bond for the identification of ownership of walls meeting at right angles. For a full discussion of the Aqd see footnote 78 on page 174 of the author's book, first cited in note 12 above.

27. One of the elements which established this unity was the predominant use of the concept of a building surrounding its open courtyard, especially for houses — despite the fact this plan arrangement is not suitable for cold climates experiencing heavy snowfall. But because of its legitimacy as part of the Sunnah, we find its application and use in distant cities like Kabul in Afghanistan where heavy snowfall is experienced rendering this model inefficient and cumbersome for its users.

28. See Chapter 2 "A design language: urban and architectural elements" in Hakim: *Arabic-Islamic Cities*. Pages 98-101 are comprehensive tables of terms which were the common linguistic Urf in Tunisia.

29. See Chapter 1 "Islamic law and neighborhood building guidelines" in Hakim, *Arabic-Islamic Cities* for a complete discussion of these principles and behavioral guidelines.

30. See Chapter 4 "Conclusions" in Hakim, *Arabic-Islamic Cities*, and Hakim "Islamic Architecture and Urbanism" in *Encyclopedia of Architecture* (cited in note 24 above), especially pp. 97 to 102.

31. The early 1980's (ushering the year 1400 A.D. and the 15th Islamic century) witnessed a number of conferences, such as the 'International Symposium on Islamic Architecture and Urbanism' held in January 1980 at King Faisal University, Dammam, Saudi Arabia. The first awards of the Aga Khan Awards for Architecture were given in 1980, and the seminars sponsored by the Awards Program were held in various locations. Shortly after that the King Fahd Award for Islamic Architecture was launched — for students work only. Magazines appeared addressing this concern, such as *MIMAR* which is funded by the Aga Khan, and *AL-BINA* which is privately published in Saudi Arabia.

32. The term "Arab Architecture" is not valid, whereas "Arab-Islamic" is. This author has discussed the basis for this terminology in the Introduction of his *Arabic-Islamic Cities*. The Arab League and its organizations tend to promote this designation. In Iraq a conference was held in September 1980 entitled 'International Symposium on Arab Architectural Heritage and our Contemporary Architecture.' Then in February 1981 a conference sponsored by the Arab Towns Organization entitled 'The Arab City' was held in Medina, Saudi Arabia. The bi-monthly journal *al-Madinah Al-Arabiya* was launched in the early 80's and is published by that organization.

33. This term was first postulated by Alexander Tzonis and Liane Lefaivre in 1981, and subsequently codified by Kenneth Frampton into a theory (references are cited in note 35 below). Recently two International Seminars on "Critical Regionalism" were held. The first in January 1989 at the College of Environmental Design, California State Polytechnic University, Pomona, followed by the second at the Delft Technical University in Holland in June 1990. A third seminar is planned to be held in 1991 at the Milan Polytechnic.

34. This author has been teaching an introductory course in History and Theory for undergraduate architecture students since 1986 at King Faisal University, Dammam, where the emphasis is on uncovering principles and patterns which have occurred in various cultures. For details refer to his paper "Teaching History by Searching for Emics and Ethics" published in proceedings of 77th Annual Meeting of the Association of Collegiate Schools of Architecture, held in Chicago, March 1989, pp. 167-180. It was subsequently published in *Design Studies*, Vol.12, No.1, January 1991, pp. 19-29. The course was one of three winners of the American Institute of Architects (AIA) 1990 Education Honors Award.

35. The two pertinent articles by Kenneth Frampton on this topic are: (1) "Towards a Critical Regionalism: Six Points for an Architecture of Resistance" in *The Anti-Aesthetic*, edited by Hal Foster, Bay Press, Washington, 1983, and (2) "Place - Form and Cultural Identity" (in Italian and English) in *Domus* #673, June 1986, pp. 19-24.

36. A number of people have addressed these issues, such as John F.C. Turner in his various articles on housing, and especially in his seminal book *Housing by People*, Marion Boyars, London 1976. More recently by N.J. Habraken in a theoretical treatise entitled *Transformations of the Site*, Awater Press, Cambridge, Mass., 1983. This author has addressed some of these issues as part of a larger framework of concerns in the article "Recycling Positive Aspects of Tradition in Contemporary Cities: Some Issues for Consideration," in the proceedings of *The Second International Conference on Urbanism in Islam*, held in Tokyo, Japan, November 1990. A revised version is published in the journal, *Cities*, Vol.8, No. 4, November 1991, pp. 274-277.

37. Christopher Alexander and his colleagues have tried to do this by amalgamating ideas rooted in various cultures in their extensive collection of patterns as published in *A Pattern Language*, Oxford University Press, N.Y., 1977. For how some of those patterns exist in an Arab-Islamic village, see the Conclusions, pp. 154-160 of *Sidi Bou Sa'id: Tunisia* (cited in note 25 above).

38. See the author's articles "Islamic Architecture and Urbanism" in *Encyclopedia of Architecture* (cited in note 24 above) and "Recycling Positive Aspects of Tradition in Contemporary Cities: Some Issues for Consideration" (cited in note 36 above).

ACKNOWLEDGEMENTS

This paper was originally presented at the "International Conference on Urbanism in Islam," held in Tokyo, Japan, October, 1989. It was subsequently presented at the "Islam and Public Law" conference organized by the School of Oriental and African Studies and held in London, U.K., June, 1990.

The author is most grateful for the assistance of Mr. Yahya Al-Najjar for drawing the final illustrations, at a time when it was impossible for the author to allocate the time to undertake this task.

AUTOBIOGRAPHICAL SKETCH

Besim S. Hakim, AIA, AICP, has extensive experience in architecture and urban design as a professor/scholar and as a consultant/practitioner. He was educated at Liverpool University, U.K. and at Harvard. He has practiced and taught in Canada, the U.S., and the Mid-East. His teaching experience started in 1967 at the Technical University of Nova Scotia, Halifax, Canada and he has also lectured and taught at numerous universities in the U.S. and abroad — including, for several years during the latter half of the 1980's, in Saudi Arabia. Professor Hakim has published extensively in professional literature, and received a Citation for Research in 1987 from *Progressive Architecture* for his book *Arabic-Islamic Cities: Building and Planning Principles*. He was also awarded the American Institute of Architects 1990 Education Honors Award for a course he has been teaching on the History/Theory of Architecture.

Printed in Great Britain
by Amazon

56625920R00143